D0855657

The Road of Danger, Guilt, and Shame

A. E. Housman, 1911. Mansell Collection/TimePix.

The Road of Danger, Guilt, and Shame

The Lonely Way of A. E. Housman

Carol Efrati

Madison • Teaneck
Fairleigh Dickinson University Press
London: Associated University Presses

Associated University Presses
440 Forsgate Drive
Cranbury, NJ 08512

Associated University Presses
16 Barter Street
London WC1A 2AH, England

Associated University Presses
P.O. Box 338, Port Credit
Mississauga, Ontario
Canada L5G 4L8

The paper used in this publication meets the requirements of the American National Standard for Permanence of Paper for Printed Library Materials Z39.48-1984.

Library of Congress Cataloging-in-Publication Data

Efrati, Carol, 1939–
    The road of danger, guilt, and shame : the lonely way of A.E. Housman / Carol Efrati.
        p.   cm.
    Includes bibliographical references and index.
    ISBN 0-8386-3906-2 (alk. paper)
    1. Housman, A. E. (Alfred Edward), 1859–1936—Criticism and interpretation.   2. Homosexuality and literature—England—History—20th century.   I. Title.

PR4809.H15 E47   2002
821′.912—dc21   2001040225

To the living spirit of A. E. Housman
and
to the memory of my Friend, Robert,
this work is gratefully dedicated

But if you come to a road where danger
          Or guilt or anguish or shame's to share,
Be good to the lad that loves you true
And the soul that was born to die for you,
          And whistle and I'll be there.

                                        (MP 30)

.

Contents

Preface

I

A. E. HOUSMAN'S PLACE IN THE RANKS OF ENGLISH AUTHORS HAS HAD ITS ups and downs over the hundred plus years since *A Shropshire Lad*, rejected by the commercial press and published at the author's own expense in 1896, slipped quietly into the hearts of readers. It did not arrive with a splash of publicity accompanied by booming sales, although it received a fair amount of critical praise in the reviews. Its readership grew steadily if slowly, although it was only during World War I and in the twenties that Housman's poetry became generally popular. Following the Wilde debacle, the most popular poet in England was Rudyard Kipling, whose work was closely associated with the reins of Empire, followed by A. E. Housman, whose *A Shropshire Lad* "was taken for open-air poetry of the healthiest kind" (Croft-Cooke, *Feasting with Panthers*, 290). On hearing of his death, Virginia Woolf said that England had lost its greatest contemporary poet. Housman was definitely part of the literary landscape and a passport-holding citizen of Parnassus, quite an achievement for a man who in his own lifetime had published only two small collections of poetry and roundly declared that he was a professor of Latin and not a poet by profession.

Following his death in 1936, however, Housman's poetic reputation went into decline although his lyrics never lost their hold on the popular heart. Perhaps this was the reason for the snubbing they received from the *doyens* of literature. How could poetry known and loved by the masses, poetry that accompanied the soldiers into the trenches of the Great War and solaced them under the barrage of German shells, poetry that was primarily written in everyday language (despite Sinclair's opinion that Housman insisted "on a self-consciously 'poetic' vocabulary" and deliberate archaisms [*A. E. Housman*, 7]) and could be understood by the uneducated and semiliterate, be good poetry? Indeed, I believe Kit Wright is correct in suggesting that "his popularity may have counted against his critical reputation" ("Never Mind What It Means," 15). Critical acclaim was ultimately awarded to Eliot's "The Waste Land," published in 1922, the year Housman's *Last Poems* appeared, but that acclaim was withheld

from Housman's lyrics. After all, everybody knew that good art and literature came wrapped in enigmas that required knowledge and study—and
authorial and/or critical footnotes and commentary—to unravel. Housman's poetry did not need such aids, so how worthwhile could it possibly
be? And how much scope could it offer for the demonstration of critical
acumen? Housman himself seems to have believed that there was an antithesis between good poetry and popular poetry. In 1922 he wrote to a
correspondent, "The book [LP] is selling at such a rate that I am afraid I
cannot be such a very good poet after all" (Maas, "Additions and Corrections," 35). Again, in Kit Wright's words, "A feature that has not en-
deared him to critics is that . . . there is not a great deal to be said about
him; by its transparent inevitability, the poem puts the critics out of
work." My contention, of course, is that Wright is wrong and that there
is indeed "a great deal to be said" about both him and his poetry, for
Housman's poems are not in fact as simple and accessible as they seem.
He habitually alternated between "studied artifice of phrasing," the "self-
consciously 'poetic' vocabulary" Sinclair noted, and a chatty, sardonic,
colloquial style that is framed in the commonplace vernacular (Nash,
"Diffugere Nives"). Robertson remarked that Housman's poetry "can
justly be called both great and popular" ("Housman and Hopkins," 94),
although the popularity was not immediate and the exact nature of the
greatness—or indeed if it can really be called 'great' at all—is a matter of
dispute.

Although these poems have "the seeming simplicity of verse written
for children" (Robbins, "Curious Construction," 147), this "simplicity"
is only "seeming." Like a deep pool on a windless day, the surface of his
poetry is limpid and comprehensible, and it reflects the image of the person looking into it. As with that pool, however, there is an entire world
below that reflecting surface that is hidden from the casual glance but
that richly rewards those who go to the trouble of plumbing its depths,
which are replete with wonders. There are, for example, countless half-
concealed allusions drawn from Housman's classical scholarship, knowledge of the scriptures, and wide reading in English and continental literature. Whatever he read was gripped firmly by a retentive and exact
memory, which rendered it up again at need, transformed by the poet's
associative imagination into "something rich and strange" which yet retained its homely surface familiarity. One can, as Davis noted in "Blue
Remembered Hills," read and understand almost all of Housman's poems
without knowing other work; his vast learning is so internalized that it is
seldom overt, nor is it necessary to identify or understand these references
in order to apprehend the text. Explicating literature by seeking for its
hidden meaning (or subtext), pattern, complexity, and significance is the
traditional function of critics, but until fairly recently they have not fully

done their job in respect to Housman's poetry, the critical consideration of which has been both unsatisfactory and fragmentary.

There are several editions of the poetic corpus, primarily consisting of the three volumes of poetry (*A Shropshire Lad* and *Last Poems*, published during his lifetime by the poet himself, and *More Poems*, published shortly after his death by his brother Laurence). The corpus also includes the supplementary selection of previously unpublished poetry (commonly cited as *Additional Poems*) included in Laurence Housman's memoir of his brother, and some translations from the Greek playwrights that were done for his friend, A. W. Pollard, for his edition of *Odes from the Greek Dramatists*. The corpus was first printed in a single-volume edition by Jonathan Cape in 1939 as *The Collected Poems of A. E. Housman*, edited by John Carter. Since then, the complete poems have been available in this format in hardback and paperback, in expensive and low-priced editions, either apparently unedited or edited by John Sparrow and later by Christopher Ricks.

The corpus has often been reprinted for the general reader, and more or less scholarly editions are available. The newest—and now standard—scholarly edition is *The Poems of A. E. Housman* edited by Dr. Archie Burnett for the Oxford University's Clarendon Press, published in 1997. This edition also includes the poetry not usually regarded as part of the corpus (parodies, light verse, juvenilia, and manuscript poems). Most of this noncorpus poetry has previously not been easily accessible and has been ignored by the critics, with the notable exceptions of Laurence Housman, Tom Burns Haber, and William White. Burnett's edition makes all this material accessible, but it omits single lines and couplets so does not quite replace Haber's *The Manuscript Poems of A. E. Housman* (1955). A limited selection of the comic verse (published in 1995 by The Housman Society as *Unkind to Unicorns: The Comic Verse of A. E. Housman*, edited by J. Roy Birch) has been reedited by Burnett and was reissued in 1999.

The poetic corpus is thus available in both noncritical and scholarly annotated versions. Indeed, *A Shropshire Lad* has never been out of print since its first publication, and new editions are constantly being published. In 1994 Woodstock Books issued a facsimile reprint of the first edition. In addition, Tom Stoppard's play about Housman, *The Invention of Love*, was produced at the National Theater in 1997 and revived in the West End the following year. In the winter of 1999–2000 it was also produced on both coasts of the United States (in Philadelphia and San Francisco). Clearly, there is a continuing interest in both the poetry and the poet. Housman's verse is, and has been from the beginning, accessible to the general public, even to those who are not particularly fond of poetry in general, even to those for whom the classical allusions and references are a closed book. The poems can be read with great enjoyment by everyone, although, as with any literature, the more one brings to it the more one gets from it.

The second generation of critics attributed the popularity of Housman's verse partly to its "adolescent" quality and subject matter: nature, hopeless love, military gallantry, suicide, etc. Just why these are considered exclusively adolescent concerns I fail to understand, but such critics as George Orwell, in a 1937 essay, prided themselves on having outgrown (although never forgotten) Housman's poems. Much critical attention was also devoted to the burning question of whether Housman was a "romantic" or a "classical" writer. Both these issues soon faded into history, although they never entirely disappeared, and were largely replaced with serious consideration of the poetry itself, its sources, influences, echoes, versification, order of composition, and so on. But there was one aspect missing.

Housman was a homosexual and, as with other homosexual writers, there has been, in general, a "critical refusal to consider [Housman's] homosexuality a factor . . . in the makeup of the literary self" (Martin, *Homosexual Tradition*, xvii). This "critical refusal" is no longer universal however. There has been at least one unpublished dissertation on Housman's poetry in which Randy Lynn Meyer, as Mr. Naiditch informs me, "has cogently argued that it was in part Laurence Housman's revelation [in *More Poems* and *Additional Poems*] of A. E.'s homosexuality that led to . . . [his] decline in popularity." In addition, Thomas Allen Culpepper wrote his doctoral dissertation, *Homoerotic Poetics in Housman, Owen, Auden, and Gunn*, in 1998. The interface between Housman's poetry and his homosexuality has clearly begun to be considered academically. Only recently, however, has the author's sexual orientation been brought out of the closet and applied in published form to the study of his work, albeit in fragmentary fashion.

Most early critics, Victorians that they were, were silent about the entire issue of sexuality, as were those who wrote the early memoirs on which all biographical studies of Housman are grounded. Shortly after his death, a book of *Recollections* was issued by his alma mater, the Bromsgrove School, in aid of the Housman Memorial Fund. The contributors to this slim volume of reminiscences were his sister Katharine Symons, his brother Laurence, his college roommate and friend, A. W. Pollard, his colleagues R. W. Chambers and A. S. F. Gow (names still to be conjured with), his nephew N. V. H. Symons, Alan Ker, and John Sparrow of Oxford University. All but the last two were the poet's relatives or personal friends. Laurence's long memoir of his brother, *A. E. H.*, appeared a year later in 1937 (a year after the poet's death), as did Gow's *A. E. Housman: A Sketch*. In 1940 Percy Withers, a friend of long standing, added *A Bur-*

ied Life to the list of seminal biographical materials, and in 1941, the poet's friend and publisher, Grant Richards, added *Housman: 1897–1936*, with an introduction by Katharine Symons, to the bookshelf. The basic building blocks of the Housman biography were all in place.

These early memoirists and protobiographers of Housman have been succeeded—but not superceded—by others who, as Tennyson would have said, "knew not him." Only in 1967 was the fact, as opposed to the rumor (hotly denied by both Katharine Symons and Grant Richards) of Housman's homosexuality made public. Laurence Housman, who died in 1959, had earlier written an article—published posthumously in *Encounter*—which revealed unequivocally to the world that his brother had been homosexual. In 1957 George L. Watson published the first nonpersonal account of the poet's life. He wrote *A. E. Housman: A Divided Life* with the aid of some of Housman's relations and associates, although Laurence refused him access to Housman's own private papers and diary. Watson suspected that the poet was homosexual, and he aired his suspicions in his book. Unfortunately, he was neither a sympathetic nor an objective biographer, and the relevant material is treated only by implication with snide, sniggering innuendo. Watson's own self-righteous rectitude breathes from every page. A year later, Maude M. Hawkins's account of Housman's life was published. It was written with the active input of Laurence Housman. Her fault is the opposite of Watson's; she gushes. She dramatizes. Her lush, purple prose and uncritical acceptance of whatever Laurence (whose memory at the best was not exactly reliable and who was himself inclined to dramatize rather than simply report events) told her—and he chose to tell her the great secret—make her book also less than satisfactory. Her stylistic excesses are combined with a habit of leaving out parts of quoted letters without notice and combining parts of other letters into a hybrid that never existed. These faults make her work thoroughly unreliable and, in its way, as distasteful as Watson's. Thus, neither biography can be trusted uncritically.

Fortunately, fuller and more critical and scholarly work has since appeared. In 1958 the first book by a reputable British scholar was published. In *A. E. Housman: Scholar and Poet*, Norman Marlow provided a considered treatment of Housman and his work covering a broad spectrum of relevant aspects. Among other areas, he explored the question of the biographical content of the poems. In 1967, Twayne Publishers brought out Haber's *A. E. Housman*. The next notable publication was Henry Maas's *Letters of A. E. Housman*, which came out in 1971. Parenthetically, Burnett is currently engaged in compiling a fuller edition.

In 1973 the Housman Society was established in Bromsgrove and in 1974 began publishing a yearly journal. At first amateurish and overloaded with personal reminiscences of the "I once saw Housman walking down the street" variety, it has progressed and developed into a fine scholarly publication. The first of the Housman Society's own publications was John Pugh's *Bromsgrove and the Housmans*, a combination of family and local history that is invaluable. A biography by Richard Perceval Graves, A. E. *Housman: The Scholar-Poet*, appeared in 1979, and Norman Page's A. E. *Housman: A Critical Biography* followed in 1983. Both took his sexuality into account. There have been further additions to the biographical Housman bookshelf. Keith Jebb's A. E. *Housman* (1992) deals briefly but reasonably well with the problem of the poet's sexual orientation. Jeremy Bourne's *The Westerly Wanderer* (1996) is an introduction to Housman's life and poetry for the general reader. All of the more recent books accept Housman's homosexuality as part of his life but, excepting Jebb's book, do little to connect it to his poetry. And despite the number of biographical studies, the definitive Housman biography has yet to be written.

The interested reader, then, has a wide choice of editions of the poetry and memoirs and biographies among which to choose. Much of Housman's prose writing is also easily available, either combined in a single volume with the poetry, *Collected Poems and Selected prose*, edited by Christopher Ricks, or published as a strictly prose selection of his work, A. E. *Housman: Selected Prose*, edited by John Carter. Unfortunately, the 3 volume edition *Classical Papers of A. E. Housman* has long been out of print and is almost impossible to find except on the shelves of university libraries, although copies occasionally come onto the market.

Many of these memoirs and biographies also contain critical discussions of some of the poetry, including (especially in the accounts of Laurence Housman and Katharine Symons) many poems not part of the corpus. Thus, there is a great deal of commentary available within them. For the reader who wants more—and more concentrated—commentary, in 1992 the Critical Heritage series brought out a volume on Housman, edited by Philip Gardner, in which are collected most of the important reviews and critical material through 1940, plus a few later pieces.

In addition to the commentary, criticism, and explication contained in the biographical materials and formal biographies, and that collected in the Critical Heritage volume, there are several books available on Housman's poetry. Among the older commentaries are those by Nesca Robb (*Four in Exile*, 1948), Robert Hamilton (*Housman the Poet*, 1949), Oliver Robinson (*Angry Dust*, 1950), and Ian Scott-Kilvert (A. E. *Housman*, 1955, revised and re-issued in 1977). There are also many more recent commentaries. Haber's 1966 companion volume to his edition of the manuscript material, *The Making of A Shropshire Lad*, although not precisely commentary, is still valuable for the comments on the poems in that volume, although his treatment of the manuscript material itself has been largely superceded by Burnett's edition. There are two books by B. J. Leggett, *Land of Lost Content* (1970) and *Poetic Art of A. E. Housman* (1978). P. G. Naiditch's *A. E. Housman at University College, London*, dealing with a large number of biographical cruxes, came out in 1988 and was followed in 1995 by a collection of short essays, *Problems in the Life and Writings of A. E. Housman*. In addition to these books, recent studies of Housman and his poetry have been written by, among others, Piers Browne (*Elegy in Arcady*, 1989), John Bayley (*Housman's Poems*, 1992), Humphrey Clucas (*Through Time and Place to Roam*, 1995), and Terence Hoagwood (*A. E. Housman Revisited*, 1995). *A. E. Housman: A Collection of Critical Essays*, edited by Christopher Ricks, had appeared in 1968, and in 1999 Macmillan brought out a follow up volume, *A. E. Housman: A Reassessment*, edited by Alan Holden and J. Roy Birch. Some of these books are far more reliable, incisive, and important than are others.

In addition to single volumes and the collections of essays, there is a mass of critical articles scattered through the professional literature about Housman's life, philosophy, pessimism, classicism, romanticism, and pastoralism. His academic and poetic achievements and his place in letters and literature have been assessed. His use (and misuse) of the Bible has been analyzed. So have his diction, style, and prosody. There have been some studies of selected areas of his characteristic imagery in individual poems. There are studies of his psychology and his poetic theory, both with and without reference to his own poetry. His moral (or immoral) stance and his attitude toward suicide have been examined. His knowledge of geography, astrology and astronomy has been evaluated. Single poems have been explicated, and the structural unity of *A Shropshire Lad* is the theme of more than one book. Holden, in the introduction to *A. E. Housman: A Reassessment*, has provided an excellent overview of "the main thrusts of these commentaries from 1896 on" (xiv).

Standards and tastes have changed. The first generation of readers and critics have left the stage to their successors, and influence has gradually ceased to be the source of anxiety as the fathers have given way to the grandsons. Reputations in decline have recovered their health, and healthy ones have fallen sick. Today Housman, like Kipling, is in the process of reclaiming his place among the citizens of Parnassus. A cursory look at the anthologies published over the last century or so shows that both the amount of space given to Housman's lyrics and the number of poems included have steadily grown. It is unlikely that today he would be included in the ranks of such minor Victorian poets as William Ernest Henley, John Davidson, and Lionel Johnson, as he was as recently as 1965 in *Nineteenth Century British Minor Poems*, edited by W. H. Auden. Although he certainly is not as important as, and is unlikely ever to be ranked with, Tennyson, Browning, and Arnold (despite Skutch's opinion that in spite the narrow range of Housman's poems, "the perfect harmony of mood and expression places them . . . in the realm of great poetry" [*A. E. Housman*, 12]), he is just as certainly infinitely more important in the annals of poetry than Henley, Davidson, and Lionel Johnson. Although Coulthard considers that "he is a minor writer not only in the circumscribed emotional and philosophical universe of his poetry but in its limited stylistic achievement as well" ("Flawed Craft," 31), he is allied only with Orwell in denigrating the craftsmanship of the poetry. There is thus no general agreement about Housman's importance, although Coulthard's evaluation is certainly the minority judgement.

The term "minor poet" covers an entire gamut from the not-quite-great to the never-heard-of. The question is where, in this continuum, is Housman's proper place. It is true his emotional and philosophical range is narrow, although not nearly as narrow as some have supposed. It is true that his dominant theme (although not his only theme, as Sinclair thinks), is pessimism, although he defined himself not as a pessimist but as a pejorist. It is true that he is repetitive. It is true that he wrote, in Clucas's phrase, "a few silly poems" ("Note on A. E. Housman," 93), although there is no critical agreement about just which ones are "silly" and a poem thought inane by one competent critic will be hailed as excellent by another. However neither narrow range, limited themes, nor repetitiveness are lacking in some major poets. I might suggest that Wordsworth can be arraigned on all three counts, and the silly poems written by him are notorious. No one, however, disputes Wordsworth's rank as a major poet. The stated criterion for major status is poetic development, and Housman did not develop. There is little change from the poetry of *A Shropshire Lad* to that of the latest entries in the notebooks (so far as the order of composition of the notebook material can be definitively determined). This criterion, however, is based on the concept of poetry as an intellectual expression reflecting the poet's intellectual development, and for Housman poetry was, as is well known, not what is said but rather the way it is said. It is ingenuous, therefore, to apply this criterion in determining his status. As for the concept of development, or progress, in verse form and control, there can be no question of the improvement from the juvenilia to the adult productions. Nor is Housman's poetic technique narrow or limited, as too many assume without taking the trouble to really look at the poems themselves. Indeed, his poetic palette is extraordinarily wide and varied.

What, then, is the single most important determining factor? I would suggest that it is sheer bulk, provided that the poetic bulk is competently written and often inspired. Housman's poetic production is obviously far less than even that of Hardy or Kipling, although of course they were professional, full-time writers and Housman was a professional, full-time

professor of Latin who also wrote poetry. Is he then to be compared with
Matthew Arnold, a professional, full-time inspector of schools who also
wrote poetry? Not quite, for in addition to quantity of short—or
shorter—poems, the writing of at least one long poem of sustained poetic
worth seems to me a central, if unstated, criterion. Housman never wrote
an epic, as Milton did, nor an extended allegory, as Spenser did, nor a
long poetic ramble, as Wordsworth did. He did not write a multibook
opus, as did both Browning and Tennyson, nor a poetic drama, as Hardy
attempted to do and Arnold succeeded in doing. His longest poem ("Hell
Gate," LP 31) is only 104 lines, and his second longest ("The Merry
Guide," ASL 42) is only 60 lines, and this seems to be central. "Great
poets write a very large number of outstanding poems, including at least
one long one" is not a criterion stated, but it is somehow assumed.

It has been said that one can tell if a poet is a major figure very simply;
if there is an entire undergraduate course of at least one semester's duration on his work, he is, ipso facto, a major poet. There is some truth to
this, in that there are full courses on Chaucer, Milton, and of course
Shakespeare, and I do not think there would be many who disagreed with
their ranking at the very top of the poetic totem pole. It is with the second rank that this definition begins to break down. There are courses in
Renaissance poetry, but none on Spenser or Sydney individually; on Neo-
Classical poetry, but none on Pope or Dryden individually; on Romantic
poetry, but none on Wordsworth, Coleridge, Shelley, Keats, or Byron individually; on Victorian poetry, but none on Tennyson or Browning individually. Yet all of these are granted major poet status with relatively little
argument. It is with the third rank that intense disagreement enters the
picture, for there is indeed no critical agreement about the exact place of
others. Are Donne, Arnold, Hardy, and so on minor or major poets? I
would say that they are on the fault line. It is with these poets, at the very
top of the third level, that I would rank Housman. More people have read,
enjoyed and reread Housman's poetry than have read Milton, Spenser,
and Wordsworth combined. As Lionel Trilling pointed out in reference
to Wordsworth, if his poetry (and that of Milton and Spencer, I would
add) were not part of the university curriculum, few indeed would read
them for pleasure, as they read Housman (Stevenson, "Durability of
Housman's Poetry," 613). Like the poems of Tennyson (whose "Charge
of the Light Brigade" is both overwhelmingly popular and overwhelmingly bad), and those of Kipling, Housman's poems live "more in the
hands of readers than in those of critics" (Clucas, "Note," 93), and if his
poetry is minor, it is at that point on the continuum where "minor"
comes very close to "major." Housman misses major status by no more
than a hair.

Readers' guides and literary encyclopedias show the same increase in the amount of space devoted to A. E. Housman as general anthologies of poetry and anthologies of Victorian poetry do in the number of his poems they include. In the earliest ones, pride of place went to his brother Laurence (some of whose plays are still occasionally produced), whose poetry tends to be mystical and "difficult." The early entries on Laurence Housman ran to a column or a column and a half, and A. E. Housman was "brother of the following," with a scant inch. The proportions reversed over time, and today it is the poet who has columns and Laurence, with a scant inch, who is "brother of the above," if he is mentioned at all. Michael Schmidt's *Lives of the Poets* (1998) devotes seven pages to A. E. Housman (including commentary, criticism, and biography), and does not mention Laurence Housman at all. We have, it seems, learned to value simplicity more than obscurity and accessibility more than difficulty for difficulty's sake. We have also learned to accept a poet as an integrated gestalt, every aspect of whose being—including sexuality—is relevant to his lyrics.

A mass of critical work has accumulated over the century since *A Shropshire Lad* appeared; Ehrsam's 1941 bibliography lists approximately 584 items, and in the last fifty-plus years the amount of commentary has grown enormously. Despite this, an integrated approach to any aspect of the poetry (let alone the homosexual subtext), one which draws not just on the poetic corpus but on all the other lyrics as well, has never been attempted. The present book, intended to fill both gaps at once, is at least the beginning of such an integrated consideration of Housman's poetry in toto. It includes not only the poems in the corpus but also those excluded from it (manuscript poetry, juvenilia, and comic verse), to see what light these bodies of poetry throw on each other. The work of many other authors (ancient and modern) is drawn upon for comparison and illustration, as is Housman's prose. My discussion combines a close reading of a large number of Housman's poems (from all sources) with attention to the inter-locking imagery, metaphors, and symbols which I suggest have their source in Housman's unconscious thought processes. Much emphasis is given to the techniques of light verse, with special notice of puns, many of which are buried in the diction. Excavating these buried puns often reveals a poem very different from the one customarily assumed to exist.

I both draw on the analyses of many other critics and present my own readings. The full text and designation of each poem is given at the first lengthy discussion of it. Thereafter, that poem is freely referred to and quotations from it integrated into consideration of other lyrics without its being again designated. Those lyrics from which only a few lines are quoted, or to which only passing reference is made, or to which I refer before the primary discussion, are always identified by the standard designation (ASL for *A Shropshire Lad*, LP for *Last Poems*, MP for *More Poems*, and AP for *Additional Poems*, the four collections of poems which are included in all editions of the collected poetry), as the interested reader will have no difficulty in obtaining the full texts.

My approach is unashamedly and unfashionably text-oriented. However, I combine a new critical emphasis on the text with biographical and historical context, consideration of workshop material, Freudian theory, feminism, and whatever else serves to aid in understanding the final texts. The various critical theories are, it seems to me, a tool basket from which the competent critic will select that most appropriate to the specific piece of literature under discussion and to the purposes of that discussion. Whatever critical tools are chosen, however, I believe that as thorough an understanding of the text as possible is a prerequisite for discussion. I have followed where the text led me without worrying greatly about this or that critical theory, preferring to be eclectic and flexible. I am therefore presenting close readings within the historical and biographical context of the poetry. This approach involves certain assumptions that should be clarified at the start.

Any worthwhile text is many-layered; understanding the obvious surface meaning of the text at the time of writing, no matter what changes in the language have introduced later alterations in the meaning, is only part of the work. Below the denotation there are layers of connotations, constituting the subtext. These subtextual layers of connotation are felt even if the reader does not analyze them. They spring from many sources. They come from the author's choice of words and rhythms, from what he excludes as well as what he includes, from what he implies as well as what he overtly states, and from the echoes he consciously or unconsciously evokes of the works of other authors. There may well also be meaningful echoes of the author's own earlier work in addition to foreshadowing of his later work. Some of the connotations that lead into the subtext will result from the author's deliberate intentions, but some of them will be the result of his subconscious or unconscious thought processes. The subtext thus produced will be the most meaningful for a complete understanding of the work since its source is the deepest levels of the writer's being. For Housman, this source is, I am positing, his sexual orientation and his own ambivalent attitude toward it.

At a time when homophobia was rampant, no matter what he actually did in his private life all overt signs of his sexual preference had to be excluded from his published writing as a matter of self-preservation. The Labouchere Amendment that outlawed all homosexual manifestations was passed into law in 1885 (eleven years before the publication of *A Shropshire Lad*) and remained in force until it was at last repealed in 1967. This was the law under which Oscar Wilde was prosecuted (and persecuted) in 1895. Clearly, any manifestation of Housman's male-oriented libido had to be suppressed and his sexual preferences prevented from showing on the surface of his work. What is overtly suppressed, however, may yet manifest itself in other ways. Sexual desire, whether for men or women, is one of the driving forces of the personality and will seek to express itself somehow. If the object of desire is forbidden, the expression of that desire will simply be disguised. St. Theresa had her erotically symbolic dreams. Housman had his poetry, and his desire was manifested by way of the subtext. His homosexuality, like his knowledge of literature, "is absolutely central . . . , but it is hidden in plain view, there to be recognized" by some and unnoticed by others (Davis, "Blue Remembered Hills," 3).

II

In the late Victorian period, even after the passage of the Labouchere Amendment, there was a flourishing, half-underground homosexual literary coterie in England. One manifestation of it was the Society of Chaeronea, a secret society the name of which indicates its orientation. Laurence Housman was a member; A. E. Housman was almost certainly not associated with it in any way (Naiditch, *Problems*, 58, note 2). I think that as a matter of general policy he kept his brother's friends at arm's length—a very long arm's length. This is suggested to me by the well-known account of how Housman was accosted in Cambridge one day by a man who introduced himself as an acquaintance of Laurence Housman. A. E. Housman responded stiffly, "Knowing my brother Laurence is no introduction to *me*," and walked off (L. Housman, *A. E. H.*, 91). The identity of this man is not known, and perhaps I am reading more into this incident than it warrants, but it seems to me to indicate that he was leery of his brother's associates and preferred not to have any contact with them.

In general, homosexual writers in the late nineteenth century were either "shamefaced or noisily defiant about their love for other men." Those who were open about their orientation, such as Symonds and Wilde, "sought by the power of their . . . talents to give colour, meaning and beauty to their own sexual idiosyncrasies, . . . to make the everyday male whore a Hyacinthus, and . . . to create hinterlands of erotic fantasy and call them ancient Greece. . . . Symonds . . . was a fake when he applied 'Greek ideals' to his affairs with gondoliers and Swiss peasants" (Croft-Cooke, *Feasting with Panthers*, 2–3). Symonds coined the term "Urnings" to designate homosexuals, but the primary literary expression of homosexuality was the work of a small number of poets known collectively as the Uranians, which was part of the cultural landscape from 1889 through 1930. They stressed the "Greek ideal," "the worship of young male beauty without sex" (Fussell, *Great War*, 284). Although they were not precisely "shamefaced," their poetry was often printed anonymously. Their books were printed in small private editions for a limited readership, or, where commercially produced, disguised the subject by substituting females for males as objects of desire (a technique which Byron had also used to make his work commercially acceptable). Inevitably, the movement attracted some whose worship of "young male beauty" did not exclude sexual expression of their worship. The only authors in this group whose names are still known to more than a tiny number of specialists are Edward Carpenter, John Addington Symonds, Baron Corvo (Frederick Rolfe), and Lord Alfred Douglas. Neither Oscar Wilde nor A. E. Housman could be considered a Uranian. Although Laurence Housman had ties to many of the poets thus designated, especially through his association with *The Yellow Book*, A. E. Housman kept his distance. Most of the Uranian writers, then as now, were known only within their own circle, and their poetry is something less than inspired. In addition to authors who wrote poems celebrating the "love of comrades," in Whitman's phrase, there were some Uranians who wrote poems celebrating the charms of prepubescent boys. This overt cult of pederasty produced pedestrian verse at the best and some thoroughly nasty effusions of boy-love at the worst. In short, the creations of the Uranians are as different as possible from those of Housman in every respect, even as to the open expression or alternative regendering of the object of desire. Housman customarily simply used gender-free words instead of either direct expression or elaborate disguises, as we shall see.

A homosexual author writing in the 1890s had to make certain choices. If he wanted his work to be published and appeal to the general public, he had to disguise or obscure the object of desire. Not only did he have to discretely conceal his actual life, if he were to write of his experiences at all, he had to invent a heterosexual version or analogue of his actual homosexual life. If he chose to express himself openly, he forfeited a general readership and risked prison and exile, like Wilde. Or, of course, he could skip prison and go directly into voluntary exile on the Continent, where he would be free to write as he chose. In that case, however, he had to cut himself off from home, family, and friends. If he chose not to do this, he had to be content with private printing in a small edition for a limited readership while still running the risk of attracting the unwelcome attention of the guardians of public morality and following the path of Wilde. During Wilde's trial, his friends "either went abroad or kept their heads well down," and homosexual poets either ceased to publish or "took good care that their art concealed their craft, like A. E.

Housman" (Reade, *Sexual Heretics*, 53). Housman chose the first course, reached a general readership, and retained all his social and familial ties as well as his university standing while escaping to the freer air of the Continent for his holidays. The very different poetry of Wilde and Housman has the same aim; both authors attempted to express same-sex love through the use of what has been called a "poetic code." Housman's strategy was one of tight control, whereas Wilde overtly expressed his "fascination with youth and male beauty," although they shared this fascination (Robbins, "Curious Construction," 147). Ultimately, Housman's strategy was obviously more successful.

Writing under these restraints Housman was forced to be allusive and symbolic rather than direct. He might well have chosen this course in any event, as he was an intensely private person who did not want his personality to obtrude itself into the surface, at least, of his poetry. He wrote to an American correspondent that his work was far more interesting than he was. It is notable that his more overtly gay poetry was never published in his lifetime but waited hidden in his notebooks until he was dead. Laurence Housman ultimately included this poetry in the two posthumous collections of his brother's lyrics. Had Housman not been working under such constraints, it is entirely possible that his poetry would not have been nearly as good as it is.

Some clearly homosexual poetry is by any standards great. One need only think of the classical writers (whose work was in Victorian times deliberately mistranslated to remove the expression of homosexuality) and of Walt Whitman. Long before the Labouchere Amendment, however, when in about 1867 Swinburne and others wanted to bring out an English edition of Walt Whitman's *Leaves of Grass*, entire sections, and most notably "Calamus," had to be excised because of its openly homosexual content. What could be tolerated among the few could not be offered to the many, and Housman's work appealed to the many rather than the few. Housman's orientation was largely hidden even from those most sympathetic to it, although many men now known to have been homosexual, including E. M. Forster, read and understood the subtext. Indeed, Forster, after reading *A Shropshire Lad*, developed what "might . . . be called an unrequited love for its author" (Gardner, "One Fraction of a Summer Field," 162). He made a bid for Housman's attention by writing to him but was rebuffed.

Whitman's sexual orientation was not nearly so well disguised as Housman's. From at least 1877, "Whitman" was used by many as a code word for illicit homosexual desire. Whitman's robust celebration of "comradeship" was indeed difficult to misread. In Robert K. Martin's opinion, he "intended his work to communicate his homosexuality to his readers, and . . . homosexual readers have from the very beginning understood his ho-

mosexual meanings" (*Homosexual Tradition*, 3). Certainly John Addington Symonds did. He was sure of his own interpretation of *Leaves of Grass*
and began corresponding with Whitman. He wrote to Whitman asking
for a clear confirmation of his homosexuality, but Whitman "would never
make an open admission of just what he meant and felt about his chum,
his mate, his comrade." Symonds was puzzled by Whitman's immediate
denial of homosexuality. What we call "Victorianism" was not limited to
England, and the Victorians, including Whitman, "had many defenses
against criticism or interference with their secret lives . . . [and] concealed
their activities under cover of Christian love for their fellows" (Croft-
Cooke, *Feasting with Panthers*, 128–29). Edmund Gosse, who anxiously
concealed his nature until he told Symonds "the not very startling truth
in a burst of confidence" (ibid., 3), wrote that Whitman had "a staggering
ignorance, a perhaps wilfull non-perception, of the real physical conditions of his nature. But the truth about him (the innermost truth) escapes
from almost every page for those who can read" (cited ibid., 129). Whitman himself may simply not have known what he was and have believed
his denial, difficult as it may be to credit this thesis.

Although there were penalties in America for homosexuality (and in
some places these penalties were horrific), there was no national law.
Even so, Whitman made considerable concessions, censoring himself by
altering his poems and even removing passages that were too blatantly
homosexual. For example, before publication of "Once I Pass'd through a
Populous City" he changed "I remember only the man who wandered
with me there for love of me" to "I remember only a woman I casually
met there who detain'd me for love of me." Housman would probably
have written "friend" or "companion" and thus sidestepped the issue entirely. Although Whitman had more artistic freedom than his English
comrades, because of social pressures he protected himself by changing
pronouns and other gender-specific words. The success of his (only partial) self-censorship is indicated by the almost complete silence in American criticism concerning this aspect of his work (Martin, *Homosexual
Tradition*, 7). His artistic freedom came with a price tag. In his art as in
his life, he was forced to act an artificial role in order to conceal his actual
concerns. This artistic freedom was precisely the freedom that Wilde had
claimed, and his downfall was also its downfall.

Whitman's "adhesiveness" was recognized in England, Jeremy Bourne
assures me, as sublimated homosexuality. However, even though the subtext of his poetry was clearly discernible, his term adhesiveness "could be
interpreted as the state of loving anybody of either sex" (Reade, *Sexual
Heretics*, 3). Whitman was not universally praised either by homosexuals
or by other "sexually deviant" writers. Symonds, Hopkins, and even
Swinburne (who was not homosexual but rather fascinated by flaggela-

tion) all used "Whitman" as a code word for homosexuality. Their response to him, however, was ambivalent, either because of his compromises (the means by which he moderated the overt homosexuality of his poetry) on the one hand, or because they were insufficiently thoroughgoing, on the other hand. Indeed, Gerard Manley Hopkins wrote to Robert Bridges on 18 October 1882 that Whitman was "a very great scoundrel" for transgressing "the prohibition of genital contact between men" (Dellamora, *Masculine Desire*, 88). Swinburne turned against Whitman after the passage of the Labouchere Amendment and repudiated him, but in 1887 "Whitman" was still his code word for homosexuality, which he at that time characterized as a disease (ibid., 92). Housman certainly knew Whitman's poetry and was influenced by it, but he avoided becoming a code word for anything except irascible and scathing remarks about other scholars in his own field.

Walter Pater was a friend of Swinburne's, and was introduced by him to the homosexual painter Simeon Solomon, whose idealized pictures of youths Pater admired. Pater's *Studies in the History of the Renaissance* revealed his own susceptibility to male beauty only too clearly. The innuendoes to which the "conclusions" gave rise prompted him to censor himself, removing this chapter from the second edition because, as he said in his introduction to the third edition, "it might possibly mislead some of those young men into whose hands it might fall." His novel *Marius the Epicurean*, however, dealt in a different form with the same ideas, and in it male friendships, dependent on physical attraction and thus erotic, are some of the strongest emotions described (Reade, *Sexual Heretics*, 20).

Of all the homosexual authors of "that curiously inconsistent half-tolerant, half-hostile" period, the one poet who stands out from the rest is Housman, in whose poetry "there is no place for sensuality." It is Housman's "acceptance of the social conventions of the period which provides the poetic tension" (ibid., 48–49). In the posthumous collections of Housman's poetry, this acceptance is muted or absent, and thus the poetic tension is of another sort.

III

The area of gay literary studies is a relatively new one. Only since about 1970 has it stepped, via the pages of gay publications, into the pages of scholarly and critical studies and made its way into the college curriculum. Perhaps the breakthrough was heralded by Steven Marcus's *The Other Victorians: A Study of Sexuality and Pornography in Mid-Nineteenth-Century England*, published in 1966, which, however, had a great deal more to say about pornography than about sexuality. Rupert Croft-Cooke's *Feasting with Panthers: A New Consideration of Some Late Victorian Writers*, which deals, among others, with Symonds, Walt Whitman, Walter Pater, and Oscar Wilde, taking full account of their homosexuality, appeared in 1967. Timothy d'Arch Smith's study of the Uranians, *Love in Earnest*, was published in 1970. The same year saw the appearance of both the first book I can find on gay studies from a reputable university press, *The Perverse Imagination: Sexuality and Literary Culture*, a collection of essays edited by Irving Buchan, published by New York University Press, and an excellent anthology of gay Victorian writing, *Sexual Heretics: Male Homosexuality in English Literature from 1850–1900*, edited by Brian Reade. Reade also provided an excellent fifty-six-page introduction that surveys in exhaustive detail the Victorian homosexual scene. He discusses such authors as Symonds, Whitman, Tennyson (for certain passages in "In Memoriam"), Hopkins, Swinburne, Pater, Baron Corvo, Housman, and Wilde, among others. He describes the homosexually charged atmosphere of the academic world of prep schools and colleges, and he also considers the artistic scene, dealing in great detail with Simeon Solomon and Henry Scott Tuke (a painter who created many pictures in the "naked boys bathing" mode). The interested reader can consult Reade for more information on these aspects of the Victorian scene.

Once the gate was opened, more serious studies followed. In 1977 the Athlone Press issued Jeffrey Meyers' study, *Homosexuality & Literature 1890–1930* (reissued in 1987). It deals with Wilde, Gide, Mann, Proust, Conrad, Forster, T. E. Lawrence, and D. H. Lawrence. In 1979 Meyers's study of homosexual prose writers was joined on the bookshelves by a study of homosexual American poets, Robert K. Martin's *The Homosexual Tradition in American Poetry*, issued by the University of Texas Press. Ten years later, in 1987, Gregory Woods's *Articulate Flesh: Male homo-eroticism & modern poetry*, was issued by Yale University Press. Meanwhile, in 1984, Phyllis Grosskurth's edition of the memoirs of John Addington Symonds was brought out in both England and the United States.

Only in the 1990s did the slow but steady trickle of studies of the homosexual element in literature become, if not a spate, at least a steady stream, as even a cursory examination of the catalogues of the various university and commercial presses will demonstrate. It would be tedious to list all the relevant works. This is in itself an indication of the growth of the field of gay studies. Two books should, however, be mentioned. Richard Dellamora's *Masculine Desire: The Sexual Politics of Victorian Aestheticism*, was brought out by the University of North Carolina Press in 1990. Dellamora deals with Whitman, Pater, Swinburne, Wilde, Hopkins, and Ruskin, but, significantly, there is no mention whatsoever of

Housman. In 1995 the Cambridge University Press issued *Cultural Politics at the fin de siecle*, edited by Sally Ledger and Scott McCracken, which included an essay by Ruth Robbins, " 'A very curious construction': masculinity and the poetry of A. E. Housman and Oscar Wilde." This is a serious, if limited, consideration of the homosexuality underlying Housman's poetry.

More recently, the field of gay studies has concentrated on exploring the conditions of the emergence of homosexuality as a distinct category of human behavior in Western culture and the consequences of its emergence from the general spectrum of human possibility. The attempt has been to delineate homosexuality as a specific portion of the spectrum and separate it from its near neighbors. Discussion centers on whether homosexuality is a matter of self-identification, emotion, or behavior, and what its relationship is to the concept of masculinity. It deals with the processes and problems of self-affirmation and self-definition. Freud's 1905 theory of sexuality is at the center of much of this concern (Cohen, "Double Lives," 85–87). One central aspect of gay studies is that of the gradations between friendship, nonphysical love, physical attraction, noncoital sexual expression, and coital sexual activity. Where, on this continuum, does "homosexuality" begin? This is not my problem, and I am happy to leave it to experts in the field.

Studies of the homosexual aspects of modern literature are a very recent phenomenon, and yet to ignore a fundamental aspect of an author's life is to ignore one of the fundamental sources of his writing. The present study demonstrates the importance of reading Housman's poems in the light thrown on them by his life. It focuses on the elements in his poems, including light verse and poems not directly on the love theme, which are the expression of his own tormented and ambivalent eroticism. It began as a doctoral dissertation (not the first one on the homosexuality of a given author, and perhaps not even the first one on this aspect of Housman's poetry). I trust that it will have something valuable to say to the nonspecialist as well as being stimulating to the specialist.

IV

I wish to express my appreciation to Dr. Burnett and Mr. Naiditch for providing me with photocopies of articles I was unable to locate, and for their general assistance and friendship. The dissertation on which this book is based has been read and criticized at various times by many people. The comments of Professor John Bayley of Oxford University, Professor Jerome Mandel of Tel Aviv University, the late Professor Emeritus Robert Friend of the Hebrew University in Jerusalem, Mr. Alan Holden of The Housman Society, and Mr. Paul G. Naiditch of the UCLA Library Special Collections Department, have been most welcome and appreciated. Professor Friend, Professor Mandel, and Mr. Naiditch were especially helpful in offering not only general criticism but also specific suggestions and corrections of errors. Dr. Burnett and Mr. Naiditch have also read and provided suggestions concerning the preface, suggestions for which I am grateful. What is worthwhile in the book is partially to be credited to all of those who have read the manuscript in whole or in part; any errors remaining despite their assiduous efforts are my own.

Acknowledgments

THE AUTHOR AND PUBLISHERS WOULD LIKE TO THANK THE FOLLOWING for permission to reprint copyrighted material: The Society of Authors as the Literary Representative of the Estate of A. E. Housman for the poetry and prose of A. E. Housman; Henry Holt for poems from "A Shropshire Lad" authorized edition copyright 1924, 1965 by Henry Holt and Co., poems from "Last Poems" copyright 1922 by Henry Holt and Co., copyright 1950 by Barclays Bank Ltd., poems from "More Poems" copyright 1936 by Barclays Bank Ltd., © 1964 by Robert E. Symons, all from *The Collected Poems of A. E. Housman* c 1965 by Henry Holt and Co., reprinted by arrangement with Henry Holt and Co. LLC; and poems from "Additional Poems" from *My Brother, A. E. Housman* by Laurence Housman, copyright renewed © 1965, 1966 by Lloyds Bank Ltd., reprinted with the permission of Scribner, a division of Simon and Schuster. We would also like to thank Ms. Devi Chapman for permission to reprint Sylvia Bruce's translation of Heine; Prof. Willis Barnstone for permission to reprint his translations of two poems by Sappho; Ms. Jean Cantu for permission to reprint several poems by Robert Friend; and Mary Holtby for permission to reprint her poem "A. E. Housman (1859–1936)," taken from *How to Become Absurdly Well Informed about the Famous and Infamous*, edited by E. O. Parrott and published by Penguin Books. Poems from *The Complete Works of C. P. Cavafy*, copyright ©Kyveli A. Singopoulo 1963 and 1968, translation Rogers, Coleridge and White © Edmund Keeley and Philip Sherrard 1975 and 1984, are reproduced by permission of the Estate of Cavafy, the translators c/o Rogers, Coleridge & White Ltd., 20 Powis Mews, London W11 1JN, and the Hogarth Press as publisher. "Eloi, Eloi, Lama Sabachthani?" by D. H. Lawrence from *The Complete Poems of D. H. Lawrence*, edited by V. de Sola Pinto & F. W. Roberts, copyright © 1964, 1971 by Angelo Ravagli and C, M. Weekley, Executors of the Estate of Frieda Lawrence Ravagli, is reprinted by permission of Viking Penguin, a division of Penguin Putnam Inc., The Estate of Frieda Lawrence Ravagli, and Laurence Pollinger Limited. Parts of W. B. Yeats's "Sailing to Byzantium" and "A Dialogue of Self and Soul" from *The Collected Poems of W. B. Yeats*, Revised Second Edition edited by Richard J. Finneran, copyright 1928, 1933 by Macmillan Publishing

Company, copyright renewed © 1956 by Georgie Yeats, and 1961 by Bertha Georgie Yeats, are reproduced by permission of Scribner, a division of Simon & Schuster, and A. P. Watt Ltd. on behalf of Michael B. Yeats. We would also like to thank The Mansell Collection/TimePix for the photograph of A. E. Houseman and permission to reproduce it both on the dust jacket and as a frontispiece. A part of chapter 10 first appeared in a somewhat different form as "The Horses and the Reins" in *Victorian Poetry*, 34 no. 1 (1996). Small parts of Chapters 4 and 8 first appeared in a somewhat different form as "Housman's Escape from the Turning Mill" and "Housman, Hardy, and the Boer War Elegy" in the *Housman Society Journal*, 24 (1998) and 25 (1990), respectively. I would also like to thank both publications for their agreement to the re-use of this material.

Introduction

The POETRY OF A. E. HOUSMAN IS FAR MORE COMPLEX AND INNOVATIVE than has been generally recognized. It is marked by an apparent stylistic simplicity in dealing with the traditional subjects of poetry and an ambiguous approach to timeless poetic themes. Nature, love, the function of poetry, and poetic immortality are all here, but Housman's treatment of them tends to be subtly original. He raises fundamental issues obliquely, setting the reality against the ideal and exposing the implicit falseness of stereotypical assumptions. Often in seeming to uphold the accepted values of traditional middle-class Victorian culture, he in fact undermines them. Housman is the poet of "what is" as opposed to "what is assumed to be" or "what ought to be."[1] Thus, there is a tension between the mode of expression and the surface meaning on the one hand, and the underlying thrust of the thought on the other.

The traditional forms of poetry, mainline English literary expression, and the overt text are played against the realistic appraisal of the subject matter as seen through Housman's very private eyes. He combines acceptance of the traditional "rules" of poetry with his own untraditional interpretation of the subject matter, quite often in the form of implicit or explicit parody, although the parodic element in much of his poetry is so subtle as to be easily overlooked. Quite often, what the poetry seems to mean is very different from its actual import. This combination of outer conformity with implied inner nonconformity results in an unexpected view, which turns the accepted terms upside down or inside out. Housman has, par excellence, the knack of seeing the world from a different angle and communicating his vision so subtly that its implications can easily be overlooked. His poetry presents a mirror world that has as much reality as the real one of distorted absurdity in which assumptions are made that, however false, are extremely comforting, especially those assumptions concerning the relationship of the sexes. This is most apparent in his humorous verses and in his avowed parodies, only a few of which are easily available. It is, however, perceptible elsewhere if one is on the alert for it. Even his humorous verse is written with a straight face, though with a twinkle in the eye, fusing the strictest conventionality with the wildest originality, and even in his most serious verse, the skewed vision manifests itself.

Outwardly in conformity with poetic tradition, much of the thrust of Housman's poetry undercuts this same tradition. This duality mirrors his double persona. The public, outer man was a crusty and forbidding university don whose unapproachability and rudeness were legendary. This public persona functioned as a mask for the private, inner man, agonizingly shy, vulnerable, and defensive. There is no dearth of contemporary evidence for this dual personality. J. D. Duff, in a letter cited by Naiditch, described Housman as "quite gentle and friendly in ordinary intercourse" (*Problems*, 46). On the other hand, Richard Aldington as a student encountered Professor Housman and has recorded the poet's lack of casual intercourse and ease with the students and his general standoffishness and churlishness. He says, "the real reason for his extraordinary behavior was that he was hopelessly and helplessly shy and sensitive, as well as proud and exacting." However, he adds, "on rare occasions when Housman was able to break through the unnatural barriers holding him aloof from his fellow creatures, he could be and indeed was . . . a genial companion . . . [with] the gift of laughter" (*Housman*, 7–8). W. R. M. Lamb, a friend for almost twenty-five years, found in him "a lively, sensitive nature, with a special clearness and accuracy in his dealing alike with books and things and persons. . . . In his ordinary talk, the sting of a strangely pungent remark would be softened by a genial smile and a twinkle" ("Housman," 822). He notes that "his warm humanity . . . showed itself, rather shyly, at moments of happy companionship." Such moments did not always occur. William Rothenstein, the artist who painted Housman's portrait more than once and became a friend, records that he "neither looked nor talked like a poet . . . but was grim and dry" and recalls how a guest at his house, having met Housman, remarked to him, "Well, William, so far from believing that man wrote *The Shropshire Lad*, I shouldn't even have thought him capable of reading it!" (*Men and Memories*, 2:39).

One of Housman's most perceptive friends, Dr. Percy Withers, commenting on the contrast between the man and the mask, wrote:

> Housman assumed a shell of callousness, and hid so well beneath it that one might have met him long and familiarly on the beaten path, and never suspected the disguise. His chiselled speech . . . , his sardonic quips, his biting satire, his easy resort to mockery and scoffing: of such was this outward vestment composed. And it was a grim deceit. Underneath beat as warm and generous a heart . . . as I have ever known." (*Buried Life*, 76–7).

Wilfrid Scawen Blunt in his diary for Sunday, 26 November 1911, recorded a walk that he took with Housman:

> He shows no trace now of anything romantic, being a typical Cambridge Don, prim in his manner, silent and rather shy, conventional in dress and

manner, learned, accurate, and well-informed . . . talking fairly well, but not brilliantly or with any originality, depressed in tone, and difficult to rouse to any strong expression of opinion. Nevertheless, I like him. . . . We had much pleasant talk all day, and sat up again till twelve at night telling ghost stories. He takes an interest in these. . . . [He] would, I think, be quite silent if he were allowed to be.

On hearing of Blunt's comment, the poet remarked that it was quite true. He gave an impression of aloofness which one Cambridge man called "Olympian airs."[2]

Despite this aloofness, this unease in social intercourse, this Olympian detachment, when Gertrude Stein and Alice B. Toklas visited England, and the latter was seated at dinner next to Housman, he "struck up a lively conversation with her" (Mellow, *Charmed Circle*, 211). And despite the shyness, he proved a most genial host to Cyril Clemens, Mark Twain's cousin, who visited him in Cambridge. In the Housman memorial issue of the *Mark Twain Quarterly* the obituary notice includes the following comment: "We have had the great honor of dining with Housman . . . , of walking and talking with him beside the Cam, and of joking and drinking whiskey and soda with him" (Clemens, "Editorial," 1). Clemens says that "Housman was a striking man . . . [with] keen, piercing, kindly grey eyes. . . . His smile was of a rare sweetness, and the twinkle in his eye gave evidence of a keen sense of humor" ("Housman as a Conversationalist," 9). Contemporary comments from many others, acquaintances, students, friends, relatives, all indicate the same disjunction. In this respect, Housman was comparable to Walter Pater. Both were "secret and paradoxical" men, men "of intense feeling, of emotions that writhed out of sight," and like Pater Housman appeared to be "a dull stick, a . . . reticent scholar who had no words to waste on mere conversation," a man of "reserve" (Croft-Cooke, *Feasting with Panthers*, 181).

This dual personality has, of course, also been noted by those who know him only through the reminiscences of others. As early as 1936, in a double review of *More Poems* and A. S. F. Gow's Memoir, the reviewer of the *Times Literary Supplement* remarked on "the sensitive and affectionate spirit that lay concealed behind an exterior which was both prim and grim" ("A. E. Housman," 845). George A. Taylor in the same year noted the contrast between the "pessimistic strain" of the poetry and "this laughter-loving, genial Fellow of St. John's, Oxford, and of Trinity, Cambridge—this university Professor, whose talk at the dinner table of the Fellows' hall was invariably . . . of the nature that brought about a laugh." ("Housman," 389) Nor have more recent critics dropped the matter. In 1990 Piers Browne wrote, "he paradoxically hid a loving sympathetic heart beneath a stiff and starchy exterior" (*Elegy in Arcady*, 86).

Housman was aloof and friendly, shy and animated, rude and kind, brusque and patient, sharp and gentle, depending on whose testimony one wishes to accept. In fact, he was all of these things—to different people.

The less the likelihood of intimacy, the easier he found it to relax and be genial. Thus, with Alice B. Toklas and Cyril Clemens, whose visits to England were brief and unlikely to be often repeated, he was able to take off his mask and be his natural self. With others, those with whom he was in daily contact, it was far more difficult. Intimacy was a threat to the mask. Housman lived a double life. The public man in England conformed to a socially mandated and acceptable role from which he regularly escaped to the freer atmosphere of France and Italy, where he could periodically lay aside this public mask and be himself. It was only through his poetic personae that in England he could express himself (albeit guardedly) in a way that was impossible to the public mask he so assiduously cultivated.

It is now no secret, although it was during Housman's lifetime and for many years after his death in 1936, that he was a homosexual. This truth was revealed only at the end of 1967. His only surviving brother, Laurence Housman, had, in 1942, long before his own death in 1958, left a packet with the trustees of the British Museum to be opened twenty-five years thereafter and made available for publication. In accordance with his instructions, the packet was opened and the contents published, edited by John Carter, in *Encounter* in October 1967, as "A. E. Housman's *De Amicitia*." The packet contained the text of an article in which the truth about the poet was at last made public. Housman's was a naturally conservative nature. As Henry Maas, the editor of his letters, noted, "at heart he defied the world; but outwardly, circumstances and a naturally conformist temper of mind preserved an appearance of rigid propriety. He hid his emotions and . . . felt the bitterness of the frustration" (Maas, *Letters*, 22). The sexual orientation that tormented him was the source of a deep and endless conflict between what he wanted to be and what he could not help but be.

Critics writing before Laurence Housman's revelations concerning his brother's sexuality were hard put to explain the air of unhappiness which permeated the poetry.[3] They could only postulate an unhappy (heterosexual) love affair, as did Louis Gillet, who assumed there had been a cruel and hopeless separation from a woman ("une femme") on the other side of the world, who probably never knew of the distress that she caused, the great silent love that was never confessed, and never returned. Oliver Robinson, like Gillet, in his 1950 study of Housman's poetry speculated that he had had an early, unhappy love affair, or that "perhaps his brother and sister are withholding information of some . . . psychological eccentricity that would completely explain his bitterness." (*Angry Dust*, 49) This bitterness, he was sure, had nothing to do with his male friendships since "it is impossible to connect the vicissitudes of friendship in the poems with Housman's life as we know it" (ibid., 52) and his closest friend, Moses Jackson, "was apparently not a disappointment to Housman" (ibid., 52). It is notable that Robinson suspected that a secret had been kept by Katharine Symons (who in fact knew nothing of her brother's inner life) and Laurence Housman (who did) and sensed that the facts of Housman's life "as we know it" were incomplete. He had no suspicion at all as to the actual nature of the "secret." Like that of Wilfred Owens, Housman's poetry "absorbs homoerotic passion into technique and tempers intimate excitement until it becomes an ally of English literary tradition" (Fussell, *Great War*, 298). Brian Reade wrote that *A Shropshire Lad* "is like a beautiful ruin built over an invisible framework [of homoeroticism] and Housman obscured the framework so well that until recently not many readers of the poems seemed to guess that it was *l'amour de l'impossible* which haunted many of them" (*Sexual Heretics*, 48–49). This is rather overstated, even ignoring the comparison to "a ruin." It is questionable, whatever the self- or culturally imposed blinkers of Housman's contemporaries, whether it is only recently that readers have ceased to be that naive. Or, indeed, if they ever were.

In any case, some more perceptive critics seem to have had some intuition of the truth. Sensing the underlying erotic impulse of *A Shropshire Lad* and understanding its nature, Edmund Gosse commented on "its secret beauty, which enslaved the ear as some subterranean music of goblins might do, heard at twilight in a sequestered glade" ("Shropshire Lad," 21). E. M. Forster was certain that a personal experience underlay *A Shropshire Lad* and that Housman had fallen in love with a man (Gardner, " 'One Fraction of a Summer Field' "). They were not the only ones who certainly sensed the homosexual subtext of Housman's poetry.

Since the article in *Encounter*, the problem has been not to solve the assumed mystery but to integrate the solution into an understanding of the poetry. There have been only a few serious attempts to do so, and they are, for the most part, tentative and limited. Indeed, the importance of Housman's homosexuality to a full understanding of his poetry is still implicitly denied by some. There have been only a few worthwhile full-length articles published on the topic, those by Auden ("Jehovah Housman and Satan Housman," 1968), Robert K. Martin ("A. E. Housman's Two Strategies: *A Shropshire Lad* and *Last Poems*," 1984), Laurence Perrine ("Housman's 'Others, I am not the first' ," 1990), and Efrati ("Horses and the Reins," 1996). Robert K. Martin responded to those critics who dealt with the poems *in vacuo*, commenting that "no one seems to consider the possibility that the "private" life will be given shape in the art"

("A. E. Housman's Two Strategies," 14 n. 4). He proceeded to do so himself, saying, "A *Shropshire Lad* was indeed a deeply personal work, the poetic consequence of Housman's love for Moses Jackson and his recognition of the impossibility of fulfilling that love in life. Housman found an adequate means of rendering his love only through the effective exclusion of the personal self from the poems" (ibid., 14). He then proceeded to analyze the difference in tone between the two official collections, and adequately to account for it, in the light of Housman's sexual orientation.

Laurence Perrine used the knowledge of Housman's homosexuality brilliantly to explicate a single phrase of one poem. He noted that this knowledge "illumines and deepens the meaning of many Housman poems, to an extent that we might almost judge these poems as incomplete without it" ("Housman's 'Others,'" 37). And in his book *Housman's Poems*, John Bayley took Housman's sexuality into account, considering it "does much to determine the depth and complexity of his poetic being: the personality of his poetry, and the individual nature of his romanticism, come to light in the ways it declares itself" (29). However, he merely scratched the surface of "the ways it declares itself." Haber wrote that accepting Housman's homosexuality provides a new depth and understanding "of the main dynamic of his . . . work" because "many portions of his poetry are more closely related to his biography than had been supposed" (*A. E. Housman*, 13). This book explores that "dynamic" and that relationship.

Indeed, had Housman not been homosexual, it is probable that few of his poems would ever have been written. Discussing nineteenth- and early-twentieth-century homosexual prose fiction, Jeffrey Meyers pointed out that "the clandestine predilections of homosexual novelists are both an obstacle and a stimulus to art, and lead to a creative tension between repression and expression. The novels become a raid on inarticulate feelings, and force the authors to find a language of reticence and evasion, obliqueness and indirection. . . . [They] are characteristically subtle, allusive and symbolic" (*Homosexuality and Literature* 1). He ascribed the subtlety of such writing to the authors' "constant anxiety, fear, and sense of doom [that] intensifies isolation and introspection, heightens the intellectual defiance of the social outcast who is forced to question and challenge conventional ideas about morality and art, and encourages him to control the potentially dangerous element in his character through the order and form of art" (10). And so with poetry, especially lyric poetry. Meyers has provided a perfect and accurate description of Housman's work.

It may be noted parenthetically that such eighteenth-century homosexual poetry as that of John Wilmot, Earl of Rochester, seems (like mod-

ern, undisguised homosexual poetry such as that of Thom Gunn, Robert
Duncan, Robert Friend, and Alan Ginsberg) rather crude when compared
with the best such poetry of the nineteenth and early twentieth centuries,
that of Walt Whitman, Hart Crane, and A. E. Housman. To be sure,
these characteristics are not limited to literature written by homosexuals.
Subtlety, allusiveness, and symbolism are characteristic of good writing,
whoever the author. As Robert Browning said, "Art remains the one way
possible / Of speaking truth. . . . Art may tell a truth / Obliquely" (Browning, *Ring and the Book*, Book 12, 628). Telling the truth "obliquely"
means being subtle, allusive, and symbolic. Obliquity has lost ground as
"homosexuals have gained more and more courage to be honest about
their lives and this change is reflected in their art" (Martin, *Homosexual
Tradition*, xvi), which has not necessarily benefited from the change. Directness, as is obvious from Forster's *Maurice*, does not necessarily con-
tribute to artistry and may well militate against its achievement.

It is obviously true that in poetic language "each word will be apt to
have two, three, or even many meanings or implications. . . . Of these
various meanings one may be the primary denotation, the others secondary, suggested, or connoted. One may be the apparent or surface meaning,
the others latent. But often the surface meaning will be of less importance than the latent ones; the idea having true poetic significance and
bearing the emotional emphasis will be not said but suggested, and . . .
the secondary meaning may be the one of prime importance" (Prescott,
"Imagination," 38). If this is the case in normative poetry during a time
when there are few or no subjects forbidden to art and literature, how
much truer it must have been during the Victorian period when so many
subjects were of necessity barred from appearance in poetry unless
swathed in veils of obfuscation. It must have been even truer still for
poetry written by homosexuals, like Housman, who preferred to be even
more ostensibly silent than others about sexuality, especially their own,
since the truth that the homosexual poet or writer wished to tell had to
be more carefully hidden than other truths. This entailed an extreme degree of "self-censorship (. . . in which metaphor [is] extensively used as a
means of concealment, a mask)," and "clearly, where homosexual desires
and acts are punishable . . . , homo-erotic literature will tend to be metaphorical and oblique" (Woods, *Articulate Flesh*, 47, 195).

It must never be forgotten that the end of the nineteenth century was
a period of rigid official adherence to the prescribed forms, and woe to
those who defied the social conventions. Homophobia was rampant, as
demonstrated by the popular reaction to the Wilde trial, and "the extent
to which Housman's life and work were determined by the almost patho-
logical fear of homosexuality which prevailed in late Victorian Britain
goes unconsidered" in most commentaries (Wells). I think that this pub-

lic attitude and Housman's consequent dread of having his secret brought to light explain why he was such an intensely lonely man. For homosexual authors like Housman, it was essential to disguise their sexual preferences and to give the impression of "normalcy." There were "consequences for their personal lives of the discrepancy between an apparent public heterosexuality and a private homosexuality (expressed publicly in indirect ways) . . . [and] the emotional price for such concealment was high, although the tensions created by the need for a constant disguise may also have been the source of a certain artistic strength" (Martin, *The Homosexual Tradition*, 91). Housman paid that emotional price for his artistic strength.

T. E. Lawrence described himself in *Seven Pillars of Wisdom*: "There was my craving to be liked—so strong and nervous that never could I open myself friendly to another. The terror of failure in an effort so important made me shrink from trying." In a review of Lawrence's book, next to the citation of this passage, according to the testimony of Laurence Housman, his brother had written in the margin, "This is me" (L. Housman, *De Amicitia*, 39). As Cyril Clemens said a few years after Housman's death, in him "there seemed to be always something of a suffering without hope. . . . It is safe to say that his deepest need was affection; he won more of it than he knew" ("A. E. Housman and His Publishers").

It is not, after all, the outer events of Housman's life that reveal him best, but his poetry. It is almost as if Housman were following Cavafy's advice: "Try to keep them, poet, / those erotic visions of yours, / . . . Put them, half-hidden, in your lines" ("When They Come Alive"), for that is what he did, and this writer is, again in Cavafy's words, using those lines to understand him. "From all I did and all I said / let no one try to find out who I was / . . . From my most unnoticed actions, / my most veiled writing— / from these alone will I be understood" ("Hidden Things"). As Otto Skutsch said, "the human springs" of his "passion, which the man concealed and the scholar had no cause to uncover, lie open to view in his poetry." (*A. E. Housman*, 1).

The Road of Danger,
Guilt, and Shame

Clio

1

The Bogle of the Hairy Weid

HOUSMAN'S HOMOSEXUALITY MAY BE THE TRUE EXPLANATION OF THE dream poem in his manuscript notebook "D," which was certainly written after the start of 1925. The entry is recorded, including the prose preface, the brackets, and the footnote, thus:[1]

I dreamt I was reading a passage of George Eliot, in which was quoted, printed in italics as prose, the verse

The bogle of the [hairy weid]*
That beast nor man hath trod
Must not be seen of you nor me
Nor aught but hell and God.
*understood as a heath or moor

George Eliot, too, presumably underwent an internal conflict. The strict conventional morals of her upbringing and her age proscribed sexual relationships unless they were sanctified and sanctioned by the marriage ceremony. This moral code is evident in her novels, most notably perhaps in the case of Maggie in *The Mill on the Floss*, who is ostracized by society for the mere appearance of sexual transgression. And yet, George Eliot's personal life was hardly in conformity with this moral code; she lived for years with a man to whom she was not only not married but who was, in fact, officially married to another woman. Thus, in a dream, Housman could easily project his conflict onto George Eliot, whose situation was not dissimilar in strict morality from his own. I would suggest that the "hairy weid" may represent the arena where this conflict is played out, an area unknown to the animal creation and still largely unexplored by man (Freud's *On Dreams* of 1914 being very recent), one "that beast nor man hath trod." It is what we would today call the subconscious. Why "hairy"? I would suggest that it is pubic hair, of which the Victorians seem to have had a horror, which was unseen even in nude serious paintings, being visible only in avowed pornography.

A "bogle," according to Katherine Briggs (30–33), is a generic phantom, a night specter, an undefined creature of superstitious dread, a frightening and dangerous tormentor of mankind (including woman-kind). The "bogle" haunting the "hairy weid" is then the specter of the tormented dreamer's forbidden, and dangerous, sexuality, which must be hidden from society. "Must not be seen of you nor me" may mean either that we—society in general—must not see such things or that such things must not be seen concerning us. No matter how carefully hidden it is, it plunges its unfortunate victim into a personal hell of self-condemnation. Those who were guilty of sexual transgressions were, in the popular esti-mation, literally doomed to a physical hell after death, as well as what in many cases must have been a living hell in life. Yet Housman's dream poem suggests that, ultimately, God may not reject such people. Again, there is an ambiguity, as the last line may be read to mean either that such transgressions cannot be hidden from God or that there is no need to hide them from Him. This poetic ambiguity well reflects Housman's own attitude toward his sexual deviation from the accepted mode. I be-lieve that this conflict underlies many of his overtly "normal" love poems as well as the ostensibly nonerotic and comic verse. It is the ultimate source of the idiosyncratic vision so apparent in his "unofficial" verse and so obscured, deeply buried but nonetheless felt, in his "official" poetry. It permeates all his work. Indeed, it might be said that his life was a meta-phor for his poetry, and his poetry a metaphor for his life.

I am using the term "official" to designate the poetry which the author himself chose to publish during his lifetime and under his direct supervi-sion: A Shropshire Lad (ASL), Last Poems (LP), and scattered contribu-tions to newspapers, journals, etc. The term "unofficial" poetry refers to More Poems (MP) and Additional Poems (AP), posthumously published, as well as to verses included in the various memoirs written about him by his friends and relatives (verses written for their private amusement and delectation), poems reconstructed from his notebooks, which were edited and published in 1955 by Tom Burns Haber and in 1997 by Archie Bur-nett, and other scattered remains. The canon consists of both types of poetry. It includes the official collections (A Shropshire Lad, Last Poems, and three translations that Housman contributed to Pollard's Odes from the Greek Dramatists in 1890). It also includes the two unofficial collec-tions taken posthumously from the complete—or nearly complete—poems in the notebooks and published by Laurence Housman (More Poems and Additional Poems).

Much of Housman's work consists of dramatic monologues. Unlike Tennyson or Browning, however, Housman did not choose to speak from behind the mask, or through the mouth of, literary, mythical, or histori-cal personages, even anonymous ones. His primary mask is Terence Hear-say, the "Shropshire Lad" himself, a contemporary figure of no particular note except among his rural neighbors, for whose country dances he provides the music and who entertains them with his poetic compositions. Terence as a character would have been quite comfortable in one of Hardy's novels. He functions as Housman's alter ego and mouthpiece and is the putative author of the poems in *A Shropshire Lad*. As John Keble wrote, "poetry is the indirect expression . . . of some overpowering emotion . . . the direct indulgence whereof is somehow repressed."[2]

Housman's solution to the problem of expressing and repressing himself at the same time was this persona, a mask through whom he could simultaneously be seen and remain hidden, speak and remain silent. Terence, as Housman explained to a correspondent, "is an imaginary figure with something of my temper and view of life. Very little in the book [*A Shropshire Lad*] is biographical."[3] The poet's sister Katharine Symons confirms this: "It is a mistake to try to identify A. E. H. personally with his phantom lads of Shropshire. . . . Where his poems can be identified with himself they are quite foreign to the Shropshire series" (*Recollections* 25 U.K., 33 U.S. ed.). Laurence Housman concurred: "wherever they [the poems] are least like 'A Shropshire Lad' they are most deeply and truly like the man he really was who wrote them" (Graves, *A. E. Houseman*, 112, quoting Laurence Housman's introduction to *A Shropshire Lad*). The term "biographical," however, needs extremely careful consideration. It is true that the incidents and characters in the Shropshire cycle are imaginary and in that sense they are not biographical. Indeed, I find a large element of parody in this group of poems. However, in another sense, they do reflect those aspects of Housman's personality that were assiduously hidden from the general view. They thus indeed function as a kind of biographical mirror, reflecting if not expressing their author, but the reflection is only partial, the reflection of a distorting mirror. However, the personae, Terence and the other anonymous characters, acted as a safety-valve that made it possible for Housman to relieve the pressure for self-expression, which would otherwise have been intolerable, without at the same time revealing himself naked to the world. Thus, the various personae both are and are not Housman himself. Terence is his spokesman. He says, ". . . since the world has still / Much good, but much less good than ill, / And while the sun and moon endure / Luck's a chance but trouble's sure, / I'd face it as a wise man would, / And train for ill and not for good" (ASL 62). Housman, here I think speaking for himself, unmasked, says the same thing.

> I to my perils
>> Of cheat and charmer
>> Came clad in armour
>>> By stars benign
> Hope lies to mortals
> And most believe her,
> But man's deceiver
>> Was never mine.
>
> The thoughts of others
>> Were light and fleeting,
>> Of lovers' meeting
>>> Or luck or fame.
> Mine were of trouble,
>> And mine were steady;
> So I was ready
>> When trouble came.

(MP 6)

The grimly realistic thought is expressed with a relish, a zest and verve, which exhilarates rather than depresses. Yes, "trouble's sure" but if one "trains for ill" one will be "ready" when it comes, "clad in armour" to meet it. This is what the poem says, and the idea is universally applicable, but only because "trouble" is a general, all-embracing term. As soon as one asks what the word "trouble" means in Housman's poetry, one realizes that it is not a vague concept but a very specific one, for that "trouble" is a thread that runs all through his lyrics; it is the "cursed trouble" (MP 21), the "ancient evil' (AP 12) that "the stars have . . . dealt me" (AP 17), the fate of the "star-defeated" (ASL 15) man who is not like other men and is also hopelessly in love with one who does not return that love.

The "perils" to be faced are those of "cheat and charmer," three lines further identified as "Hope" and personified as feminine ("most believe *her*"), a liar, and "man's deceiver." 'Man's deceiver' is "woman," and has been so since Eve tempted Adam to eat the fruit of the tree. The "perils" are the dangers that the feminine constitutes for the masculine. "But man's deceiver / Was never mine." Others think of "luck," but Housman and his lads are "luckless" (AP 20), fundamentally different from those "others" who think also of "lovers' meetings" (an ambiguous term, but one that readers would presumably identify as applying to heterosexual lovers). These stars that provide the "armour" by which one can survive the "trouble" they themselves have allotted as one's portion are the only "benign" ones in Housman's poetry. Ironically, they have at the same time endowed the speaker with his "trouble" and armed him against the "deceiver" by making him immune to her charms. The ambivalence thus hinted at surfaces in other poems to be discussed later. The "armour" is both a symbol of the poet's immunity to the feminine "cheat and charmer" and the mask behind which his face is hidden.

He donned that mask as a very young man and never again removed it. One aspect of it is his persona Terence, who also "trained for ill." Indeed Housman's poetry in general is the expression of this mask, as is the poetry of his contemporary, the Alexandrian poet C. P. Cavafy, who wore the same mask for the same reason. Cavafy wrote, in "Aimilianos Monae, Alexandrian, A.D. 628–655" (*Collected Poems*, 88),

> Out of talk, appearance, and manners
> I'll make an excellent suit of armor;
> and in this way I'll face malicious people
> without the slightest fear of weakness.
>
> They'll try to injure me.
> But of those who come near me none will know
> Where to find my wounds, my vulnerable places,
> under the deceptions that will cover me.

There is no proof that Housman knew Cavafy's poetry, but it is at least possible. In any case, they were writing at the same time about many of the same concerns. It is clear from Housman's own statement that "very little" is biographical, and from the statements of his sister and brother as well, that in some of the poems, at least, there are biographical aspects and thus sometimes and in some places we hear Housman's own voice. Having subtracted the greater part, which is not ostensibly biographical, the residue consists of that "very little" which is.

However, it is not always clear whether in any given poem we are, in fact, eavesdropping on the speech and thoughts of a persona, or we are admitted into the poet's relatively unmasked presence. In the unofficial verse, the likelihood that Housman is speaking *in propria persona* is far higher than in *A Shropshire Lad* or even *Last Poems*. However, there are several unofficial Terence poems. There are also some official poems in which the poet to a greater or lesser extent drops his mask and refers to his private dilemma. In these, however, he often confuses matters by the use of gender reversal or, more commonly, by simply not designating gender at all, simply using such general terms that the true subject is not explicit. As Thom Gunn said, "most homosexual writers until at least the 1960's dealt with autobiographical and personal material only indirectly. One method was for a poet to address his work to an unspecified 'you.' . . . Another method of indirection was . . . to change the gender of a character into its opposite." The comment might have been made specifically about Housman.

It is not always easy to decide whether we are dealing with a fully developed persona or with the poet unmasked to a greater or lesser extent, but there are some indications that may act as a guide. Of course, the use of the first person pronoun is not such an indication. We must turn to the content to help us to determine how close the poetic voice is to Housman's own. Where Terence himself or another of the cycle characters is named, we are clearly in the Shropshire cycle. Specific reference to Shropshire geography may also be an indication that the "I" is fictive, but this is a good deal less sure. And where the speaker is Terence himself, it is always possible that he is speaking for his creator, and what he says may reflect Housman's own mind. When the grammar of the noncomic poems is substandard, we may assume with some assurance that we are dealing with a persona. We can have the same assurance when the poem is cast as a dialogue between the speaker and an auditor, or when it indicates that the speaker has an agricultural background. Where there is a discontinuity between the facts given in the poem and the facts of the poet's own life, where for example the speaker is a soldier or a sportsman, we can also assume that we are dealing in some degree with a persona. Where the speaker is a criminal, however, the matter is more complex. According to the laws of England at that time, Housman was indeed a criminal, and at any moment he could have been arrested, tried, and sentenced to prison, as was Oscar Wilde, and for the same offense. Thus, psychologically if not actually, in those poems where the speaker is a felon he may also be a closer projection of the author's self than are the soldier personae. It is noticeable that we are never informed what crime any of Housman's felons committed. The reader is free to assume what crime he will, but for the poet, the crime is "nameless," the term used in AP 18 for the offense of Oscar Wilde, as we shall see.

The most problematic poems are those which indicate that the masculine "I" is romantically involved with a woman. On the face of it, these would seem to be clearly fictive, but it is not difficult to write "she" where the heart whispers "he," and I suspect that this was often Housman's practice. However, I have accepted his diction and those poems in which the female gender of a character is specified but that are not linked to the Shropshire cycle have been grouped together in chapter 7. There are some poems in which Housman is clearly speaking for himself. These include the poems referring to his brother Herbert's death in the Boer War, the poems in memory of his friend Adalbert J. Jackson, the "Epithalamium" for his friend Moses J. Jackson's marriage, the poem bidding farewell to Venice (one of Housman's regular vacation venues) in which his gondolier is mentioned by name, and the poem he composed to be sung at his own funeral. All except the last will be discussed either in chapter 8 or chapter 9. This leaves many poems with a question mark. Shortly after Housman's death, Louis Gillet remarked, *apropos* Terence and the other personae, that the figure of the persona is evidently the author's double. It is the image or the projection of the core of his personality onto that "other" which each of us carries within himself, and which is our deepest secret, unknown even to ourselves. It is, he said, difficult to distinguish, in the case of Housman, which of these personalities is the disguise and which the true entity, whether it is the persona or the professor who is actually the mask. He wondered whether the poetic creation was not more an evasion or a revelation, or if it did not serve rather to preserve the author's "incognito." Where the poem consists of an interior dialogue, or where there is ambiguity or self-mockery, it seems quite reasonable to consider the speaker as more factive than fictive. On the whole, where the knowledge of Housman's personal situation adds depth and meaning to what is otherwise cryptic or shallow, it seems to me to be acceptable to assume a biographical reference.

There is much testimony from well-known authors to indicate that literary works can, do, and perhaps must have a biographical basis. In *Shirley* Charlotte Brontë's character remarks, to explain why she writes poetry even though she knows it is not particularly good, that the "gift of poetry . . . was, I believe, granted to allay emotions when their strength threatens harm," and in Anne Brontë's *Agnes Gray* the titular character says, "When we are . . . long oppressed by any powerful feelings which we must keep to ourselves, for which we can obtain and seek no sympathy from any living creature, and which, yet, we cannot, or will not wholly crush, we often, naturally, seek relief in poetry . . . in our own attempts to give utterance to those thoughts and feelings" (232–33 and 100, respectively). Who can doubt that these characters are speaking for Charlotte and Anne? And in *The Way of All Flesh*, Samuel Butler says, "Every man's work . . . is always a portrait of himself, and the more he tries to conceal himself the more clearly will his character appear in spite of him" (60). A single sentence from W. H. Auden's "The Virgin and the Dynamo" ("A poet can embody his private experiences in a public poem," 66) seems to sum up the position. Indeed, the canon of English literature does not lack for examples of both poetry and prose that are either totally meaningless without knowledge of the author's biography or, at best, far less meaningful. One might mention Thomas Wyatt's love for Anne Boleyn, Shakespeare's knowledge of practical stagecraft, Milton's blindness, the Brontë sisters' scapegrace brother Branwell, Dickens's childhood experience in the blacking factory, Tennyson's love for his dead friend Arthur Hallam, C. S. Lewis's conversion to Christianity, Yeats's love for Maude Gonne, and the ambivalence of James Joyce toward Ireland and

Catholicism. This list could obviously be extended *ad infinitum*. There is then no question that this "connection between the life and the work of a writer often leads to a fuller understanding" of the work (Stevenson, "Durability of Housman's Poetry," 616).

Biographical interpretation, however, presents its own problems. It is dangerously easy to slip into the habit of treating every narrative as factually based, and in 1967 C. S. Lewis could write, "even today there are those (some of them critics) who believe every novel and even every lyric to be autobiographical" (*Discarded Image*, 213). C. S. Lewis is a critic whose strictures must be taken seriously, and he also said that, "at best . . . we meet the poet, even in the most personal lyric poetry, only in a strained and ambiguous sense. . . . The character presented is that of a man in the grip of . . . emotion: the real poet is a man who has already escaped from that emotion sufficiently to see it objectively . . . and to make poetry of it" ("Personal Heresy in Criticism," 13). The poet may be present only in Lewis's "strained and ambiguous sense," but in that sense he is indeed present. Wordsworth's "emotion recollected in tranquillity," to which Lewis alludes, must once have had a real existence in order to be recollected at all.

E. M. W. Tillyard's warning, however, must still be heeded. "The mixture of biography and criticism, even when most justified by the nature of the author," he says, "has its besetting danger: it is all too easy for the reader to use biography as an illegitimate short cut into the poet's mental pattern as revealed in his poems" ("Personal Heresy in Criticism," 16). George T. Wright has delved deeply into this matter and reached the following conclusion. The poem reveals the poet, but neither the persona nor the implicit poet (the poet's projection of himself as poet) is the poet himself; however, "either of them may serve, *and may be intended to serve*, as approximate representations of the poet himself" (*Poet in the Poem*, 29, emphasis mine). There is clearly a sliding scale from an almost completely fictive persona with a touch of the poet to an almost completely factive poet with a touch of the persona.

Leggett is clearly unhappy about the application of biographical data to the poetry (the idea "that Housman's personality must be seen as the key to his poetry"). However, he is reluctantly constrained to admit, "Housman, like all poets, relied heavily on his personal experiences and emotions to provide the materials for his art." While arguing that "scholarship must turn from Housman's life to his art to explain the nature of his achievement as a poet," he concedes that "no one would deny the value of biographical . . . scholarship" (*Land of Lost Content*, 5–9, 135). Indeed, even if it is accepted as a general principle that the "writer's private life is no concern of critic or reader, [Housman must be excepted from its application because] such an important facet of his personality

. . . is bound to leave its traces in his work and . . . ought not to be entirely overlooked. Housman's poetry owes a great deal to his reticence on the subject, on what he is careful not to say" (Whitehead, " A. E. Housman," 133), or at least not to say clearly and unambiguously.

I consider the best solution to be hermeneutic. As Leslie Fiedler wrote, it is essential "to move constantly back and forth between life and poem . . . in a meaningful spiraling" because there is a "complementary relationship . . . [between] the life and work of the poet" ("Archetype and Signature," 395). It seems to me, then, not only legitimate but actually necessary to use the biographical facts to throw light on the literary production, and—cautiously—to use the literary production to illuminate the biographical facts, although to use the poetry to add to the known facts is something else. Oscar Wilde's "The Portrait of Mr. W. H." is a tour de force of this kind of pseudocriticism. Thus, to ignore Housman's sexual orientation in a study of the erotic aspects of his poetry would be to ignore the significance of the poetry itself. It is therefore necessary to consider his life, without direct reference to his poetry, in some detail.

Alfred Edward Housman was born in 1859 in Fockbury but the family soon moved to Bromsgrove, both suburbs of Birmingham, just east of Shropshire. He was the eldest of seven children in a High Church, Tory family; both of his grandfathers were Anglican clergymen, although his father, a younger son, was a solicitor. He was educated as a day student and thus never exposed to a boarding-school environment, although even day scholars spent most of their waking life at school, returning home only at night. Devoted to his mother, Housman was devastated when she died on his twelfth birthday. To exacerbate the loss, he was not at home at the time, having been sent on a visit to his godmother. This was his first great blow, and all his life he treasured such mementos of his mother as remained to him. At this time the older Housman, following his wife's death, decided to circumcise all his sons. For a boy barely entering adolescence who had just had a shattering blow, this must have been a traumatic experience.

His father, perhaps feeling unable to cope alone with a large family of young children, remarried, taking as his second wife his cousin, who had been a close friend of his first wife and had, in fact, introduced Housman's parents to each other. Housman's relationship with his stepmother was completely amicable, and remained so during her entire life. He was a leader among his siblings, lively, amusing, and highly successful at his studies, and he was not lacking in close friends—both male and female—of his own age. Indeed, when Housman developed a friendship with anyone, that person was likely to remain his friend so long as they were both alive.

In 1877, he entered St. John's College, Oxford, where he read classics and for two years was brilliantly successful in all ways. He was one of the moving spirits of, and prolific contributors to, *Ye Rounde Table*, a university humor magazine, took a lively interest in politics, and in 1879 received first-class honors in classical moderations. He also formed a strong friendship with two other students, A. W. Pollard and Moses J. Jackson. During their final year, 1880–81, these three young men took rooms together.

Then came his second blow. In 1881, his father had a stroke and his recovery was doubtful. The family's financial situation was not good, and it was confidently expected that Housman would receive a First and recoup the family fortunes through his undoubted genius. But he failed classical greats, left Oxford without taking his degree, and had no prospects whatsoever. Possibly, he had not been fully informed of either the seriousness of his father's illness or his family's money difficulties. When he reached home and was told exactly what the situation was his sense of guilt must have been excruciating. Rather than bringing home academic glory and recouping the family fortunes, he had brought home only academic disgrace and an extra mouth to feed at a time when money was so scarce that the entire family was confined to a single small room, all they could afford to heat.

The question of *why* he failed his examinations has been widely debated. Housman disliked philosophy and history. Consequently, as he himself said, he ignored many of the texts set for the examination because they bored him.[4] Skutsch suggested that part of the cause was his "revolt against the vague and high-sounding, which tends to disregard what is clearly ascertainable" (*A. E. Housman*, 2). Gow suggested that the less than inspired teaching at St. John's failed to imbue him with an interest in the curriculum, and he chose to spend his time laboring over the text of Propertius rather than studying the required texts. He may have chosen to write nothing rather than write what he knew would be inadequate answers to the questions posed. He may have been sufficiently arrogant to believe that he had no need to study assiduously for his examinations, for while Pollard was poring over his books Housman and Jackson were engaging in long, pleasant conversations. Or Housman may simply have been unable to resist the attraction of those conversations.

On his return home after being "ploughed" (and Housman later conceded that he had done so badly that the examiners had no other choice), his personality and behavior were completely altered. His brother Laurence records that "he came back from Oxford a changed character. It was probably the blow of his failure which caused him to withdraw completely into himself" (*A. E. H.*, 56), and his sister noted that "the change was instantaneous and baffling. He returned home a stricken and petrified brother, who, from that time, was withdrawn from all of us behind a barrier of reserve which he set up as though to shield himself from either pity or blame" (introduction to Grant Richards, *Housman*, xv). Or, perhaps, from curiosity? The mask was in place, and in place it publicly remained for the rest of the poet's life.

The only contemporary explanation offered for this mask was Laurence and Katharine's attribution of it to the pain and shame of his academic failure, and no doubt that was part of it. P. G. Naiditch, convinced that no other explanation is necessary, informs me in a letter of 18 December 1996, that he "can easily conceive of someone killing himself over such a failure, or having a nervous breakdown as its result, or (what happened to Housman) withdrawing into himself." It seems unlikely to me, however, that this alone would have produced such a radical, life-long, and complete change of character. Many people have undergone equally painful experiences and rebounded from them. Housman did not, not even upon achieving distinction as the greatest Latinist of his generation, not even upon receiving the Chair of Latin at Cambridge, not even upon being offered the highest honors both academia and the Crown could offer (honors which he invariably refused). If the primary cause of this metamorphosis in his personality was academic shame, academic honors should have ameliorated it. They did not. Housman had scant regard for the praise of others, and one who is unmoved by praise is unlikely to be so deeply and permanently affected by the lack of praise. Since the only academic approval that mattered to him was his own, the only disapprobation that affected him deeply would also have been his own. He does not seem to have felt academically shamed by his failure; indeed, on applying for a post at University College, London, he calmly stated, "I failed to obtain honours in the Final School of Litterae Humaniores. I have since passed the examinations required for the degree of B. A." (Naiditch, *Housman at University College*, 14). Although Naiditch has remarked to me in a letter of 20 May 1998 that Housman had little choice since the facts were included in his entry in the Oxford University Calendar, this still does not sound to me like the language of a man racked by academic guilt over academic failure, even if the dry manner of stating the verifiable fact can be interpreted as a mask covering deep guilt and suffering. I still believe, as do most of the biographers, that there was something more, and that something more was almost certainly his realization that he was deeply, hopelessly, and irrevocably in love with his friend and roommate, Moses J. Jackson. The excerpts from Housman's diary included in Laurence Housman's posthumous article of 1967 bear witness to the depth, the hopelessness, and the irrevocability of that love.

Whether Jackson was aware of his friend's feelings at this time (or indeed, ever) is moot. One of Housman's poems ("Because I liked you better," MP 31) suggests that Jackson did know, disapproved, and wrung a promise from his friend "To throw the thought away," or at least not to force the matter onto his attention. But of course the poem may reflect Housman's conception of Jackson's possible (or probable) reaction to the knowledge rather than an actual occurrence.

Jackson received an important position in the Patent Office in London, to which he moved, ultimately taking rooms together with his younger brother Adalbert, a student reading classics at University College, London. Housman himself remained at home for a year, occasionally teaching at his own alma mater, while studying for a pass degree and also to himself take the civil service examinations. There is no record of his corresponding with Moses Jackson during this year, but it seems to me likely that letters passed between them.

Housman succeeded in the examination for his pass degree and also did well in the civil service examinations. He was then offered a post in Dublin, which, to the chagrin of his family, he refused. He promised to take the next position offered to him, whatever and wherever it might be, and the next offer was—a post in the London Patent Office. Either this was the result of Moses Jackson's intervention on his friend's behalf or it was an extraordinary twist of fate. Until 1992, no one had ever suggested that Jackson was in any way involved. It was always assumed that it was the merest chance.[5]

In November of 1882, after his first professional paper (on Horace) was published, Housman moved to London to take up his post, and almost immediately (in December) he joined the Jackson brothers in their lodging. This arrangement continued until November 1884, when Adalbert Jackson took his degree and returned to Ramsgate. Housman and Moses Jackson continued to share rooms for approximately a year, and then in the autumn of 1885, Housman disappeared and was missing for a week. Moses Jackson was frantic and went to the lengths of writing to Alfred's father in Bromsgrove to know if his friend had for some reason gone home. At the end of this missing week, Housman returned to the lodgings as suddenly as he had left, only to move out soon thereafter to take lodgings alone. His new address was just around the corner. Later he moved farther away.

Housman's first London address was 15 North Place, in Bayswater, where the Jackson brothers were already settled. This indicates that either Housman wrote Jackson asking him to arrange lodgings for him in the vicinity or, at the very least, knew where Jackson was living and took pains to be as close as possible. Otherwise we are stretching coincidence to the breaking point. In either case, Housman obviously knew Jackson's address, which is *prima facie* evidence of some correspondence between them during the year Housman was immured in Bromsgrove. Once in London, Housman remained in North Place for only a few weeks before joining the Jackson brothers in their lodgings at 82 Talbot Road, presumably at their invitation, although it is certainly possible that Housman broached the idea first. As Housman's salary was a good deal lower than Jackson's, this arrangement made excellent economic sense and this provided an ostensible motive for the invitation and acceptance (or for the request and agreement). In any case, Housman was already established in Talbot Road by early in 1883. After the mysterious week's absence, he left, but only to move to 39 Northumberland Road, "round the corner and down the street from 82 Talbot Road," where Moses Jackson continued to live. There Housman remained "for a number of weeks" until in 1886 he removed to Highgate. Naiditch (*Problems*, 18) and Shaw (*Housman's Places*, 64–65) both give the addresses, and both note the proximity of the Northumberland Road rooms to those on Talbot Road. Shaw, in a private conversation with me, has also remarked on this.

It has been conjectured that, deliberately or accidentally, Housman had revealed his feelings to Jackson, that a flaming row had resulted, and that this quarrel was the cause of the week's disappearance and Housman's subsequent removal to separate lodgings. Piers Browne, speaking for a host of commentators, sums up this generally accepted interpretation of the recorded events by saying, "It is presumed that somehow Housman must have opened his heart to Moses, who possibly was deeply shocked, rejecting the advances of his friend" (*Elegy in Arcady*, 16). It is "presumed" and it is "possible," but there is no actual evidence on which to base this assumption as to the cause of the events. It might indeed have been so. Moses Jackson's obvious worry might have been due to fear and guilt—fear that his rejection had driven Housman to commit suicide and guilt if that were indeed the case—or simply to remorse that he had driven him away. It might as easily be due to simple ignorance of why his friend had left and where he had gone. Neither of the "flaming row" scenario explanations of Jackson's agitation explains both why Housman returned—and was welcomed back—after a single week, and his removal shortly thereafter to temporary lodgings only a few steps distant from the lodgings of his friend. Maas certainly rejects this dramatic scenario, holding that it is extremely unlikely that Housman had "ever talked about . . . [his sexual inclinations] even to his closest friends, let alone to Jackson" ("On Editing Housman's Letters," 20).

There was certainly a break in their friendship at this time, although of course they continued to see each other regularly at the Patent Office. However, in light of the strong friendship and affection that Jackson continued to manifest toward Housman, the probability of such a dramatic scenario seems to me doubtful. It seems at least possible that Housman, fearing to alienate his friend by just such a revelation, and feeling himself incapable of continuing to be with him constantly without making just such a revelation, simply panicked and bolted, leaving Jackson deeply hurt by this unexplained and (to him) inexplicable flight. This seems to me a reasonable explanation of the disappearance, Jackson's appeal to Mr. Housman in Worcestershire, and Housman's moving, first out of the quarters in which he was alone with Jackson (and the unbearable temptation this entailed) and then far away from even the neighborhood where temptation dwelt. Such a desertion could only create a certain coolness in Jackson's attitude, which explains the temporary break in their close friendship without making its subsequent renewal unlikely if not impossible. It is, of course, also possible that Jackson was indeed aware of Housman's feelings, perhaps even reciprocated them, but was unprepared to go further than the Platonic ideal of nonphysical affection, thus creating in reality the situation depicted by E. M. Forster in the school chapters of *Maurice*. It may be noted that Housman's flight coincided with the passage of the Labouchere Amendment, the law under which all homosexual activities, and not only the act of sodomy, became illegal.

In December of 1887, Moses Jackson took up a new post as the director of a school in Karachi, as far from England as was practical, and went out to the eastern reaches of the British Empire. By this time, he had met a young widow, Rosa Chambers, proposed marriage to her, and been accepted. In 1888 Jackson moved to India (as it then was), and it was not until the end of October that he wrote to Housman. The poet, who had refrained from being the first to write, replied to this letter in the middle of December, three weeks after receiving it. No further correspondence is recorded in Housman's diary. If the flaming row scenario is correct, it is hard to understand why Jackson chose to renew the friendship. If the break was the result of hurt feelings, it is far less unlikely that he should take the first step to heal the breach by writing to Housman. It might be significant that Housman had continued his friendship with Adalbert Jackson, a most amiable young man, and conceivably it was at his brother's prompting that Moses Jackson wrote to Housman.

In October of 1889, Moses Jackson returned to London where he married in December. Housman was neither invited to the wedding nor even informed of it. Again, one must wonder why. If the break had been so complete that Jackson never thought to invite him, or if the break was indeed caused by the alleged flaming row four years earlier, it is curious that the friendship resumed after Jackson and his bride returned to India. It is at least within the bounds of possibility that Jackson neither invited Housman to the ceremony nor informed him of it in order to spare him the pain of witnessing what would for him have been a far from happy event. Laurence Housman indeed suggests that it may have been "intended kindness." And, just perhaps, Jackson would have himself felt rather uncomfortable standing at the altar with Housman's eyes on him.

Page notes that the diary entries relating to Moses Jackson's stay in London suggest that he deliberately avoided a tête-à-tête with Housman. To him, this "strongly suggests that Jackson was well aware of Housman's feelings for him but—whatever his earlier sentiments may have been—now preferred to pretend that they did not exist" (*A. E. Housman*, 59).

Jackson and his bride returned to India. Housman carefully traced the progress of their journey via the shipping news. Although Housman wrote to Jackson in January, immediately after being informed of his marriage (possibly by Adalbert?) and wrote again in June and November, Jackson apparently did not write to Housman at all in 1890 (ibid., 60). However, at some point after this, the friendship must have been renewed. When one recalls that during his first absence in India it was Jackson who first wrote to Housman, and also that he had failed to reply to three letters Housman wrote to him during 1890, one may tentatively assume that it was Jackson who finally revived the correspondence. In any case, the correspondence did continue since there is a diary entry for 18 June 1891, "Wrote to him by today's mail," which—like the other Jackson entries—is written in ink whereas the non-Jackson entries are in pencil (Carter "Corrigenda and Agenda," 3).

The most notable aspect of the diary entries is that, whereas other friends are mentioned by name ("Add," that is Adalbert Jackson, and friends in the Patent Office), Moses Jackson's hardly appears at all, only one or two entries referring to "Mo." Moses Jackson is almost always "he," "him," or "his." To Housman, there was only one "he." The only letter from Jackson found among Housman's papers after his death was the last one, and the letters Housman wrote to Jackson are reportedly preserved in the family (although Burnett informs me that the last one is in a private collection) and have never been published.

In 1892, two events of great importance occurred within two months. At the beginning of October, Housman took up the appointment as Professor of Latin at University College, London, which he had received the previous June. Shortly thereafter, early in November, Adalbert Jackson, with whom Housman had maintained a close and warm relationship, died of typhoid fever. After his death there was no one with whom Housman could talk intimately about Moses Jackson, no one with whom to share the news from India or through whom casual messages could be passed.

Jackson returned to London in 1894 for a visit, by which time he had two sons. A third was born early in 1895, and it would seem that during this or Jackson's next visit the breach was completely healed, for when in 1900 a fourth son was born, Housman stood godfather to the infant Gerald. Clearly, if Jackson was in fact aware of his friend's feelings, he was neither horrified nor repulsed by them, or he would not have sanctioned such a relationship with his son. Being a godparent was then taken far more seriously than it is today, and even today it is not a light thing.

In 1895, Oscar Wilde was tried for homosexuality, found guilty, and given the heaviest sentence permitted under the law for his offense. The judge, in passing the sentence of two years in prison at hard labor, stated that he regretted it was so light. Shortly after this, a young cadet at Woolwich, who may have been a homosexual, killed himself. Housman was deeply moved by the young man's death and retained the newspaper account of the inquest, including the text of the suicide note. At Housman's death, this clipping was found in his own copy of A *Shropshire Lad* (published in 1896, the following year).

In 1897, Housman traveled for the first time to Europe, where he visited Paris, Rome, and Naples. Thereafter, he went to the Continent almost every year. That winter, Jackson returned to London for an extended visit, and in 1898, while he was on his way back to Karachi after an abortive attempt to be appointed to a professorship in London, Housman (presumably aware of his friend's desire to return to England) added his name to the list of applicants for the position of Headmaster of University College School. Housman himself was the convener of the committee that considered the various applicants, but despite his best efforts another man was appointed. Although bitterly disappointed at the board's decision, he could do nothing. Ironically, it was Housman who was deputed by the board to inform Jackson that his application had been rejected. The letter is extant and shows clear signs of Housman's agitation.

In 1898, Jackson was again in England. Both he and Housman stayed for a few days with Pollard, reviving their Oxford association. During this visit, someone made apple-pie beds for all three of the men. No one ever admitted to being responsible for the prank, but it has all the earmarks of Housman's puckish sense of humor.

In 1901, the poet's youngest brother, George Herbert (always called "Herbert" but named, Stephen Housman informed me, for the poet), was killed fighting in South Africa, and four years later his eldest brother, Robert, died from pneumonia. Housman's father had died in 1894. By this time, in addition to other scholarly work on Greek and Latin literary texts, Housman had already begun editing Manilius's *Astronomica*, an extremely obscure and difficult Latin poem in five books, which is actually not nearly as dull as it is reputed to be. This labor occupied him for nearly the remainder of his life. In 1903, the first book of Manilius was published, and it is dedicated to "Sodali Meo," Moses J. Jackson.

Jackson continued to visit London every few years until in 1911 he moved his family to Vancouver, British Columbia, Canada, where he took up farming. In that same year, Housman was offered the Kennedy

Chair of Latin at Trinity College, Cambridge, which he accepted and retained until his death.

One of Housman's nephews, a son of Katharine Symons, was killed during the Great War. This nephew, on his last home leave, had become engaged, and among Housman's first reactions to the news of his death was pity for the bereaved fiancée ("that poor young girl" he wrote in his condolence letter to his sister).

It was in 1920 that Housman was informed that Moses Jackson was gravely ill in Vancouver. On 5 September of that year he queried his publisher, Grant Richards, about the timing of a new book of poems, asking how long it would take from the receipt of the manuscript until publication. Richards was enthusiastic, but Housman put him off, indicating that it had been only an idle question. It was not. On 9 April 1922, he informed Richards that a second volume of poetry was "practically certain." He had learned that Jackson had stomach cancer and there was no hope of recovery.

In the preface to his new volume, Housman wrote, "About a quarter of this matter belongs to April of the present year . . ." which is to say the period immediately after receipt of the dolorous news from Canada.[6] *Last Poems* was published on 19 October 1922, and less than three months thereafter Moses Jackson was dead. He had survived just long enough to receive a copy of the new volume and the author's accompanying letter, in which Housman wrote, "you are largely responsible for my writing poetry," and to acknowledge the gift. Jackson's letter thanking Housman for the volume of *Last Poems* was faintly written in pencil, beginning "Dear Old Hous" (an address both affectionate and intimate),[7] and Housman carefully traced it in ink, wrote on it "Mo's last letter," and preserved it among his most cherished possessions. This is the only one of Jackson's letters to Housman which Laurence Housman specifically records finding after his brother's death,[8] and he reportedly destroyed it. Laurence Housman says "No (other) letter from Jackson to my brother remains" ("*De Amicitia,*" 36). It is always possible that Housman, feeling the approach of death, destroyed the letters himself to ensure these very private communications remaining so but lacked the will and the heart to destroy this particular letter. Jackson died in January of 1923.

It took some time for the news to cross the Atlantic and reach Housman. From March of that year (when word of Moses Jackson's death seems to have arrived) through May, he was continuously ill. During the remaining fourteen years of his life, Housman wrote almost no new poetry, fulfilling the prophecy of his preface: "I publish these poems, few though they are, because it is not likely that I shall ever be impelled to write much more."[9]

It is abundantly clear from the dates and the preface that *Last Poems* was written as a tribute to his dying friend, and that with Moses Jackson's death, died Housman's poetic muse. Many years later, when visiting Housman's rooms at Trinity, his brother Laurence noticed two pictures on the walls, one of a young, and the second of a middle-aged, man. The first was a portrait of Adalbert, the second of Moses. Laurence asked about the latter portrait. A. E. Housman replied "in a strangely moved voice . . . 'That was my friend Jackson, the man who had more influence on my life than anybody else' " (L. Housman *A. E. H.* 61).

Housman continued to teach, to work on Manilius, and to travel regularly to France and Italy. Once the Manilius edition was finished, however, he had no great desire to keep on living. He once remarked that he continued to run up the forty-four stairs to his rooms (in the tower on the Sidney Street side of Whewell's Court) two at a time in hopes that he would drop dead from exertion before reaching the top of the flight. He did not, and he was eventually persuaded to move to different rooms on the ground floor of Trinity Great Court. Due to his deteriorating health, he was periodically forced to enter a nursing home, and there in 1936 his godson, Gerald Jackson, visited him for the last time. He died on 30 April of that year, having outlived almost all of his closest friends and relatives.

At the time of his death, Housman left four notebooks containing anything and everything: odd phrases and lines, work sheets and fair copy of both published and unpublished poems, unpublished poems in various stages of composition, oddments of classical essays, and random notes on various matters. The work sheets include many phrases and lines that were ultimately rejected (often those that would have made the poems more obviously personal). A typical example is the change from the original variants "To sleep with friends one knows" and "To lie by lads one knows" to the final published version, "A choice of friends one knows." In the same poem, "I sleep with these or those" was rejected and replaced by "Asleep with these or those" ("Hughley Steeple," ASL 61). All variants can be found in Burnett's *The Poems of A. E. Housman*. The final choices were far less open to sniggering innuendo.

In his will, A. E. Housman designated his brother Laurence as his sole literary executor. His instructions were to destroy all prose manuscripts in whatsoever language, to publish, if he saw fit, any completed poems which did not fall below the general level of those in the two published collections, and to destroy everything else. Laurence Housman interpreted these instructions liberally. In *More Poems* (MP) and *Additional Poems* (AP), he published many poems that were not, in fact, completed, finalizing the texts from among the alternatives that had been left open. In an appendix to *More Poems*, and as footnotes to *Additional Poems*, he did, however, provide for a few lyrics some of the alternative readings that he had rejected. Among these poems are to be found those that are most personal. Laurence Housman made a rough (very rough) guide to the notebooks, listing what was on each page of each notebook, in order, and numbering the pages. This guide is carelessly done and inaccurate, some page numbers being repeated and other pages left without any code number. In addition, the contents noted do not always match the writing on the page, and some notations are maddeningly vague, such as "Fragments" or "Unpublished poem." A. E. Housman, for whom accuracy was holy, would not have been amused.

Laurence Housman then cut up the pages, destroying indeed any fragments with unpublished material on both sides. Those which had published material on one side and unpublished material (heavily scored over and theoretically thus obliterated) on the other, he pasted onto mounting sheets, leaving visible only the parts relating to published material, including the work sheets. In the process, he ignored the order of the notebooks, mixing fragments of them indiscriminately. Having thus cannibalized the notebooks he sold most of the dismembered remains to the highest bidder, an American who donated them to the Library of Congress in Washington, D.C. There in due course the backings were removed and the scraps, some the size of postage stamps and some almost entire pages, were cleaned and remounted so that both published and unpublished material were visible. They were then microfilmed. Additional fragments survive elsewhere.[10]

Ultimately, Tom Burns Haber transcribed many of the remains at the Library of Congress and reconstructed parts of the notebooks for publication in 1955 (*The Manuscript Poems of A. E. Housman*) and 1966, (*The Making of "A Shropshire Lad"*). In 1997, Archie Burnett used the original manuscripts for his edition of *The Poems of A. E. Housman*, and the readings in this volume are almost always superior to Haber's. Since Burnett did not include single lines and couplets, however, Haber's book is still needed. Because many details are visible in the original that cannot be seen in the photocopy of the microfilm that I have, in this book references to the notebook material will be, when possible, to Burnett's edition, and for material not therein included to Haber's volumes, rather than to the manuscripts themselves. Where both Burnett and Haber have omitted notebook material, reference will be made directly to the manuscripts. These were received by the Library of Congress in six packets designated "A" through "F." Each envelope contained scraps from all four notebooks. Reference therefore is to the packet designation, the place of the scrap within the packet, and its numeration in the entire collection. Thus, "F–2, sheet 152" from the sixth packet ("F") is a work sheet of ASL 39 ("Tis time, I think, by Wenlock town"), originally a part of the first notebook.

There are dates on only a few of the fragments. For dating the notebook material, therefore, I have relied on Burnett's meticulous scholarship and, to a lesser extent, on Haber. Both have recreated the notebooks using Laurence Housman's guide and John Carter's summary, plus what clues there are in the fragments. It should be remembered, however, that poems may well have existed in preliminary form (or even complete form) in Housman's mind well before being entered in the notebooks. The notebook dates are, therefore, a last possible date of composition and not necessarily the date of inception. *A Shropshire Lad* was published in 1896, and most of the poetry in it had been written during the previous year. Much of the poetry in *Last Poems* dates from the same period, the rest having been newly written or completed from earlier beginnings after the news of Jackson's terminal illness reached Housman. Although it is impossible in most cases to be completely sure exactly when a poem was actually composed, it is abundantly clear that what Housman described in the preface to *Last Poems* as "the continuous excitement under which in the early months of 1895 I wrote the greater part of my other book [ASL]" occurred some time after Jackson's marriage and removal to India.

The nature of that "continuous excitement" referred to in the *Last Poems* preface has inspired a certain amount of conjecture. It has usually been understood to refer to Housman's emotional state in 1895. In 1927, in a letter to Paul L. Love (Leggett, "Unpublished Housman Letter," 48), he explained the phrase: "The excitement was simply what is called poetical inspiration." This seems to fit the context perfectly and put an end to speculation about his emotional life at the time of writing *A Shropshire Lad*. However, Housman's words could be disingenuous. The emotional "excitement," it is undeniably true, was not roused by any events of 1895. It was the result of events that had taken place in earlier years.

As an old man, Housman wrote to Maurice Pollet, "I did not begin to write poetry in earnest until the really emotional part of my life was over" (*Letters*, 329). The emotions engendered in those earlier years germinated in the "hairy weid" and years later erupted as "poetical inspiration." Thus, his emotion, recollected in (relative) tranquility, indeed provided that "continuous excitement." Housman was a master at concealing the truth by telling it. That the word can connote a state of sexual arousal is clear from the fact that Hardy used it thus in *The Woodlanders* ("Fitzpiers, now thoroughly excited, was not going to let her escape him"). Thus, the "continuous excitement" to which Housman refers may refer back to the period in which he and Moses Jackson were sharing a residence in the close daily intimacy of living together, even if not "living together." The "poetical inspiration" of his explanation was the constant physical presence and psychological intimacy of the young men. And indeed, the "*fons et origo* [of Housman's poetry] lay in the thwarted, largely unrequited, and almost totally repressed love for two golden-limbed lads of his youth—the Jackson brothers" (Hunt, "Immortal Memory," 57).

Thalia

2
Be Kind to Unicorns

Housman's double vision, his "intelligence . . . characteristically inseparable from an unfailingly and playfully imaginative sense of the absurd" (Burnett, "Poetical Emendations," 296), was expressed in parody and mock-logic. Housman created an irreverent, often perverse, world on the surface, but as one begins to consider them, many of the nonsense verses take on a darker coloring. Behind them is discernable the shadow of Housman's own particular "weid." It is these verses, and this shadow, which I wish to consider here. Victorian England itself was a world of self-contradictions. It was a world that excoriated Oscar Wilde while sending its sons to public schools in which homosexuality was rampant. If all guilty of Wilde's offense had been sent to prison, much of the student body at Eton, Harrow, Rugby, etc., would have been moved *en masse* to Pentonville and Holloway,[1] with not a few masters to keep them company. And Housman would have been with them.

This was a world in which appearance was primary, and reality, provided it was hidden behind a facade of respectability, did not exist. The primary areas of reality that lacked official existence were those that humanity shared with the rest of the animal world: elimination and procreation. The genitals, and anything associated with them, were *verba non grata*. In a world that took words, spoken and written, so seriously, it is another inner contradiction that this was the great age of two types of literature that, unlike the novel, were not in harmony with the prevailing middle-class ethos. One was pornography. This world took itself and its morals very seriously, yet produced an effusion of sometimes brilliant (but far more often dull and inane) sexually explicit stories and verse, much of which is a good deal less erotic than the majority of books on late-twentieth-century best seller lists. Some of the best of Victorian erotic fiction has been republished and can be purchased at any major bookstore today. Housman certainly collected pornography, but he did not write it. The second type of out-of-harmony literature he relished in the writings of others (especially Carroll and Lear) and also created himself. I refer, of course, to nonsense verse. The Victorian Age produced an effusion of wonderful nonsense unmatched in any other time or place.

These seeming contradictions may have been a logical necessity. The pressure of constantly maintaining seriousness, earnestness, and moral rectitude in one's public bearing, aspirations, interests, beliefs, and behavior, must have been a considerable strain; both pornography and comic verse offered a measure of private relief. Where the pressure is unbearable, a means of relief will not be lacking, and Housman availed himself of all means of relief available. Nonsense verse, by its very nature, overturns the status quo. One of its methods for doing so is the ubiquitous pun, and Housman could pun with the best.

Although Housman's puns could be merely the source of fun, in his mature poetry they are usually quietly inserted into his serious poems where they may well pass unnoticed. I. A. Richards noted long ago that "humour is perhaps the last thing that is expected in lyrical poetry" (*Practical Criticism* 139), and it is readily overlooked in consequence. A good example is in ASL 50: The penultimate line is ". . . doomsday may thunder and lighten" where the word "lighten" refers both to the lightning that accompanies the thunder and to the lightening of the load of life, which is "This luggage I'd lief set down." This nonhumorous use of puns—or perhaps multivalued words would be a better term in the context—is typical of Housman's poetry. It might be compared with that of Walter Savage Landor, in whose poem "Age" we find, "[Death] strikes all things, all alike / But bargains: those he will not strike." Housman's technique "is not simply a recurring image but a playing upon various meanings and associations, literal and metaphorical, that attach themselves to that image. So far from being . . . a poet of simplicity . . . [he] is prepared to exploit the rich suggestiveness of language" (Page, *A. E. Housmen*, 196). Or, as Ricks has expressed it, in many of Housman's more powerful poems, "the force comes from what is submerged. . . . He was fond of that particular kind of pun or anti-pun which creates its double meaning by invoking but [at the same time] excluding," so the method of his serious verse is that of nonsense verse: "indirections, disparities, and emotional cross-currents. . . . What is said is not what is meant, but something is certainly meant" ("Nature of His Poetry" 174, 173).

A comic effect may be produced by the immoderate use of alliteration, intentionally (or unintentionally, as is often the case with Swinburne and occasionally with Housman as well), or by other types of word-play, such as ingenious and unexpected rhymes. There was, as Ricks notes, "a supple effrontery and insouicience" in his rhymes ("Nature of Housman's Poetry," 108). Laurence Housman says in "A Poet in the Making" that "ingenious rhymes . . . were a constant feature of his light verse" (116) from his childhood when he and his siblings amused themselves by writing it. Katherine Symons notes that "outrageous rhyming was a feature" in his comic verses which were "frankly devoid of literary pretension, spontaneous and unpolished" (Symons et al., *Recollections* 20 U.K., 22 U.S. ed.).

Another of the methods of comic verse is to juxtapose the ordinary and the fantastic, which results either in the fantastic's becoming ordinary or the ordinary, fantastic. Katherine Symons tells us that her brother "was quick to see humour in things about him, or to give grim things a humourous turn" and that his nonsense verse is characterized by "pungency and dryness of humour" (ibid., *Recollections* 20 U.K., 23 U.S. ed. 2nd part not in U.K. ed., 25 U.S. ed.).

The out-of-place detail or anachronism both startles and delights by throwing the background into bold relief, or alternatively by reducing it to the reality of a theatrical flat, exploiting the incongruity of union between things that are normally antithetical. In Housman's version of the nursery rhyme Jack and Jill, for example, Jack sports a vaccination mark. Since its values are not the usual ones, nonsense verse implicitly suggests that other views are possible. By the very fact of mocking normative assumptions and expressing the unconventional view, it is subversive of the conventional one. J. Hillis Miller, considering Dickens, wrote: "The comic view is . . . like the perspective of the outcast. Both see the world from the outside, from the point of view of someone who is not part of what he sees" (*Victorian Subjects*, 109). And Housman viewed himself as a generic outsider, "a stranger and afraid / In a world I never made" (LP 12).

There is, as George R. Creeger says of Lewis Carroll, an "impulse toward chaos" which is "somehow always held together" (Auden, *British Minor Poets*, 373). It may have its roots in the disruptive but controlled libido of the poet, a disruptiveness that is kept from interfering with his life by being channeled into equally disruptive but controlled verbal form. Ricks says of Housman that "nonsense-verse is not meaningless, and the sense of it matters; its emotional force comes from the disparity between the absurdity or falsity of what is said and the emotional truth of what is felt. The childishness or cruelty is combined with a jauntiness, wit, and aplomb of style and movement" ("Nature of Housman's Poetry," 116).

Housman's humor, like his poetry in general, welled out of his subconscious. The end of his lecture "The Name and Nature of Poetry" (A. E. Housman, *Collected Poems and Selected Prose*, hereafter cited as NNP) in which he describes his method of poetic composition is well-known, but it will bear repeating (370–71):

I would go out for a walk of two or three hours. As I went along, thinking of nothing in particular, only looking at things around me and following the progress of the seasons, there would flow into my mind, with sudden and unaccountable emotion, sometimes a line or two of verse, sometimes a whole stanza at once, accompanied, not preceded, by a vague notion of the poem which they were destined to form part of. Then there would usually be a lull of an hour or so, then perhaps the spring would bubble up again. . . . When I got home I wrote them down, leaving gaps, and hoping that further inspiration might be forthcoming another day. Sometimes it was, if I took my walk in a receptive and expectant frame of mind; but sometimes the poem had to be taken in hand and completed by the brain, which was apt to be a matter of trouble and anxiety . . . sometimes ending in failure.

An examination of the notebooks shows the accuracy of this description. Almost always, some verses of a poem are written with hardly a blot, while others are so worked over that the final version has been squeezed into an empty corner of the page. Both the ease of the poetry that "bubbled up" from the subconscious and the "trouble and anxiety" of the poetry that was "completed by the brain" are clearly evident. The following couplet came in a dream, bubbling up directly from the poet's subconscious, as had the "bogle" quatrain: (Burnett, *Poems*, 560)

> Above the soldier's grave there twine
> The Woodbine and the Concubine.

Page suggests that the "unfeeling manner conceals feelings to which he [Housman] was unwilling to give direct, naked expression" (*A. E. Housman*, 113).[2] The only other comment on this couplet, and one which is far more perspicacious, is Bayley's. He notes the deadpan humor and says, "It suggests a striking mixture. . . . Entwining together woodbine and concubine is startling . . . and mingles in a sort of brisk languor the pastoral and military, classic and commercial." Two heraldic flowers, woodbine and columbine, are transposed, woodbine turning into its other sense, and columbine becoming a camp-follower. "The punning transpositions give the couplet its curious charm, while drawing no direct attention to themselves" (*Housman's Poems*, 12).

In these two lines, then, are most of the elements discussed above: the pun, the "impulse toward chaos," the melding of incongruous details into a unity all its own, and the wittiness. The couplet also suggests something else: that the soldier should not be deprived of his creature comforts, tobacco and women, even in death. When, during the Great War, there was a movement to deprive soldiers in the field of the latter, Housman opposed it. He was against the regulation of sexuality for others as well as for himself, for heterosexuals as well as homosexuals.

The twining of the oddly assorted pair provides another pictorial element which Bayley has neglected to mention, the concubine with tobacco smoke twining around her, and another implication, that the tobacco and the woman mourn the soldier who loved them and are still faithful to him. It is a common motif in folk tale and folk ballad (and Housman was a great admirer of the Scottish border ballads and thoroughly conversant with them) that out of dead lovers' graves there grow plants that, twining about each other, symbolize the eternal union of the dead couple. "Out of her breast there sprung a rose, / And out of his a briar. / They grew as high as the church-top, / 'Till they could grow no higher, / And then they grew in a true lover's knot" ("Fair Margaret and Sweet William," in *English and Scottish Popular Ballads*, Childe, 74, A, 1:201, verses 18 and 19). Here, the same elements, the dead lover and two plants, are rearranged in Housman's subconscious to provide this suggestive (in more senses than one) dream poem.

A moral, or antimoral, may be hidden in the most surprising places. Often, in Housman's nonsense verses, the guilty party may escape all punishment by sheer accident, and the offended party may be the one to receive a shock. This is not always true, of course, in Housman's poetry any more than in reality, but it is true often enough to suggest that it reflects the poet's deepest belief, or at least wish-fulfillment. Here, the innocent offender is saved by chance, and the offended party is left to consider his loss (Burnett, *Poems*, 261–62).

> Away with bloodshed, I love not such;
> But Jane Eliza snores too much.
>
> I bought a serpent that bites and stings
> For three-and-sixpence or four shillings.
>
> When Jane Eliza began to snore
> I put it under her bedroom door.
>
> The serpent had neither bit nor stung,
> It had only just put out its tongue,
>
> When Jane Eliza fell out of bed
> And bumped upon it and killed it dead.
>
> It showed off none of its pretty tricks
> That cost four shillings or three-and-six;
>
> It had no time to sting or bite
> Nor even to utter the words "Good night".
>
> So three-and-sixpence at least is gone,
> And Jane Eliza she still snores on.

Housman's comedy here arises partly from the enormous disparity between the "crime" and the intended "punishment." Snoring is after all a

perfectly natural phenomenon, however annoying to one doomed to listen to it, and it is something over which the offender has no control. The
avenging speaker has philosophic objections to murder—at least to messy
murder ("Away with bloodshed, I love not such")—but is quite prepared
to ignore his own distaste given the insupportable provocation ("*But* Jane
Eliza snores too much", emphasis mine). So he introduces a snake into
the scene. It is possible to have a snake without its presence calling up
the shade of that other snake from Eden, but we must always remember
that Housman was steeped in the Bible and for him that biblical reference would be likely always to hover in the background.

If snoring is taken as a metaphor for sexuality, especially forbidden sexuality (a reprehensible but natural action performed in bed—and what
Victorian hero or heroine can be imagined either snoring or indulging in
sexual relations at all, prohibited or licit?), this snake is the punishment
for it rather than the cause. The poor snake has not even time enough
before expiring to speak his last farewell. The offender's killing of the
snake is then the defeat of artificial conscience by a natural process. The
concentration on the price of the snake gives us a clue to the underlying
meaning. Pounds, shillings, and pence (and it seems sometimes most especially the pence) are the prime concern of the clerical, mercantile, and
professional Victorian middle class, the disciples of Bentham and wor-
shippers at the shrine of Utilitarianism. This group prided itself on its
hardheaded practicality as well as its respectability. It embraced conformity. One recalls Dickens's Mr. Gradgrind in *Hard Times* and Charles
Pooter of *The Diary of a Nobody*, two good examples of this money-con-
scious class. The persona who is so anxious to wreak vengeance on Eliza
Jane for her reprehensible activity may be a representative of this mind-
cast, the archetypical representative of conventional morality.

Numbers, whether in reckoning prices or in more general mathemat-
ics, may represent practical, scientific knowledge (as in "When first my
way to fair I took" [LP 35]) or the unpleasant inevitabilities, such as death
(in "Loveliest of trees" [ASL 2]), which are ultimately unavoidable.
Housman habitually uses numbers to indicate "real" as opposed to "ideal"
life that is presumably emotional, imaginative, artistic, and instinctive,
anything but practical and useful. As both a professor of Latin (one of
the more useless of the liberal arts, said the Benthamites) and as a writer
of poetry which was neither didactic nor morally uplifting nor intended
to be socially reforming (another useless art, said they), and as one who
objected to the destruction of natural beauty (as per his letter to *The
Standard*, quoted in full in chapter 5), Housman had every motive for
practical opposition to this class. He also had a constitutional dislike for
their dogma. He describes London in 1866 as "the gross world of London,
enslaved by commerce, respectability, and middle-age."[3] The persona,

preoccupied with the price of his snake and willing to kill provided the murder can escape public notice, would then in Housman's opinion fit in perfectly in "the gross world of London." He objects to a natural activity because it is outside what he considers proper behavior, and he can be seen as a personification of that respectable (and often hypocritical) group, Victorian middle-class society.

Whatever the actual price, the speaker has thrown away his money and has not achieved his aim. His aim is unachievable. Human nature cannot be killed, only forced to go under cover (or under the covers to muffle the snoring?), driven into the closet, or confined underground. Housman's nonsense poetry can be deadly serious.

As I said above, in Housman's nonsense verse the offender often escapes the consequences of the offense. Jane Eliza certainly does, but others are not so fortunate. William is one of the unlucky ones (Burnett, *Poems*, 284).

Purple William
Or
The Liar's Doom

The hideous hue which William is
Was not originally his:
So long as William told the truth
He was a usual-coloured youth.

He now is purple. One fine day
His tender father chanced to say
"What colour is a whelp, and why?"
"Purple" was William's false reply.

"Pooh" said his Pa, "You silly elf,
It's no more purple than yourself.
Dismiss the notion from your head."
"I, too, am purple" William said.

And he *was* purple. With a yell
His mother off the sofa fell
Exclaiming "William's purple! Oh!"
William replied "I told you so."

His parents, who could not support
The pungency of this retort,
Died with a simultaneous groan.
The purple orphan was alone.

These verses are a part of the contemporary mode best known today through Gilbert's *Bab Ballads*, verses that are "funny but also curiously macabre in their imperturbable accounts of disasters" (George H. Ford, *Norton Anthology*, 2:1613). William's self-revelation is indeed a disaster. The pain underlying this cautionary tale rises to the surface if one takes it as an allegory. William is a "hideous hue," an unnatural color. He was a perfectly normal boy so long as he conformed to the mandated rules and "told the truth," at least the truth his parents (or society) expected to hear; however, when he broke those rules by lying (or perhaps by telling a deeper truth), his difference became manifest. His parents could not accept this revelation, and "The purple orphan was alone," cut off from other people, doomed to a life of isolation and rejection.

I am not the only one to see William's purpleness as a metaphor for homosexuality. Bayley says of this poem that the "matter-of-fact information has echoes of sin and lost happiness, of the discovery of the dreadful in oneself, of being sent to prison for the color of one's hair" (*Housman's Poems*, 98). He is referring to the far more serious piece of nonsense verse inspired by the Oscar Wilde trial in which it is "the colour of his hair" which makes the subject different (AP 18). "Purple William" can thus be read as an allegory of Housman's own situation, with William's unacceptable and unusual color as a metaphor for homosexuality.

Disobedience to the established authority leads another of Housman's characters into an experience as strange as Alice's (Burnett, *Poems*, 282–83).

Aunts and Nieces
Or
Time and Space

Some nieces won't, some nieces can't
Imbibe instruction from an aunt.
Eliza scorned her good Aunt Clare.
Where is Eliza now? Ah, where?
   "Avoid, at the approach of dark,
Eliza, the umbrageous park.
During the daytime, lairs and dens
Conceal its direr denizens.
But when that brilliant orb, the Sun,
His useful journey nearly done,
Approaches the horizon's verge,
They will, my dearest niece, emerge;
And forth the cockatrice will frisk,
And out will bound the basilisk,
And the astoundingly absurd

Yet dangerous cockyoly-bird
Will knock you, with its baneful beak,
Into the middle of next week."
     "Pooh," said Eliza, "that it can't.
Still, if you think so, thank you, Aunt.
Now, after this exhausting talk,
I think that I will take a walk."
     She therefore fetched her parasol,
Her gloves and reticule and all,
And need I specify the spot
Which drew her footsteps? I need not.
"Eliza," said her aunt, "is late.
Jane, place the crumpets by the grate.
What was that distant crow I heard?
Was it the cockyoly-bird?
I think so. There it goes again.
You may remove the crumpets, Jane."

     Meanwhile Eliza took the air.
(Shall I?—I will not—mention where),
And as the afternoon progressed
She sat upon the grass to rest,
Drew from her reticule a bun,
And bit it in the setting sun.
Soon, with her mouth full, she perceives
Movements and rustlings in the leaves
Which spoil the situation's charm
And tend to substitute alarm.
She dropped the bun and said "Dear me!
I fear I shall be late for tea."
Then, from behind, a vicious peck
Descended on Eliza's neck.
Eliza into the azure distance
Followed the line of least resistance.
In the middle of next week
There will be heard a piercing shriek,
And looking pale and weak and thin
Eliza will come flying in.

    The comedy here is the result of interfacing decorum and zaniness. The background of social convention is breached, and social convention ignores the breach, swallowing it up and converting it to the normal. Aunt Clare's imperturbability at the realization that Eliza has indeed been "knocked into the middle of next week," the only result of which is that the crumpets are returned to the larder, indicates the same "punctilious ritualism" that is the psycho-dynamic style of Carroll's characters. In

Carroll, as here, "an excessive or unexpected event occurs within the strict confines of convention. . . . But the incident evokes *no reaction or only a muted one*. All personae remain . . . dignified . . . , preserving the rule of normality (Paglia, *Sexual Persona*, 552, 548, emphasis in original). It is not only the style that is Carrollean; the basic joke is one he used as well, part of the Mad Gardener's Song from *Sylvie and Bruno* (303):

> He thought he saw a rattlesnake
>   That questioned him in Greek:
> He looked again, and found it was
>   The Middle of Next Week.

The "middle of next week" was a cliche, and "Housman was a specialist in using cliches in an unexpected context, or the wrong way round, in order to defamiliarize them into making a startling point" (Bayley, *Housman's Poems*, 131). This is precisely what the Mad Gardener does. Presumably, this harrowing experience will inculcate into Eliza the principle that rules must be obeyed. Succumbing to the lure of the forbidden (all the more alluring because forbidden) is to bring down on one's own head the consequent retribution. This, after all, is the great purpose of such stories (Zipes, *Fairy Tales*, 113).

Just what is this cockyoly-bird, one devastating knock of whose beak can cause such complete disorientation? It is "absurd" and at the same time "dangerous" and it comes out of its lair in the hours of darkness. The question answers itself. The name of the cockyoly-bird (cock-and-hole-y bird? cock-in-hole-y bird?) is sex. It is another avatar of the "bogle" and its presence turns the pleasant park into the "hairy weid."

The cockyoly-bird is Housman's only foray into the creation of an entirely new creature (albeit a very ancient one as the ear, if not the eye, attests). His usual habit, as one might expect it would be, was to look at more mundane creatures, already present either in folk lore (like the unicorn), classical literature (like the amphisbaena), or the mundane zoological garden, from a new angle (Burnett, *Poems*, 263).[4]

The Elephant
Or
The Force of Habit

> A tail behind, a trunk in front
> Complete the usual elephant.
> The tail in front, the trunk behind
> Are what we very seldom find.

If you for specimens should hunt
With trunks behind and tails in front,
That hunt would occupy you long.
The force of habit is so strong.

The solution of the riddle Housman poses is, clearly, to reverse the angle from which one is observing, for when one looks at the elephant from the other direction, every elephant will answer the description. When one stands facing the tail, the tail becomes *ipso facto* the "head," now "in front" being closer to the observer. However, this is just what is so difficult to do. In order to reverse one's perceptions, to look at a known thing from a fresh angle, to see it in a different light, one must break the habits of perception instilled from the cradle. What at first reading sounds a strange and exotic beast is in fact the same old elephant we have always known. The difference is in us, not in it. Is Housman perhaps suggesting, consciously or not, that differences in what constitutes normality in people, as in elephants, are no differences at all?

If there is confusion between the two ends of the elephant, really quite different in appearance, what does one do with a serpent which has two heads (not like those of Cerberus or the Hydra growing from a single neck, but one at each end) and can therefore, in Dr. Johnson's words, "move with either end foremost"? What do you do if you encounter an amphisbaena? And what is its underlying meaning? (Burnett, *Poems*, 269–70)[5]

Thomasina and the Amphisbaena
Or
Horrors of Horticulture

"In the back, back garden, Thomasina,
    Did you recently vociferate a squeal?"
"Oh, I trod upon an amphisbaena,
    And it bit me on the toe and on the heel.
        Yes, it bit me (do you know)
        With its tail upon the toe
    While it bit me with its head upon the heel."

"How excessively distracting and confusing.
    Pray, what, Thomasina, did you do?"
"Oh, I took the garden scissors I was using
    And I snipped it irretrievably in two.
        And it split with such a scrunch
        That I shall not want my lunch,
    And if you had heard the noise, no more would you."

"And where, Thomasina, are the sections
    Of the foe that you courageously repressed?"
"Oh, they ran away in opposite directions
    And they vanished in the east and in the west.
        And the way they made me squint,
        It would melt a heart of flint,
And I think that I will go upstairs and rest."

As in "Aunts and Nieces," part of the fun derives from the completely matter-of-fact acceptance of the fantastic serpent and the immediate progression to practical matters of correct procedure. Part arises from the diction with its swings from the overblown poetic ("vociferate," "trod," "irretrievably," "foe that you courageously repressed") to the rather slangy colloquial ("scrunch," "no more would you," "squint"). Part is due to the sudden introduction of a cliche ("melt a heart of flint"). And yet another part is based on the chiasmus of the tail-to-toe and head-to-heel attack.

The nonsense is delicious, but I suspect that the amphisbaena so summarily divided into two halves is emblematic of something more. Instead of having both head and tail, as ordinary serpents do, the amphisbaena has two heads. It is therefore not limited to a single direction but can go either way. It may thus function for Housman as a symbol of general human sexuality, which can also go in two directions, homosexuality and heterosexuality. Thomasina divides the serpent into two pieces, each of which can only move in a single direction. Its bimobility (or metaphorical bisexuality) is thus destroyed. The homosexual potential and the heterosexual potential (or alternatively the male potential and the female potential) are sundered. Specialization sets in. The destroyer of the amphisbaena is Thomasina. Clearly, Thomasina is a feminine name, but by incorporating the masculine "Thomas," it represents the accepted union of male and female upon which society insists. I would hesitate to state categorically that the amphisbaena and Thomasina should be read as another pair of metaphors for the homosexual outcast and heterosexual society, but there is something to be said for this interpretation. When Thomasina forcefully cleaves the snake into its two component parts, she renders it harmless. It is no longer a threat to her, or symbolically a threat to the social status quo. As I said, I do not insist on this reading, but it does provide a subtext that is typically Housmanian in a typically Victorian manner. It aligns this poem with Christina Rossetti's "Goblin Market," which also has a highly charged sexual subtext in what appears on the surface to be a charming fairy tale. As Housman wrote two separate poems on the amphisbaena, it is reasonable to assume that it held some special meaning or significance for him.

Unlike the amphisbaena, the crocodile is not the inhabitant of a myth-ical pseudozoological garden. Housman treats it as having the same de-gree of reality as the amphisbaena, no more—but no less. Housman's verses have a certain charm, yet this poem too is not without its subtext (Burnett, *Poems*, 277–78):

The Crocodile
Or
Public Decency

Though some at my aversion smile,
I cannot love the crocodile.
Its conduct does not seem to me
Consistent with sincerity.

Where Nile, with beneficial flood,
Improves the desert sand to mud,
The infant child, its banks upon,
Will run about with nothing on.
The London County Council not
Being adjacent to the spot,
This is the consequence. Meanwhile,
What is that object in the Nile
Which swallows water, chokes and spits?
It is the crocodile in fits.

"Oh infant! oh my country's shame!
Suppose a European came!
Picture his feelings, on his pure
Personally conducted tour!
The British Peer's averted look,
The mantling blush of Messrs. Cook!
Come, awful infant, come and be
Dressed, if in nothing else, in me."
Then disappears into the Nile
The infant, clad in crocodile,
And meekly yields his youthful breath
To darkness, decency, and death.
His mother in the local dells,
Deplores him with Egyptian yells:
Her hieroglyphic howls are vain,
Nor will the lost return again.
The crocodile itself no less
Displays, but does not feel, distress,
And with its tears augments the Nile;
The false, amphibious crocodile.

"Is it that winds Etesian blow,
Or melts on Ethiop hills the snow?"
So, midst the inundated scene,
Inquire the floating fellaheen.
From Cairo's ramparts gazing far
The mild Khedive and stern Sirdar
Say, as they scan the watery plain,
"There goes that crocodile again."
The copious tribute of its lids
Submerges half the pyramids,
And over all the Sphinx it flows,
Except her non-existent nose.

The keys to the underlying meaning seem to me to be found in the first verse and in line twenty-six ("darkness, decency, and death"). In the first verse are two clear statements: the speaker is averse to insincerity, and the crocodile's conduct is insincere. Later in the poem, the crocodile presents itself as the guardian of public morals and public decency, the local (self-appointed) substitute for the London County Council. The implication concerning Housman's opinion of the guardians of public morals need not be underlined. The child, on the other hand, is an innocent in the state of nature, and his lack of concern for conformity with public standards, and especially his display of his genitals (his normal sexuality) throws the crocodile into fits. The crocodile proceeds to instill the missing consciousness of public decency into the child, and offers itself as the obvious solution to the problem. Do not offend the public eye; it is better to hide oneself in the mantle of public conformity than to be seen as one actually is, even though this means death, physical, spiritual, or emotional. Decency, proper public behaviour, is equated with the darkness of the crocodile's interior—or of the closet—and the death of one's innate being. One must let oneself be absorbed by the forces of conformity.

The British Peer's look might well be averted, unwilling as he would be to acknowledge publicly the existence of an aspect of life which was denied by the official ethos. The crocodile tears shed by the beast of public morality that has devoured the natural child can be matched in the Victorian (and modern too, for that matter) press, pruriently gloating over the details of scandals reported with the appearance of gravest disapproval. And the indifference of the Khedive and the "Sirgar," the constituted authorities, to the crocodile's murder of the child reflects the Victorian reality where the transgressions of the noble and powerful were winked at while those of the middle and lower classes were treated with the utmost severity. Especially in matters of sexual behaviour, the upper classes could (usually) ignore the crocodile. And so the crocodile tears submerge the country, except the sphinx's "non-existent nose", nonexistent perhaps because it has been eaten away by syphilis. But the sphinx keeps its own secrets.

This poem is clearly, like so many others of Housman's, far more than it seems. It is a reaction to nineteenth-century social conventions. The crocodile "devours the naked children of Egypt in the interest of decorum . . . [and] the poet affects surprise that society should be amused at his disliking a creature who performs such an acceptable social function" (Bayley, *Housman's Poems*, 97–98). At the same time there is a decided ambivalence. The poem "shows how children, made ashamed of naked-ness [physical or psychological], sacrifice themselves when the crocodile calls. . . . Such poems . . . are not lacking in personal feelings; their force comes from the fact that no man could have had a more rigid sense of Public Decency than had Housman, even though in one vital respect it oppressed his deepest feelings" (Ricks, "A. E. Housman," 174). Housman had indeed permitted himself to be swallowed by the crocodile of public conformity, had more or less willingly immured himself in the closet, and in this poem he manages the trick of hunting with the hounds while at the same time running with the hare.

People and animals, real or imaginary, are not alone the subjects around which Housman could let his imagination rove. He could even invest a geometrical form with personality—of a sort (Burnett, *Poems*, 272–73).

The Parallelogram
Or
Infant Optimism

The parallelogram, and what
The nature of its earthly lot,
Are themes on which a light we seek
From Euclid, the intrepid Greek.

That dauntless sage describes it as
A quadrilateral which has
(How he found out he does not tell)
Its opposite sides parallel.

And seemingly the fact is such.
Oh, when I recollect how much
Strange information, true or no,
To that geometer we owe—

Surprising things, which I, alone,
Unaided, never should have known,—
My cheeks have often been bedewed
With tears of thoughtful gratitude.

And cause of thankfulness I find
Abounding in my infant mind,
Whenever I consider what
The parallelogram is not.

It is not (as it might have been)
A monster of appalling mien:
The hand of Providence confines
Its form by parallel straight lines.

It does not scratch, it does not bite,
It does not make a noise at night;
It would attempt these acts in vain:
And why? because it is a plane.

Nor let me peevishly repine
And wish its peaceful life were mine:
It suffers, blameless as it is,
From many disadvantages.

Wherever placed, it matters not
In how unsuitable a spot,
The parallelogram must stay:
It is too weak to crawl away.

If with a syringe you should go
And water it, it would not grow;
And nothing else can it become,
Not even a trapezium.

Then morn and evening let me raise
My little hands in duteous praise,
Because a Christian child I am,
And not a parallelogram.

Geometrical forms are, then, preexisting entities, each with its own nature and characteristics, discovered by Euclid in the same way as previously unknown (but existing) animals, plants, or chemical elements were discovered and described by tireless Victorian investigators of natural science. Darwin springs instantly to mind, but he was only one of a host. The Royal Geographic Society sponsored exploration, and Euclid becomes an early version of Dr. Livingstone. Thus, he is a provider of "strange information, true or no," a "geometer" in the same mold as the Victorian "geographer," albeit one of those ancient authors of whom Southey wrote in "My Days among the Dead Are Past." Housman here parodies this poem by simply inserting Southey's lines into a different context:

> With them I take delight in weal
>   And seek relief in woe;
> And while I understand and feel
>   How much to them I owe
> My cheeks have often been bedew'd
>   With tears of thoughtful gratitude.

The parallelogram, unlike some of those forms discovered in remote parts of the world by the geographers, is neither a dangerous nor a disturbing monster, but a weak, blameless, suffering entity ("if my ways are not as theirs . . . When did I make laws for them?") rooted in a single, perhaps unsuitable, spot (it "cannot fly / To Saturn nor to Mercury"). It is incapable of growth or development. Nor can it change itself into something else, something it is, by its very nature, not. In fact, as the inset quotations from LP 12 ("The laws of God, the laws of man") indicate, the parallelogram is not unlike A. E. Housman, who would have been quite happy not to be a "parallelogram," had the choice been his. It was not.

As an adult homosexual, he knew that he was not a "monster," but still he felt himself "confined" by prison bars (potentially actual and certainly psychological), those "parallel straight lines." Although not dangerous to others, he suffered; his environment could not be fled however uncongenial it was. The geometrical figure cannot undergo growth and change, and is thus, I would suggest, a metaphor for sterility, one of Housman's ubiquitous themes and one of his code words for homosexuality. As a child, Housman certainly did not think that he was basically in any way different from other boys; thus the otherwise inexplicable subtitle, "Infant Optimism."

One of the best-known composite creatures, a creature very much alive in literature through the present, is the unicorn, the animal that is in every respect a normal horse save one: it has a horn. Predictably, Housman projected himself into this mythological beast, and created his own version of it (Burnett, *Poems*, 280–82).

Inhuman Henry
or
Cruelty to Fabulous Animals

> Oh would you know why Henry sleeps,
> And why his mourning mother weeps,
> And why his weeping mother mourns?
> He was unkind to unicorns.

No unicorn, with Henry's leave,
Could dance upon the lawn at eve,
Or gore the gardener's boy in spring,
Or do the very slightest thing.

No unicorn could safely roar
And dash its nose against the door,
Nor sit in peace upon the mat
To eat the dog or drink the cat.

Henry would never in the least
Encourage the heraldic beast:
If there were unicorns about
He went and let the lion out.

The lion, leaping from its chain,
And glaring through its tangled mane,
Would stand on end and bark and bound
And bite what unicorns it found.

And when the lion bit a lot
Was Henry sorry? He was not.
What did his jumps betoken?
Joy. He was a bloody-minded boy.

The Unicorn is not a Goose,
And when they saw the lion loose
They grew increasingly aware
That they had better not be there.

And oh, the unicorn is fleet
And spurns the earth with all its feet:
The lion had to snap and snatch
At tips of tails it could not catch.

Returning home, in temper bad,
It met the sanguinary lad,
And clasping Henry with its claws
It took his legs between its jaws.

"Down, lion, down!" said Henry, "Cease!
My legs immediately release."
His formidable feline pet
Made no reply, but only ate.

The last words that were ever said
By Henry's disappearing head,
In accents of indignant scorn,
Were "I am not a unicorn."

And now you know why Henry sleeps,
And why his mother mourns and weeps,
And why she also weeps and mourns;
So now be kind to unicorns.

The Lion and the Unicorn, as every reader of *Through the Looking Glass* is aware, are both heraldic beasts, the Lion symbolizing England and the Unicorn Scotland. On one level, of course, this is part of the fun in Housman's treatment, as in Carroll's, and one could easily provide a political interpretation of the poem. But Housman's poem works on a deeper symbolic level than the political, the level of wish fulfillment. The unicorn, we are told, has certain habits that annoy Henry, that very proper defender of home and hearth and hater of unicorns. Its primary crimes seem to be that it "dances upon the lawn at eve" and "gores the gardener's boy in spring." The lawn dancing is perhaps derived from the habits of fauns and satyrs in classical mythology. Fauns and satyrs are symbols of unbridled sexuality. As for goring the gardener's boy, if the horn is seen as a phallic symbol, the nature of the sexuality can hardly be left in doubt.

Establishmentarian Henry calls out his lion, his "legion of decency," and sets it loose to destroy the unicorn. The mob rampages, and the unicorns flee (perhaps, as many "Oscarites" did, to Europe), leaving the furious mob foiled. The lion then turns on his master and destroys him. Henry, we have already been told, is metaphorically "bloody-minded." His erstwhile pet, the lion, renders him literally "sanguinary." He may say "I am not a unicorn," but the mob, once roused, wants blood, and innocent blood is just as acceptable as the guilty variety. Henry is "hoist on his own petard." Thus, the element of wish fulfillment. The last line then becomes a rather wistful plea for tolerance. As the title suggests, it is actually Henry who is "inhuman" rather than the unicorn.

William Blake's use of the tiger as a symbol of experience, especially of carnal experience, magnificent and frightening, is the basis of another of these thinly-masked poems. In this one, Housman acknowledges his debt to the earlier poet, whom he greatly admired, in the same way as he had done with Southey: by including a direct quotation in a very different context (Burnett, *Poems*, 212–14):

Oh have you caught the tiger?
    And can you hold him tight?
And what immortal hand or eye
Could frame his fearful symmetry?
    And does he try to bite?

Yes, I have caught the tiger,
    And he was hard to catch.
O tiger, tiger, do not try
To put your tail into my eye,
    And do not bite and scratch.

Yes, I have caught the tiger,
    O tiger, do not bray!
And what immortal hand or eye
Could frame his fearful symmetry
    I should not like to say.

And may I see the tiger?
    I should indeed delight
To see so large an animal
Without a voyage to Bengal.
    And mind you hold him tight.

Yes, you may see the tiger;
    It will amuse you much.
The tiger is, as you will find,
A creature of the feline kind.
    And mind you do not touch.

And do you feed the tiger,
    And do you keep him clean?
He has a less contented look
Than in the Natural History book,
    And seems a trifle lean.

Oh yes, I feed the tiger,
    And soon he will be plump;
I give him groundsel fresh and sweet,
And much canary-seed to eat,
    And wash him at the pump.

It seems to me the tiger
    Has not been lately fed,
Not for a day or two at least;
And that is why the noble beast
    Has bitten off your head.

Housman seems to be playing on the alternate meanings of the word "frame." Blake used it to denote "create." Housman uses it to denote "circumscribe" or "put limits to." The attempt to limit sexuality, to "tame" it and "civilize" it, here by feeding it on food fitted for innocent lambs and innocuous birds, backfires and destroys the optimist who attempts it, for not even an "immortal hand or eye" could do so. What cannot be "framed" or circumscribed is the tiger's "fearful symmetry." Does "fearful" here mean "filled with fear" or does it mean "inspiring fear"—or both? Since "symmetry" denotes a configuration that is the same on both sides, it would be superfluous to indicate just what type of sexuality Housman is indicating cannot ultimately be tamed, fenced in, and circumscribed, although it may appear to be so for a time. One cannot help but suspect that the true author of Housman's best nonsense poems was the "bogle of the hairy weid," and that bogle their true subject.

It may be noted that those verses that are most revealing and least dis- guise Housman's own sexual identity and attitude are found only in Lau- rence Housman's memoir. It is at least possible that he was the only one to see these poems during his brother's lifetime. Housman, with his mask and his well-developed instinct for self-protection, may have been less careful with his brother (who was himself homosexual, although the brothers seem never to have discussed this matter) than with others. In fact, Housman never actually confided his sexual preference to his brother, but Laurence Housman wrote to Gow after his brother's death, "I have known for many years what Alfred's tendency was. He knew that I knew . . ." (Page, *A. E. Housman*, 2).

3

State the Alternative Preferred

THERE IS A TRADITION AT CAMBRIDGE THAT TWO DONS, ONE OF THEM
Housman, took a walk one spring day to Madingley. A bird was singing
loudly, and one of the examiners exclaimed:

> "O cuckoo, shall I call thee bird,
> Or but a wandering voice?"

To which Housman responded:

> "State the alternative preferred,
> With reasons for your choice."[1]

If true, this anecdote indicates his sometimes donnish pedantic humor,
as well as his intimate familiarity with English poetry and his years in
the classroom (for every teacher will recognize the parody of a standard
examination question as well as the parody of Wordsworth). It also illustrates his facility at producing parody and rhyme at a moment's notice.

Indeed, much of Housman's parody consists in reproducing the original
poem—with the alteration of a few words to devastating effect. This is
precisely what he did with Frances Cornford's "O why do you walk
through the fields" in a letter of 22 March 1910 to his artist friend, William Rothenstein (A. E. Housman, *Letters*, 109):

> O why do you walk through the field in boots,
> Missing so much and so much?
> O fat white woman whom nobody shoots,
> Why do you walk through the field in boots,
> When the grass is soft as the breast of coots
> And shivering-sweet to the touch?

The alteration of the rhyme words changes a rather sentimentally simplistic poem into a devastatingly sardonic one. The "fat white woman" is
metamorphosed from a pathetic spinster observing carefully all the nice-

ties of social convention into a rather horsey, overbearing dowager. One walks abroad in the fields wearing gloves, and (alas!) nobody loves her, while her parodic twin tramps through the fields in boots, and (amazingly!) nobody shoots her. The crowning touch is the substitution of "coots," which sound old, eccentric, and cranky, for "doves" which sound (in both meanings) poetic, mournful, and lovelorn. The woman takes on the aura of the bird, and Mrs. Cornford's lorn maiden is rendered as ridiculous as the coot simply by altering three words of the original. This is a prime example of what Burnett calls Housman's "urge . . . to debunk and reject falsely idealized emotions" ("Poetical Emendations," p. 293).

Of course, Housman was not limited to inserting quotations into inappropriate (or perhaps ironically appropriate) new settings or to altering a few words to produce a parody. He could do far more. (Burnett, *Poems*, 210)

> The shades of night were falling fast,
>   And the rain was falling faster,
> When through an Alpine village passed
>   An Alpine village pastor:
> A youth who bore mid snow and ice
>   A bird that wouldn't chirrup,
> And a banner with the strange device—
>   "Mrs. Winslow's soothing syrup."
>
> "Beware the pass," the old man said,
>   "My bold, my desperate fellah;
> Dark lowers the tempest overhead,
>   And you'll want your umberella;
> And the roaring torrent is deep and wide—
>   You may hear how loud it washes."
> But still that clarion voice replied:
>   "I've got my old goloshes."
>
> "Oh, stay," the maiden said, "and rest
>   (For the wind blows from the nor'ward)
> Thy weary head upon my breast —
>   And please don't think I'm forward."
> A tear stood in his bright blue eye,
>   And he gladly would have tarried;
> But still he answered with a sigh:
>   "Unhappily I'm married."

The addition of truly execrable puns and almost dialectical colloquialism to Longfellow's poetic diction, the insertion of the unheroic mundane umbrella and galoshes into the high romantic drama, and the

substitution of an innocuous advertising slogan for Longfellow's mysterious, blood-stirring "Excelsior!," all combine to inject realism into what
Arnold Bennett called in *Clayhanger* (book 3, chapter 12, 380) "a pretty
thing, charming in its thin sentimentality." To add one more nail to the
coffin of sentimentality, Housman adopts and adapts the climax of Lear's
"The Courtship of the Yonghy-Bonghy-Bo" (*Nonsense Verse*, 90):

> Lady Jingly answered sadly,
>   And her tears began to flow, —
>   "Your proposal comes too late,
>   Mr. Yonghy-Bonghy-Bo!
> I would be your wife most gladly!"
> (Here she twirled her fingers madly)
>   "But in England I've a mate!"

Of course, the roles of male and female, pursuer and pursued, are reversed by Housman, but both the basic situation and the "punch line"
are the same; even Lady Jingly's tears are (in)appropriately transferred to
Longfellow's hero. When Housman's comic realism is set beside both
Lear's "pure comedy" and Longfellow's "pure romance," the effect is to
parody both forms, and "the distorted image mirrored in the parodist's
glass is somehow closer to the truth than the original" (Battestin, introduction to Fielding's *Joseph Andrews*), or, in this case, than to either of
the originals. The comic effect of this role reversal in parody becomes a
source of ambiguity in Housman's serious poetry. Even here, the final line
is ambiguous, meaning either "Unfortunately, I'm already married," as in
Lear, or "My marriage is unhappy." For Housman, it may be that there is
no difference between these two formulations.

A rich source for Housman was the nursery rhyme, together with its
companion, the fairy tale, nor were they a basis for parody only. He could
use such material deftly in making a point in textual criticism. In his edition of book 3 of Manilius's *Astronomica*, Housman comments on an
anomaly in the Latin poet's method for computing the ecliptic by con-
flating Little Red Riding Hood with the Goose and the Gosling. He
thereby reduces Manilius to a childish and imperceptive fool: "The wolf,
to whom in his proper shape you [Manilius] denied admittance, has come
back disguised as your mother the goose, and her gosling has opened the
door to him."[2]

From this source, in 1899, Housman contributed a single couplet to a
rhymed version of "The Story of the Seven Young Goslings," written by
his brother Laurence, as a substitute for what Laurence Housman himself
admitted was a "quite bad couplet, dealing with the widowing of the
Mother Goose" (L. Housman "Poet in the Making," 122):

> Entombed in a wolf was her husband the gander,
> And the painful event had completely unmanned her.

Laurence Housman had the grace to add, in the same article, that "friends to whom I have revealed the origin of those two lines assure me that they are the best in the whole poem" (122). Judging by Laurence Housman's unaided poetry, his friends were probably correct. The pun on "unmanned" is typically Housmanian. We remember the child clad in crocodile when considering the gander entombed in wolf.

It is possible that when he appealed to his brother for help with his versified fairy tale, Laurence Housman was remembering that many years earlier before entering Oxford, A. E. Housman had made up the following nonsense verse to amuse his young brothers and sisters:[3]

> Little Miss Muffet sat on a tuffet
> Opening her mouth very wide.
> There came a great spider; she opened it wider;
> And the spider ran down her inside.

This is most interesting because, although written before Housman was faced with his own sexuality, it reflects attitudes consistent therewith. As Desmond Morris has demonstrated (*Naked Ape*, 234–37), the spider, like the snake, is a symbol of male sexuality. The female's "opening her mouth very wide" and then, when a male arrives, even "wider," needs no expertise to explicate in sexual terms. Disguised as a nursery-rhyme parody, we have a metaphoric description of the male/female sex act in terms that make the concept extremely distasteful. We have the female as an insatiable trapper, swallowing up the male whose role is that of self-destructive trappee. And this is in the disguise of "nonsense verse" to amuse younger children! Christina Rossetti's own "Goblin Market" is hardly more innocent on the surface, or nastier underneath. As with the Cornford poem, Housman reverses the character of the female subject. Dainty, modest Miss Muffet, Miss Every-Victorian-Young-Lady, fleeing the (male) spider, is transformed into a sort of female ogre intent on first capturing, then swallowing, and ultimately absorbing and destroying its natural prey. Already, Housman's unconscious hostility toward and fear of the generic female is evident.

The realm of children's literature was the source of another poem which combines burlesque of a certain literary style with a parody on the relationship of the sexes. "Jack and Jill," used to illustrate the grammatical point that adjectives follow nouns, as Jill does Jack, was the second part of a poem included in a paper on Erasmus Darwin that Housman gave at a meeting of the University College, London, Literary Society.

Housman said it was "intended to convey to the reader, in language at once appropriate to the subject and intrinsically beautiful, the information that adjectives agree with their substantives in gender, number and case" (Laurence Housman, *A. E. H.*, 229).[4] The text is found in Burnett, *Poems*, 265–67.

Fragment of a Didactic Poem on Latin Grammar

> See on the cliff fair Adjectiva stand,
> Roll the blue eye and wave the ivory hand;
> Her amber locks resplendent rubies deck
> And orient emeralds wind her whiter neck.
> She marks afar the much-loved youth pursue
> O'er verdant meads the bounding kangaroo.
> " 'Tis he! 'tis he! your wings, ye Zephyrs, give!
> Waft, waft me, breezes, to my Substantive!"
> She speaks, and, headlong from the dizzy height,
> Prone to the plane precipitates her flight.
> Three Nymphs attend her in the airy chase,
> The Nymphs of Number, Gender, and of Case;
> The vine, the myrtle, and the rose they twine
> To bind thy victims, Concord, to the shrine.
> The startled youth, in momentary dread,
> As the fond fair descends upon his head,
> Shouts: the high rocks his vigorous outcry swell
> And teach the obedient echoes how to yell.
> From distant seas emerge the finny tribe
> And in the air parabolas describe;
> Barks the pleased hound, spectator of the sport,
> And hippopotami forget to snort.
> On dove-borne car descends the Paphian queen,
> And hovering Cupids vivify the scene.
> The clasping pair confess their mutual flame,
> In gender, number, and in case the same;
> Embowering roses screen their transports fond,
> And simpering Syntax waves her jewelled wand.
> So, up the steep side of the rugged hill,
> Companions in adventure, Jack and Jill
> With footing nice and anxious effort hale
> To the moist pump the necessary pail.
> The industrious pair their watery task divide,
> And woo the bashful Naiad side by side.
> The sturdier swain, for arduous labour planned,
> The handle wielding in his practised hand,
> With art hydraulic and propulsion stout
> Evokes the crystal treasure from the spout.

The maid, attentive to the useful flow,
Adjusts the apt receptacle below;
The gelid waves with bright reflections burn,
And mirrored beauty blushes from the urn.
Now down the hill their hands, in triumph gay,
The liquid plunder of the pump convey,
And seek the level land: incautious pair!
Too soon, alas, too soon shall ye be there.
The hero first the strong compulsion feels,
And finds his head supplanted by his heels;
In circles whirled he thunders to the plain,
Vain all his efforts, all his language vain,
Vain his stout boots and vain his eyebrows dark,
And vain, oh vain, his vaccination-mark.
The inverted pail his flying form pursues,
With humid tribute and sequacious dews
(So, through affrighted skies, o'er nations pale,
Behind the comet streams the comet's tail).
The prudent fair, of equilibrium vain,
Views, as he falls, the rotatory swain.
Exhilaration heaves her bosom young,
Tilts the fine nose, protrudes the vermeil tongue,
Bids from her throat the silvery laughters roll
And cachinnations strike the starry pole.
Gnomes! her light foot your envious fingers trip
And freeze the titter on the ruby lip.
The massy earth with strong attraction draws,
And Venus yields to gravitation's laws;
From rock to rock the charms of Beauty bump,
And shrieks of anguish chill the conscious pump.

Kenneth Baker remarks about the "Jack and Jill" part of the poem (which is all that he considers) that "Housman's satire is aimed not so much at any single poet as at the Augustan style in general, with its tendency to long-windedness and complacency" (*Unauthorized Versions*, 403). Housman was, in fact, not greatly enamoured of the Augustan style, considering it not in fact real poetry but

"sham poetry, a counterfeit deliberately manufactured and offered as a substitute. . . . The literature of the eighteenth century in England is an admirable and most enjoyable thing. It has a greater solidity of excellence than any before or after. . . . But the human faculty which dominated the eighteenth century and informed its literature was the intelligence, and that involved, as Arnold says, "some repressing and silencing of poetry." . . . The writing of poetry proceeded, and much of the poetry written was excellent literature, but excellent literature which is also poetry is not therefore excellent poetry. . . .

To poets of the eighteenth century high and impassioned poetry did not come spontaneously. . . . The way to write real poetry, they thought, must be to write something as little like prose as possible; they devised for the purpose what was called a correct and splendid diction, which consisted in always using the wrong word instead of the right, and [they] plastered it as ornament . . . on whatever they desired to dignify. . . . It was in truth at once pompous and poverty-stricken. It had a very limited, because supposedly choice, vocabulary, and was consequently . . . [unable to] describe natural objects with sensitive fidelity to nature; it could not express human feelings with . . . variety and delicacy." (NNP, 354–57)

Housman's "Fragment of a Didactic Poem on Latin Grammar" is a perfect example of these strictures; it could almost have been written to illustrate them. Indeed, it may have been. No commentary on it could be as exact as Housman's own. It is certainly filled with "splendid poetic diction" which is "as little like prose as possible" and unlike Housman's usual practice, it does not "describe natural objects with sensitive fidelity to nature." Jack is a noun (presumably a proper noun, as he is capitalized), and Jill is an adjective (not necessarily a feminine adjective, either). Number, gender, and case are nymphs that might almost have migrated from Pope's *The Rape of the Lock*. And the noun, a very young man, is momentarily afraid of the precipitate maiden. Both grammatical concepts and young lovers (?) are treated in a very Neo-Classical style, but what could be more delightfully out-of-place and absurd than noun-Jack's first appearance in pursuit of a kangaroo, witnessed by the hippopotami as well as by adjectival Jill? Only his having been vaccinated against disease but not, obviously, against losing his balance when in the company of a girl.

Part of the fun lies in matching the florid expressions to the dry grammatical rules they illustrate and represent, and in the second part one cannot but hold the original phrasing in mind while reading this spoof. It is a tour de force of far-fetched simile and metaphor, expressed in terms of Augustan poetic diction. Gender, case, and number become the votaries of Concord, and the adjective its "victim," laid out on a sacrificial altar. The water from the pump is the gift of a "bashful Naiad" who must be "wooed" to give it. It is "the crystal treasure," and "liquid plunder" of the pump, which turns the pump into Aladdin's or Ali Baba's cave, or to another possibility to be discussed in a moment. The homely pail becomes an "urn," and tumbling after Jack, a comet's tail following the comet. The "massy earth" is a magnet, and Jill is Venus. The most ingenious metaphor is, of course, implicit in the treatment, that which transforms a grammatical principle into a romantic idyll and a simple nursery rhyme into the elaborate and artificial mock-epic. This is to Pope's *The*

Rape of the Lock (which Housman in *NNP* called the most "perfect" poem in English "of greater than lyric length," 355) as Hardy's *Wessex Tales* are to his novels: shorter but of recognizably the same species.

Housman's grammatical allegory could serve as a "how not to" example of poetic speech, both the Augustan variety and its Victorian equivalent. It is a practical application of Lewis Carroll's "advice" to a would-be poet: "look at all things / With a sort of mental squint" ("Poeta Fit, Non Nasciter," 791). "Verdant meads," "precipitates her flight," "airy chase," "fond fair," "finny tribe," "Paphian queen" for Venus (alias Jill, in the second part), "embowering roses screen their transports fond," "gelid waves," "humid tribute and sequacious dews," "prudent fair," "cachinnations"— all of these and others are drawn from the poetic diction of the previous century. And what could be better than "art hydraulic" for a Victorian equivalent? Perhaps only "Venus yields to gravitation's laws." In the midst of this high-flown terminology, Housman brings us down to earth, like Jill herself, with a quite literal "bump" as the "charms of Beauty" come tumbling after "the rotatory swain."

In this poem, Housman also puns delightfully on "vain": all that Jack has (his language, boots, and eyebrows) or can do is in vain, and Jill for her part is vain of her equilibrium. Truly, here, pride goeth before a fall. But Housman is not only creating a parody of poetic diction, He is also creating an allegory of both heterosexual (in Jack and Jill) and homosexual (in the identically gendered noun and adjective) union. Considering that the liquid "crystal treasure" is forced out of the "spout" by manual handling, it is difficult not to make the following equation: water = ejaculate, pump = penis, and the "apt receptacle below" = the girl's genital "bucket" which she positions and re-positions to best receive "the useful flow" which has been produced by the swain's vigorous masturbatory activity.[5] Note that read this way, the lines imply that the girl's cooperative receptivity is insufficient to evoke the youth's ejaculation; this can only be produced by manual stimulation by a male hand, even if that hand must be his own. Jill has no part in operating the "pump."

> Companions in adventure, Jack and Jill
> With footing nice and anxious effort hale
> To the moist pump the necessary pale.
>
> . . . .
>
> The handle wielding in his practiced hand,
> With art hydraulic and propulsion stout
> Evokes the crystal treasure from the spout.
> The maid, attentive to the useful flow,
> Adjusts the apt receptacle below;

They may be "companions in [sexual] adventure," but their union is a matter of mechanics and not of affection, as is all too clear from Jill's unsympathetic mirth at Jack's fall. The other side of the allegory is that although the noun and adjective must be of the same gender, Jack and Jill are most assuredly not. And since the adjective must change its form to match the noun, presumably adjective-Jill, whose arrival fills noun-Jack with dread, metamorphoses into a masculine form so that they can become an "enamoured pair" confessing a "mutual flame" ("in gender, [as well as in] number, and in case the same"). The conversion of adjective-Jill to the masculine gender results in "transports fond" that are, in good Victorian fashion, discreetly screened from observation by roses.

The same-gender couple's "transports fond" are in marked contrast to the intergender relationship that develops quite naturally in the second half, not only in its sexual implications but in its surface meaning as well. In Housman's version, the familiar nursery rhyme is greatly expanded by the amplification of the action and the addition of circumstantial details. Jill sticks out her tongue ("protrudes the vermeil tongue") and laughs at Jack's sad plight (for which lack of sympathy the "gnomes" punish her by tripping her and sending her "tumbling after" him). Housman also adds a detailed description of the scene. At first, Jack and Jill are partners, each doing the work for which he or she is best fitted. Jack pumps and Jill steadies the pail, their "watery task" divided between them. They begin in harmonious agreement, unlike "Adjectiva" who, lushly female, is not at all in agreement with the young male Substantive. When Jack slips, however, all sympathy, equality, and agreement vanish. His fall is accompanied by Jill's "titters," and whereas Jack poetically "thunders to the plain," falling with a Miltonic grandeur implied by the nature of the language in which it is narrated, Jill prosaically "bumps."

Housman was invariably fair to his female students (even though he had difficulty in remembering their names), but the women of whom he approved were those who ran their homes competently, provided good food for their families and guests (especially when he was one of the guests), and in general conformed to the Victorian ideal of the "angel of the house." It is no surprise that he first visualizes the adjective in a feminine role, altering herself to match the specifications of her male companion, nor is it surprising that the substantive that determines the form of his dependent is seen as a male. Nor, finally, is the implication that the male can only find bliss with another male surprising. Although Jill tumbles after her "youth," by the end they are a discordant couple, in language as well as in sympathy, unlike the couple who agree in gender, number, and case, whose concord ends the first half.

As implied by the venue in which the poem was presented, in addition to being a parody of Augustan poetry in general, it is a sustained parody specifically of Erasmus Darwin's *Loves of the Plants*, "in which elaborate . . . poetic diction is applied to a theme totally unsuited for poetry. . . .

All Darwin's grandiloquence and stilted diction are there—the correct adjective, the absurd periphrasis, the dead apostrophe, the jargon . . . , the comic rhetoric" (Marlow, *A. E. Housman*, 176).

To me, it is self-evident that good parody can only be written by one who knows and loves the original. Overstatement is the heart of the fun in "Jack and Jill." If it relies on an elaborately overblown style for its comic effect, Housman could get just as much fun out of an underblown style. In 1907, when he heard that his brother Laurence "'was engaged in writing the libretto of an opera, he sent me—wishing to be helpful, and calling it 'Model for young librettists'—the following:" (L. Housman, *A. E. H.*, 229). The text is in Burnett, *Poems*, 257–59.

Fragment of an English Opera
(designed as a model for young librettists)

Dramatis Personae: Father (bass), Mother (contralto), Daughter (Soprano)
Scene: a Room. *Time*: Evening.

Fath.   Retire, my daughter;
            Prayers have been said:
        Take your warm water
            And go to bed.
Daught. But I had rather
            Sit up instead.
Fath.   I am your father,
            So go to bed.
Daught. Are you my father?
Fath.   I think so, rather:
            You go to bed.

Moth.   My daughter, vanish:
            You hear me speak:
        This is not Spanish,
            Nor is it Greek.
Daught. Oh, what a bother!
            Would I were dead!
Moth.   I am your mother,
            So go to bed.
Daught. Are you my mother?
Moth.   You have no other:
            You go to bed.

Fath.   Take your bed-candle
            And take it quick.
        This is the handle.
Daught. Is this the handle?

Fath.	No, that's the wick.
	This is the handle,
	At this end here.
	Take your bed-candle
	And disappear.
Daught.	Oh dear, oh dear!
F. and M.	Take your warm water,
	As we have said;
	You are our daughter,
	So go to bed.
Daught.	Am I your daughter?
F. and M.	If not, you oughter.
	You go to bed.
Daught.	I am their daughter;
	If not I oughter:
	Prayers have been said.
	This is my mother;
	I have no other:
	Would I were dead!
	This is my father;
	He thinks so, rather:
	Oh dear, oh dear!
	I take my candle;
	This is the handle:
	I disappear.
F. and M.	The coast is clear.

Housman was a lover of the music hall rather than the opera house, but he has caught perfectly the repetitive nature of an operatic libretto, much of which consists of reiterating the same inane phrases *ad nauseum* (which may explain why operas are admired for their music and not for their lyrics). And this is a very Victorian libretto indeed, with its emphasis on parental authority and proper daughterly obedience. Many, if not all, of the great operas are stories of passionate love and lurid passion, but in true Victorian fashion the male and female here are a married couple, very respectable parents in fact. It is only in the last line that we find out *why* they are so anxious for their child to retire: "The coast is clear." One need hardly emphasize that they are not concerned with the weather at Dover Beach, despite the possible nod to Matthew Arnold. And thus, in true Victorian fashion, the marital relationship, like that of the union between the noun and the adjective, but unlike the coast, is obscured.

It will not have escaped observation that Housman was far from being a feminist. Perhaps this is why he was so strongly attracted to the Biblical story of Adam and Eve and the fall from Eden that he returned to it several times, once in a poem printed in the canon (AP 3) and at other times in a jocular (?) vein. The canonical poem does not concern us here, as its purport is the inborn restlessness of Adam's sons, taking perhaps a hint from Herbert's "The Pulley" ("The heart of man, for all they say, / Was never happy long"). The other treatments might have been designed to rouse the ire of all members of the feminist movement (of which, inter-estingly enough, both his brother Laurence and his sister Clemence were among the founding parents). These poems, needless to say, were not published by either the poet or his brother. The following verse (Burnett, *Poems* 175) will indicate why.

> When Adam of the apple ate
> He had [?no] friend to keep him straight;
> God to a wife: 'twas hopeless odds.
> Friends are a deal more help than gods.

Obedience to God would have kept Adam "straight." That is, his behav-iour would have been in accordance with the "rules" ("the laws of God"). However, in the struggle between God and woman for Adam's allegiance, God does not stand a chance (" 'twas hopeless odds"). Had Adam had a male human friend to advise him, it is implied, he would not have fallen, for "Friends are a deal more help than gods" in resisting the allure of woman and keeping a man "straight." For Housman, the meaning of "straight" here is the diametrical opposite of the modern one.

There is another brief, rather nasty, "Adam" verse ("When Adam day by day," *Poems*, 257). This verse merely underlines the idea that all the guilt is Eve's and all the punishment Adam's ("Eve from scenes of bliss / Transported him for life"), but the last of these "Adam" poems takes a different view of the fall. It was written in the late 1890's for M. R. James, to whom Housman sent some "Specimens of a Proposed Illustrated Edi-tion of the Bible" (Burnett, *Poems, 264*).

Genesis
Chap. II

AEH Fecit

> The forms which you do not perceive
> Are those of Adam and of Eve.
> To draw them would not do at all.
> How providential was the Fall!

This rather ingenuous quatrain not only expresses the concept of the "Fortunate Fall," it is also a wry comment on middle-class Victorian prudery. During this period, there was a popular movement to "dress" representations of the nude in both painting and sculpture. This was the "fig leaf" era during which many older works of art, both Classical and Christian, were made "decent," obscuring the human figure by adding artfully arranged draperies or foliage (in fact far more erotically suggestive than the unadorned nude, which "would not do at all"), in the case of mythological representations, or the placing of strategically positioned leaves where what was pictured was the prelapsarian population of two. In either case, reality, and all that the word implies, could not be perceived.

Until the end of his poetic life, Housman took pleasure in intricate metrical arrangements and audacious rhymes. Some of his light verse and parodies, not here considered, are purely playful, but much of it has deeper and more somber undertones, as I have tried to demonstrate. "A. E. Housman's light verse is not nearly well enough known. . . . [He] shows in his comic stanzas and parodies how playful he can be" (White, *Centennial Memento*, 36). And he also shows how well he can disguise his personal concerns beneath a covering of froth.

Euterpe

4

The Garland

DURING THE VICTORIAN PERIOD, THERE WERE TWO OPPOSITE IDEAS about the proper function of poetry. One, derived from the Romantics and especially Wordsworth's long quasi-autobiographical poetic excursions, was the exploration of the poet's own mind. The other, derived from the Victorian devotion to earnestness and practicality, was the public service. Housman did not subscribe to either of them. He was emphatically not interested in spreading his psyche out for public view, nor did he write uplifting poetry, designed to inspire or improve the reader. His ideas about the proper function of poetry were very different. He held other, and older, theories of poetic function.

One of the things which poetry traditionally does is make the poet's name immortal, thus immortalizing the subject of the poem. If the poem lives on, both live on with it. This is one of the constant themes of Shakespeare's sonnets. Keats is remembered in his own right and not as the subject of Shelley's "Adonais." The same may be said for Arthur Hugh Clough and Matthew Arnold's "Thyrsis" and "Scholar Gypsy," but who would remember the name of Edward King had Milton not written "Lycidas" or Arthur Hallam had Tennyson not written "In Memoriam"?

This immortalizing power of poetry is a theme running not through Shakespeare's sonnets alone but through a great deal of later poetry as well, great, mediocre, and execrable alike. This potential power of poetry to preserve both poet and subject in imaginative life, despite physical death, is a theme that Housman touched often, and in his own way. It is not the name (usually an apparently impersonal "you" or "he") that he immortalizes but the concept of youth and (masculine) beauty frozen and preserved by death. This was one of the great themes of Latin literature with which he was of course intimately acquainted. Housman builds on a line from one of Horace's odes (book 4, no. 2), "And some brave youth's too early funeral mourns," (275) creating a Pindaric ode which celebrates rather than mourns the "brave youth's too early funeral."

To an Athlete Dying Young

The time you won your town the race
We chaired you through the market-place;
Man and boy stood cheering by,
And home we brought you shoulder-high.

To-day, the road all runners come,
Shoulder-high we bring you home,
And set you at your threshold down,
Townsman of a stiller town.

Smart lad, to slip betimes away
From fields where glory does not stay
And early though the laurel grows
It withers quicker than the rose.

Eyes the shady night has shut
Cannot see the record cut,
And silence sounds no worse than cheers
After earth has stopped the ears:

Now you will not swell the rout
Of lads that wore their honours out,
Runners whom renown outran
And the name died before the man.

So set, before its echoes fade,
The fleet foot on the sill of shade,
And hold to the low lintel up
The still-defended challenge cup.

And round that early-laurelled head
Will flock to gaze the strengthless dead,
And find unwithered on its curls
The garland briefer than a girl's.

(ASL 19)

There is an implicit parallel between art and early death. In a painting, a statue, a Grecian urn, time is frozen. As it is by art, "old Time" is halted by death. Both artistic representation and early bodily mortality circumvent the decay wrought by time and preserve the moment of perfection.

The world of art is replete with statues and paintings memorializing youth, and Greek art concentrated on the youthful athlete. For both Winckelmann and Pater—and presumably Housman—the ideal of beauty was the Greek statue of an adolescent male where all the bodily organs were molded (Dellamora, *Masculine Desire*, 112). In classic Greek art, "the beautiful boy was always beardless, frozen in time. . . . His beauty would not last and so was caught full flower by Apollonian sculpture" (Paglia, *Sexual Personae*, 114). Thus, we have "the wry turn by which the poet [or rather the persona] finds consolation in praising the dead youth for his 'ingenuity', as though he had 'decided' to die young to avoid disillusionment" and the fading of his physical perfection, both inevitable accompaniments of aging (Rosenthal and Smith, *Exploring Poetry*, 432). The imagery implies that death is the final goal to which the young athlete has beaten his competitors, winning the race in a double sense (Brooks and Warren, *Understanding Poetry*, 267). Indeed, a "smart lad!"

The beautiful pubescent boy was also, in classical Greece, a sex object. Thus, Housman's poem can be read either as "a serious fictionalization of history, made palpable for its very real concern for the death of an adolescent male" or it can be read as "a . . . pederastic ode, made publishable by its historical seriousness" (Woods, *Articulate Flesh*, 76). There is no need to belabor the point. For Housman, it was both, although I would not use the word "pederastic" since this term refers specifically to preadolescent boys rather than those in the first flush of their burgeoning masculinity, and what evidence there is indicates that Housman preferred adult men.

It is clear from Housman's reaction to a proposed illustration for ASL 5I ("Loitering with a vacant eye"—"Fancy selecting a *mutilated* statue!" [Grant Richards, *Housman* 182])—that the physical perfection of the youth whose statue was depicted was important to him and relevant to his poetry, as relevant to this poem about a Greek athlete as to the one about a Greek statue, to be discussed later. The last line suggests that "the love for a young man . . . prevails over death in a way that the rose garland of heterosexual love cannot. . . . [The poem] suggests that it is the purity of boy-love which preserves it from time and mortality" (Martin, "Two Strategies," 16). One should note, however, that there is nothing inherently "pure" about "boy-love" (pederasty), and it is not quite the same thing as "the love for a young man." There is no indication whatsoever that the "you" of this poem is a prepubescent boy rather than a fully developed youth.

The imagery, which Housman used so suggestively, was also drawn from Greek traditions. The laurel is the poet's crown, the crown of bays. It is also the athlete's victory crown. The laurel is associated with both male athletic triumph and poetic fame. In a poem that will be considered shortly, Housman's farewell at once to his art and his friend, the controlling image is that of laurels cut down. The dead laurels are the symbol not only of the poet's creative death but also of the physical death of his friend, once an athlete.

As the laurel is symbolic of male perfection, so the rose is of female beauty. The laurel is appropriate to the poet because it does not wither. It is appropriate to the young athlete because, growing early, it symbolizes the beauty of youth, which, according to Greek aesthetic theory, was at its peak in adolescence. Unlike the laurel, the rose is notoriously short lived, whether in terms of feminine beauty or in terms of horticulture. It is these associations which Housman exploits in having the early-growing and lasting laurel (as the symbol of athletic championship) wither even before the short-lived rose. This year's athletic record is bettered next year. Thus, glory on the sports field "does not stay" and the record is always being "cut." This youth, however, "takes . . . the unwithered laurel with him" to the grave (White, "*A Shropshire Lad* in Process," 261).

The rose-crowned maiden will decay, but the laurel-crowned youth will remain "unwithered." Even in the "shady night," the darkness of death inhabited by the shades of the earlier dead, the boy carries with him the laurel wreath with which the poet has crowned him. It is "the poet's assertion of the permanence of art (and memory). . . . He [the athlete dying but not dead] remains alive because he wears a laurel that will not wither, a garland of words," this very poem (Martin, "Two Strategies," 16). This laurel wreath is more than a symbol of athletic victory. It is more than a symbol of poetic preeminence. It is a gift of love. That it is "unwithered" is an implied assertion of the immortality of the poem and of the "lad," "the wreath [of words] which guarantees a life beyond death" (ibid., 15).

The poet's laurel is symbolic of poetry, but poetry is not universally appreciated, at least the sort of poetry that Housman, in the guise of Terence, writes. For some, it may be not bays but bains.

> "Terence, this is stupid stuff:
> You eat your victuals fast enough;
> There can't be much amiss 'tis clear,
> To see the rate you drink your beer.
> But oh, good Lord, the verse you make,
> It gives a chap the belly-ache.
> The cow, the old cow, she is dead;
> It sleeps well, the horned head:
> We poor lads, 'tis our turn now
> To hear such tunes as killed the cow.
> Pretty friendship 'tis to rhyme
> Your friends to death before their time
> Moping melancholy mad:
> Come, pipe a tune to dance to, lad."
> Why, if 'tis dancing you would be,
> There's brisker pipes than poetry.
> Say, for what were hop-yards meant,

Or why was Burton built on Trent?
Oh many a peer of England brews
Livelier liquor than the Muse,
And malt does more than Milton can
To justify God's ways to man.
Ale, man, ale's the stuff to drink
For fellows whom it hurts to think:
Look into the pewter pot
To see the world as the world's not.
And faith, 'tis pleasant till 'tis past:
The mischief is that 'twill not last.
Oh I have been to Ludlow fair
And left my necktie God knows where,
And carried half-way home, or near,
Pints and quarts of Ludlow beer:
Then the world seemed none so bad,
And I myself a sterling lad;
And down in lovely muck I've lain,
Happy till I woke again.
Then I saw the morning sky:
Heigho, the tale was all a lie;
The world, it was the old world yet,
I was I, my things were wet,
And nothing now remained to do
But begin the game anew.
     Therefore, since the world has still
Much good, but much less good than ill,
And while the sun and moon endure
Luck's a chance, but trouble's sure,
I'd face it as a wise man would,
And train for ill and not for good.
'Tis true, the stuff I bring for sale
Is not so brisk a brew as ale:
Out of a stem that scored the hand
I wrung it in a weary land.
But take it: if the smack is sour,
The better for the embittered hour;
It should do good to heart and head
When your soul is in my soul's stead;
And I will friend you, if I may,
In the dark and cloudy day.
     There was a king reigned in the East:
There, when kings will sit to feast,
They get their fill before they think
With poisoned meat and poisoned drink.
He gathered all that springs to birth
From the many-venomed earth:
First a little, thence to more,

> He sampled all her killing store;
> And easy, smiling, seasoned sound,
> Sate the king when healths went round.
>   They put arsenic in his meat
> And stared aghast to watch him eat;
> They poured strychnine in his cup
> And shook to see him drink it up:
> They shook, they stared as white's their shirt:
> Them it was their poison hurt.—
> —I tell the tale that I heard told.
> Mithridates, he died old.

                                                            (ASL 62)

The poem opens with a protest against the verses Terence makes. Terence is the nominal author of *A Shropshire Lad*, of which this is the penultimate poem, so the protest is specifically against this collection of poems. The friend who lodges this protest is one of Terence's mates, a rural Shropshireman (as is Terence himself, but certainly not Housman) who prefers drinking beer and dancing to thinking, and Terence's lighter to his more serious poetry. We meet him or his like many times in the Shropshire cycle. There is no need to seek for a face behind the mask, as one of Housman's biographers did. Watson speaks of "the hypothetical reader (whose extrovert qualities were palpably drawn from a certain model)" (*A. E. Housman*, 157). In fact, nothing is known about the attitude of that "certain model" to his friend's lyrics despite Gerald Jackson's remark that his father did not care for poetry. Housman dedicated the first book of his Manilius to Moses Jackson, and he therein addressed his friend as "sodali meo M. J. Jackson harum litterarum contemptori," which has been translated by Leofranc Holford Stevens as "To my comrade M. J. Jackson, who pays no heed to these writings." However, as Naiditch notes ("Review of Burnett's edition," 114), "contemptor" can also mean one who scorns or despises. This alternate meaning may have been intended—and intended jocularly—although it is not clear whether what was scorned or despised was Latin poetry, Manilius, or poetry in general. If it was meant jocularly (which would have been very much in Housman's vein), it may in fact indicate the reverse of what it seems to, whatever that is. In any case, it does not seem to me necessary to posit a specific model for the persona in "Terence, this is stupid stuff." That having been said, the speaker may indeed be based in some way on Jackson if he is identified as Terence's friend Ned, as will be discussed in the next chapter.

The heart of the poem is Terence's defense of his kind of poetry. This defense is logically developed, beginning with the comparison of poetry to pewter pots as a container for intoxicating contents. It is, after all, just as possible to be drunk on poetry as on ale, but without the unpleasant aftereffects. "Under the influence," a man is blind to reality, seeing "the world as the world's not," and when he does eventually sober up, it is to the realization that he has made rather a beast of himself ("down in lovely muck I've lain"). Being drunk on poetry lacks these drawbacks. Reading Milton may produce eyestrain but never a night spent snoring in the mud beside the road. Ludlow Fair, as will be discussed later, is one of Housman's metaphors for the material world. Those who prefer it to the world of imagination, "fellows whom it hurts to think," would be most unlikely to appreciate his poetry, bitter and sour, preferring his rhymes, light and frothy.

Terence's poetry is "not so brisk a brew as ale"; its purpose is not to promote conviviality and good fellowship ("a tune to dance to"). Its function is instead medicinal; like an inoculation, it gives the auditor (or reader) a minor dose of reality ("a belly-ache") as a protection against a major and catastrophic case of reality poisoning. Its "smack" is "sour" or "bitter" in more than one sense: it has a bitter taste in the mouth (like bitter beer) and it provides a painful impact (a smack on the face) (Lea, "*Ironies and Dualities*," 76). Another meaning of the word "smack" is also relevant: a tinge or a small amount, the meaning that links the Mithridates story to the first part of the poem, making it a parable.

It is generally assumed that in his defense of his poetry Terence is speaking for an unmasked Housman, and Terence's speech is accordingly interpreted. When Terence/Housman says that "the stuff I bring for sale / Is not so brisk a brew as ale," he is foreshadowing the image in ASL 63 in which he says of his flowers/poems that he took them to sell at the fair but found no buyers. This poem will be considered shortly.

One phrase of Terence's defense has generated an undue amount of explication: "out of a stem that scored the hand / I wrung it in a weary land." There was a lively discussion in the pages of *The Explicator* concerning this phrase, and many and ingenious were the explanations offered for the metaphor. Kane suggested the image of a hand squeezing a bunch of grapes over a wine-cup, and considered the Bible the source of this image as well as the phrase "weary land." (Kane, *Explicator* Q 7) Another explicator demurred, saying that as the word "it" refers to Housman's poetry, the "weary land" is the source of his poetry ("trouble and suffering"). He added that the "stem" might be a pen, as "in the emotion of expressing suffering in poetry, the stem (or pen) might well "score the hand.'" Another possibility, he suggested, is that, in accordance with the pastoral tone of *A Shropshire Lad*, it may be a shepherd's pipe, a panpipe played with a sort of "wringing motion." Such a pipe might be made from a "bine stem," specifically the stem of the hop plant used in making beer, the beverage with which the poetry is associated by the imagery (Griffith, *Explicator*, 13, #16). A third commentator suggested that the two preced-

ing and the two following lines make it clear that "it" "refers to a drink.
. . . Through the 6 lines the pronoun refers to a brew, and obviously not
to a pen or a musical pipe. Besides, one does not wring a pen or a musical
pipe, and they do not 'score the hand' " (Werner, *Explicator*, 14, #2A).
Dudley brought the discussion to a close by pointing out that the raw
material of experience is more painful than either the grain used to brew
ale or wine grapes. Since panpipes, pens, and hopstems all make the
image absurd (none of them could "cut or scrape" Terence's hand), there
is no need to seek for a "literal referent" at all. Specifying one only acts
"to demolish a fine, stern metaphor" (if you don't want to, or can't, think,
then drink. If you want to face reality "then sip . . . the medicinal drops
painfully extracted by Terence from the scrawny weeds of experience"
[Dudley, *Explicator* 14, #2B]).

When a single image gives rise to so many diverse and mutually exclu-
sive interpretations, it is more than likely that the source of the image is
the "hairy weid," and the most satisfactory explanation one that would
shock the Victorians (and all too many moderns, as well). If a referent is
sought, and I believe the metaphor requires one (and not beer), I would
suggest the nettle, which is Housman's repeated symbol for the bitterness
and sterility of his lifestyle. It most certainly "scores the hand" in the
literal sense. As a metaphor for bitter experience it is perfect in the literary sense. It is the plant that grows on the "graves of lovers / That hanged
themselves for love" (ASL 16). It is also "the leaf that hurts the hand"
for "touch it and it stings" (MP 32). The "weary land" from which both
Housman's poetry and the nettles in his life grew is the "hairy weid."

The "wringing the stems" image is to be found in Manilius (*Astronomica*, 321). Goold translates the pertinent line as, "and stems he will
squeeze together, and distil mixtures therefrom." The "mixtures" are per-
fumes and unguents. Although Housman may not at that time have yet
read the Latin poet, it is a short step from Manilius' literal description
of distilling perfume to Housman's metaphorical one of distilling poetry.
Whichever of the explanations one prefers, it is abundantly clear that
like the wreath of laurels which was metamorphosed into the poem that
crowned the athlete, the poetry that Terence defends is metaphorically a
natural growth and a medicine that will "do good to heart and head." It
carries in solution all the help that Terence can offer: companionship in
suffering ("I will friend you if I may"), the suffering implicit in the preceding line. "When your soul is in my soul's stead" is a quotation from
Job 16:4, with "when" substituted for "if," and it refers to Job's sufferings.
The story of Mithridates is drawn from Pliny who relates in full the tale
that Housman summarizes. One commentator links the ideas of the
poetry, the medicinal dose, and the story of Mithridates to suggest, with
perhaps unintentional humor, that "Housman should be taken in small
doses" (Hamilton, *Housman the Poet*, 25).[1]

Unlike most other poets, Housman predicts ultimate oblivion for himself, his poetry, and (by implication) his subject: "The world will last for
longer / But this will last for long" (AP 4). The innate futility of poetry
is voiced not only by Housman, the actual poet, but also by his alter ego
in another of the cycle poems. This one, like "Terence, this is stupid
stuff," stands slightly outside the narrative line of the Shropshire cycle
although some of the minor characters (Dick, for example) are met in
other poems.

Fancy's Knell

When lads were home from labour
   At Abdon under Clee,
A man would call his neighbor
   And both would send for me.
And where the light in lances
   Across the mead was laid,
There to the dances
   I fetched my flute and played.

Ours were idle pleasures,
   Yet oh, content we were,
The young to wind the measures,
   The old to heed the air;
And I to lift with playing
   From tree and tower and steep
The light delaying,
   And flute the sun to sleep.

The youth toward his fancy
   Would turn his brow of tan,
And Tom would pair with Nancy
   And Dick step off with Fan;
The girl would lift her glances
   To his, and both be mute:
Well went the dances
   At evening to the flute.

Wenlock Edge was umbered,
   And bright was Abdon Burf,
And warm between them slumbered
   The smooth green miles of turf;
Until from grass and clover
   The upshot beam would fade,
And England over
   Advanced the lofty shade.

The lofty shade advances,
    I fetch my flute and play:
Come, lads, and learn the dances
    And praise the tune today.
To-morrow, more's the pity,
    Away we both must hie,
To air the ditty,
    And to earth I.

(LP 41)

"Terence, this is stupid stuff" (ASL 62) opens with his friend's plea for him to "pipe a tune to dance to." Here, a volume of poetry later, and in almost the same position in *Last Poems* as the prior poem occupies in *A Shropshire Lad*, Terence complies with this request, to the general satisfaction of his companions.

The parallel placement seems quite deliberate and, taken together with the inherent commentary of the one poem upon the other, seems designed to encourage regarding them as companion pieces. This poem is the reverse of the wares Terence formerly brought to market, for this stuff is indeed as "brisk a brew as ale." It is not only poetry, it is verbalized dance music, unsurpassed "for delicacy and breathlessness of rhythm" (Stauffer, *Nature of Poetry*, 218) in which the "shifting cadence evokes . . . the village dancers stepping lightly to the flute" (Deutsch, *Poetry in Our Time*, 17).

The flute is Terence's chosen instrument. Rather than participating himself in the boy-girl pairing off, he plays it for their benefit. This flute is the instrument on which *Punch*, in a well-known cartoon greeting the appearance of *Last Poems*, the volume in which Housman took his farewell of his friend, depicted him piping, returning to the temple of the Muses twenty-six years after his first appearance there. There is little reason to doubt that Terence is voicing his creator's own farewell to the Muse whom *Punch* depicts joyfully welcoming him home. This flute is also Housman/Terence's equivalent of the oaten pipe of the classical pastoral shepherd, and it is one of the understated elements that link Housman's poetry to the ancient pastoral tradition. In addition, the flute is the most phallically shaped of musical instruments (Woods, *Articulate Flesh*, 60), and, from the way it is played, the most suggestive of homosexual phallicism. It "might also be interpreted as a symbol of fellatio" (Reade, *Sexual Heretics*, 30). It is peculiarly appropriate to Housman, and his choice of it as the symbol for his poetry is probably not accidental. With the death of Moses Jackson half a world away, Terence laid aside his flute; Housman symbolically laid aside his instrument.

The change from the past tense in which the bulk of the poem is written to the present and future tenses of the final verse seems to sum up Housman's poetic history. He played his flute in college, creating "a tune to dance to," the comic verse in *Ye Rounde Table*. "The lofty shade" began to advance in *A Shropshire Lad* with its "sour smack" of "bitter brew," and in *Last Poems* the "lofty shade," the shadow of night and death, completes its advance. No more tunes would be publicly played on the flute, and few more even privately composed. "Tomorrow" that shade would blot out all dancing, all music, and all Housman/Terence's poetry, together with the life of the man who had inspired them.

The form in which this poem ends is extremely unusual. In her book on poetic closure, Barbara Smith does not include any comments on it in particular, but her general remarks apply to it more than, perhaps, to any other poem in English literature: "This sort of explicit announcement [of the end of a poem] can only rarely be accommodated by a poem's thematic structure. . . . Explicit self-closural references are, in fact, only rarely encountered" (*Poetic Closure*, 172). Yet here, Housman has perfectly "accommodated" this poetic rarity to his theme. The end of the poem is the end of Housman as a poet, of Terence as a piper and spokesman for poetry, and of Housman's poetic inspiration.

The ephemerality of poetry was articulated by Horace in the *Ars Poetica*: "Death claims both us and our works. . . . The works of men's hands must perish, much less can the glory and charm of words endure undecaying" (*Complete Works*, 399, trans. by Edward Henry Blakeney). In fact, "away we both must hie," I and my music/poetry together with the setting sun, my airs to the air where they will diminish and die away (as the scansion of the poem itself does), leaving not even an echo to be heard, and "to earth I," to death, the grave, and oblivion. This is, after all, "Fancy's Knell," the passing bell that announces the death of "fancy." The word means both "imagination" and "preference," here specifically preference in (female) sweethearts ("the youth toward his fancy / Would turn his brow"), and it does indeed toll the death of both.

A poem can be a metaphorical urn, entombing the subject. Housman does not use this metaphor at all. It is inappropriate for his poetry. For him, poetry is like a flower, an organic growth. We have already seen his account of how poetry would germinate in him until it was born fully formed from the matrix of his unconscious mind, a process for which flowers are metaphorically a most appropriate image. A flower germinates from a seed. It grows, changes, develops, and dies. However, although the individual blossom will fade and wither, its seeds will in time germinate and blossom in another year. Thus flowers and poetry are alike both ephemeral and eternal.

Like the seed of a dead flower, a dead poem may inspire a later poet to create a new burst of beauty. This aspect of flowers is one that Housman exploits in many poems as a symbol of poetry that, for him, could defy time and death, up to a point, but was not exempt from the ultimate darkness. It could delay, but not defy, final decay.

Housman is but one of many who have utilized the metaphor of flowers for literature.[2] We have seen this metaphor at work already in his lyrics. The poem is a medicine brewed from bitter plants, and the poem is the athlete's and poet's crown of bays. The wreath may be, instead of a crown of victory, a funeral offering, and as just such a votive offering to the dead the metaphor is frequently used. Swinburne so used it in his elegy for Beaudelaire, "Ave Atque Vale": "For thee, O now a silent soul, my brother, / Take at my hands this garland, and farewell" (*Swinburne*, 86, verse 18), a fitting offering indeed for the author of *Les Fleurs du Mal*. Tennyson, too, used the image in "In Memoriam" 8: 5 and 6 (*Tennyson*, 353) in much the same way, and with much the same purpose, as did Housman.

> ". . . this poor flower of poesy
> Which, little cared for fades not yet.
>
> But since it pleased a vanished eye,
> I go to plant it on his tomb,
> That if it can it there may bloom,
> Or dying, there at least may die."

Heine, a poet Housman greatly admired and who influenced Housman's work, also made use of this image, and Housman adapted Heine's work. He began with a free translation of the German poet's brief verse, reversed the order of Heine's images, and built on it to create his own poem. Heine's poem, "Lyrisches Intermezzo 62" ("Am Kreuzweg wird begraben"), has been translated thus by Sylvia Bruce (*Essays*, 42):

> At the cross-roads lies buried
> The man who did himself in.
> There grows a flower, blue,
> For the poor fellow's sin.
> At the crossroads I stood and sighed;
> Cold and mute was the night.
> Hangdog in the moonlight
> Moved, slow, the flower of rue.

This quite literal translation may be compared with Housman's expansion of it:

Sinner's Rue

I walked alone and thinking,
    And faint the nightwind blew
And stirred on mounds at crossways
    The flower of sinner's rue.

Where the roads part they bury
    Him that his own hand slays,
And so the weed of sorrow
    Springs at the four cross ways.

By night I plucked it hueless,
    When morning broke 'twas blue:
Blue at my breast I fastened
    The flower of sinner's rue.

It seemed a herb of healing,
    A balsam and a sign,
Flower of a heart whose trouble
    Must have been worse than mine.

Dead clay that did me kindness,
    I can do none to you,
But only wear for breastknot
    The flower of sinner's rue.

                                                    (LP 30)

From Heine, Housman took the blue color of the flower, its association with the graves of suicides at the crossroads, and a part of its name. Heine's trembling moonlight becomes Housman's faintly stirring night wind. And that is all. Every other detail—the flower's color-change between night and morning, its use as a symbol "of healing, / A balsam and a sign," and most important the conversion of the flower into an offering from the dead to the living and back into the poem offered by the living to the dead (for the literal flower is picked by the persona and fashioned into a "breastknot" which we are reading)—all this Housman added to Heine. He thus enriched the poem, deepened its significance, and thereby made it his own.

The significance of the funeral at the crossroads may be seen in the graphic description of such an interment that Thomas Hardy included in his short story "The Grave by the Handpost": ". . . at the junction of the four ways . . . a grave was dug" for old Sergeant Holway, who "had shot himself" and whose corpse was thrown into the grave by four men who "shoveled in and trod down the earth." No mound was raised over it.

There was no funeral, and he was buried "like a dog in a ditch" in "an accursed place," with " 'a new six-foot hurdle-saul [a stake] drough's body' " (*Selected Stories*, 121–133) In dealing with suicide, Housman shows the same sympathy that is evident in Hardy's treatment. It is not the fact of a man's death that arouses their pity, but rather "the life which he [the suicide] must have found so intolerable" (Molson, "Philosophies," 211). Katharine Symons tells us about her brother that "to a painful degree, he was capable of compassion for suffering, and resentment against the cruelties of the world," and his "philosophical agonies . . . drove him into sympathy with murderers and suicides" (Symons, et al, *Recollections*, U.S. ed. 33, not in U.K. ed.).

The half-buried pun on "springs" in conjunction with "bury" three lines above suggests that the dead man is a seed from whose body the flower has sprung. There is also a half-buried pun on "flower," as (depending on how one pronounces it) it can mean that which springs from seed or that which flows from a spring. This suggests that whereas rue as a flower symbolizes regret—or that remorse that must, of course, be worn with a difference—rue is also, potentially at least, the purifying water that flows from the springs of compassion. It washes away the dead man's guilt. Whether the guilt is for whatever led the suicide to this last gesture or for simply having killed himself remains ambiguous. Probably both are intended. The blossom is an agent of healing or reconciliation, and it is "a sign" that by definition must have some greater significance than itself. Perhaps it is intended to be a symbol of divine compassion and, thus, of hope for final forgiveness of both the implied sources of guilt. It is in this sense that the "dead clay" can be said to have done the persona a "kindness," extending a promise of reconciliation with the very Author of the law against self-slaughter.

The poetry symbolized by the flower can thus be a mutual gift, from the dead to the living and from the living to the dead. The seed was, in a sense, Heine's gift to Housman. The flower that grew from it is Housman's gift to an anonymous suicide. Not all suicides are anonymous. One, whose name is known, and whose cause of guilt Housman conjectured, also received a votive offering of flowering poetry from Housman.

On 6 August 1895, Maclean, a young cadet at Woolwich, shot himself, leaving a note that was the seed from which, within two months, a poem sprang. The circumstances were touched on in the first chapter, and it is well to examine them more closely. The coroner's inquest was held on 9 August. The eighteen-year old boy's body was found in a hotel in London. He was lying in a pool of blood in his room with a bullet wound in his forehead. He had clearly destroyed some photographs and a letter before he shot himself, and there were traces of handwriting on the remains of the letter. It was assumed that the boy killed himself because of some sort of love trouble. Despite the assumption that the handwriting was that of a woman, the conclusion was that the grounds for the boy's suicide were unknown.[3] The case was fully reported in the London daily paper *The Standard* on 10 August 1895. Housman read their account, including the full text of the boy's suicide note, which read in part:

> the main reasons that have determined me. The first is utter cowardice and despair. There is only one thing in this world that would make me thoroughly happy; that one thing I have no earthly hope of obtaining. The second . . . is . . . I have absolutely ruined my own life; but . . . I have not morally injured—or "offended," as it is called in the Bible—any one else. Now I am quite certain that I could not live another five years without doing so . . . it is final, and consequently better than a long series of sorrows and disgraces.

Housman clipped and saved the account and his clipping is extant.

Whatever the truth about the gender of the handwriting on the note that was not carefully enough destroyed, Housman clearly connected the boy's suicide with the Oscar Wilde trial of 25 May 1895, and he "(perhaps wrongly) attributed the [boy's] depression to a recognition of irresistible homosexual tendencies" (Nosworthy, "Woolwich Cadet," 352). The key is the Biblical word "offended" which may refer to a variety of transgressions but, however interpreted later, does not specify homosexuality (which is designated an "abomination" rather than an "offense"[4]). In the context of the note, however, this interpretation is not unreasonable.

The suicide note proved to be another seed, and it grew into the following votive wreath, a crown of bays and laurel, the victor's—and the poet's—crown. The notebook records an earlier version of the second line of the last verse: "And take the wreath of verse I've made":

> Shot? So quick, so clean an ending?
>   Oh that was right lad, that was brave:
> Yours was not an ill for mending,
>   'Twas best to take it to the grave.
>
> Oh you had forethought, you could reason,
>   And saw your road and where it led,
> And early wise and brave in season
>   Put the pistol to your head.
>
> Oh soon, and better so than later
>   After long disgrace and scorn,
> You shot dead the household traitor,
>   The soul that should not have been born.

Right you guessed the rising morrow
        And scorned to tread the mire you must:
Dust's your wages, son of sorrow,
        But men may come to worse than dust.

Souls undone, undoing others,—
        Long time since the tale began.
You would not live to wrong your brothers:
        Oh lad, you died as fits a man.

Now to your grave shall friend and stranger
        With ruth and some with envy come:
Undishonoured, clear of danger,
        Clean of guilt, pass hence and home.

Turn safe to rest, no dreams, no waking;
        And here, man, here's the wreath I've made:
'Tis not a gift that's worth the taking,
        But wear it and it will not fade.

                                        (ASL 44)

The echoes from the Woolwich cadet's suicide note are woven so
smoothly into the text that, were the note itself not available for comparison, it would be impossible to determine which phrases were Housman's
and which were derived from the boy's words. There are five echoes, one
in each of the first five verses. There are no echoes in the last two verses,
and this I think is the key to what is, on the surface, a self-contradictory
attitude, a blanket recommendation that the best course of action for homosexuals is to commit mass suicide. Since the boy's note echoes the
ethos of the times, I would suggest that these first five verses represent the
general attitude toward homosexuality ("not an ill for mending," "saw
your road and where it led," "long disgrace," "guessed the rising morrow,"
"souls undone, undoing others"). The last two verses are Housman's own
comment on the event. In the last verse, "Housman expressed his real
sense of comradeship" with the dead boy (Bayley, "Housman and Larkin," 158).

The voice of society commiserates with the dead boy, shedding crocodile tears over his grave. We have already encountered the crocodile as a
symbol of social rectitude whose invitation to the death of the spirit
proved irresistible to the Egyptian child of nature. Here, the demand of
the voice of moral rectitude for the bodily death of the Woolwich cadet
proved equally irresistible, and the boy, like his nonsense counterpart,
died in obedience to that peremptory invitation.

In commemorating a death that was "a welcome release from a life that

has been a tragedy" (Robinson, *Angry the Dust*, 28), Housman transformed the Woolwich cadet, as Martin says,

> from pathetic victim to hero. . . . A suicide is praised as if he were a military
> hero . . . and his death becomes the means of new life. For it is the poet's act
> of love . . . that creates the laurel of the last stanza. . . . Although Housman
> in 1895 was perhaps incapable of imagining a homosexual life, he was capable
> of recognizing his own obligation to preserve the memory of those who died
> for their sexuality, in the hope that his wreath might last "unwithered" to
> another age where it might give hope to other "luckless lads."

Martin suggests that Housman felt he had a "mission . . . to write the
works that could preserve the memory of those who could not speak"
("Two Strategies," 16). I would hesitate to state this quite so categorically.

Housman's determination to preserve his own mask, to stay in the
closet in the modern phrase, would, I think, have militated against his
feeling any such obligation. He was clearly much moved by this boy's
death (his preserving the newspaper account of it indicates as much), but
probably did not expect his readers to remember it or to connect it with
the poem. His Oscar Wilde poem he did not publish, although Laurence
Housman was under the distinct impression that his brother wished it to
be published and the truth about himself made known—once he was
safely in the grave (L. Housman, "*De Amicitia*").

The "wreath" Housman fashioned for the boy is identical to the "garland" that he fashioned for the athlete who also died young. He has
awarded the crown of bays to both of them. The living laurel is an appropriate symbol for victory against death, but when death is the victor,
Housman uses a very different botanical metaphor. The seed is from
Shakespeare's "Not a flower, not a flower sweet, / On my black coffin let
there be strown" (*Twelfth Night*, 2: 4), part of a song on the subject of
hopeless and unrequited love, and from this seed grew what is titled in
Housman's notebook, although without a title in *A Shropshire Lad*,

(A Winter Funeral)

> Bring, in this timeless grave to throw,
> No cypress, sombre on the snow;
> Snap not from the bitter yew
> His leaves that live December through;
> Break no rosemary, bright with rime
> And sparkling to the cruel clime;
> Nor plod the winter land to look
> For willows in the icy brook

To cast them leafless round him: bring
No spray that ever buds in spring.
    But if the Christmas field has kept
Awns the last gleaner overstept,
Or shrivelled flax, whose flower is blue
A single season, never two;
Or if one haulm whose year is o'er
Shivers on the upland frore,
—Oh, bring from hill and stream and plain
Whatever will not flower again,
To give him comfort: he and those
Shall bide eternal bedfellows
Where low upon the couch he lies
Whence he never shall arise.

(ASL 46)

If the "ironic model" for this poem is "Lycidas," as Martin suggests ("Two Strategies"), it is of significance that Milton was commemorating his dead friend. What is Housman's poem commemorating? This poem is indeed "wrung . . . in a weary land" from "a stem that scored the hand," but whose grave, or better what grave, is it that is to be strewn with "whatever will not flower again"? The flower of sinner's rue was blue in the morning, and also blue is the "shrivelled flax." But whereas the rue seems to acquire an eternal color, the color of the flax will last "a single season, never two." I would suggest that this is the grave of hopeless love, as suggested in the song from *Twelfth Night*. That the hopeless love is specifically homosexual is suggested by the sterility of the plants laid on it ("no spray that ever buds in spring"). Love between heterosexuals is assumed to bring forth new life, to "flower again" in the children sprung from the union, but homosexual love, no matter how great, how tender, how complete, must of its very nature be eternally sterile. What could be more appropriate for the grave of unrequited sterile love than plants that will neither bud nor flower again? Knowing Housman's penchant for buried puns, the identity of the buried "he" that "never shall arise," in the last line, can be easily conjectured on this basis.

This is not to negate the more general reading that emphasizes the suitability of dead plants for the grave of the dead, despite the elegiac pastoral tradition in which perennial flowers (and other perennial plants), symbolizing immortality, are customary. As Leggett notes, the "conceit is that the appropriate symbols of death are not the green living plants which survive the winter and are reborn in the spring. Eternal Death's proper emblem is 'whatever will not flower again' " (*Land of Lost Content*, 122). Nor is this intended to negate the implicit denial of personal immortality that many critics have noted.[5] This reading is intended to add another layer of significance to those generally recognized.

Housman's own explication of his flower imagery is combined with as clear a statement of his poetic purpose as could be expected in the metaphor that closes *A Shropshire Lad*.

> I hoed and trenched and weeded,
>   And took the flowers to fair:
> I brought them home unheeded;
>   The hue was not the wear.
>
> So up and down I sow them
>   For lads like me to find,
> When I shall lie below them,
>   A dead man out of mind.
>
> Some seed the birds devour,
>   And some the season mars,
> But here and there will flower
>   The solitary stars,
>
> And fields will yearly bear them
>   As light-leaved spring comes on,
> And luckless lads will wear them
>   When I am dead and gone.
>
> (ASL 63)

That the flowers in question are in fact the poems that Housman wrote is beyond dispute. It has been suggested that the rejection of the flowers at the fair reflects the rejection of *A Shropshire Lad* by the first publishing house to which Housman offered it. This, I have been assured by P. G. Naiditch, in a letter of 1 January 1997, is indeed so, but it does not negate Martin's contention that the poem is a metaphorical account of Housman's "own life and art."

The speaker makes an offering of his love and labor, but it goes "unheeded." He then "sows" the seeds of his first offering, which is to say, he creates the poems that are the product, or seed, of the love once proffered and refused. That seed will yield new flowers and come to adorn "other unlucky lads." . . . In this poem, more than in any other of this collection, Housman is open about the homosexual meanings of his heritage: the flowers that he sows are to be worn by other lads. In that way, his own love, so hopeless and so painful, becomes a source of hope and comfort. For the love, once transformed into art, is able to transcend time and prejudice until it finds its rightful place. ("Two Strategies," 15)

Since on other occasions Housman used an unacceptable color to represent homosexuality ("Purple William" perhaps and the Oscar Wilde poem about "the colour of his hair" certainly), the fact that here the poems/flowers are rejected because "the hue was not the wear" supports this interpretation.

Just what flowers are intended, and why are they not named? It is possible, of course, that they are a mixture of kinds, simply generic "flowers." But it is also possible that the image behind these blooms is that of the scarlet poppy, which, "for late Victorians and Edwardians, . . . was associated specifically with homoerotic passion," an association that "had been conventional" (Fussell, *Great War*, 248). If the hue of Housman's anonymous flowers was scarlet, then indeed it was "not the wear," and if his flowers were, in his own mind, poppies, there was good reason for not indicating it.

There is a note of optimism, unusual for Housman, in the final lines of the poem. If at the beginning when "I" offer these flowers of a color whose "hue was not the wear," the stigmata of homosexuality, they are rejected, the flowers—or the orientation itself—will not be eradicated ("And fields will yearly bear them / As light-leaved spring comes on"). And the end looks forward to a future when, even though "I am dead and gone" and it is too late for "me" to wear my own flowers publicly, those flowers will be openly sported even if those who wear them are still "luckless" ("And luckless lads will wear them").[6] It is pleasant to see in today's Gay Pride parades the fulfillment of this covert prophecy. And just perhaps the red favors that are today's symbol of AIDS awareness and support for the gay community are indeed Housman's metaphor made palpable.

The key phrases, as often in Housman, are from the Bible (Matthew 13:3–9, and repeated Mark 4:3–9). The passage is so relevant that it must be cited in full:

Behold, a sower went forth to sow; And when he sowed, some seeds fell by the way side, and the fowls came and devoured them up: Some fell upon stony places, where they had not much earth: and forthwith they sprang up, because they had no deepness of earth: And when the sun was up, they were scorched; and because they had no root, they withered away. And some fell among thorns; and the thorns sprung up, and choked them: But other fell into good ground, and brought forth fruit. . . . Who hath ears to hear, let him hear.

This is a parable, and as such means something other than—or more than—it says. In the Bible, the sower and seed analogy explains that speech is itself a parable. Therefore, the poem also may be reasonably taken as a parable, its message "cast . . . in a secret tongue. The male love which gave rise to the poems would survive in them until it could flower again," and, like flowers, they "contain the means of their own continuation. The poet sows their seeds so that they may flower again another year. By this capacity for regeneration, they are able to survive the poet himself" (Martin, "Two Strategies," 15). Without the homosexual reference, this interpretation has been offered many times. In short, "poetry itself provides the poet a means to transcend his own mutable nature. Poetry as a product of the mind of man has a permanence which is denied man himself" and represents "the final triumph of art over the forces of change. . . . [The poet] has overcome time through a metaphorical conception of the immortality of art" (Leggett, *Land of Lost Content*, 89). This concept we have already considered.

What, then, does the homosexual interpretation add to it? There is still another dimension to the image. As was remarked in the discussion of "A Winter Funeral," flowers bring forth seed. Therefore we can add children to the already existing equation of flowers, love offerings, and literature. Katharine Symons wrote to Grant Richards that "Alfred found he was 'creating' something. He was indeed begetting *A Shropshire Lad* . . . that would do for him in the place of progeny." In a later letter to Richards, she wrote that her brother "found the inhibitions of chastity and celibacy compensated . . . as he believed himself producing immortal progeny." Richards accepted this metaphor and himself referred to Housman's begetting a Shropshire lad, which was the "offspring of his brain and destined to act for him as progeny to perpetuate his name." Katharine Symons also wrote to another correspondent that "when, early in 1895, he found himself writing poems of unaccustomed force, he became excited with the conviction that he was producing immortal progeny" (Wysong, "Housman's Surrogate Son," 148–49). There seems no doubt that Housman considered his poems as his children, and *A Shropshire Lad* was his firstborn, for whom he felt the tenderest pride and affection. This nicely explains why he refused permission to dismember the book by anthologizing individual poems from it and refused to accept royalties from its sale. Housman may well have felt, as his sister said, that his poems were his children. Thomas Hardy felt the same way, using the same metaphor in "Panthera" (*Selected Poetry*, 237):

> I had said it long had been a wish with me
> That I might leave a scion—some small tree
> As channel for my sap . . .

Nesca Robb approaches the answer to this question of what the homosexual interpretation adds to those already offered, but she does not have the information revealed in Laurence Housman's *Encounter* article that is needed to completely articulate it. She says that the poet "can look into the future and see his verses strewn about the world as 'herbs of healing' for later sufferers" (*Four in Exile*, 41–42). She is quite right about the poems being "herbs of healing," "balsams and signs," but was not in a position to know who those "later sufferers" were. They are the "luckless lads" who find, perhaps to their amazement and horror, that they are attracted physically to men rather than women. This being so, the additional dimension must be added to the poetry/flower analogy.

The scattering or sowing of seed is an agricultural or horticultural image, but it is also an image of "husbandry," and of the function of the husband in marriage: sexual love and the physical expression (expression in its most literal possible sense) of seed. Indeed, in literature, "one of the most frequent guises of the male genitals is as a plant or flower" or flower (Woods, *Articulate Flesh*, 33), returning us to the ambiguity of the word *in vacuo*, which we have already seen. Woods suggests that artistic creativity is a homosexual substitute for having children, one's stake in the future. The homosexual poet thus projects his (or her) love "forward in time" in two ways: love is made to outlast life, and death is not the end. For an afterlife of love in heaven, the homosexual substitutes an afterlife in art. We have seen this motif before, but it is even more potent with homosexual poets where art is the only "access to immortality" (ibid., 81–85). Flowers and children are not the only things that spring from seed; Housman's poems are the flowers that grew from his seed; they are his children, the palpable offspring of his love.

In a real sense, the poems can thus be considered the children of the poet, fathered on him by—whom? By the Muse, in the older tradition, or by some one person who has inspired them and for whom they were written, like Shakespeare's sonnets, which were dedicated to "the onlie begetter of / These issuing sonnets / Mr. W. H." The modern version is the words that Housman addressed to Moses Jackson in the inscription of the copy of *Last Poems* Housman sent to him in hospital from "a fellow who thinks more of you than anything in the world . . . you are largely responsible for my writing poetry" (Graves, *A. E. Housman*, 230).

Appropriately, Jackson's impending death lies behind the image of the felled bays in what is perhaps the most haunting of all the lyrics in the canon, written in April 1922:

> We'll to the woods no more,
> The laurels all are cut,
> The bowers are bare of bay
> That once the Muses wore;
> The year draws in the day
> And soon will evening shut:
> The laurels all are cut,
> We'll to the woods no more.
> Oh we'll no more, no more

To the leafy woods away,
To the high wild woods of laurel
And the bowers of bay no more.

(LP prefatory poem)

Like others we have seen, this lyric too grew from a seed, the seed of a medieval French ronde. In notebook fragment no. 107, the poem is given its French title ("Nous n'irons plus aux bois"), the first line of Theodore de Banville's poem ("Nous n'irons plus aux bois, les lauriers sont coupes . . . / Les lauriers sont coupes, et le cerf aux bois / Tressaille au son du cor: nous n'irons plus aux bois"). In his treatment Housman omitted all the picturesque details that mythologize the lyric, such as the Loves and the clustered Naiads, simplifying and universalizing it by using only the transposed refrain.[7]

The laurels are cut, and there are no more bays. What is the difference between these two designations of the same plant, or is there one at all? If the "laurel" is the tree and the "bay" is the leaf, as Professor Friend suggested to me, I must wonder about the green bay tree and the laureled head. In one of her songs, "Oh roses for the flush of youth," Christina Rossetti, whom as a poet Housman admired more than he did her brother, differentiates them thus: "Laurel for the perfect prime. . . . And bay for those dead in their prime" and, for Housman, Moses Jackson was perfection dead in his prime, the two images fusing into a single model. The three-dimensional equivalent of the image is the Kennedy Memorial outside Jerusalem, where the American president, cut down in his prime, is symbolized by a felled tree. The term "in his prime" is indefinite and perhaps more applicable to Kennedy than to Jackson, who was in his sixties when he died, but for Housman Jackson would always be "in his prime,"

Who are the "we" of the first line? If the poem is merely a rumination, then the "we" is "me, myself, and I." But if it is more than Housman's final farewell to poetry ("the bowers are bare of bay / That once the Muses wore"), if it is a farewell taken because the "shady night" is in the process of blotting out the morning and the glad day, if it harks back to the long walks in the country around Oxford and later around London that Housman was accustomed to take in Moses Jackson's company (as I believe), then the "we" is precisely that: "we." It is "you" for whom this is written, and "I" who am writing it for you. We will never again be together, and you will inspire no more poetry from me. This lyric is, in fact, a compressed version of "Fancy's Knell."

The intense private grief of which this is the cryptic expression explains clearly what many critics have felt without, perhaps, quite knowing why. The poem has the "power to pierce the breast with unutterable emotion" (Tinker, "Housman's Poetry," 94), it has "a mournful intensity that has rarely been equalled" (Hamilton, *Housman the Poet*, 65), and it "conveys depths of tragic intensity" (Schneider, *Aesthetic Motive*, 96). The penultimate line, keening and wailing, is "almost like a cry in the dark" (ibid., 99). It is, literally, just that: "a cry in the dark" such as another Alfred, Lord Tennyson, had voiced for his lost friend ("An infant crying for the light / And with no language but a cry," (*Tennyson*, "In Memoriam" 54:5, 395). After this half-strangled, half-inarticulate cry, Housman fell silent. There would be no more laurels, no more comradeship, no more light in his life, and no more poetry.

Five times in twelve lines the words "no more" echo. This phrase had a special meaning for Housman. Commenting on Milton's line in *Comus* ("Nymphs and shepherds, dance no more") many years later in *Name and Nature of Poetry*, Housman said that the words "can draw tears . . . have the physical effect of pathos. . . . [They] find their way to something in man which is obscure and latent, something older than the present organization of his nature" (369). Was it only Milton's line that had such a strong effect on him, or had the line from *Comus* merged with his own to recreate the desolation he felt at his friend's death? Unlike Browning or Tennyson, Housman could not look forward to a reunion with his dead love in a heaven in which he did not believe. Even were there such a reunion after death, it was not he who could say with Browning, or even silently hope, "O thou soul of my soul! I shall clasp thee again." For him, the silence was eternal, and the beloved voice would be heard no more.

Art and scholarship are, for Housman, in the last analysis meaningless. Time will in the end sweep all things away, art, monuments, literature, and love itself, for love is no more exempt from this fate than poetry or any other human creation. For him, unlike the other poets, although love is longer lived than the lover, it too is, in the end, mortal. As Strozier penetratingly comments, "Here Housman plays down the immortality of love . . . , for love in the lyric (and elsewhere) usually takes on the cloak of immortality. The earlier stanzas . . . lead the reader to believe Housman is interested in this point too" but "by reversing the usual form of presentation of the adjectives—stronger before strong, longer before long [where] the comparative leads us to expect the superlative," he reverses the usual comments about love ("Image, Illogic and Allusion," 261)

> It is no gift I tender,
>   A loan is all I can;
> But do not scorn the lender;
>   Man gets no more from man.
>
> Oh, mortal man may borrow
>   What mortal man can lend,
> And 'twill not end tomorrow
>   Though sure enough 'twill end.

> If death and time are stronger
>   A love may yet be strong;
> The world will last for longer
>   But this will last for long.

(AP 4)

Love itself is transitory, but the art that it inspires (the "this" that "will last for long") is another incarnation of the crown of bays that has been so ubiquitous in Housman's poetry. "This" in the final line refers to both the scorned love, the "gift" of the first line, and to the poem itself that "will last for long," although not forever. Love may die, but the "idea that art preserves [it] by transforming love from the transitory realm of the real into the eternal world of the imagination" is a persistent theme (Martin, "Two Strategies," 15).

The ambiguity of "Man gets no more from man" is typical of Housman's treatment in poetry of his own sexual preferences. It is an old adage that "man" embraces "woman." When Housman was writing, the modern version of "Newspeak" had not become mandatory (persondatory?), so the line can be read (as can the "mortal man" repetition in the second verse) to mean, "A woman can get no more from a man than the loan of his love." But this is a loan with a time limit on it. In the second verse, a heterosexual reading would indicate that the mortal man and the mortal woman each loans the other his/her love. This reading is excessively awkward to verbalize. The clear and obvious meaning of the lines is homosexual. Early drafts (Barnett, *Poems*, 151 bottom) make it clear that the "loan" of the first verse is to be identified as the "love" of the third verse, and that love is incontrovertibly homosexual:

> It is no gift I offer
>   A loan is all I may,
> But take you yet the proffer,
>   Though 'tis not made for aye.

And

> Here, take the loan I offer—
>   The gift I dare not say—
> And never scorn the proffer
>   Because 'tis not for aye.

The word "proffer" opens other possibilities, among them that what is being proffered is not only the persona's love and his poem but his body, for so long as life is in it. Here, when Housman writes "man" he means precisely that. Nor does he mean any man; the context makes it quite

clear ("do not scorn the lender," "and never scorn the proffer") to whom
this poem is addressed. The poet's love, spanning his entire lifetime, was
indeed "strong." It was strong enough to sustain him even after its (unwilling?) recipient had himself succumbed to "death and time." Like so
many of those in *Additional Poems*, this lyric gives us the poet almost unmasked.

If Housman does not claim immortality for his poetry or his love, neither does he claim universality for his poems. Their message is aimed at
those in peculiar need of his solace and consolation.

> They say my verse is sad: no wonder.
>   Its narrow measure spans
> Rue for eternity, and sorrow
>   Not mine, but man's.
>
> This is for all ill-treated fellows
>   Unborn and unbegot,
> For them to read when they're in trouble
>   And I am not.
>
> (MP prefatory poem)

Burnett has chosen "Rue for eternity" in the third line in preference
to the more usually printed "Tears of eternity." This strikes me as psychologically correct, since rue appears in several of Housman's lyrics and tears
are far less common. Housman was given to wry, bitter regret ("rue"), but
not to self-pity ("tears"). He wrote, "With rue my heart is laden," but
never "With tears my eyes are burning."

In his reprinting of this lyric in "*De Amicitia*," Laurence Housman itali-
cized the first word of the second verse: "*This* is for all ill-treated fellows."
Burnett does not italicize the word, but such emphasis would have been
consistent with the poetic metaphors that we have been examining. *This*,
this poem, this body of poetry, is for—whom? Who are these "ill-treated
fellows"? The answer may be clear by now, arrived at by intuition and
analogy with other poems, but this is not necessary. It is clearly spelled
out in the manuscript where the second line reads, "For he that spells it
scans." The word "spell" as used here can carry the older meaning of
"reading with understanding" or "decoding." The original fifth line is "I
make it for [unlucky/unhappy] fellows" (*Burnett Poems*, 113 bottom), for
boys like the Woolwich Cadet, in short. The first thought, as in other
poems, has consistently been altered to an impersonal form, or, as Horwood remarked, in Housman's poetry "particular situations and tempera-
ment are raised to the level of the universal" (A. E. Housman, *Poetry and
Prose*, 15).

Housman usually worked from his immediate personal reaction toward universality ("Not mine, but man's"), but the remarks about the use of the masculine noun made in the preceding poem are also applicable here. The term "luckless lads" refers to "men steeped in perplexity about their atheism or homosexuality, or both. The beauty of the lyric is that the lucklessness might as readily have been caused by anything, and could be taken to refer to anything, or nothing" (Browne, *Elegy in Arcady*, 74). Or, as Reynolds has phrased it, Housman's "serious poetry was simultaneously a personal outlet for his own sorrow and an impersonal expression of every man's misery" ("Housman's Humor," 164). It is clear from this and other poems that "to reach and give succour to the suffering homosexual . . . , as well as to act as a balm to those who had experienced the agony of unrequited love, must have been among Housman's aims" (Browne, *Elegy in Arcady*, 22).

Nor did Housman limit the balm that poetry could offer to those in his own peculiar position. He saw poetry as a balm for other sorrows than those that afflicted him personally. When his nephew was killed in action during the Great War, Housman sent his sister a copy of his poem "Illic Jacet" (LP 4), written many years earlier, perhaps for Herbert, dead in the Boer War. This poem, about the death of a soldier, concludes ". . . far from his friends and his lovers / He lies with the sweetheart he chose." In the accompanying letter, that in which his sympathy was extended to his nephew's bereaved fiancée, he wrote, "Well, my dear, it is little I or anyone else can do to comfort you, or think of anything to say that you will not have thought of. . . . I do not know that I can do better than send you some verses that I wrote many years ago; because the essential business of poetry . . . is to harmonize the sadness of the universe, and it is somehow more sustaining and healing than prose" (A. E. Housman, *Letters*, 140–41).

Tennyson had seen poetry as a way to ease his own pain at the loss of his friend: "For the unquiet heart and brain, / A use in measured language lies; / The sad mechanic exercise, / Like dull narcotics, numbing pain" (*Tennyson*, "In Memoriam" 5:2, 349). Housman turns outward where Tennyson turned inward, offering his verse to ease the pain of others. His own was unassuageable.

"To harmonize the sadness of the universe" while unable to assuage his own inner torment was Housman's avowed aim. It is explicit in the poem that Laurence Housman printed at the beginning of *More Poems* and implicit in a host of others. One has the impression that Housman to a large extent succeeded in achieving it.

5

What Tune the Enchantress Plays

I<small>N THE PRECEDING CHAPTER, WE CONSIDERED HOUSMAN'S USE OF FLOWERS</small> as a controlling metaphor for his own poetry, and much of his most characteristic imagery is drawn from the realm of nature. Nature is, of course, traditionally a female figure, variously embodied as Gaea, Ceres/Demeter, the Great Mother of prehistory, and our own half-jocular Mother Nature, to name but a few of her incarnations. Given Housman's ambivalent feelings about women, ranging from his adoration of his own mother through his comment to his brother that women were "the deplorable sex" (L. Housman, *Unexpected Years*, 299), it is not surprising that in his poetry this ambivalence is reflected. For Housman, nature functions, on the one hand, as the personified female, mistress (inspiration, refreshment, and beloved), muse, mother, and harlot; on the other hand she is an impersonal, unconcerned, and changeless backdrop for the round of human life. As the abstract female principle personified, she always carries an erotic charge, either positive or negative. When she is a mere background, this charge is absent. It is the first group that concerns us here. The sensuous evocation of nature is evident in one of Housman's earliest poems (Burnett, *Poems*, 203).

Summer

Summer! and over brooding lands
The noonday haze of heat expands.
A gentle breeze along the meadows
Lifts a few leaflets on the trees;
But cannot stir the clouds that lie
Motionless on the dreaming sky,
And cannot stir the sleeping shadows
As motionless upon the leas.

Summer! and after Summer what?
Ah! happy trees that know it not,
Would that with us it might be so.

And yet, the broad-flung beech-tree heaves
Through all its slanting layers of leaves
With something like a sigh. Ah no!
'Tis but the wind that with its breath
To them so softly murmureth;
For them hath still new sweets in store
And sings new music evermore;
Only to us its tones seem sighs,
Only to us it prophecies
Of coming Autumn, coming death.

The languorousness of the imagery in the first verse, inchoate and inconsistent as a whole, seems in each separate detail to create a sense of postcoital relaxation. The heat overlies the earth and expands. The trees are stirred by the wind. The clouds "lie / Motionless" on the dreaming, and therefore at least half-asleep, sky. The shadows are also asleep and lie motionless on the meadow. And in the second verse this erotic underlayer continues. The "happy" beech-tree (and as we shall see later the mature Housman, at the end of his poetic life, chose this, his favorite tree, on which to inscribe the bitterness of unrequited love) "heaves" with a "sigh." The words hold an erotic connotation in suspension. The same sighs that recall the aftermath of copulation almost immediately metamorphose into the sighs of despair at the coming of autumn and death. None of this imagery is organized or developed, but it is there in embryo.

The pathetic fallacy is given vivid expression in the first fourteen lines and then abruptly denied, refuted, and rejected. Nevertheless, the objectively confuted concept is still accepted as subjectively valid. Terence can utilize it even when Housman disavows the "conception of nature as a living and sentient and benignant being, a conception as purely mythological as . . . Dryads and Naiads" (*NNP*, 363). And for Terence, it is the maternal aspect of nature that is preeminent.

In my own shire, if I was sad,
Homely comforters I had:
The earth, because my heart was sore,
Sorrowed for the son she bore;
And standing hills, long to remain,
Shared their short-lived comrade's pain.
And bound for the same bourn as I,
On every road I wandered by,
Trod beside me, close and dear,
The beautiful and death-struck year.
Whether in the woodland brown
I heard the beechnut rustle down,
And saw the purple crocus pale

Flower about the autumn dale;
Or littering far the fields of May
Lady-smocks a-bleaching lay,
And like a skylit water stood
The bluebells in the azured wood.

(ASL 41:1–18)

Here the identification of nature as the female mother is overt. The concept is, of course, embedded in our language (we constantly refer to Mother Earth as well as Mother Nature), but this is more literal; the persona calls himself "the son she bore." Fertility is associated with the female; the very contours of the gently rounded female body resemble the landscape's hills and dales (Paglia, *Sexual Personal*, 7–8). There is, in Housman's poetry, a constant yearning for the hills, and his sense of banishment from them may be a (subconscious) reflection of both his sexual alienation from the female and of his "beautiful and death-struck" mother. In poem after poem, he "substituted landscape for the maternal figure" (Perkins, *History of Modern Poetry*, 199). And, as we shall see, in poem after poem the emphasis in the course of the poem shifts from dawn to sunset, from fertility to barrenness, from life to death, from happy— and heterosexual—coupling to the barrenness of homosexuality.

The lady-smocks on the "fields of May" are, of course, from the song that closes Shakespeare's *Love's Labour's Lost*. Housman acknowledged Shakespeare's songs as one of the major influences on his own poetry. To his silver-white flowers, Housman has added the "bleaching," which may subliminally suggest exposed bones "littering" the ground, the bones of "lady's smocks," women's bodies, whited sepulchres. But are they "lady-smocks" or "ladies' mocks?" Is this an ear pun? It may well be so intended.

Nature is not only the benign mother figure; she is also the Great Mother of prehistoric religious belief, both the giver and taker of life. Housman was an acquaintance of George Frazer and, indeed, contributed to *The Golden Bough*, so it is hardly conceivable that he was unaware of this avatar of the goddess. In one incarnation, she is also the triune goddess Artemis, the goddess of the moon, queen of the night, who, in her third phase as Hecate, is the queen of the dark of the moon, of black nights and black magic. In this form, she is the malign queen of evil enchantment, the overlady of Shakespeare's Weird Sisters.

Her strong enchantments failing,
Her towers of fear in wreck,
Her limbecks dried of poisons
And the knife at her neck,

> The Queen of air and darkness
>   Begins to shrill and cry,
> "O young man, O my slayer,
>   To-morrow you shall die."
>
> O queen of air and darkness,
>   I think 'tis truth you say,
> And I shall die to-morrow;
>   But you will die to-day.

(LP 3)

Although Skutsch identified the queen of air and darkness as "cowardly sloth," Housman himself identified her as the spirit of evil. As Heap has pointed out, the source of the phrase is Biblical, from Ephesians 2:2, where we find "the prince of the power of the air," and 6:12, where we find "principalities, . . . powers, . . . the rulers of the darkness," and in both quotations the dark power is unambiguously male. In Housman's poem, the symbol of evil has been metamorphosed into a female, an enchantress. She is the malign side of female sexuality incarnate, and she has no power over the "young man" whose "knife" is at her neck. Her poisons have dried up, her weapons rendered ineffective. Her "strong enchantments" have failed, and what are a woman's "enchantments" but her sexual allure? The implication here is plain; the persona is immune to the appeal of the feminine, and this indicates that he is homosexual. The gender of the "prince of the power of the air" *had* to be changed if Housman's persona was to be immune to the enchantment.

The implications of the "knife" will be taken up more fully in chapter 9. It is sufficient here to note that a knife can be (though it need not be) a phallic symbol. The "young man's" knife is at the queen's throat, not subject to her will, and she is terrified ("begins to shrill and cry"). The threat she resorts to depends, in this reading, on the Elizabethan submeaning of "die." He will not die for her or because of her. He will "die" after she has left the scene, but his consummation will be independent of her. Being immune to her enchantments he alone is a threat to her continued power. This is not to say that Housman was immune to the charm of nature, far from it. But he tended to find his most characteristic imagery in her unpleasant manifestations and to be skeptical about her more obvious charms.

There are two contrasting image clusters in poetry; beauty, fertility, richness, spring, youth, and life are set against ugliness, sterility, poverty, winter, age, and death. In Housman's poetry, however, the alignment is different. Beauty, fertility, richness, spring, and youth are associated with death, and ugliness, sterility, poverty, winter, and age with life.

Housman was unusually sensitive to and appreciative of the beauty of nature, but his way of expressing his ecological commitment, typical of his driest style, could (just possibly) be misinterpreted by the literal minded. His objection to the destruction of natural tracts has been mentioned in reference to his opposition to the utilitarian ethos. The letter he wrote to *The Standard* in response to such destruction (A. E. Housman, *Letters*, 30–31) is a masterpiece of indirect invective and deserves to be better known.

Sir:
In August 1886 Highgate Wood became the property of the Mayor and Commonalty and Citizens of the City of London. It was then in a very sad state. So thickly was it overgrown with brushwood, that if you stood in the centre you could not see the linen of the inhabitants of Archway Road hanging to dry in their back gardens. Nor could you see the advertisement of Juggins's stout and porter which surmounts the front of the public house at the south corner of the wood. Therefore the Mayor and Commonalty and Citizens cut down the intervening brushwood, and now when we stand in the centre we can divide our attention between Juggins's porter and our neighbours' washing. Scarlet flannel petticoats are much worn in Archway Road, and if anyone desires to feast his eyes on these very bright and picturesque objects, so seldom seen in the streets, let him repair to the centre of Highgate Wood.

Still we were not happy. The wood is bounded on the north by the railway to Muswell Hill; and it was a common subject of complaint in Highgate that we could not see the railway from the wood without going quite to the edge. At length, however, the Mayor and Commonalty and Citizens have begun to fell the trees on the north, so that people in the centre of the wood will soon be able to look at the railway when they are tired of the porter and the petticoats. But there are a number of new red-brick houses on the east side of the wood, and I regret to say that I observe no clearing of timber in that direction. Surely, Sir, a man who stands in the centre of the wood, and knows that there are new red-brick houses to the east of him, will not be happy unless he sees them.

Sir, it is spring: birds are pairing, and the County Council has begun to carve the mud-pie which it made last year at the bottom of Waterlow Park. I do not know how to address the Mayor and Commonalty; but the Citizens of the City of London all read the *Standard,* and surely they will respond to my appeal and will not continue to screen from my yearning gaze any one of those objects of interest which one naturally desires to see when one goes to the centre of a wood.

I am, Sir, your obedient servant

A. E. H.

The style of this letter would place it comfortably in either chapter 2, where it could have joined the reversed elephant, or in chapter 3, where it could have served as an admirable parody of the Gradgrind style of com-position and habits of thought, but its subject matter places it irrevocably in the present discussion. Housman did not make a habit of writing let-ters to the editor, and that he did so in this case indicates his intense opposition, couched in terms of scathing sarcasm, to the ongoing destruc-tion of his local patch of woodland in the heart of London. Not only had he passed his boyhood in a rural setting, but also throughout his life he habitually took long daily walks in the countryside, noting the progress of the seasonal changes in flowers and foliage.

Few poets have observed nature so closely or so sympathetically, and few have reflected in their work such a unified sense of her simultaneously promising fulfillment and failing of her promise. This does not negate nature's beauty and ability to renew and refresh the spirit, at least for the moment.

> When green buds hang in the air like dust
>   And sprinkle the lime like rain,
> Forth I wander, forth I must,
>   And drink of life again.
>
> Forth I must by hedgerow bowers
>   To look at the leaves uncurled
> And stand in the fields where cuckoo-flowers
>   Are lying about the world.

(MP 9)

The fifth line was left open in the manuscript (Burnett, *Poems,* 120 bot-tom), where it exists in two forms, that which Laurence Housman (and Archie Burnett) chose, and this one: "Forth I must to the wild wood bow-ers." This version utilizes the alliteration of which Housman was so fond, and it neatly sets the woods off from the fields two lines later. It also cre-ates a contrast between walking in the woods to look at the uncurled leaves of the forest trees and standing in the meadows to look at the newly sprung field flowers, a contrast that is lost by using "hedgerow." One may also note that "bowers" are not commonly an element in hedge-rows but are in wooded areas. The "wild wood" line was the original one, and both Laurence Housman and Dr. Burnett chose to use an alternate that had been written above it. However, Housman quite often tried one or more alternate phrasings and was just as likely to ultimately choose the original version as to adopt a later variant, so this is no real basis for choice or justification of the variation now universally printed.

Had the final text been determined by the poet rather than by his brother, I have no doubt that such would have been the case here. The phrase "drink of life again" links this poem to the persona of "Spring

Morning" (LP 16) who "drinks the valiant air of dawn" although his be-loved "rouses from another's side." It seems to me there is little doubt that the persona is one of Housman's "luckless lads" (luckless because, among other things, he is doomed to love without being loved in return), or that he is speaking in the poet's voice. He certainly expresses exqui-sitely Housman's own "sensitiveness to the beauty of the world" (Marlow, A. E. *Housman*, 2) and his response to the "green buds" of spring. On 16 March 1890, Housman made the following typical entry in his diary, indicating his close attention to the progress of spring. "Catkins on hazel; calendine in bud; a green flower out, whose name I do not know, buds on hazel (green with red tips) and blackthorn (reddish); hawthorn, wild roses, and lilac buds unfolding; lords and ladies new (some just coming up); hayriff and wild parsley new; crocus fading in some cases" (L. Hous-man, "*De Amicitia*," 37). This is one of the twenty seasonal entries. An-other, a fall entry, is equally detailed: "Hawthorne yellow and reddish, very fair amount of leaves. Ash green and not much thinned. Oak russet yellow. Plane . . . thinned but green" (Haber, "A. E. Housman's 'Secret Grief' "). Between the lines of these terse entries, his love for nature's gifts can be clearly felt. He himself found some "comfort in the fields and the woods" (Sparrow, introduction to A. E. Housman, *Collected Poems*, 13).

What nature has to give, then, in the way of comfort, is only "a fleeting revelation of beauty that mocks at the hope it seems to offer" (Hamilton, *Housman the Poet*, 26). And that this is indeed a mockery is made mani-fest by the pun with which the poem closes, for the cuckoo-flowers are not only "lying about the world" in contrast to the persona who is stand-ing in the fields, but they are "lying" about the hope they symbolize. Also, let it not be forgotten that the very word "cuckoo" with its echo of "cuck-old" has long had the connotation of "betrayed husband" or, perhaps, lover. Nature's flowers, her speaking symbols, as Housman's own poems are his flowers, cry "cuckold" in the ears of her lover. She is not only his mistress, she is his faithless mistress.

> Tell me not here, it needs not saying,
>   What tune the enchantress plays
> In aftermaths of soft September
>   Or under blanching mays,
> For she and I were long acquainted
>   And I knew all her ways.
>
> On russet floors, by waters idle,
>   The pine lets fall its cone:
> The cuckoo shouts all day at nothing
>   In leafy dells alone;
> And traveller's joy beguiles in autumn
>   Hearts that have lost their own.

On acres of the seeded grasses
   The changing burnish heaves;
Or marshalled under moons of harvest
   Stand still all night the sheaves;
Or beeches strip in storms for winter
   And stain the wind with leaves.

Possess, as I possessed a season.
   The countries I resign,
Where over elmy plains the highway
   Would mount the hills and shine,
And full of shade the pillared forest
   Would murmur and be mine.

For nature, heartless, witless nature,
   Will neither care nor know
What stranger's feet may find the meadow
   And trespass there and go,
Nor ask amid the dews of morning
   If they are mine or no.

                        (LP 40)

Many critics have discussed the imagery's erotic force. Empson focused on the persona's amorous description and his jealousy at the end (Empson, "Rhythm and Imagery"). Both Page (*A. E. Houseman*, 199–200) and Bayley (*Housman's Poems*, 175) dismiss the second point. Bayley finds not so much the jealousy of a betrayed lover as the "wry worldliness of the disillusioned lover—'I wonder who's kissing her now?'" Ricks, Brooks, and Page have all provided fine analyses of the tone of the poem. Each of them noted, although with slightly different emphases, the identity of the persona as an old and cast-off lover whose carnally erotic attitude toward his unfaithful mistress, the enchantress Nature, is unrequited by her, an identity emphasized by the repeated "possess" and "mine." The indifference of the beloved is a gloss on unrequited love. The reader senses "by the end of the poem that it may after all be about another kind of love as well as (not instead of) love of nature."[1] Nature, however, is not really "indifferent." Rather she is "heartless" and "witless." "The vocabulary is from the language of betrayal" (Friedman, "Divided Self," 32) and continues the implicit metaphor of a love affair. The persona's "love for nature is the more passionate for being unrequited," and the poem is "a tragedy of unrequited passion and unfulfilled yearning" (Watts, "Poetry," 123).

Enough has been quoted to demonstrate that the erotic force lying behind the poem has been felt by a remarkably diverse group of commentators who have, among them, considered the problem from every viewpoint and come to the same conclusion. The poem is indeed about the persona's love for nature and the indifference which she bestows in return (Page, A. E. Housman, 199), but it is about something more.

Even if Robbins is correct in asserting that "A Shropshire Lad is informed largely by a fear of emotional commitment," she errs in stating that "only the love of nature is a love without risk—all other forms of attachment will be disappointed" because the love of nature is inevitably a love that will not and cannot be returned ("Very Curious Construction," 149). The love of nature is a paradigm for unrequited passion. In this poem, nature is presented as accepting the persona's homage but not responding in kind to his devotion. She (or is it really he?) is not precisely unfaithful, for where there has been no troth there can be no unfaithfulness, no betrayal. The persona knows this intellectually, of course, but emotionally, that is quite different. "I knew all her ways" in one sense refers to the paths and byways of the forest, the "waters idle" and "leafy dells" as well as the harvested fields on its outskirts. In another sense, they are the methods used by the enchantress, the "tunes" with which she entraps hearts. I am not suggesting that "nature" is a code for Moses Jackson. I am, rather, suggesting that Housman endowed the persona with an emotional response to nature that reflected his own feelings about his friend, who was neither "heartless" nor "witless" but who was, in the last analysis, unresponsive to him in one of the most basic and most meaningful ways in which one human being can be responsive to another, the requiting of devoted love.

Nature's attitude is, on the surface, quite similar to that which Matthew Arnold ascribes to her at the end of "Youth of Nature." Man and Nature exist on such different time scales that although their interaction may be supremely meaningful to a human being, it cannot but be a matter of sublime indifference to Nature for whom a person is fleetingly ephemeral and all but beneath her divine notice. The concept is common to both these and many other poems, but the erotic intensity is unique to Housman. It is Housman's farewell to Nature, his unfaithful mistress. It was written in April of 1922, immediately after Housman informed Richards that he was almost certain to have a second volume of poems ready for publication in the autumn, and represents his final surrender of all that had given beauty and meaning to his life. The "dews of morning" are indeed also the "dues of mourning" for something gone beyond recall.

Housman can also treat natural phenomena metaphorically, and the ramifications of his metaphor reward careful consideration.

> On Wenlock Edge the wood's in trouble;
> His forest fleece the Wrekin heaves;
> The gale, it plies the saplings double,
> And thick on Severn snow the leaves.

'Twould blow like this through holt and hanger
     When Uricon the city stood:
'Tis the old wind in the old anger,
     But then it threshed another wood.

Then, 'twas before my time, the Roman
     At yonder heaving hill would stare:
The blood that warms an English yeoman,
     The thoughts that hurt him, they were there.

There, like the wind through woods in riot,
     Through him the gale of life blew high;
The tree of man was never quiet:
     Then 'twas the Roman, now 'tis I.

The gale, it plies the saplings double,
     It blows so hard, 'twill soon be gone:
To-day, the Roman and his trouble
     Are ashes under Uricon.

                                        (ASL 31)

That this poem is a satellite of the Shropshire cycle is clear not only from its geographical references (Wenlock Edge itself, the Wrekin, and the Severn) but also from the persona's self-identification as a "yeoman" who may reasonably be identified as Terence. As we have already seen, this persona often verbalizes his creator's thoughts. The physical wood and physical wind of the first verse become a metaphor for the human species and the forces of life and fate, respectively. Wind throughout A Shropshire Lad is a metaphor for the force of life, variously the "breath of life" (ASL 38), the "stuff of life" (ASL 32), and here "the gale of life" (Leggett, Land of Lost Content, 109). It has been suggested that the link between man and tree that underlies the imagery is that when burnt, both are reduced to ashes (Stallman, Explicator). This seems to me a needlessly narrow linkage. Everyone is a branch of a specific tree, a family tree, and if one traces a family tree back far enough it will include all people somewhere on its branches. Thus "the tree of man" is an image of humanity in the aggregate, and the wind that makes the Wrekin "heave" and "bends the saplings [the young of the species] double" can be, among other things, the force of uncontrolled passion, of "emotional turmoil" (Rosebury, "Three Dimensions," 225).[2] The wind which shakes the forest, one of Housman's favorite metaphors, changes its value constantly in his poems, the literal wind metamorphosing into the force of human passion, the spirit of life, the connection with one's past, and the forces of destruction, all of which have a part in this lyric.

The "trembling" suggested by "fleece" is intensified to "heaves" in the second line and the "heaving hill" in the tenth line, where it suggests, as in the very early verses glanced at above, a sexual encounter between the wind and the trees, "a sapling Daphne prostrated beneath the wind. . . . The inner and invisible strife of sex [is] made visible in the heaving forest" (Bayley, *Housman's Poems*, 37). That forest is, however, specifically masculine ("His", not "its"); it is not "a sapling Daphne" at all, but her masculine counterpart. It is specifically the "tree of *man*," although I have been careful above to use the gender-free "humanity." The Roman, an inhabitant of a world in which homosexuality was accepted, whose "thoughts" and "blood" "hurt" and "warmed" him in the past, had the same thoughts and blood as the persona in the present. As LeMire puts it: "The Roman . . . felt the same winds of passion [as Terence], and they posed for him the same problems" ("Irony and Ethics," 123). Those problems are not only the Roman's and Terence's, but Housman's as well.

The terrible aloneness of Housman's luckless lads in a world of heterosexual couples is evoked again and again, especially in poems ostensibly celebrating the spring. This is perhaps inevitable, as spring is the season of courtship and coupling in much of nature's domain, not excluding the human. Spring is the traditional time for couples to pair off, but not for Housman's personae. A poem will begin with a magnificent description of spring. The speaker seems in harmony with his world, in harmony with nature. Then his terrible loneliness, his basic separation from the natural world, intrudes and reverses the mood of the opening.

March

The Sun at noon to higher air,
Unharnessing the silver Pair
That late before his chariot swam,
Rides on the gold wool of the Ram.

So braver notes the storm-cock sings
To start the rusted wheel of things,
And brutes in field and brutes in pen
Leap that the world goes round again.

The boys are up the woods with day
To fetch the daffodils away,
And home at noonday from the hills
They bring no dearth of daffodils.

Afield for palms the girls repair,
And sure enough the palms are there,
And each will find by hedge or pond
Her waving silver-tufted wand.

> In farm and field throughout the shire
> The eye beholds the heart's desire;
> Ah, let not only mine be vain,
> For lovers should be loved again.
>
> (ASL 10)

The first verse, with its astrological references, cannot help but be compared to the opening of Chaucer's *Canterbury Tales* where "the yonge sonne / Hath in the Ram his halve cours yronne" (ll. 7–8, *Chaucer's Poetry*, 5), but Housman's zodiacal reference is far more elaborate.[3] The "silver Pair" that the Sun "unharnesses" from his chariot are a pair of fish, which is why they are silver in contrast to the gold of the Ram, and why they "swam" before "his chariot." They "swam" there "late" because they are the sign of Pisces, which precedes Aries, "the Ram," the sign of March, which the sun had already half traversed when the Canterbury pilgrims set out. The two fish may be assumed to be male and female, a heterosexual pair (unlike Gemini, where both halves of the constellation are male). The Ram, on the other hand, Housman's own zodiacal sign, is uncompromisingly male—and alone.

In Roman mythology, the arrival of Aries heralds the start of the year, or, as Manilius put it, "Turn now your gaze upon heaven as it climbs up from the first cardinal point, where the rising signs commence afresh their wonted courses, and a pale Sun swims upward from the icy waves and begins by slow degrees to blaze with golden flame as it attempts the rugged path where the Ram heads the procession of the skies" (*Astronomica*, 156–57), leading the way "resplendent in his golden fleece" (ibid., 25). He has golden fleece because this is the very ram that the Argonauts sailed to Colchis to find.

Another poet who used a similar zodiacal description for the same purpose is Thomas Hardy, at the opening of "The Year's Awakening" (*Selected Poetry*, 220):

> How do you know that the pilgrim track
> Along the belting zodiac
> Swept by the sun in his seeming rounds
> Is traced by now to the Fishes' bounds
> And into the Ram, when weeks of cloud
> Have wrapt the sky in a clammy shroud

None of these descriptions can match Housman's for the pure splendor of the pictorialization. Nor are they comparable in the "depth of erudition" that "underlies such apparently artless lyrics" (Ferguson, "Belligerent Don," 658). The image of Pisces as drawing Apollo's chariot through the thicker (because more watery) air in February when the sun is low in the sky yields to that of Apollo riding on the golden back of Aries. In the second verse, Aries the astrological Ram becomes the domesticated ram in field and pen.

The second verse also has its parallels in other work. In "God's Funeral" (*Selected Poetry*, 230), Hardy writes "To start the wheels of day" without any rust having accumulated during the off time. And, most notably, Robert Browning's "Old Pictures in Florence" opens with "The morn when first it thunders in March / The eel in the pond gives a leap, they say" (*Poetry*, vol. 1, 656). Housman's "brutes in field and brutes in pen" cannot but be more evocative of the universal joy of spring than Browning's "eel in the pond." This was not, however, Housman's original conception of the line. One of the draft variants is "trout in brook and herd in plain," carrying on the Pisces-Aries theme. Housman abandoned this version of the line, possibly because he found the "plain/again" rhyme unsatisfactory, possibly because he had decided to move away from the astrological opening theme, possibly in order to incorporate the agricultural image of the penned livestock, and possibly for all (or none) of these reasons. For whatever reason he made the alteration, I think it is to be regretted as the first draft is to my mind superior as an evocation of that rebirth of gladness that springtime symbolizes, the "regeneration of man's spirit. . . . The winds force the warmth of the sun, symbolic of life and fertility, to deepen nature's creatures' instincts for living, their spirit of joy" (Kowalczyk, "Horatian Tradition," 230–31).

Many critics have found the opening quatrain of the poem magnificent and felt that the remainder is pedestrian and clumsy. One asks,

> Why no dearth of daffodils? The answer: because of the alliteration. . . . Why is it that the boys who started going to the woods end up by returning from the hills? Boys, to be sure, will be boys and there is no telling in which direction they will scamper off when given the chance, but here their energetic wanderings seem to be primarily caused by the fact that hills rhymes with daffodils. This being the case, it becomes rather difficult to believe in their substantial existence." (Firchow, "Land of Lost Content," 113–14).[4]

It might be well to remember that the "boys" here are not children but adolescents. It might also be well to remember Housman's early-honed facility for rhyme, a facility that makes it unlikely that he would use a word for this purpose alone. He chose his words carefully, never seizing on the first (and obvious) one to present itself. Why, then, do the boys indeed go to the woods and return from the hills? Is it too simplistic to suggest that these woods, like those of Wenlock Edge, are located on the hills? There are times when the obvious explanation is quite sufficient.

Haber, who finds in this poem a "lack of unity, . . . faltering sequence, and . . . inconclusive ending," attributes these failings, despite his rejection of biographical interpretation, to its having "probably" been written in March. March was not only the month in which Housman was born but also that in which his mother died on his twelfth birthday, and Haber considers that "these poignant memories . . .entered disturbingly into the composition" (*Making of "A Shropshire Lad,"* 76). This, I would suggest, is assuming altogether too much. It is assuming that the poem was written in a single session and that that session was in March. It is also assuming that Housman (who was a meticulous self-critic who would work over a poem for years until he felt it was right, and who was quite willing to abandon a poem that he could not polish to his own satisfaction) was unaware of these faults and/or did not see fit to remove them by revision before including the poem in his first volume. I say nothing of the assumptions about the "poignant memories" that "entered disturbingly" into the poem and disrupted its unity. It might be more productive to look again at these verses and try to see why Housman was satisfied with them.

March is not characterized only by its zodiacal sign. It has many other associations, one of which is the renewal of life. This association with renewal is integral to spring in religion (where Easter celebrates the resurrection of bodily and spiritual life) and in folklore, a debased remnant of older forms of religion. In religion and folklore we find the roots of the motifs used in the third and fourth verses. Both the daffodil and palm are associated with Easter, the palm most obviously in the religious rituals of Palm Sunday and the daffodil in the folk belief that it "dies on Easter Day" (ASL 29). Housman's "waving silver-tufted wand" which can be found near ponds is a willow wand, the spring symbol gathered by girls, including Tess Darbeyfield. "In addition to the distinction of a white frock, every woman and girl carried in her right hand a peeled willow-wand, and in her left a bunch of white flowers." This is a depiction of a traditional spring celebration, descended from the "May-Day dance," one of the "old customs" lingering "in a metamorphosed or disguised form" (Hardy, *Tess of the d'Urbervilles*, 49–50). These wands are thus part of an ancient spring fertility rite, and Housman's poem is drawn from the same tradition as Herrick's "Corinna's Going A-Maying."[5] These ritual symbols of fertility rites lead directly into the desolate cry at the end of the last verse ("lovers should be loved again"). If this is "lack of unity," "faltering sequence," and "inconclusive ending," then what is required to give it tight sequential unity leading inevitably to the ending?

The daffodil that "dies on Easter Day," mentioned above, is the controlling motif of another spring poem.

The Lent Lily

'Tis spring; come out to ramble
        The hilly brakes around,
For under thorn and bramble
        About the hollow ground
        The primroses are found

And there's the windflower chilly
        With all the winds at play,
And there's the Lenten lily
        That has not long to stay
        And dies on Easter day.

And since till girls go maying
        You find the primrose still,
And find the windflower playing
        With every wind at will,
        But not the daffodil,

Bring baskets now, and sally
        Upon the spring's array,
And bear from hill and valley
        The daffodil away
        That dies on Easter day.

(ASL 29)

The irony with which "March" ends, the aloneness of the persona in a world of couples occupied with the worn-down remnants of fertility rites, here is extended from the human to the natural world. Easter and spring, the celebration of the triumph of life over death, is associated with the "Lent Lily," the daffodil that then dies. Nor is there here any implication of the renewal of life the following year. The effect is to detach Easter from the concept of eternal life. The poem that opens with the joy of life, as a personified young Spring emerges from her winter sleep to ramble the countryside, is almost immediately invaded by death.

The "hollow ground" is a tumulus, an ancient burial place. The primroses may be found about it, but its chill spreads through the poem like an echo from the grave. Ultimately, the new life of spring is as hollow as the ground to which the auditor is invited. This poem is an invitation to join in the ritual greeting to spring, and it has the same pagan background and underpinnings as the previous poem, but it adds the grave that lies literally beneath the spring flowers and figuratively behind, and before, the celebrants.

Another spring morning, this one in April, begins with life and it, too, ends in quite another key, the same key of loneliness, the same desolation with which "March" closed.

Spring Morning

Star and coronal and bell
    April underfoot renews,
And the hope of man as well
    Flowers among the morning dews.

Now the old come out to look,
    Winter past and winter's pains,
How the sky in pool and brook
    Glitters on the grassy plains.

Easily the gentle air
    Wafts the turning season on;
Things to comfort him are there,
    Though 'tis true the best are gone.

Now the scorned unlucky lad
    Rousing from his pillow gnawn
Mans his heart and deep and glad
    Drinks the valiant air of dawn.

Half the night he longed to die,
    Now are sown on hill and plain
Pleasures worth his while to try
    Ere he longs to die again.

Blue the sky from east to west
    Arches, and the world is wide,
Though the girl he loves the best
    Rouses from another's side.

(LP 16)

The "hope of man" is both the personal hope that spring inspires in humanity and a glance back to Easter. We are still in the same cycle of associations. And again, this is about a young man whose love was "vain," who was not "loved again." He may "drink the valiant air of dawn" after a sleepless night spent gnawing on his pillow and longing to die, but inevitably after trying other pleasures (though "the best are gone") he will "long to die" again. The world may retain its beauty and its ability to "comfort" the lad, but the comfort can only be superficial and temporary because "the girl he loves the best / Rouses from another's side." As the poem reads, the young man's idol has married another man. There is no ambiguity here, or is there?

Bayley has shown a fine sensibility in reading Housman but he has not considered how easily the monosyllabic "girl" may be written in place of the equally monosyllabic "lad." He writes, "It might seem obvious to point out that the poems possess an eroticism in no way confined to his own source of unhappiness; but it is important to do so, for effect depends on the rapid alternation between a simple sexual self—the poet's own— and the longing and sadness of an intense, disembodied sympathy. Housman can transform the griefs of sex . . . without losing any of their erotic intensity" (*Housman's Poems*, 57).

But Housman's spring morning renews the "hope of *man*," of one of the "luckless lads" for whom he specifically wrote. And those lads were not mourning for the loss of a beloved girl. This is a "spring morning," but is it not equally, despite Graves' characterization of it as "cheerful" (*A. E. Housman*, 219), a spring "mourning"?

> My heart, my heart is silent;
>   The larks sing loud and shrill;
> High, high the larks hang singing;
>   My heart, my heart is still.
>
> High spring the leaves and grasses;
>   Then I was no more proud;
> My heart, my heart is silent
>   Although the larks sing loud.

Here (Burnett, *Poems*, 174), the heart's winter invades the year's spring. In another fragment, the reverse occurs, and "Spring came to trespass in the winter field" (*A. E. Housman*, *Manuscript Poems*, 78). In both, we find the implicit contrast between the joy that seems to be expressed in the lark's song in spring and the joylessness of the one listening to it (whose heart is "a winter field," a region of which winter is the lawful possessor where spring is an interloper). This is a common emotional experience. For Housman, it seems to have been not a temporary mood but a settled emotional state.

In "My heart, my heart is silent," there is a certain incompleteness in the thought, suitable to an incomplete poem. "Still" in the fourth line, as "silent," stands in contrast to the loud singing of the larks above it, and as "motionless" it is in contrast to the vegetation that "springs" in the following line. "Then" in the sixth line implies that at some earlier period the now silent heart was proud and also sprang "high," but this pride was that which "goeth before a fall" and the proud heart had been

felled (by a very Housmanian wind, perhaps). This adds a contrast between the rising of the singing lark and the falling of the silent heart (or
the falling silent of the heart) which is poetically very satisfying and links
this lyric to "When summer's end" (LP 39) below. The music of the larks
may be understood as poetry, that of man and that of nature. The silent
heart can then be understood as a poetic silence. To be sure, this lyric
dates from 1893 or 1894, but its mood imbues much of Housman's later
poetry.

I have spoken above of the contrast between nature's fecundity and the
sterility with which Housman's poetry endows her, and of the concept of
the poems themselves as flowers. We have already looked at "A Winter
Funeral" (ASL 46) and its implications in this regard, and these concepts
in tandem illuminate others of Housman's poems.

> Their seed the sowers scatter
>   Behind them as they go.
> Poor lads, 'tis little matter
>   How many sorts they sow,
>   For only one will grow.
>
> The charlock on the fallow
>   Will take the traveller's eyes,
> And gild the ploughland sallow
>   With flowers before it dies,
>   But twice 'twill not arise.
>
> The stinging-nettle only
>   Will aye be found to stand:
> The numberless, the lonely,
>   The filler of the land,
>   The leaf that hurts the hand.
>
> That thrives, come sun, come showers;
>   Blow east, blow west, it springs;
> It peoples towns, and towers
>   About the courts of Kings,
>   And touch it and it stings.
>
>   (MP 32)

I suggested above that the nettle is indeed the "stem" that scored Terence's hand, Housman's recurring symbol of the bitterness of life from
which his poetry was brewed. Housman's nettles in the courts of kings
echoes the biblical image of Jerusalem laid waste as punishment for her
sins, implying that man's life is fated to be barren and bitter, but as a
punishment for what sins? The Woolwich cadet could have answered.
The nettle's growth mocks the fertility of heterosexual love, and does so

in a wry affirmation of the ubiquity of homosexual attachments that thrive in all times, all places, and all levels of the social hierarchy, even "about the courts of kings." The reference to "the numberless, the lonely," otherwise cryptic, is abundantly clear in this reading.

Like so many of the lyrics in *Last Poems*, the next poem is a farewell to the past and Housman's muse in both the figurative and literal senses. The end of summer that is "nighing" in it is the approaching end of Moses Jackson's physical—and of A. E. Housman's emotional and cre- ative—life. The poem is a litany of loss in which every word is freighted with looming finality. We have: summer's end, evening, skies at evening cloud, sunset, lose, last of day, hues of evening died, night, nightfall, ashen, darkness, lost, close, are not, no more, end, autumn, and, with the heaviest cargo of all, parting. Almost every word is a harbinger of death. And what of those words which are not? They are even more final than the closural words. What is the "air of other summers" that carried hope if not the Christian promise (and premise) of eternal life after death, a promise which we know Housman rejected (it came, and was, and is not, and comes no more anew). This is why "now," in the penultimate verse, "the years and seasons" ahead must be "worse and few." For him, there was not even hope of a meeting as Tennyson phrased it, "behind the veil." It was " 'Adieu, adieu' for evermore" (*Tennyson*, "In Memoriam", 56:7, and 57:4 respectively, 400–401).

When summer's end is nighing
    And skies at evening cloud,
I muse on change and fortune
    And all the feats I vowed
    When I was young and proud.

The weathercock at sunset
    Would lose the slanted ray,
And I would climb the beacon
    That looked to Wales away
    And saw the last of day.

From hill and cloud and heaven
    The hues of evening died;
Night welled through lane and hollow
    And hushed the countryside
    But I had youth and pride.

And I with earth and nightfall
    In converse high would stand,
Late, till the west was ashen
    And darkness hard at hand,
    And the eye lost the land.

The year might age, and cloudy
    The lessening day might close,
But air of other summers
    Breathed from beyond the snows,
    And I had hope of those.

They came and were and are not
    And come no more anew,
And all the years and seasons
    That ever can ensue
    Must now be worse and few.

So here's an end of roaming
    On eves when autumn nighs:
The ear too fondly listens
    For summer's parting sighs,
    And then the heart replies.

                       (LP 39)

As was suggested above, there is a link between this poem and the manuscript lyric "My heart, my heart is silent." That link is pride. In the past, "I was young and proud." I made vows, and in "How clear, how lovely bright" (MP 16) we see the futility of making vows that have never been, and never will be, kept. Once, "I had youth and pride," but time leached that pride away, and "then I was no more proud." The larks may still sing, but autumn has followed summer, and "my heart is silent." Its reply is that silence, the silence of approaching death, the silence of eternal regret.

How clear, how lovely bright,
How beautiful to sight
    Those beams of morning play,
How heaven laughs out with glee
Where, like a bird set free,
Up from the eastern sea
    Soars the delightful day.

To-day I shall be strong,
No more shall yield to wrong,
    Shall squander life no more;
Days lost I know not how,
I shall retrieve them now;
Now I shall keep the vow
    I never kept before.

—Ensanguining the skies
How heavily it dies
    Into the west away;
Past touch and sight and sound,
Not further to be found,
How hopeless under ground
    Falls the remorseful day.

(MP 16)

The image of the sun rising from the sea and going down to traverse the underground is of classical origin and Housman uses it as a metaphor for the life of man; birth and death, or sunrise and sunset, act as a frame for the span of life or day. And this span consists of false starts, broken pledges of reformation, and waste, leading only to final remorse. To "squander life" is not only to waste time but also to spill the seed of life. The reference may therefore be to masturbation. "Squandering life" evokes the combination of sterility, futility, and remorse that is so endemic in Housman's poems.

The West

Beyond the moor and mountain crest
—Comrade, look not on the west—
The sun is down and drinks away
From air and land the lees of day.

The long cloud and the single pine
Sentinel the ending line,
And out beyond it, clear and wan,
Reach the gulfs of evening on.

The son of woman turns his brow
West from forty counties now,
And, as the edge of heaven he eyes,
Thinks eternal thoughts, and sighs.

Oh wide's the world, to rest or roam,
With change abroad and cheer at home,
Fights and furloughs, talk and tale,
Company and beef and ale.

But if I front the evening sky
Silent on the west look I,
And my comrade, stride for stride,
Paces silent at my side.

Comrade, look not on the west:
'Twill have the heart out of your breast;
'Twill take your thoughts and sink them far,
Leagues beyond the sunset bar.

Oh lad, I fear that yon's the sea
Where they fished for you and me,
And there, from whence we both were ta'en,
You and I shall drown again.

Send not on your soul before
To dive from that beguiling shore,
And let not yet the swimmer leave
His clothes upon the sands of eve.

Too fast to yonder strand forlorn
We journey, to the sunken bourn,
To flush the fading tinges eyed
By other lads at eventide.

Wide is the world, to rest or roam,
And early 'tis for turning home:
Plant your heel on earth and stand,
And let's forget our native land.

When you and I are spilt on air
Long we shall be strangers there;
Friends of flesh and bone are best:
Comrade, look not on the west.

(LP 1)

The first point to note is that this poem opens *Last Poems*. Moses Jackson was Housman's "friend and comrade" (LP 24), the other half of Housman's wistful "we,"[6] the one to whom this volume is silently addressed, the man preparing to journey to the "West." In European folklore, mythology, and literature alike, the "West" is the locale of the "Isles of the Blessed," the island of Avillion. The setting sun points the way to the land of the dead, as the rising sun comes from the lands of morning.

From the perspective of England, the sun rises from and sets into the sea. Thus, swimming is both a return to the environment in which the soul existed before birth (in modern parlance, a return to the womb) and a plunging into the final unknown. Metaphorically, the swimmer is the soul, his discarded clothing on the sand the dead body on the earth. And Moses Jackson is the object of the plea to "plant your feet on earth and stand," "look not on the west," and "send not on your soul before" [me, to where I cannot follow you]. This is the heart's plea, valid even while the intellect knows it is nonsense. Or perhaps it is an incantation against inevitable death. The very terms used in the poem recapitulate the history of their friendship: "Change abroad and cheer at home, / Fights and furloughs, talk and tale." There is also the buried pun on "pine" in the "single pine" that stands "sentinel" alone at "the ending line" between the lands of life and death, the empty "gulfs of evening," a pun expressing the poet's own emotion. In effect, Housman *is* the isolated pine tree pining for his friend. In the fifth verse, "comrade" expands to include an added concept: "grief" ("Grief and I abode the nightfall" MP 46). The silent shadow of Moses Jackson and the grief for what had never been were Housman's constant companions throughout his adult life.

Housman's last, and uncompleted poem, mentioned above, in which I am reproducing Burnett's reconstruction (*Poems*, pp. 184–85) while indicating most of the open alternates, unites many of the themes we have been exploring. Here we find the association of Nature with love, and especially thwarted love, the sense of betrayal and abandonment, and the loneliness, the terrible loneliness.

Here, in the beechen forest,   [I sealed for years and ages]
    When spring and love were
               new,
I took my knife last April,
    I carved the names of two.

November comes, and carries
    More than the leaves away.   [What months have spilt and shed]
                                [What lived but months and days]
                                [Eternal things away;]
                                [Love with the leaves away;]
                                [What lived a briefer day:]
                                [What lived a little day:]
                                [What months have seen decay]
                                [What months have worn away]
Eternal things are perished,   [Lost is the letters' meaning,]
                                [The sense has left the tablet]
                                [Lost is the letters' meaning,]
                                [Still, though the sense is perished]
    Their tablet shall not stay.   [The tablet yet is read.]
                                [Letter and tablet stay]
                                [And still the tablet stays.]

So here I bring the auger,
    And in the hole I drill
I pour out of the vial
    The vitriol sure to kill.

Next May in one green woodland
   Shall stand a naked tree,
When spring comes north and
          islands
   Turn leafy in the sea.

Haber seems rather puzzled by the poem. "Long before psychology was a name," he writes, "the human heart knew its own bitterness; and the earliest shocks of it are often the deepest and the longest felt. There is in A. E. Housman's life no factual record of a disastrous youthful romance. But his poetry is filled with the record. Perhaps the beech tree poem is his final memorial" to this early hypothetical romance.[7] One must wonder why it is so difficult to believe that one man's love for another man can be just as intense, just as faithful, just as devoted, and just as "disastrous" as some other man's for a woman. That the emotion is autobiographical, neither Haber nor I doubt for a moment. That "there is no factual record of a disastrous youthful romance" is true only if one insists that such a "romance" must of necessity be heterosexual. However one reconstructs the poem, the parallel with Trollope's Johnny Eames and Lily Dale is clear.[8] Nor need one wonder what two names had been carved.

Clearly, Housman never intended this poem to be published, and equally clearly this was because it was intensely personal and the personal reference had not been universalized, as was his wont in other poems. The unalloyed bitterness of this is rare in his verse. It is clear that the islands that "turn leafy in the sea" are to be contrasted to the "naked" beech tree that is the other face of nature, the face that is aligned with human passion. This aspect of nature is freighted with the same hopelessness—and the same yearning—as we have seen in the "larks" poem where there was no alloy of bitterness.

The following poem well illustrates the danger of making biographical assumptions on the basis of the poetry alone.

      In midnights of November,
         When Dead Man's Fair is nigh,
     And danger in the valley,
        And anger in the sky,

     Around the huddling homesteads
        The leafless timber roars,
     And the dead call the dying
        And finger at the doors.

Oh, yonder faltering fingers
    Are hands I used to hold;
Their false companion drowses
    And leaves them in the cold.

Oh, to the bed of ocean,
    To Africk and to Ind,
I will arise and follow
    Along the rainy wind.

The night goes out and under
    With all its train forlorn;
Hues in the east assemble
    And cocks crow up the morn.

The living are the living
    And dead the dead will stay,
And I will sort with comrades
    That face the beam of day.

                      (LP 19)

The reference to "Ind" could easily be read to mean that Moses Jackson had died in that country, as Housman's brother had actually died in "Africk," did we not know otherwise. The references are in fact biographical, but while the one to Herbert Housman is literal, that to Moses Jackson is metaphorical. It was not Jackson that died in "Ind" but something else. It could be interpreted to mean that Housman's love for him died when he went to India, did we not know otherwise. We shall return to this point in chapter 10.

Housman created a lyric expressing a "deep physical longing for comrades or brothers now dead," a "haunting" poem of "intimacy" and "communion in death." "Left in the cold" refers to "those who have failed to find a place on the social scene, or fit in on an amorous one. Here it is the literal fate of the dead," whose fingers, in folk lore and ballad, tap "at doors, crying to be let in; but these are the hands of friends or lovers, their touch once loving" and now "alive and warm again" in the imagination (Bayley, *Housman's Poems*, 132–33).

If the hands of the dead (or dying?) are "hands I used to hold," are we to understand them as the hands of his small brother (which would be eminently reasonable) or the hands of Moses Jackson (and what happens then to the "flaming row"), or both? And what are we to make of the two following lines, in which the persona characterizes himself as a "false companion" whose inattention or neglect is responsible for their banishment from life and who is therefore filled with remorse? It is a known fact that survivors of a disaster, whether the Holocaust or a natural catastrophe, or a mundane train or airplane crash, or a deadly disease, feel great guilt at still being alive when others have perished. Is this what is expressed here? Does the persona feel somehow that had he been alert instead of "drowsing" he could have prevented the deaths of those he loved? He also characterizes himself as "dying." Is this a case of "for whom the bell tolls," or does the poem imply that the deaths of those he loved have resulted in his own spiritual or emotional death and that henceforth he will be one of the living dead, determined to shortly follow them? The last verse rejects this emotional despair and turns determinedly toward the future, abandoning the ghosts of the past. And yet, the tone of the entire poem, as with other poems that end similarly, negates this resolution. One feels that the midnight emotion is not so easily banished as the persona might hope.

The Romantic poets celebrated wild nature, uncultivated and rough land haunted by wailing demons and ghosts, threatening, exhilarating, and uninhabited. The earlier Augustan poets had celebrated tamed nature, controlled, man-cultivated or manicured landscapes, gardens and parks, inhabited, soothing, safe and reassuring. Housman's ideal landscape is neither wild nor yet tamed, but self-cultivated, the country fields and woods, natural woods, natural meadows, the hedgerows of the quiet English countryside.

> 'Tis time, I think, by Wenlock Town
>   The golden bloom should blow;
> The hawthorne sprinkled up and down
>   Should charge the land with snow.
>
> Spring will not wait the loiterer's time
>   Who keeps so long away;
> So others wear the broom and climb
>   The hedgerows heaped with may.
>
> Oh tarnish late on Wenlock Edge,
>   Gold that I never see;
> Lie long, high snowdrifts in the hedge
>   That will not shower on me.
>
>   (ASL 39)

In Housman's poetry, the gold inevitably tarnishes, the drifts of white mayflowers give way to the snowdrifts of winter, and the joy of spring is for others, others who will "wear the broom" and "climb the hedgerows." Spring, with its promise of fertility, its promise of renewal and courtship, is invariably for others to enjoy, not for Housman's persona, or for Housman. Only one poem in the canon is an avowed translation rather than a hybrid in which Housman has grafted his variations onto a translated base, as with Heine's poem (discussed in the preceding chapter) or Sappho's (to be discussed in chapter 10). It is titularly a spring poem, and it held some special meaning for Housman. In it, "we sense the presence of deeply held, personal concerns in what is ostensibly a translation" (Nielsen and Solomon, "Horace and Housman," 327). One of his students recalled that "he read the ode aloud with deep emotion, first in Latin and then in an English translation of his own. 'That,' he said hurriedly, almost like a man betraying a secret, 'I regard as the most beautiful poem in ancient literature,' and walked quickly out of the room. A scholar of Trinity . . . [said to me] 'I was afraid the old fellow was going to cry' " (Grant Richards, *Housman*, 289). Why could this poem all but move Housman to tears?

Diffugere Nives Horace—Odes, IV 7

The snows are fled away, leaves on the shaws
    And grasses in their mead renew their birth,
The river to the river-bed withdraws,
    And altered is the fashion of the earth.

The Nymphs and Graces three put off their fear
    And unapparelled in the woodland play.
The swift hour and the brief prime of the year
    Say to the soul, *Thou wast not born for aye*.

Thaw follows frost; hard on the heel of spring
    Treads summer sure to die, for hard on hers
Comes autumn, with his apples scattering;
    Then back to wintertide, when nothing stirs.

But oh, whate'er the sky-led seasons mar,
    Moon upon moon rebuilds it with her beams:
Come *we* where Tullus and where Ancus are,
    And good Aeneas, we are dust and dreams.

Torquatus, if the gods in heaven shall add
    The morrow to the day, what tongue has told?
Feast then thy heart, for what thy heart has had
    The fingers of no heir will ever hold.

When thou descendest once the shades among,
    The stern assize and equal judgment o'er,
Not thy long lineage nor thy golden tongue,
    No, nor thy righteousness, shall friend thee more.

Night holds Hippolytus the pure of stain,
    Diana steads him nothing, he must stay;
And Theseus leaves Pirithous in the chain
    The love of comrades cannot take away.

(MP 5)

The first six and a half verses are, not surprisingly, a loose translation of Horace's Latin, what Nash calls "Englishing" rather than translating the text, but then something happens. The last two lines, with their "contrast, couched in emotionally powerful form, of a desire prompted by love" and "a failure and futility that are seen as inevitable" are Housman's own.[9] "The poignant desperation of that last line is a sheer addition, not belonging in the Latin of Horace at all" (Hoagwood, "Poetic Design," 11). Housman "radically transformed . . . [the ode] in ways that reveal . . . [his own] conscious or unconscious concerns"; one of his concerns was the "climate of censure for homosexuality," the "manner in which the centuries had twisted homosexual or homoerotic love from a normal experience to a serious crime deserving of cruel punishments." He thus introduced an ambiguity at the end of the poem: "Is it a chain that is unremovable or a love that is unremovable even if the chain holds the loved one?" (Nielsen and Solomon, "Horace and Housman"). In contrast to Housman's translation of the last section, it is instructive to look at that of Samuel Johnson (*Horace*, 285), where the translation may be more faithful but the passion is missing:

> Hippolytus, unjustly slain
> Diana calls to life in vain;
> Nor can the mighty Theseus rend
> The chains of Hell that hold his friend.

The phrase "the love of comrades" is itself derived, not from Greek literature but from American. It has been traced back to Walt Whitman's poetry of the early 1860s, whence both John Addington Symonds and Edward Carpenter adopted it. Housman's certainly knew Whitman's use of the phrase;[10] Housman's own marked copy of *Leaves of Grass* is in the Adelman Collection at Bryn Mawr College near Philadelphia. For all three, the phrase denotes the love that "passes the love of woman" and is thus appropriate to the writer whether implied in the original myth or not.

The meaning of this poem for Housman was, I am quite sure, not in the spring, nor in the Nymphs and Graces, nor in the images of autumn and winter (much as Housman must have relished them). It was in the last two lines into which he infused his own emotion, the lines that evoke deathless friendship helpless against death. This was the image that, "almost . . . betraying a secret," could make him look as if he "was going to cry," could force him to leave the room "quickly"—before the tears forced their way to the surface and the secret was indeed betrayed. This leads us into the next section of this study, the direct consideration of friendship, and of love.

Erato

6
Rose Harland

Mᴜᴄʜ ᴏꜰ ᴛʜᴇ ᴘᴏᴇᴛʀʏ ᴛᴏ ʙᴇ ᴅɪꜱᴄᴜꜱꜱᴇᴅ ɪɴ ᴛʜɪꜱ ᴄʜᴀᴘᴛᴇʀ ᴄᴏɴꜱɪꜱᴛꜱ ᴏꜰ Housman's version of the pastoral tradition. It is concerned with life— and death—in rural England, a preindustrialized England inhabited by yeomen who farm the land or graze sheep upon it. They are sturdy border youths fond of their beer and their girls, the high point of whose year is the great agricultural fair held on May Day in Ludlow. Uneducated and unsophisticated, they are direct descendents of Colin Clout and cousins germane of Forster's country boys. As with Forster, for whom it was a standard homoerotic motif, Housman's poems are imbued with the theme of "the sudden death of boys," boys who "meet inexplicable sudden deaths" (Fussell, *Great War*, 285) or die in battle or are hanged for un- specified crimes. Housman's "lads" are emphatically not related, except in the most tenuous way, to the Corydons and Phyllises of the more di- rectly classical pastoral, except in one respect. As in the classical pastoral, the center of interest in the Shropshire cycle is the untutored songsmith– cum–musician, in this case Terence Hearsay who, like his remote Greek antecedents, plays a pipe—in his case a flute—and composes poetry. Housman's characters inhabit a specifically English Arcadia rather than Lodge's Anglified but basically Greek realm, and they are part of the con- tinuum that runs from Spenser via Wordsworth and Forster to Housman and beyond. There is also a connection to Edward Carpenter's long four- part prose-poem *Towards Democracy*, written between 1883 and 1905 and thus contemporary with much of Housman's own writing. Carpenter's poem is "a celebration of 'comradeship' among pastoral youths uncor- rupted by industrialism and undeformed by 'education'," and is itself part of "the main prewar tradition of homoerotic poetry [that] runs from Whitman to Hopkins to Housman" (ibid., 281).

We have met Terence Hearsay in several poems where he functions as a spokesman for A. E. Housman. It is time to look at him in his native environment, rural Shropshire, and at the cycle in which he holds center stage. Although many poems in the cycle are peripheral, there is a clear narrative line concerning the affairs of the rustic "eternal triangles," the main characters in which are Terence himself ("I"), Fred, Dick, and Ned (his friends-cum-rivals), and Rose, Fan, and Nancy (their girls).[1] Many of the poems are, as one would expect, in *A Shropshire Lad*, but some of them are in *Last Poems*, some in the other collections, and some— incomplete—in the notebooks. These last provide much of the story, but it would seem that Housman tired of the game and dropped it. However, it is quite possible to combine the published poems and the notebook fragments, and from them construct the plot of the mock epic.

It seems to me that this is an apt description, as from the first there is a certain tone of parody, which is strongest in the notebook fragments, though also present elsewhere. The spoof of stereotypical romantic themes and gender roles is usually characterized by an exaggerated, some- times flippant, tone that, absent or muted as it is in many individual poems (especially those in the canon), becomes quite obvious when all of them, fragments included, are read consecutively. The cycle also in- cludes the poems about trips to Ludlow Fair and what happens there. We have seen some of this already in Terence's description of one such excur- sion. Other poems about the fair are filled with regretful nostalgia rather than comedy. Ludlow Fair itself functions as Housman's metaphor for the everyday world, the world of pounds, shillings, and pence, his version of "Vanity Fair" where everything, including love (or at least a facsimile thereof) is for sale, if one is willing to pay the price.

This theme is interwoven with the narrative thread to create a portrait of the world in which things are often not what they seem. It is not true, as has been suggested, that *all* of Housman's poetry was written "with his tongue in his cheek; . . . a clever fake" (Watts "Poetry," 118). It is true, however, notably in these poems, that the "uproarious humour which breaks out in Housman's prose can also be found . . . in the poetry, adding a zest to unhappy themes with its touch of parody" (Wells, "Hidden and Unmasked," 11).

It might be well, first, to present the dramatis personae of the cycle and a rough outline of the plot. First, of course, is Terence, "I", who stands at its center. The use of the first person singular pronoun is prima facie evi- dence that the speaker is Terence (unless there is good reason to think otherwise). This is certainly so in *A Shropshire Lad* and those poems where names associated with Terence are mentioned, and provisionally so in other poems that have the same tone and/or Shropshire locales. Among Terence's mates are Maurice, who has been murdered, and his unnamed brother, who has murdered him. The story is told to Terence by the murderer himself in ASL 8, and the cause of the murder, as is manifest in an excised verse still extant in the notebooks, was their ri- valry over Lucy. Then we have another unnamed "lad" executed in Shrewsbury jail, on the night of whose execution Terence keeps watch outside the prison (ASL 9). This may be Maurice's brother, the murderer. These poems are not included here both because they are well known and easily available, being among the most popular of the lyrics, and because they stand a bit outside the main narrative development.

Terence's rival, at the beginning of the cycle, is Fred Loughton, and the girl they both want is Rose Harland. The result of this rivalry, or at least the resolution of it, is Fred's death (ASL 25 and notebook fragment). Terence steps into his shoes (ASL 27) and walks with his love until her death shortly thereafter (ASL 21). The young swain seems to have no difficulty in replacing her (ASL 26). Eventually, however, he is rejected by a girl (perhaps Fan) whom he is pursuing. In a fit of pique he joins the army (ASL 5 and ASL 34).[2] He goes to London for a time before being sent overseas (ASL 37 and ASL 41). Meanwhile, Ned Lear, one of his drinking buddies and fair-going companions, his rival for Fan's favors, has become involved with Nancy, who is thrown out of her father's home, perhaps because she is—or thinks she is—pregnant (notebook fragments only). Ned serves for a time in the army with Terence, either to avoid marrying Nancy or, having married her, to escape his new responsibilities.

In the army, Terence proves a rather less than satisfactory soldier although he is apparently not brought to book for his dereliction of duty (MP 39 and notebook fragments). After leaving the army, he returns to Shropshire where he writes poetry and plays his flute at country dances (ASL 62 and LP 41). At one dance, Fan, once the bone of contention between Terence and Ned, pairs off with Dick, and Nancy, faithless to Ned, with Tom. This precipitates a fight between Tom and Ned. In the course of the resulting brawl, Dick is badly injured. Ned is sent to jail, perhaps for causing severe bodily harm during the fracas, perhaps for something else. Dick dies, and Ned, in jail, also dies (ASL 58, titled "The Return of the Native" in the printer's copy of *A Shropshire Lad* although Housman apparently changed his mind and in the final copy the poem is left untitled, ASL 59, and LP 20).

Back in his old haunts, Terence is haunted by his memories (notebook fragments only) and by Ned's ghost (notebook fragments only). He is left to go to Ludlow Fair and get drunk alone (LP 21, 35, and 34). He ruminates on the fair, on the difference between how it seems to a young man and how it appears to one who is old(er) and alone, with nothing to look forward to except death (ASL 50). After he dies, Terence is conducted to Hell where he again encounters Ned Lear, who proceeds to rescue them both from Satan's capitol city (LP 31). They go off together in silent companionship, communion, and contentment.

Bayley has suggested that, since Housman's full name was Alfred Edward Housman, and since "Ned" is a nickname for "Edward," Ned is in some way Housman himself. Ned the character may in part be "a sardonic self-portrait" of the poet, "a fantasy self-projection" in which "Pirithous-Ned Housman [is] rescued from his heart's Hades . . . by himself by shooting dead Hell's master" and becomes "a couple who then come home together" ("Housman and Larkin" 156–57). I do not accept this identification of Housman with Ned. Housman's sister Katharine called him Alfred, and Laurence called him Fred. To Moses Jackson he was "Hous." He called himself A. E., and it was thus he signed his letters, even those to his closest relatives. It might also be noted that Edward was his father's name, and Housman's own surrogate in his poetry, his 'fantasy self-projection,' is Terence, the persona of "Hell Gate," whom Ned rescues. It seems then that Ned must then be a fantasy portrait of Moses J. Jackson, the friend who had it in his power, had he so chosen, to rescue Housman from his personal hell of rejection and loneliness, but is he? Ned (or Moses Jackson) would thus be the "I" of "Terence, this is stupid stuff," the friend whom "it hurts to think." As already remarked, this identification has been suggested, but I do not accept it. Even if, as seems likely, Moses Jackson lies at the heart of Ned Lear, Ned is not a portrait of Moses. To return to the idea that Ned is Housman, I confess that I cannot, stretch my imagination as I may, conceive of Housman ever thinking of himself as "Ned" even in a fantasy or daydream (in which he is already present as Terence), or suddenly doubling his mask. No, I think Bayley here is entirely mistaken.

We thus have not one but several triangles, all of which end in tragedy, tragedy that quickly degenerates into farce. One such "plot" may be serious, but the multiplicity of them points the entire cycle in the direction of lampoon. It is almost too close to farce to be called satire.

It is possible to arrange the above poems in a different sequence, or to substitute other poems for those I have used (some of which might not be admitted into the sequence at all). I have, however, based the "plot outline" on internal indications as well as on the logic of the situation, and I believe it is defensible as the most likely scenario. This is, obviously, not the sequence that Housman gave the poems when they were printed. However, he may have quite deliberately confused the narrative by mixing the order of the poems, deciding not to finish and include some of the "chapters," and interspersing other poems that are not part of the main narrative line, all in order to obscure the import: the inherent instability of heterosexual relationships in contrast to the enduring affection of male friends for each other.[3] An unrelated example of this intent to mystify the critics is the order of composition of the verses in "I hoed and trenched and weeded" (ASL 63). Why not, then, a similar intent in regards to a series of poems, especially when the thrust of the complete narrative posed a threat to his public mask?

The key word for heterosexual relationships is "fancy," a passing preference without deep roots.[4] This word runs like a motif through the cycle. It is never applied to friendships between males. The key word for male friendships is "lad," a word that is notoriously ubiquitous in Housman's poetry. Lad may be Housman's equivalent of Wilde's "boy," emphasizing "both maleness and youth" (Robbins, "Very Curious Construction," 151), but not, I think, of Robert Nichols's "boy." Nichols used "boy" for erotic effect (Fussell, *Great War*, 296–97). The problem with reading "lad" as Housman's equivalent in English of the Greek *ephebe* is that the word has apparently always been used in British English (as indeed it still is) without this connotation. Anyone who habitually listens to the news on British television is accustomed to hearing police chiefs and athletic coaches and mothers talking about their "lads." Attractive as is the idea that in Housman "lad" equals "*ephebe*," and as plausible as that may sound to those accustomed only to American English, it simply will not do. I have spoken to many English friends, including specialists in Housman, and all are agreed that "lad" is normative English and not a code word denoting homosexual interest. Fussell suggested that in the diction of the Great War, different degrees of erotic heat were connoted by the words "men" (largely neutral), "boys" (a little warmer), and "lads" (very warm indeed). However, his suggestion that "as *men* grow more attractive, they are seen as *boys*, until finally, when conceived as lovers, they turn into *lads*" (ibid., 283, his emphasis) could only have been written by someone not immersed in the British variety of English, and it is roundly rejected by Burnett. Jeremy Bourne suggested to me that these words indeed have different (nonerotic) connotations in the context of officer-soldier relations. An officer's using "men" indicates an atmosphere of discipline, stiffness, and starchiness, whereas calling the troops "boys" or "lads" connotes an atmosphere of warmth, support, and approval but in no way has an erotic undertone. What "lad" does seem to me to connote is a combination of affection for—and some degree of authority over—the one so designated.

The term "lad" appears from time to time in noncycle poems, and there are a few cycle poems in which it does not appear. On balance, its presence, especially when used more than once within a single poem, indicates that the poem is connected to the cycle even if only peripherally. It may be regarded, like the use of other colloquialisms, as a constant aspect of Terence's vocabulary and an occasional one of Housman's. It is clearly Terence speaking when "The chestnut casts his flambeaux, and the flowers / Stream from the hawthorne on the wind away, / The doors clap to, the pane is blind with showers. / Pass me the can, lad; there's an end of May" (LP 9, with its notorious "Whatever brute and blackguard made the world").

In whatever order we arrange these or substitute poems, whatever other poems are used in place of them, we clearly sense the commitment of men to each other in contrast to the strictly heterosexual game of "musical beds." Taken as a connected narrative, as I have outlined it here, the plot elements (each of which separately, except the last, can be found in countless serious Victorian novels as well as in melodramas) prove when combined quite outrageously ludicrous. Taken together, there is a fragmentary lampoon on Victorian mores and values.

One of Housman's most popular poems serves as a prologue to the cycle, both in its theme and its imagery.

> When I was one-and-twenty
>   I heard a wise man say,
> "Give crowns and pounds and guineas
>   But not your heart away;
> Give pearls away and rubies
>   But keep your fancy free."
> But I was one-and-twenty,
>   No use to talk to me.
>
> When I was one-and-twenty
>   I heard him say again,
> "The heart out of the bosom
>   Was never given in vain;
> 'Tis paid with sighs aplenty
>   And sold for endless rue."
> And I am two-and-twenty,
>   And oh, 'tis true, 'tis true.

(ASL 13)

The worksheet for this poem is one of the two that Housman himself destroyed (the other was "I hoed and trenched and weeded"). Haber thinks this destruction was aimed at the writing on the reverse of the sheet, presumably because it had some explicit reference that Housman was unwilling to chance being seen ("A Shropshire Lad," 87). This is, of course, quite possible, but it is equally possible that the first draft of the poem itself included some such reference.

More than one critic sensed the narrative underlayer of the poem. It was compared to the ballad, which leaves most of the details to the auditor's imagination. It "tells only that a story could be told, were the speaker not so reticent" (Perkins, History of Modern Poetry 199). One of the earliest of the critics, William Archer, remarked that "there is a whole heart-history" in it ("Housman," 191). The story that "could be told," the "heart-history," is the Shropshire cycle. In theory, the persona might be a woman, Rose or Nancy or Fan, rather than Terence. It is generally agreed, however, that "Housman's narrators are consistently male"

(Mandel, "Insane Narrators," 411, note 3). In addition, in this case we have the author's own word for it. Concerning the projected Fraser illustration for ASL 13, he wrote to Grant Richards: "How like an artist to think that the speaker is a woman!" (Grant Richards, *Housman* 182).

The imagery in the poem is mercantile, and the merchandise is the hearts that are bought and sold. The heart cannot be given away to one's "fancy," "for something is always gotten in return. The heart is always *sold*, and the price is 'endless rue' " (Leggett, *Land of Lost Content*, 31, emphasis his). The price paid for the sale of a heart is "sighs aplenty" unless one keeps one's "fancy" free, and one's fancy is in Housman always for a girl. Heterosexual love is something that a man will "rue." The heart may also, of course, be paid for in the same coin, the other's heart in return. It may be given in even exchange for the beloved's heart ("lovers should be loved again", ASL 10), or even "lent" to him ("It is no gift I tender / A loan is all I can," AP 4), but these possibilities are neither heterosexual nor included in this poem.

The narrative of the cycle proper begins with the rivalry between Terence and Fred for Rose's favor, as both "fancy" her. The last verse here is to be found in the notebooks as an alternative to what I have printed as the penultimate verse.

> This time of year a twelvemonth past,
>   When Fred and I would meet,
> We needs must jangle, till at last
>   We fought and I was beat.
>
> So then the summer fields about,
>   Till rainy days began,
> Rose Harland on her Sundays out
>   Walked with the better man.
>
> The better man she walks with still,
>   Though now 'tis not with Fred:
> A lad that lives and has his will
>   Is worth a dozen dead.
>
> Fred keeps the house all kinds of weather,
>   And clay's the house he keeps;
> When Rose and I walk out together
>   Stock-still lies Fred and sleeps. (ASL 25)
>
> He keeps his bed now days are warm,
>   And clay's the bed he keeps;
> When Rose and I walk arm in arm
>   Fred Loughton lies and sleeps.
>   (Burnett, *Poems*, 27 bottom)

The question is not so much "Who will 'walk out' with Rose?" as "Who is 'the better man?'" This phrase is used twice but the meaning "ironically" shifts "in the exact middle of the poem" (Page, *A. E. Housman*, 193). From the girl's point of view, one man is as good as another. From Terence's point of view, the "better man" is the one who is better with his fists; from Rose's, the "better man" is simply the one who can satisfy her need for a beau with whom to "walk out." Being fought over is a sop to her vanity, and it does not in the least matter to her who wins. The phrase "and has his will" is overtly sexual, implying that the relationship between Rose and her lover is a carnal one. Such a fight caused by the rivalry between two young men who want to "walk out" with the same girl is not exactly unknown in the serious novel. In *Adam Bede* a similar fight takes place between Adam and his good friend Arthur Donnithorne over Hetty Sorrel.

Nor is George Eliot the only one to use this plot component. In Charlotte Brontë's *Shirley* a similar battle is graphically described. "A two-three months sin', [Fred] Murgatroyd and Moses [Barraclough] chanced to meet one Sunday night; they'd both come lurking about these premises wi' the notion of counselling Sarah to tak' a bit of a walk wi' them; they fell out, had a tussel, and Fred was worsted" (149). Sarah, unlike Rose, had her own preference. She preferred Fred despite his having had the worst of it. I doubt very much that the similarity of name and phraseology in Bronte's and in Housman's descriptions is coincidental. He was an omnivorous reader with an extraordinarily retentive memory. The difference between his account and Bronte's is limited to the nature of the girl for whose favor the men fought. Sarah is not a symbol of female fecklessness; Rose is. Rose is the demure and passive Victorian Miss taken to extremes.

It has been suggested that this rivalry, like Maurice's with his brother, was resolved by murder. Mandel assumes that such is the case and, having invented a murder, proceeds to condemn it for "lack of sufficient motive . . . The speaker kills Fred" in order to get Rose, thinking this "sufficient justification" ("Insane Narrators," 412 n. 9). The idea that there has been a murder is refuted by Molson, who contends that "a suitor . . . rejected when his rival was alive, has [simply] survived him with satisfactory results" from his own point of view (Molson, "Philosophies" 207), and from hers, and by Jebb, who considers Fred's death "arbitrary" (*A. E. Housman*, 84) and does not consider the question of murder at all in his case. The result would have been just as satisfactory, from Rose's point of view, had Fred been the one to survive. To which I would add that we have had one murder resulting from a rivalry over a girl (Lucy, for whose sake Maurice's brother murdered him), and a second such event would be inartistic, besides which there is no such implication in the text. Housman's poetry so often does deal with convicted felons that I suspect a sort of carryover effect has inspired this idea.

In a way, Fred does survive, but only as a ghost who, not knowing that Terence has replaced him in Rose's bed, proceeds to question his friend about events following his demise.

>"Is my team ploughing,
>   That I was used to drive
>And hear the harness jingle
>   When I was man alive?'
>
>Ay, the horses trample,
>   The harness jingles now;
>No change though you lie under
>   The land you used to plough.
>
>"Is football playing
>   Along the river shore,
>With lads to chase the leather
>   Now I stand up no more?"
>
>Ay, the ball is flying,
>   The lads play heart and soul,
>The goal stands up, the keeper
>   Stands up to keep the goal.
>
>"Is my girl happy,
>   That I thought hard to leave,
>And has she tired of weeping
>   As she lies down at eve?"
>
>Ay, she lies down lightly,
>   She lies not down to weep:
>Your girl is well contented.
>   Be still, my lad, and sleep.
>
>"Is my friend hearty,
>   Now I am thin and pine,
>And has he found to sleep in
>   A better bed than mine?"
>
>Yes, lad, I lie easy,
>   I lie as lads would choose;
>I cheer a dead man's sweetheart,
>   Never ask me whose.

(ASL 27)

The girl "lies down lightly" and is "well-contented" with the change in swains. Who can this be but Rose who was perfectly willing to exchange her dead lover for a living one who "has his will." And "I," as always unless there is good reason to think otherwise, is Terence, Fred's friend as well as his rival. Fred may be "thin and pine" in his thin pine box, but Terence (sleeping in "a better bed" than his, i.e., Rose's bed) lies just "as lads would choose," in his dead friend's place. Something rather similar occurs in Tennessee Williams's *Cat on a Hot Tin Roof*, and for perhaps a rather similar reason. Bronowski suggests that Terence has not only replaced Fred in Rose's bed but also on the football team and is now the goalie. This is an attractive reading supported by another poem in which "Twice a week the winter thorough / Here stood I to keep the goal" (ASL 17) where the speaker may again be assumed to be Terence. Bronowski also says the speaker is a cad. To be sure, he does not think this is Terence, or any other persona, speaking. He thinks the speaker is A. E. Housman, who is rather ashamed of himself ("The Poet's Defence," 226). Any comment about this would be superfluous.

The couple in the next poem may not be Terence and Rose, but the first person male narrator as a general rule is to be identified as Terence, and we know that Rose walked with her young man, whoever he might be, "on her Sundays out." Therefore, the identification of this young couple who walked in the countryside on Sunday mornings as Terence and Rose is not unlikely.

Bredon(*) Hill

> In summertime on Bredon
>   The bells they sound so clear;
> Round both the shires they ring them
>   In steeples far and near,
>   A happy noise to hear,
>
> Here of a Sunday morning
>   My love and I would lie,
> And see the coloured counties,
>   And hear the larks so high
>   About us in the sky.
>
> The bells would ring to call her
>   In valleys miles away:
> "Come all to church, good people;
>   Good people, come and pray."
>   But here my love would stay.

And I would turn and answer
        Among the springing thyme,
"Oh, peal upon our wedding,
        And we will hear the chime,
        And come to church in time."

But when the snows at Christmas
        On Bredon top were strown,
My love rose up so early
        And stole out unbeknown
        And went to church alone.

They tolled the one bell only,
        Groom was there none to see,
The mourners followed after,
        And so to church went she,
        And would not wait for me.

The bells they sound on Bredon,
        And still the steeples hum.
"Come all to church, good people,"—
        Oh, noisy bells, be dumb;
        I hear you, I will come.

*Pronounced Breedon.   (ASL 21)

The problem that this poem raises for critics is the exact implicaton of
the last line. It is true, of course, that it is assumed that in time all will
"come to church," one way or another, but some have also assumed that
the line means the persona intends to (perhaps actually does) commit
suicide. Hamilton (*Housman the Poet*, 62–63), Leggett (*Land of Lost Content*, 34–35), and Marlow (*A. E. Housman*, 82) all read the poem thus.
However, again this may be a carryover effect from the number of suicides
actually to be found in Housman's poetry (the Woolwich cadet, the dead
man on whose grave the sinner's rue grows, the lover on whose grave the
nettle dances [ASL 16], and so on). For one thing, if the speaker were to
kill himself, he would not "come to church" at all; he would be buried
"at the four cross ways" (LP 30). The line could as well be interpreted,
had another (and more conventionally pious poet) written it, to mean
that the persona feels his girl's death is a divine punishment for their
choosing to wander on the hills on Sunday morning rather than go to
church and is filled with remorse. He therefore vows that from this time
on he will attend Sunday services regularly, even if not in the reverent
frame of mind that is implied by "faithfully."

Assuming that the identification of the couple as Terence and Rose is
tentatively accepted, Terence obviously does not kill himself because of

his lost love. The following poem may be read as either a reprise of the preceding one or as a continuation of the story. It makes no ultimate difference. Either way, Terence replaces his lost love.

> Along the field as we came by
> A year ago, my love and I,
> The aspen over stile and stone
> Was talking to itself alone.
> "Oh who are these that kiss and pass?
> A country lover and his lass;
> Two lovers looking to be wed;
> And time shall put them both to bed,
> But she shall lie with earth above,
> And he beside another love."
>
> And sure enough beneath the tree
> There walks another love with me,
> And overhead the aspen heaves
> Its rainy sounding silver leaves;
> And I spell nothing in their stir,
> But now perhaps they speak to her,
> And plain for her to understand
> They talk about a time at hand
> When I shall sleep with clover clad,
> And she beside another lad.

(ASL 26)

If the first verse refers back to "Bredon Hill," the second makes it clear that the lonely youth has found a new love. His old sweetheart has gone to her bed of earth and he has found another girl's bed in which to sleep, or not to sleep. His inconstancy is matched by the new girl's, whom he fully expects to replace him, when he is gone, as unconcernedly as he has replaced his own former sweetheart or as Rose had done Fred.

As early as 1923, the three poems ("This time of year a twelve-month past," "Along the field as we came by," and "Is my team ploughing") were associated. They were recognized as a related group picturing

> first the lad who was beaten in fight a year ago but, now that his stronger rival is dead, walks out with Rose Harland and "has his will," and then this same lad smitten with a chill misgiving, as he walks under the aspens that perhaps their "rainy-sounding silver leaves" are telling her of a time when he too may be dead "and she beside another lad." In the third and grimmest of these little poems the dead lad asks about . . . his girl (MacDonald, "Housman," 121).

In 1936, it was suggested that "This time of year" was about Terence and Fred, "Along the field as we came by" about Terence and Rose, and "Is my team ploughing" again about Terence and Fred.[5] The idea was never further developed, nor could it be expanded successfully without the notebook material. It implicitly suggests the same linkage between the various poems that I have expanded to explicate the saga of the Shropshire cycle although both early critics arrange these three in a somewhat different order than that I have adopted. E. M. Forster, without being specific about which poems are involved or in what order, nonetheless was alert to the narrative implications, writing that the theme of Housman's poetry "involves a story. But . . . it is impossible to figure the story out and discover through what mutations it passed" ("Ancient and Modern," Gardner, *Critical Heritage*, 319). He was wrong. Using the notebook material, it is indeed possible "to figure the story out."

The love between a man and a woman may be strong at the start, but one quickly recovers from the infection.

> Oh, when I was in love with you,
>   Then I was clean and brave,
> And miles around the wonder grew
>   How well did I behave.
>
> And now the fancy passes by,
>   And nothing will remain,
> And miles around they'll say that I
>   Am quite myself again.
>
> (ASL 18)

Leggett has rightly called the tone of this poem "almost flippant" and identified its theme as inconstancy in love (*Land of Lost Content*, 38). The love in which this inconstancy exists is specifically heterosexual, a "fancy." Terence turns his eyes in a new direction, toward Fan, and there is a rival for her company as there had been for Rose's, his good friend, his drinking, brawling, fair-going companion, Ned Lear. This poem was never completed, but enough of it is extant in the notebooks to indicate the development of the "plot" (Burnett, *Poems*, 175–76).

> Ned Lear and I were drunk last week,
> Oh, dripping drunk were Ned and I,
> Too drunk to see, too drunk to speak,
> Too helpless drunk to reason why.
> You might have looked through Ludlow fair
> And never spied a tipsier pair.
>
> Off to the fair, the morn of May,
> Two lovely lads went I and Ned.

Clean shirts, blue neckties, breastknots gay,
New coats on back, new hats on head.
And who this week are wearing those
Two hats, the Lord Almighty knows.

then began
The quarrel which should go with Fan.

He called me all the names he knew,
And that was more than he could spell;
I gave him stuff to think of too,
The tale about his sister Nell
And Martin Hughes, and what folks thought
And folks expected: then we fought.

It was no one-time excursion to Ludlow fair that ended with Terence leaving his necktie "God knows where" and sleeping off the "pints and quarts of Ludlow beer" in a muddy ditch. One suspects, indeed, that the main attraction of the fair was the opportunity to enjoy good fellowship, get drunk, and end up in a glorious fight with one of his friends—over a girl, if nothing better offered. This is what constitutes a really good time, as a persona (perhaps Terence) says elsewhere. "Could man be drunk forever / With liquor, love, or fights, / Lief should I rouse at morning / And lief lie down of nights" (LP 10), although not, preferably, in the mud. "Love" is not in first place. This is an exaggeration of the Victorian definition of "manliness," just as Rose's passivity is of "femininity."[6]

Terence beats Ned for the privilege of going with Fan (who has not been consulted as to her preference). I am identifying the girl in the next two poems as Fan for two reasons. Although the name is in more than one poem, no story is told about her, and there are stories about all the other characters. If this is not in fact Fan, we must add a third—and anonymous—girl to the cast of characters, which seems needless since Fan is already present waiting in the wings for her cue to enter and take center stage. Also, we know that Terence has cast his eye on her. Let it be Fan, then. Terence finds his attempted seduction balked, not by a male friend-cum-rival this time but by the girl herself.

Ah see how thick the goldcup flowers
    Are lying in field and lane,
With dandelions to tell the hours
    That never are told again.
Oh may I squire you round the meads
    And pick you posies gay?
—" 'Twill do no harm to take my arm.
    "You may, young man, you may."

Ah, spring was sent for lass and lad,
    'Tis now the blood runs gold,
And man and maid had best be glad
    Before the world is old.
What flowers to-day may flower to-morrow,
    But never as good as new.
—Suppose I wound my arm right round—
    " 'Tis true, young man, 'tis true."

Some lads there are, 'tis shame to say,
    That only court to thieve,
And once they bear the bloom away
    'Tis little enough they leave.
Then keep your heart for men like me
    And safe from trustless chaps.
My love is true and all for you.
    "Perhaps, young man, perhaps."

Oh, look in my eyes then, can you doubt?
    —Why, 'tis a mile from town.
How green the grass is all about!
    We might as well sit down.
—Ah, life, what is it but a flower?
    Why must true lovers sigh?
Be kind, have pity, my own, my pretty,—
    "Good-bye, young man, good bye."

                                   (ASL 5)

It is not only the goldcup flowers that are "lying in field and lane"; Terence is doing quite a bit of lying himself, trying to get the girl to "lie" with him in the same fields. But this time the girl is perceptive enough to see it and prudent enough to act on her perception. The more urgent the speaker becomes, the more skeptical she becomes, and the more wary and reluctant. The tone and technique carry us back to Housman's comic verse, reminding us of his parodies, and here there is also a revision of Shakespeare's song from *As You Like It* 5.3.17–34.

    It was a lover and his lass,
        With a hey, and a ho, and a hey nonino,
    That o'er the green corn-field did pass
        In the spring time, the only pretty ring time,
    When birds do sing, hey ding a ding, ding;
    Sweet lovers love the spring.

    Between the acres of the rye, . . .
    These pretty country folks would lie, . . .

> This carol they began that hour, . . .
> How that a life was but a flower . . .

Shakespeare's charming, artless lovers become Housman's rural Lothario and the girl he is courting in the spring, walking with her in the lanes, meadows, and fields, where, it is safe to assume, in addition to the buttercups and dandelions there grow corn and rye. In Shakespeare, "they" begin the "carol" together; in Housman, it is only he who sings it, but it is the same song yet. Firchow objects to the tone. He sees the poem as an "Edward Learian jingle" but misses the implication that this is at least a semicomic poem. "What is this," he asks, "a courtship 'twixt a swain and his aunt? . . . 'Young man' introduces a false note of moralistic primness and bourgeois respectability, a note that clashes violently" with the pastoral background ("Housman's Shropshire," 109). What he does not add is that the term also serves to characterize the "moralistic," prim, and "bourgeois" young lady and differentiate her from the other girls in the cycle. Nor is Housman's Shropshire an Arcadian never-never land, but rather a countryside inhabited by real people of all types, callow youths and moralistic girls included.

If this poem is accepted as part of the cycle "plot," one may also deduce from it that Terence this time has set his cap for an older girl. She is more of a challenge because more experienced than the younger ones whose conquest has proved so easy that there is no challenge left in it. His seduction technique, effective or not as it may be, is most unoriginal.

> When the lad for longing sighs,
>   Mute and dull of cheer and pale,
> If at death's own door he lies,
>   Maiden, you can heal his ail.
>
> Lovers' ills are all to buy:
>   The wan look, the hollow tone,
> The hung head, the sunken eye,
>   You can have them for your own.
>
> Buy them, buy them; eve and morn,
>   Lovers' ills are all to sell.
> Then you can lie down forlorn;
>   But the lover will be well.

(ASL 6)

We are back in the ambience of Ludlow Fair, where anything can be had for the appropriate price. You can buy "lover's ills," and you can sell them. All the suits of love can be acquired and donned at any moment.

The signs that convinced Polonius that Hamlet was mad for Ophelia's love are easily put on—and as easily dropped once their nefarious purpose has been achieved, leaving her truly mad and not merely "mad north-north-west"; "Then up he rose and donn'd his clothes, / And dupp'd the chamber door; / Let in the maid, that out a maid / Never departed more. . . ." (*Hamlet*, 2.2.396 and 4.5.52–55, respectively). Hamlet may not have intended to seduce and abandon his sweetheart, but Terence certainly does. The fulfillment of the male's desire heralds the end of his love, upon which he forsakes the girl, no longer a maiden (Leggett, *Land of Lost Content*, 39). Terence is sensitive enough to realize that "curing" him involves the girl's ruin. Either she will find herself in love with one who no longer cares for her ("forlorn" in the sense of "deserted") or she will be "ruined" in the good old Victorian sense, as were Little Em'ly, deserted by her lover, and countless others. Terence does not have enough sensitivity, however, to refrain from the attempt. In this case, it fails. The challenge of seducing Fan is more than Terence bargained for, and more than he can meet.

The commercial metaphor for sex was brilliantly used by Christina Rossetti in "Goblin Market," where the girls who buy the wares offered by the fascinatingly ugly little men (the male organ in all its range of variation?) die from eating the fruit they sell. The same image is used by Oscar Wilde in *De Profundis*, but with a difference. "Love does not traffic in a market-place, nor use a huckster's scales. . . . The aim of Love is to love: no more, and no less" (55–56). But Wilde was not talking about heterosexual love . . .

Rejected by the object of his affections, or at least of his intentions, who, unlike Rose, does not regard herself as a prize to be automatically awarded to the champion fighter, Terence threatens to enlist in the army. This may be a final ploy to win the girl's consent to cure his affliction. His vanity has been badly wounded (Robb, *Four in Exile*, 29).

The New Mistress

"Oh, sick I am to see you, will you never let me be?
You may be good for something but you are not good for me.
Oh, go where you are wanted, for you are not wanted here.
And that was all the farewell when I parted from my dear.

"I will go where I am wanted, to a lady born and bred
Who will dress me free for nothing in a uniform of red;
She will not be sick to see me if I only keep it clean:
I will go where I am wanted for a soldier of the Queen.

"I will go where I am wanted, for the sergeant does not mind;
He may be sick to see me but he treats me very kind:
He gives me beer and breakfast and a ribbon for my cap,
And I never knew a sweetheart spend her money on a chap.

"I will go where I am wanted, where there's room for one or two,
And the men are none too many for the work there is to do;
Where the standing line wears thinner and the dropping dead lie thick;
And the enemies of England they shall see me and be sick."

(ASL 34)

The key word is "sick." The seducer was "sick unto death" as a result
of his prey's refusal to "heal" his "ail." Now, she is "sick" (nauseated) of
him and his unwelcome attentions. The Queen will not be "sickened" by
him if he only takes care to be neat and clean (we remember his and
Ned's clean shirts, new coats, and new neckties—and lost hats—and understand that Terence is a bit of a dandy who prides himself on a certain
nattiness). The sergeant may be "sick" and tired of him, but he will nevertheless supply him with the essentials (beer, a full belly, and sartorial
decorations are the extent of his essential needs), which is more than a
girl will do. The image used takes us back to the market place where love
is bought and sold. The sergeant, unlike the girl, will treat him "very
kind," and the word, as we shall see later, has sexual connotations as well
as the usual ones. If here "I" am not wanted by the girl, "I" am wanted
in the army where I will cause England's enemies to be "sick" with fear.
We may remember Thackeray's Henry Esmond, who reacted very like this
when Beatrix was beyond his reach, as well as Dickens' Joe Willet in *Bar-
naby Rudge*, who did the same thing when Dolly Varden was denied him.

So off goes Terence in a huff to London, or rather in a train. In this
poem, Terence, leaving home for London and the army, merges with
Housman, leaving home for London and the Patent Office (emotionally,
not biographically) as also in the following one that gives us his/their
reaction to London.

As through the wild green hills of Wyre
The train ran, changing sky and shire,
And far behind, a fading crest,
Low in the forsaken west
Sank the high-reared head of Clee,
My hand lay empty on my knee.
Aching on my knee it lay:
That morning half a shire away
So many an honest fellow's fist
Had well-nigh wrung it from the wrist.

Hand, said I, since now we part
From fields and men we know by heart,
For strangers' faces, strangers' lands,—
Hand, you have held true fellows' hands.
Be clean then; rot before you do
A thing they'd not believe of you.
You and I must keep from shame
In London streets the Shropshire name;
On banks of Thames they must not say
Severn breeds worse men than they;
And friends abroad must bear in mind
Friends at home they left behind.
Oh, I shall be stiff and cold
When I forget you, hearts of gold;
The land where I shall mind you not
Is the land where all's forgot.
And if my foot returns no more
To Teme nor Corve nor Severn shore,
Luck, my lads, be with you still
By falling stream and standing hill,
By chiming tower and whispering tree,
Men that made a man of me.
About your work in town and farm
Still you'll keep my head from harm,
Still you'll help me, hands that gave
A grasp to friend me to the grave.

(ASL 37)

The train, actually the Great Western Railway, follows its laid-down course through a very real countryside. It runs through Wyre Forest in southeastern Shropshire and northwestern Worcestershire. Brown Clee Hill, the highest elevation in Shropshire, and Abdon Burf, the highest part of Brown Clee Hill, the "standing hills," drop behind and are lost, together with the "falling streams" ("Teme and Corve and Severn") as the train moves toward London (Franklin, "Housman's Shropshire"). Also left behind is "the chiming tower," Ludlow Tower, which called the "good people" to church on Sunday while he and his girl(s) were sitting in the hills instead of in their pews. This is the tower whose chimes play "The conquering hero comes" on Monday, the tower that is so prominent in "The Recruit" (ASL 3), where Terence, upon joining the army, was told to "reach your friends your hand," an exhortation that he has clearly obeyed. Bredon Hill itself, which still stands although the girl he met there on Sundays is long dead, and the "whispering tree" with its "rainy sounding silver leaves" are likewise left behind. There are no other references—direct or indirect—to the female part of the population, but there is instead a great well of regret at leaving those "true fellows," Dick and Ned and his other male companions and friends, the "lads."

That Terence is going further from Shropshire than merely to London is not so clear, but can be inferred by the phrase "strangers' lands," which can mean "areas of England inhabited by 'strangers' to Terence" or "lands inhabited by foreigners," strangers even stranger than Londoners. There is also the possibility that Terence will never return to "Teme nor Corve nor Severn shore," a possibility by no means certain since it is preceded by "if." Since Terence is not severed emotionally from home, and since the train runs in both directions, there is no reason for him to think of this possibility unless at his final destination there is also a possibility of his being killed (a journey to "the land where all's forgot"). He must suspect that he "till trump of doomsday / On lands of morn may lie, / And make the hearts of comrades / Be heavy where" he dies (ASL 3). In short, the poem may be read to indicate that Terence is joining the military and going to war. For my cycle "plot" I am assuming this reading. So Terence is in London, alone, and he misses his old home and the lads who had given him such a hearty send-off.

> Yonder, lightening other loads,
> The seasons range the country roads,
> But here in London streets I ken
> No such helpmates, only men;
> And these are not in plight to bear,
> If they would, another's care.
> They have enough as 'tis: I see
> In many an eye that measures me
> The mortal sickness of a mind
> Too unhappy to be kind.
> Undone with misery, all they can
> Is to hate their fellow-man;
> And till they drop they needs must still
> Look at you and wish you ill.
>
> (ASL 41:19–32)

We have seen the first half of this lyric in the previous chapter, the half dealing with nature's sympathy for the "son she bore." Here is the rest of it. And what we find here are possibly more echoes, echoes of "The New Mistress" (ASL 34). The eye that "measures" Terence is not "kind," as he had expected the sergeant's to be, he who would supply his needs: beer, breakfast, and clothing ("a ribbon for my cap" and "a uniform of red"). For this he would have to be "measured." The owners of the eyes that do the measuring "hate" their fellows and will continue to "wish you ill" until "they drop." "Drop" is precisely what soldiers do when they become "the dropping dead." Are all of these echoes and buried puns accidental? I do not think so. Housman was too much a linguistic crafts-man and too aware of the multiplicity of meanings in words, for *all* these puns and ambiguities to have been the mere result of chance. Let us give the poet credit for knowing what he was doing, and accept the possibility that Terence has been inducted into the army and shipped abroad.

Meanwhile, life continues its wonted course in Shropshire. Ned Lear, who had shared Terence's "fancy" for Fan, has found a new love, Nancy. The notebook records of this romance are even more fragmentary than usual. Haber reconstructed the incident, providing a description of the fragment and prose links between the lines (A. E. Housman, *Manuscript Poems*, 53). He conjectured that the missing upper portion of the page "contained the beginning of the unhappy romance of Nancy and Ned, whose story is continued on the surviving fragment. Whatever the pre-liminaries may have been, we may surmise 'How many hopes, how much desire / Brought these two souls to the mire.'" As for Nancy, let us turn to the poet. (Burnett, *Poems*, 177–78).

> Her father turned her from the door
> And when, like better folks before,
> She had not where to lay her head,
> Then her heart came back to Ned.

Haber continues, "She went at night in the rain to her lover's house, where Ned was sitting alone by a waning fire thinking of his sweetheart" (A. E. Housman, *Manuscript Poems*, 53). And the poem continues in Bur-nett, *Poems*, 177–78.

> Ned at home was sitting late
> Thinking, by the embered grate.
> All the house was long abed
> But staring in the fire sat Ned.
>
> The fire was out, the [?air was chill],
> When a foot came to the sill
> And a hand afraid to knock
> Fingered faintly at the lock.
>
> Long did those two sweethearts stand,
> In love, and never lift a hand.
> Long and speechless and apart
> Still breaking heart to breaking heart.
>
> The rain blew in, the door swung wide;
> Nancy only cried and cried.

So, to continue with Haber (A. E. Housman, *Manuscript Poems*, 53), "Nancy weeping stood before her lover, who embraced her and wept with her. As they consoled each other, 'In heaven the world-wide night' dropped its tears upon them." Clearly Nancy, unlike Fan with whom Terence walked in the fields, the lanes, and the meads, did not say, "Good-bye, young man, good-bye." She said "yes," healed his "ail" and, now that he is well, she has the symptoms of love-sickness herself (or perhaps in her case it is morning sickness) and lies down "forlorn."

The night might have "dropped its tears upon them," but at some point Ned does enter the army, and when we next see Nancy in Shropshire, she is "paired" with Tom. This, therefore, seems a likely place for Ned to have followed Terence and decamped to an army camp, before or after marrying her, thus leaving Nancy to her own devices—and the attentions of a new lover. Housman's girls are not the faithful sort.

Anthony Trollope's Carrie Brattle, like our Nancy, was turned away from her father's door as "a fallen woman" in *The Vicar of Bullhampton*. The situation is a staple of melodrama. The novels and the stage reflected Victorian reality, and "the father who said in melodrama to his unmarried daughter with child, 'Do not darken my doorstep,' was not a figure of fun [or imagination] but a viable figure. The daughter had run foul . . . and had to be made to suffer," especially in the middle class (Ronald Pearsall, *Worm in the Bud*, 160). and Terence and his friends, being yeomen, may be considered at the lowest level of the middle class.

Meanwhile, Terence has not found in the army a life of "skittles and beer" and, sent to fight in "strangers' lands," he has found himself—to his great shame—to be a coward, as he explains in both the canon and the notebooks.

> My dreams are of a field afar
>   And blood and smoke and shot.
> There in their graves my comrades are,
>   In my grave I am not.
>
> I too was taught the trade of man
>   And spelt my lesson plain;
> But they, when I forgot and ran,
>   Remembered and remain.

(MP 39)

> There are ten graves, and in the ten
>   The tale of dead is nine
> There in nine graves my comrades are
>   The empty grave is mine.

There nine shrewd lads are underground,
  And all are there but I
To keep my carcase safe and sound
  And leave my name to die.

The success of this (composite) poem "obviously depends on the fictional background of the speaker's cowardice, [and] on his complicated attitude of regret and envy for his dead comrades" (Leggett, *Poetic Art*, 53). Placing it in the cycle and identifying the speaker as Terence provide this "fictional background," which the poem needs, and also explains the "complicated attitude" expressed therein. Terence would very much regret deserting his friends and not being with them in death as he had been in life; he would feel extreme guilt about it. And he would envy them for being together while he himself was left alone. The tenth grave is not, in fact, empty, for in it lie all of Terence's ideals, dreams, and self-image, in short, his name.

He soon leaves the army. Whether Terence has been given a dishonourable discharge, completed his term, or deserted is unimportant. He is out of the army, and still alive. He returns to "the forsaken west," where we have already seen him defending the "bitter brew" of his poetry and playing for the dances where "Tom would pair with Nancy / And Dick step off with Fan," each lad turning "toward his fancy" (LP 41). They are not so young as they once were, but not so very much time has passed. They are only a little older, and not much wiser. I have placed this poem here rather than in the early section of the cycle because of its valedictory tone, and for another reason, which will appear shortly.

Terence is back home, but home is not the same. Many of his friends have already gone or will soon depart, and they will not return. That last dance was indeed "Fancy's Knell."

When I came last to Ludlow
  Amidst the moonlight pale,
Two friends kept step beside me,
  Two honest lads and hale.

Now Dick lies long in churchyard,
  And Ned lies long in jail,
And I come home to Ludlow
  Amidst the moonlight pale.

(ASL 58)

Dick's romance with Fan ended what seems a long time ago with his death (he now "lies long in churchyard"), and Ned has been sent to prison. I have filled in the gap by positing that when Tom paired with

Nancy a fight started between him and Ned,[7] and that Dick was badly injured in the melee and died, either immediately or a bit later, as a result of his injuries, for which Ned was taken, tried, and sentenced to a term of imprisonment. Terence's two closest friends are gone, and his "memory of the homeward walk with friends contrasts with the wayfarer's present loneliness" (Haber, "Spirit of the Perverse," 377). Ned has not long to live in jail before he too dies (or is executed) in Portland, mourned by the alone and now friendless Terence.

The Isle of Portland

> The star-filled seas are smooth to-night
>   From France to England strown;
> Black towers above the Portland light
>   The felon-quarried stone.
>
> On yonder island, not to rise,
>   Never to stir forth free,
> Far from his folk a dead lad lies
>   That once was friends with me.
>
> Lie you easy, dream you light,
>   And sleep you fast for aye;
> And luckier may you find the night
>   Than ever you found the day.

(ASL 59)

Browne thinks this "luckless lad" was executed: "The lines . . . explain that the criminal . . . probably having committed murder, . . . had been hanged" (*Elegy in Arcady*, 90). This seems to me to assume a great deal. I have been careful to note that my reconstruction of events is tentative and to indicate the textual basis for it. There is no support for either of these assumptions in the text, and again we have what I have called the carry-over effect, doubled—the idea of murder and that of hanging. The "dead lad" I have identified as Ned, a lad who "once was friends with me," "lies long in jail," and certainly dies before Terence does. I have suggested accidental homicide as his crime. We have had enough brawling to make this reasonable. But he may indeed have murdered Dick, or someone else, or have committed any other capital crime. Since he is one of Housman's "luckless lads," he may equally well have been sentenced to jail for homosexuality and died a natural death from the rigors of his confinement, or even committed suicide, as have been hanged. The text itself does not "explain" either the reason for the imprisonment or the cause of death.

Nevertheless, Ned is now dead, and so is Dick, dead a year, thinks Cleanth Brooks, who suggests that the next poem represents the first an-

niversary of his funeral ("Alfred Edward Housman"). Bayley suggests that
the speaker might, among other possibilities, be "a comrade or an anonymous lover" (" 'Night Is Freezing Fast' "). I believe the speaker is indeed
a comrade, and that comrade is Terence.

> The night is freezing fast,
>> To-morrow comes December;
>>> And winterfalls of old
> Are with me from the past;
>> And chiefly I remember
>>> How Dick would hate the cold.
>
> Fall, winter, fall; for he,
>> Prompt hand and headpiece clever,
>>> Has woven a winter robe,
> And made of earth and sea
>> His overcoat for ever,
>>> And wears the turning globe.
>
>   (LP 20)

Gosse sensed that this poem, too, was part of an untold story, that
"below this quiet surface there is a ceaseless mystification, an obvious
sense that the half is not told" ("Shropshire Lad," 25) Indeed, and now
it has been told. "The night is freezing fast" indeed, both quickly chilling
the churchyard, which is "freezing fast," and immobilizing Dick, "freezing" him "fast," fastening him in his coffin and making it fast in the
earth.

Critical interest has focused primarily on the second verse with its
metaphysical conceit. Housman was not impressed by this mode of
poetry, a mode in which the poets of the seventeenth century excelled.

There was a whole age of English in which the place of poetry was usurped by
something very different which possessed the proper and specific name of wit:
wit not in its modern sense, but as defined by Johnson, "a combination of
dissimilar images, or discovery of occult resemblances in things apparently unlike." Such discoveries are no more poetical than anagrams; such pleasure as
they give is purely intellectual. . . . Some of the writers . . . were, by accident,
considerable poets; and though their verse was generally inharmonious, and
apparently cut into lengths and tied into faggots by deaf mathematicians,
some little of their poetry was beautiful and even superb. But it was not by
this that they captivated and sought to captivate. Simile and metaphor . . .
were their great engrossing pre-occupation, and were prized the more in pro-
portion as they were further fetched. They did not mean these accessories to
be helpful, to make their sense clearer or their conceptions more vivid; they
hardly even meant them for ornament, or cared whether an image had any

independent power to please: their object was to startle by novelty and amuse by ingenuity . . . (NNP, 353).

Just as the Latin grammar fragment examined in the third chapter was in the Augustan style, this poem is in the metaphysical style, and again Housman has provided his own commentary on it. The lecture in which Housman voiced his opinion of the "School of Donne" was delivered in 1933 and F. R. Leavis, T. S. Eliot's strong supporter, was present—and outraged. Whether so intended or not, the lecture was perceived as in many ways a direct challenge to the Eliot school of criticism, which found ultimate poetic value in the metaphysical mode. This outrage apparently amused Housman, who wrote to his brother Laurence, "The leader of the doctrinaire teachers of youth is reported to say that it will take more than twelve years to undo the harm I have done in an hour" (L. Housman, A. E. H., 185; A. E. Housman, Letters, 335). Eliot himself, on the contrary, did not so take it and reviewed the lecture favorably (Review of NNP).

The critics have reacted to the verse in accordance with their own allegiance—or lack of allegiance—to Eliot's critical precepts. Bonamy Dobree, writing in The Spectator, was predictably pleased with it. In this poem, "with that touch of metaphysical wit he so much despised, Housman burst the bounds of his own convictions" and created an "organic gem," ("Complete Housman," 24) Housman had not uttered a blanket condemnation of all metaphysically witty poetry, considering some examples of it to be "superb" poetry, but he had certainly punctured the pretentiousness of much of it. This is his own version of a metaphysical conceit, and Priestley considered it an "audacious image." It should be no surprise that Cleanth Brooks also considered this "one of Housman's finest poems" in which "Dick, his friend observes with a kind of wry humor, has outwitted winter" by turning the entire world into an "overcoat," a "commonplace and matter-of-fact" word that is "triumphantly right . . . [Clever Dick] has finally outwitted the cold [he hated in a] jest . . . characteristic of the dead youth" (Brooks, "Alfred Edward Housman," 69). On the other hand, Kreuzer finds the image "grotesque" (Elements of Poetry, 220). It is, in fact, both "grotesque" and brilliant, depending on whether one dislikes metaphysical poetry or is enamoured of it. We have already seen Housman's own attitude, and we have also seen that he enjoyed writing parodies of period styles, so it is not outrageous to suggest that this was intended at least partially as a period parody. Indeed, Bayley hints at this. He says that in this poem we find the same kind of purely intellectual and intellectually frivolous pleasures that Housman considered were given by metaphysical conceits, and that here "he seems to have used and enjoyed that undercover frivolity" (" 'The Night Is Freezing Fast,' " 18).

That the image is parodic is also suggested by the intellectual overelaboration we find here. Housman used the same basic metaphor elsewhere in a manner as reminiscent of the simplicity of Wordsworth as here it is not: "Clasp your cloak of earth around you" (LP 29). Housman considered the "Lucy" lines in which Wordsworth used the image one of his "two very best and most characteristic," one of his most purely poetic, stanzas ("Review of *The Cambridge History of English Literature*, vol. 11, 317"). He admired Wordsworth's poetry as much as he denigrated that of the metaphysical school.

Terence, having seen his closest friends buried, continues with his own life; he drinks to forget—and remembers . . . "The thought comes cold" of Dick, wrapped in his overcoat of earth and snow, and of Ned, like Dick, sleeping "fast" (Burnett, *Poems*, 178–79).

> Often, drinking, warm with ale,
> Or laughing at an idle tale,
> Into my heart the thought comes cold
> How I forget my friends of old,
> Lads that before light was gone
> Put the cap of darkness on.
> What a clod of earth am I
> Forgetting fellows when they die!
> [   ] any trifle glads
> My heart, and you forgot, my lads.
>
> And come to think [   ]
> Poor fellows, I'm no worse than you;
> I keep you in mind no more
> But you forgot me long before.
>
> Long it lasted; now it ends,
> I'll say no more that we were friends.
>
> Who could think that knew us then,
> When they and I were living men,
> And saw what friends we used to seem,
> —Who could think it, who could dream?

But it does not end. In Housman's poetry, by definition, friendship does not end, and if a relationship does end, it was *ipso facto* not real friendship at all. There is a single verse and a collection of lines and abortive verses that may be fragments of a draft of another Terence Hearsay poem (notebook manuscripts A-234–5 in the Library of Congress). If so, the poem is so fragmentary that my comments on it are extremely tentative, but it does seem to carry on the story. Terence is roused from his sleep by a well-known voice calling his name. I have placed this poem after "Often, drinking, warm with ale," but the order of these two poems can be reversed without altering the sense of the narrative. The first— completed—verse of the fragment can be found in Burnett, *Poems*, 178.

> "Hist, Terence, hist! wake up: 'tis I."
> That was a voice I know.
> Up I got and out I looked
> And saw who stood below.

It is clear from the odd lines that the voice is that of someone "dead a year." Terence tells him that it is "Better to think your friend's unkind / Than know your love's untrue." Apparently something momentous has occurred, but Terence tells his ghostly visitant that "the news will keep," "there are worse things than sleep," and sends him away. The ghost, under protest, "in the moonless night / Went back to find his grave" (Notebook A234–35).

The speaker, "dead a year," could be either Dick or Ned. I have identified him as Ned because of Nancy, certainly once his sweetheart and possibly his wife, who paired off with Tom at the village dancing, which fits in nicely with "Better to think your friend's unkind [Tom] / Than know your love's untrue [Nancy]." If the ghost is Dick's, these lines have no referent. The news that it would be 'worse than' death to know, that "will keep," could it not be of Tom's marriage to Nancy, the final triangular twist?

Having burned his candle at both ends, Terence, still a relatively young man, can look ruefully back on his life. The dream of a life of brawling, fellowship, drinking, friendship, and seduction is over for him. He has given his heart away, not once but over and over, as have his mates, and the time has come when the wise man's words echo in his thought. He has not given it but sold it for "endless rue," and now it must be paid for. "The candles burn their sockets, / The blinds let through the day, / The young man feels his pockets / And wonders what's to pay" (LP 21). He need not wonder. " 'Tis paid with sighs aplenty / And sold for endless rue." Terence, Fred, Rose, Dick, Ned, Nancy, Fan, they have all reaped the "endless rue," and Tom's turn to pay "with sighs aplenty" will presumably come. Meanwhile, Terence continues to look back on his (mis)spent youth and the time he has spent at Ludlow fair.

> When first my way to fair I took
> Few pence in purse had I,
> And long I used to stand and look
> At things I could not buy.

> Now times are altered: if I care
>   To buy a thing I can;
> The pence are here and here's the fair,
>   But where's the lost young man?
>
> —To think that two and two are four
>   And neither five nor three
> The heart of man has long been sore
>   And long 'tis like to be.

(LP 35)

The first two verses are not original. Housman knew them well in the
original Greek form in the *Palatine Anthology*. As a boy he had received
the book *Sabrinae Corolla* in which the same verses are translated into "a
jerkier rhythm":

> I was poor, but I was twenty,
> Now at three score I have plenty;
> What a miserable lot!
>   Now that I have hoarded treasure,
>   I no more can taste of pleasure;
> When I could, I had it not.[8]

And still another translation, this by A. J. Butler (Caclamanes, "Source
of a Poem,"), is:

> Poor in my youth, rich in my age and frought
> With misery in both my lot.
> When wealth had brought enjoyment, I had naught:
> Now, having wealth, enjoy it not.

A comparison of all these versions demonstrates that by using the word
"lost" at the end of the translated verses, Housman has changed the poem
from literal to metaphorical. We are no longer talking about real money
and real wares but about spending time and energy to buy hearts, time,
and life, and especially the "time of one's life" in breaking hearts. This is
even clearer in the two draft versions of the second verse where the "lost
young man" is instead the (metaphorically) "dead young man" (Burnett,
Poems, 103 bottom).

> There's less I'd care to choose today,
>   But what I would I can;
> The pence are here, and nought's away
>   Except the dead young man

> And
> Today is altered: if I care
>   To buy a thing I can;
> The pence are here, and so's the fair,
>   But not the dead young man

It is clearer yet in what Haber thinks was intended to be the fourth verse, as it "completes the idea of the poem, which as printed lacks good sequence and falls short of finality" (A. E. Housman, *Manuscript Poems*, 73).

> Because out of the womb he brings
>   And carries to the grave
> A head full of the thoughts of things
>   He will not ever have.

(Burnett, Poems, 181)

The third verse has aroused critical interest because of the entry of arithmetic into poetry. One would have to be a madman to believe that two and two is not always four; Terence is not mad. It is the very certainty that a given problem will have a given result that saddens him. He knows what the equation of his life has been, what its inevitable product, and that he and his friends were "fools." The fires of his life that burned "long ago" are only ashes now, like those of the Roman "under Uricon," (ASL 31) and the friends between whom he once walked to Ludlow fair are dust beneath Ludlow's church tower, where once the bells invited all "good people" to "come and pray." They have at last come to church, but not to pray.

The First of May

> The orchards half the way
>   From home to Ludlow fair
> Flowered on the first of May
>   In Mays when I was there;
> And seen from stile or turning
>   The plume of smoke would show
> Where fires were burning
>   That went out long ago.
>
> The plum broke forth in green,
>   The pear stood high and snowed,
> My friends and I between
>   Would take the Ludlow road;
> Dressed to the nines and drinking
>   And light in heart and limb,
> And each chap thinking
>   The fair was held for him.

Between the trees in flower
    New friends at fairtime tread
The way where Ludlow tower
    Stands planted on the dead.
Our thoughts, a long while after,
    They think, our words they say;
Theirs now's the laughter,
    The fair, the first of May.

Ay, yonder lads are yet
    The fools that we were then;
For oh, the sons we get
    Are still the sons of men.
The sumless tale of sorrow
    Is all unrolled in vain:
May comes to-morrow
    And Ludlow fair again.

                                        (LP 34)

The sexual aura of nature, which we have seen in the last chapter, underlies the opening imagery of the orchards, the plum and the pear trees. Their association with the light-hearted, carefully dressed young men, already drinking the first of the "pints and quarts of Ludlow beer" that they will consume at the fair, sheds a carnal aura over the scene. That beer so happily downed, that symbol of the fair, will be metamorphosed into Terence's poetic "bitter brew," the "sumless tale of sorrow" created "in vain." To young men, those of the past like Fred, Dick, Tom, and Ned, and those of the present alike, it is only "stupid stuff" (ASL 62). They are too vain to profit by the old story no matter how often it is retold to them. It is not only a story of foolishness, it is a count or tally of sorrows, and the sorrows "unrolled" in it are Terence's. His friends dead, his own sorry tale weighing on him, he has only the prospect of death for comfort. And once again his creator speaks through his mouth.

       Clunton and Clunbury,
       Clungunford and Clun,
       Are the quietest places
       Under the sun.

       In valleys of springs of rivers,
           By Ony and Teme and Clun,
       The country for easy livers,
           The quietest under the sun,

We still had sorrows to lighten,
    One could not always be glad,
And lads knew trouble at Knighton
    When I was a Knighton lad.

By bridges that Thames runs under,
    In London, the town built ill,
'Tis sure small matter for wonder
    If sorrow is with one still.

And if as a lad grows older
    The troubles he bears are more,
He carries his griefs on a shoulder
    That handselled them long before.

Where shall one halt to deliver
    This luggage I'd lief set down?
Not Thames, not Teme is the river,
    Nor London nor Knighton the town.

'Tis a long way further than Knighton,
    A quieter place than Clun,
Where doomsday may thunder and lighten
    And little 'twill matter to one.

(ASL 50)

This poem is generally read as an expression of "the general world-weariness of youth" (Brashear, "Trouble with Housman," 84). There seems to me nothing that smacks of youth about the poem. Rather it evokes the weariness of age, not necessarily physical years but years replete with experience, too replete. The persona is tired, tired of drinking and brawling and seduction, tired of life, tired of walking alone to Ludlow fair from Knighton, and most of all, tired of Ludlow fair itself and the innumerable things for which it stands, the "sumless tale of sorrow." The river where he expects to set down his burden is indeed "not Thames, not Teme;" it is called Lethe or Styx. And the city to residence in which he looks forward is "Nor London nor Knighton" but Ludlow, not the fairgrounds but where "Ludlow tower / Stands planted on the dead" dust of his comrades. He confidently expects that "doomsday" will not matter to "one." Whom? If himself, it will "lighten" him of the "luggage I'd lief set down" (the full ramifications of the pun have already been considered). It may not be him, but his beloved to whom his death will not matter. In either case, he is wrong.

He—or rather his ghost—is conducted to a city that is indeed not London nor Knighton. Nor is it the graveyard of Ludlow church (where, parenthetically, Housman's own ashes are buried). Terence finds himself on that broad, broad road that is proverbially paved with good intentions, but this is not the end of his story.

Hell Gate

Onward led the road again
Through the sad uncoloured plain
Under twilight brooding dim,
And along the utmost rim
Wall and rampart risen to sight
Cast a shadow not of night,
And beyond them seemed to glow
Bonfires lighted long ago.
And my dark conductor broke
Silence at my side and spoke,
Saying, "You conjecture well:
Yonder is the gate of hell."

Ill as yet the eye could see
The eternal masonry,
But beneath it on the dark
To and fro there stirred a spark.
And again the sombre guide
Knew my question, and replied:
"At hell gate the damned in turn
Pace for sentinel and burn."

Dully at the leaden sky
Staring, and with idle eye
Measuring the listless plain,
I began to think again.
Many things I thought of then,
Battle, and the loves of men,
Cities entered, oceans crossed,
Knowledge gained and virtue lost,
Cureless folly done and said,
And the lovely way that led
To the slimepit and the mire
And the everlasting fire.
And against a smoulder dun
And a dawn without a sun
Did the nearing bastion loom,
And across the gate of gloom
Still one saw the sentry go,
Trim and burning, to and fro,
One for women to admire
In his finery of fire.

Something, as I watched him pace,
Minded me of time and place,
Soldiers of another corps
And a sentry known before.
    Ever darker hell on high
Reared its strength upon the sky,
And our footfall on the track
Fetched the daunting echo back.
But the soldier pacing still
The insuperable sill,
Nursing his tormented pride,
Turned his head to neither side,
Sunk into himself apart
And the hell-fire of his heart.
But against our entering in
From the drawbridge Death and Sin
Rose to render key and sword
To their father and their lord.
And the portress foul to see
Lifted up her eyes on me
Smiling, and I made reply:
"Met again, my lass,' said I.
Then the sentry turned his head.
Looked, and knew me, and was Ned.
    Once he looked, and halted straight,
Set his back against the gate,
Caught his musket to his chin,
While the hive of hell within
Sent abroad a seething hum
As of towns whose king is come
Leading conquest home from far
And the captives of his war,
And the car of triumph waits,
And they open wide the gates.
But across the entry barred
Straddled the revolted guard,
Weaponed and accoutred well
From the arsenals of hell;
And beside him, sick and white,
Sin to left and Death to right
Turned a countenance of fear
On the flaming mutineer.
Over us the darkness bowed,
And the anger in the cloud
Clenched the lightning for the stroke;
But the traitor musket spoke.
    And the hollowness of hell
Sounded as its master fell,

And the mourning echo rolled
Ruin through his kingdom old.
Tyranny and terror flown
Left a pair of friends alone,
And beneath the nether sky
All that stirred was he and I.
    Silent, nothing found to say,
We began the backward way;
And the ebbing lustre died
From the soldier at my side,
As in all his spruce attire
Failed the everlasting fire.
Midmost of the homeward track
Once we listened and looked back;
But the city, dusk and mute,
Slept, and there was no pursuit.

(LP 31)

This, Housman's longest and most complex poem, can be read simply as a story of "friendship . . . triumphant at the gate of hell."[9] Gosse saw it as "a dream of punishment and eternal pain, mitigated only by the enduring love of those for whom error and disgrace veil not a whit the inner beauty of a soul whose sins are misfortunes and whose shame is accidental" ("Shropshire Lad," 26) Charles Williams, himself a poet and author, waxed rhapsodic over Housman's treatment of the theme of "the love between friends": "Recognizing his friend, the sentinel straddles across the way lest he should enter. . . . It is the strangest and one of the finest of Mr. Housman's poems. . . . Many things have been said at hell gate since Dante and Milton passed there, but few . . . so satisfying as that of this newcomer; to Sin's smile ' "Met again, my lass," said I.' It is as great in its way as Farinata in his burning tomb (*Poetry at Present*, 36)."

My only caveat is that this is the persona's address to "Death" and not to "Sin." Housman's "Death and Sin" render up the "key and sword" respectively, which means that in this poem, unlike Milton's, Death is the (female) portress with the key and Sin is the (male) guard who holds the sword. Housman was well aware of the gender that Milton assigned to "Sin."[10] In his introduction to Manilius, book 1, he describes the probable reaction of a certain textual critic to the enormities of one of his disciples as being "something like Sin when she gave birth to Death." His gender reversal was not the result of ignorance or carelessness but of intention. I will return to this point.

The fullest analysis of this aspect of Housman's poetry is that of Nesca Robb, who discusses, at great length, the theme of friendship as "the love that has given itself so completely that it can endure all" freeing the friends "from the oppression of evil." While romantic (i.e., heterosexual) love is essentially selfish, making demands, taking, and seeking its own satisfaction and happiness, friendship is essentially unselfish, a giving of oneself, asking nothing for itself in return, and "willing to take upon itself the sufferings of the beloved" (*Four in Exile*, 47–49 53). One sometimes thinks that Robb has confused the words "friend" and "saviour," and one sometimes wonders if she knew in 1948 what was only made public in 1967 . . . but no, her choice of terminology, which has turned out to be so literal, was clearly intended to be metaphorical. When she writes about Housman's celebration of friendship and his comparison of it to "romantic" love, not to the advantage of the latter, she has, albeit with unnecessary prolixity, articulated the basic motif of the Shropshire cycle. She may have thought that she was writing about Housman's writing about friendship in the ordinary sense of the word, but we remember what Oscar Wilde said in *De Profundis* and know that "friends" has another meaning also.

Putting this aside for the moment, on one level all these commentators are correct. The poem is certainly about "sin and hell, and hell's master defied and shot by a mutinous subject for the sake of his friend, the pair then making their escape together" (Bayley, *Housman's Poems*, 151). But it is about something more, and this too was sensed. Gosse speaks of "the shadowy passion" that passes and repasses "like the flaming sentinel," and he says of Housman's poetry as a whole: "Nothing is told right out; the emotion is veiled and discreet; we are left to conjecture what is the exact nature of it" ("Shropshire Lad," 26, 24) Watson, too, noted the "romantic symbolism," which "could not easily be deciphered" (*Divided Life*, 212–13). Yet this "symbolism" is clear enough. Haber put it simply: the poem "commemorates a man's devotion to a man" ("Downward Eye," 314 n. 9). This is drawing close but is not yet at the center of the target. One must add quotation marks around "friend" to score a bull's-eye.

"Hell Gate" is the opposite of "Heaven's Gate," and the poem is a brief anti-*Paradise Lost*. Housman here has done "more than Milton can" (ASL, 62) to justify, not God's ways to man but some men's ways with men, the ways of certain men, his "unlucky lads," with each other. Robert K. Martin has explicated this aspect of the poem with great tact and sensitivity. The expulsion from Eden "becomes the escape from Hell, the revolt against God becomes the revolt against Satan, and the original couple, Adam and Eve, are radically recast as a "pair of 'friends'." The poem is . . . [a] vision of human rebellion against an unjust world . . . the attempt by God and man to impose 'foreign laws' to make men 'dance as they desire,'" ("Two Strategies," 17) The poem's role as a trope of homosexual revolt is seen not only in the final emblem of the two "friends" but in the repetition of the word "plain," recalling Sodom and Gomorrah, the (reputedly homosexual) Cities of the Plain. In this poem,

Housman "imagines that love may conquer death, that man need not accept the fear of damnation, . . . [his] vision of a triumphant humanity, joined by what Whitman would have called 'manly love' " (ibid., 17). Or, as Graves calls it, "a moving fantasy about the birth of a world in which homosexuality is not punished by 'hell' or 'pursuit' " (*A. E. Housman*, 226).

Indeed, here we find "tyranny and terror flown," the "tyranny and terror" of society that "must still / Wrest their neighbor to their will, / And make me dance as they desire / With jail and gallows and hell-fire" (LP 12). No wonder it was W. H. Auden's favorite of Housman's poems ("Worcestershire Lad"). Bayley calls this poem Housman's "slightly amused day-dream" transforming "into wish-fulfillment the grim tale" of Theseus and Pitithous's attemp to abduct (or free?) Persephone from Hades, the tale underlying the end of "Diffugere Neves" ("Housman and Larkin," 156).

All this is very true, but what has it left out? It has ignored all the past history of Terence and Ned and all the indications of that history that I have used to construct the "plot" of the cycle. The "bonfires lighted long ago" are the same fires "that went out long ago" in "The First of May" (LP 34) along the road to Ludlow fair. Is this not then the same road? If so, Ludlow (Church) tower is the tower of the city of Satan, which implies that it is this world that is hell. The road to Ludlow was the road to the girls: "The lads in their hundreds to Ludlow come in for the fair, / . . . The lads for the girls and the lads for the liquor are there" (ASL 23), and "the bonfires lighted long ago," which also "went out long ago," can be read as the fires of lust that rage in the bones of youth and dwindle to ash with the onset of age. They mark the "gate of hell" in the Elizabethan sense of "female genitalia." The "damned who burn" in the sexual sense keep watch upon the gate, the fire that consumes them is jealousy as well as lust. And the burning sentinel is, after all, our old friend Ned who fought Terence for possession of Fan and, I have inferred, killed Dick in fighting with Tom over his attentions to Nancy.

Terence, recalling the steps on the road that has led him to hell, recounts them: battle, the loves of men, cities entered, oceans crossed, knowledge gained, virtue lost, folly done and said, and the way that led "to the slime pit and the mire." It is this history that has led me in reconstructing the "plot." Folly done and said takes us back to the attempted seduction among the "goldcup flowers" and the resulting impulse to enlist in the army. Battle, cities entered, oceans crossed, all imply this stint in the army. The loves of men, until now, has meant friendship in the usual sense and has been a prime factor in Terence's life. It can have another meaning as well. The way that led to the mire is the road to and from Ludlow where, having downed those "pints and quarts of Ludlow beer," "down in lovely muck I've lain." And the knowledge gained, the virtue lost, return us to the anti-Miltonic theme that suggests that the knowledge won is the fruit of the Tree, and Housman's tree is "the tree of man." The knowledge gained from the "tree of man" is not of sexuality in general but specifically the homosexual variety. This knowledge gained is knowledge of men in the biblical sense, the fruit of the tree of man, and lost virtue is its price, lost virtue but not "sighs aplenty" or "endless rue" (ASL 13).

Terence's first glimpse of the sentinel "Minded me of time and place, / Soldiers of another corps / And a sentry known before." This is why I have included in the scenario not only Terence's own stint in the military, which linked with "The New Mistress," as explained above, but Ned's having served with him. Ned is "one for women to admire," and implicitly one who has always seemed to respond to them, and we remember the fight between him and Terence over Fan and the story of his romance with Nancy. He is a sentry "known before," and is the word "known" here used in the modern or the biblical sense? At the point where Ned appears on the battlements, it seems that only the first possibility is intended, but then one begins to wonder. He is "nursing his tormented pride" and his heart is filled with the fires of hell. Is this hellfire that consumes him lust—or pride? Has he ever differentiated between them? Or have both he and Terence confused the desire for male admiration with both the means of attaining it, by beating the pants (metaphorically) off each other, and the ostensible object of the exhibition, the conquest of the girls? The intense bond between the rivals could have deeper roots than appear on the surface. This would explain why Ned's pride is "tormented." It has been false pride from the first, false in its intent, false in its object, false in its meaning.

The portress of the door, returning to the Shakespearean meaning of "hell's gate," is Death (we recall that "to die" was an Elizabethan expression meaning "to complete an act of (hetero)sexual intercourse," and Sin stands with her. Housman, knowing perfectly well that in Milton Sin is the mother of Death, quite deliberately reversed the genders of these two beings. Sin holds a (phallic) sword, and is male. Death holds the keys and is female, the truth beneath the masks of Rose, Nancy, and Fan. And she is foul.

Terence recognizes her without difficulty. He greets her, and it is the sound of his voice that rouses Ned from his self-absorption ("sunk into himself apart"), makes him turn around to look, "and knew me, and was Ned." It seems that Ned is only fully himself in his recognition of Terence and of the links that bind them to each other. On recognizing Terence, Ned raises his musket, the gift of hell itself, and turns it, not on the appalled (female) Death who stands as portress at the door, but on the (male) father of both Death and Sin, Satan himself, "their father and their lord." And he fires it. One need not be an assiduous hunter of Freudian symbolism to decipher this particular piece of symbolism. Sexuality is the gift of hell, and the function of the female portress, Death, is to keep men inside her precincts (the grave) from breaking out, as well as to admit new inmates. Hell is both a grave and a prison, a place of unfulfilled desire. To fire one's weapon at Satan is to defy the female in the deepest sense, and the revolt against her function frees the man she has held captive as well as the newcomer. The fall of the sexual bastion of the female is accompanied by a "mourning echo" for hell, a "morning" echo for the pair of friends who are left alone (in more than one sense). Once Terence walked to Ludlow fair "between" his pals. Now he has only one mate, and it is enough. The "everlasting fire" fades from Ned's uniform. There is no longer anything to feed it. There is nothing to arouse lust; love has replaced it. There is nothing to arouse jealousy; the friends have achieved a state of silent communion that precludes it. Two separate "I"s have become a single united "we." With the fading of the "everlasting flame" from Ned's uniform, fade the last traces of Rose, Nancy, and Fan. The girls have been rendered totally irrelevant. The world is no longer hell because two men have committed themselves to each other. Ned may have been "one for women to admire," but it is Terence who gets him in the end. As the thunder and lightning of doomsday, anticipated in the prior poem, fade into silence, Hell vanishes from their world.

Haber implicitly anticipated this reading when he wrote that the reader senses

> that the poem is in some way incomplete, that some important antecedents are missing. This feeling arises in the very first line, where we are told of a road that led onward again. The word again sets up an inquiry which holds . . . throughout the reading of the poem and recurs as often as we think of the word. Where had the road begun? Where had they set foot on it? How had they met? (*A. E. Housman*, 167–68)

I trust that I have supplied answers to these questions. Haber also implicitly supports my reading of the significance of Terence and Ned as masks for Housman and Moses Jackson, stating that "Ned, who was also the silent comrade in "The West' [already identified by Haber as Moses Jackson] . . . risks all for his friend, kills the Dark Conductor, and saves them both. This act of rescue is such as would become the idealized Moses Jackson, here and elsewhere in Housman's poetry his partner." (ibid.).

In the passage from *Seven Pillars of Wisdom* quoted in a review beside which Housman wrote "This is me," T. E. Lawrence says, "intimacy seemed shameful unless the other could make the perfect reply, in the same language, after the same method, for the same reason" (L. Housman "*De Amicitia*," 39). Here there is that perfect reply, the union of silent sympathy and instinctive understanding so complete that it does not need words.

And so ends the Shropshire cycle, only parts of which were ever published with either the author's sanction or that of his brother. A parody of Victorian mores and gender stereotypes? Yes, of course it is that, set out as I have here. But it is also something more, and that something more is the expression of what lay behind Housman's mask.

We ended the last chapter with "Diffugere Nives" (MP 5). This is Housman's answer to Horace's "Theseus leaves Pirithous in the chain / The love of comrades cannot take away." In "Hell Gate," "the love of comrades can take away the chain, at least in the world of poetry and imagination" (Bayley, *Housman's Poems*, 7). This is not a nightmare but a vision.

7

On Hero's Heart Leander Lies

THE PRECEDING CHAPTER DEALT WITH HOUSMAN'S PARODY OF THE normative relationship between the sexes. Even in this parodic setting, however, there are individual verses of beauty and rare delicacy that, standing alone, present young love in its first flowering as sweetly as anyone could wish.

> The youth toward his fancy
>   Would turn his brow of tan,
> And Tom would pair with Nancy
>   And Dick step off with Fan;
> The girl would lift her glances
>   To his, and both be mute:
> Well went the dances
>   At evening to the flute.
>
> (LP 41, verse 3)

If we did not already know Tom, Nancy, Dick, and Fan, and something of their previous history, this rural idyll would present a perfect portrait of the freshness, the shyness, and the budding wonder of first love. The girl's eyes seeking her young man's face and their mutual silence perfectly evoke the breathless tenderness of the moment. Here, Housman "has captured . . . the shyness and silence of love as yet but half-acknowledged" (Robb, *Four in Exile*, 23). The cynicism that is the reverse side of this idyllic coin has also been seen in operation within the cycle, Terence having sufficient sensitivity to understand the consequences of a successful seduction for the ruined girl, although not enough to change his plans one whit.

Housman had a reputation for being a misogynist, a reputation that I suspect he carefully cultivated, in part perhaps to protect himself from doting mamas of eligible daughters. In his poetry outside the cycle there is often a sensitivity toward women that belies this reputation as completely as the actual facts of his personal life and friendships do. As in the case of Whitman, the fact that women are not seen as sexual objects frees the poet to see women as human beings. In Whitman, we find "a strong sense of compassion for . . . suffering women" (Martin, *Homosexual Tradition*, 8). The tenderness with which Housman treats women in some of his poetry speaks for itself. When Orwell remarks that in Housman's "poems the woman's point of view is not considered, she is merely the nymph, the siren, the treacherous half-human creature who leads you a little distance and then gives you the slip," ("Inside the Whale," 23) we learn a good deal more about Orwell than about Housman's poetry. Housman treats the relationship between the sexes from several points of view, not excluding the girl's. Indeed, as has been noted by Sylvia Bruce, "in Housman the seducer, attempted or actual, is always the male, often of his best friend's girl" (*Essays*, 45).

> Delight it is in youth and May
>   To see the morn arise,
> And more delight, or so they say,
>   To read in lovers' eyes.
> Oh maiden, let your distaff be,
> And pace the flowery meads with me,
>   And I will tell you lies.
>
> 'Tis blithe to see the sunshine fail,
>   And hear the land grow still
> And listen till the nightingale
>   Is heard beneath the hill.
> Oh follow me where she is flown
> Into the leafy woods alone,
>   And I will work you ill.

(MP 18)

We have seen this same theme in a lighter mood in the last chapter ("Oh, see how thick the goldcup flowers"). Here Housman makes explicit what was implicit in that poem. The young man's courtship, idyllic as its setting may be, is based on lies, and the "sweet nothings" he whispers in the girl's ear mean nothing and are worth nothing. Alas for her if she mistakes them for true gold. The girl who succumbs to the boy's invitation to go with her wooer alone into the "leafy woods" following the nightingale can expect the same fate as hers. The nightingale is Philomela, Procne's sister, raped and then abandoned by her lover, her brother-in-law, who cut out her tongue so that she could not tell her story. Whoever follows the nightingale can expect to share her unhappy fate. Here, "the best a girl can do is to listen to a boy's lies and follow him into the leafy wood; the best the boy can do is not work her ill. . . . [This] is not so far from the actual conditions under which love is made in youth" (Bishop, "Poetry," 144). The swain knows well enough what he wants, and he is perfectly willing to "tell you lies" if thus he can get it, even if his getting it will "work you ill." The idea that this is "the best a girl can do" could only have occurred to a man. Housman can look at the event from the girl's point of view and suggest something better: she need not agree. She can instead say, "Goodbye, young man, goodbye." If she does not, if she accepts his false coin as true currency, she is sure to have a bitter awakening. As Millard notes, "the menacing effect is more that of a murderer than a seducer" ("A. E. Housman," 94).[1]

> The sloe was lost in flower,
>   The April elm was dim;
> This was the lover's hour,
>   The hour for lies and him.
> If thorns are all the bower,
>   If north winds freeze the fir,
> Why, 'tis another's hour,
>   The hour for truth and her.

(LP 22)

Watts comments that "there have been three-volume novels that have said no more in four hundred thousand words than this poem says in forty," ("Poetry," 132) some of which, like *Adam Bede*, are among the great novels of English literature. Such novels focused on the woman's point of view, excepting Hardy's *Tess of the d'Urbervilles*, tend to be written by women. Housman, like Hardy, is quite capable of seeing the consequences to the girl of the seduction so satisfactorily concluded from the man's point of view, and of making the situation crystal clear without needing to be explicit. This is one of those "bolder poems" in which "the poet triumphs over the restrictions of Victorian decorum" (Brooks, "Whole of Housman," 270). It is the hour not only for "lies and him" but for "lies with him" as well.

The vocabulary of buying and selling hearts in the poetry already discussed extends to the buying of bodies with the coin of declared, but insincere, love, so I have spoken in terms of false coin and true coin, nor am I the only one to use this metaphor. We are not in the cycle itself, but

"the penalty for love's consummation . . . is still paid with sighs . . . , with shame, remorse, and mutual accusation. Whether one pays or both, the heavy toll is exacted in the end. . . . [This] is a tragedy condensed in eight lines. . . . The hour for happiness is the man's and his only. With the help of nature, . . . the arch-seducer, he buys his pleasure of the woman with lies. . . . The hour for disillusionment belongs to the woman. The truth of love is disillusionment. The gesture in the opening of the . . . [penultimate] line is perfect: What else could follow the hour of lies? (Haber, "Downward Eye," 311).

For Housman, however, this may not be the end of the story. In the notebooks there is an odd quatrain which Haber thinks is suggestive of "Her strong enchantments failing" (A. E. Housman, *Manuscript Poems*, 38). I would suggest that it would better serve as a third verse for this poem, which it matches in meter and rhyme scheme as well as in its import (Burnett, *Poems*, 172). Payment for such an act of betrayal may be long delayed, but it will come.

> The old deceived diviner
> Awakes in hell to find
> The web of doom spun finer
> Than any mortal mind;

Sometimes the seducee and the successful seducer may be mutually disillusioned.

> In the morning, in the morning,
> In the happy field of hay,
> Oh they looked at one another
> By the light of day.
>
> In the blue and silver morning
> On the haystack as they lay,
> Oh they looked at one another
> And they looked away.

(LP 23)

"*Both* lovers" in this poem "feel the whip of shame. . . . The hour for truth is the hour of disillusionment; and now, after their long night's embrace, the lovers cannot bear to read their fault in each other's eyes" (Haber, "Downward Eye," 312. The emphasis is his). Thus far, there is no disagreement. This ostensibly simple poem, however, provoked an interesting exchange of views in the pages of *College English* between Ryley and Perrine. Ryley opened the discussion by noting that the brief poem "seemed so luminous as to need no explication whatever" but he found that he was wrong. There was an ambiguity centering on the pronoun, which might have referred to animals or people, and if people to two men, two women, a man and a woman, a man and a boy, or any other combination. "In the absence of cars and motels, an unmarried couple might spend the night together in a hayfield and . . . because of the prevailing disapproval of sex outside of marriage, they might well feel shame when their eyes met in the morning." But even if the poem is "probably about a heterosexual couple, . . . the last line is infinitely ambiguous." The couple is probably heterosexual, Ryley concludes, because Housman did not publish his poems about the other sort of love during his lifetime ("Hermeneutics in the Classroom," 46).

Perrine responded by noting that

> Housman's lovers never suffer from feelings of guilt or bad conscience. The proprieties mean little to them. Their love leads to suffering because it is unrequited. Or it ends in disillusion. Falling in love is followed by falling out of love. Disillusion . . . is the issue in this poem. Housman puts extraordinarily heavy emphasis on the fact that the aversion takes place when the lovers see each other "By the light of day." . . . A feeling of guilt over having violated accepted morality would not have to wait till morning. . . . It would not require the lovers to see one another. Disillusionment, however, comes naturally with restored sight. The lovers look at one another by morning light and think, "My God! Is that what I made love to last night!" ("Housman's Lovers," 708).

Ryley responded to Perrine's response by pointing out that the Latin *aversor* ("look away") "can imply either shame or disgust," although the English word "tends to minimize the idea of repugnance." Perrine's explication, in place of their looking away, requires at the least "a grimace or a raspberry" ("Response to Laurence Perrine," 708).

In this exchange, the idea that the couple might *not* be heterosexual sank out of sight and never rose again. However, in those poems that are explicitly heterosexual the text makes this quite clear. There may be personal names (Nancy and Fan in "Fancy's Knell,", Rose in "This time of year a twelvemonth past," or Hero in "Tarry delight," below). There may be feminine nouns such as "maiden" ("Delight it is" and "When the lad for longing sighs"), "lass" ("Oh see how thick the goldcup flowers" and "Along the field as we came by"), "girl" ("Is my team ploughing"), or "bride" ("The True Lover," ASL 53, discussed below). Or there may be feminine pronouns such as "her" ("The sloe was lost in flower" and "The New Mistress"). When the text does not make the gender clear, when the words are neuter, a homosexual relationship is usually involved, as we shall see in the next chapter.

That the same may possibly be true here is indicated by the fact that in the notebook drafts, "they" in both the third and sixth line is "faintly pencilled over" by "we." Haber asks, "The partners in this tumbling—are they *they* or *we*?" ("Downward Eye," 312. The emphases are his). Unlike so much, this alteration from "we" to "they" is still clearly visible in the manuscript. Nor need this be a "tumbling." It may be no more than a snatched kiss, one responded to—to his great astonishment and intense shame—by the other half of the "we."

Ryley concluded that the couple was heterosexual because of Housman's not having published his more obviously homosexual poems in his own lifetime. However, few of his homosexual poems are blatantly so. The tone of this one is far more like them than it is like the tone of the explicitly heterosexual lyrics that underline the gender difference of the lovers and almost invariably have at least a faint hint of mockery of one or both in the tone. In fact the tone here, as well as the content, but not the setting, are paralleled by Cavafy, whose lovers are certainly homosexual, in "Their Beginning."

> Their illicit pleasure has been fulfilled.
> They get up and dress quickly, without a word.
> They come out of the house separately, furtively;
> and as they move off down the street a bit unsettled
> it seems they sense that something about them betrays
> what kind of bed they've just been lying on.
>
> (*Collected Poems*, 8)

I would characterize Housman's pronoun in this poem as hovering ambiguity, with a vengeance.

We have seen many examples of the male lover false to his girl, and vice versa. However, this desertion of the girl may not be caused by disloyalty to her but rather by loyalty to something greater. We all know Lovelace's "To Lucasta, Going to the Wars" ("I could not love thee (Deare) so much, / Lov'd I not Honour more").[2] Housman wrote on the same theme, where the persona "rises and goes, though it is not God or country that inspires him," says Firkins ("Living Verse," in Gardner, *Critical Heritage*, 173), seemingly rather at a loss to understand what does inspire him. Honor, as one might expect, for Housman means loyalty to one's comrades, which takes precedence over all other loyalties.

The Deserter

> "What sound awakened me, I wonder,
>   For now 'tis dumb."
> "Wheels on the road, most like, or thunder:
>   Lie down: 'twas not the drum."
>
> Toil at sea and two in haven
>   And trouble far:
> Fly, crow, away, and follow, raven,
>   And all that croaks for war.

"Hark, I heard the bugle crying,
        And where am I?
My friends are up and dressed and dying,
        And I will dress and die."

"Oh love is rare and trouble plenty
        And carrion cheap,
And daylight dear at four-and-twenty:
        Lie down again and sleep."

"Reach me my belt and leave your prattle:
        Your hour is gone;
But my day is the day of battle,
        And that comes dawning on.

"They mow the field of man in season:
        Farewell, my fair,
And, call it truth or call it treason,
        Farewell the vows that were."

"Ay, false heart, forsake me lightly:
        'Tis like the brave.
They find no bed to joy in rightly
        Before they find the grave.

"Their love is for their own undoing,
        And east and west
They scour about the world a-wooing
        The bullet to their breast.

"Sail away the ocean over,
        Oh sail away,
And lie there with your leaden lover
        For ever and a day."

                                        (LP 13)

There are many ramifications to the puns that converge in the lines "My friends are up and dressed and dying / And I will dress and die." There is, of course, the obvious meaning of donning clothing, so that one is "dressed to kill" after the ranks are "dressed" (Bayley, *Housman's Poems*, 43). One also "dresses meat" after it is killed, when the "carrion" may be "cheap," unlike life at "four-and-twenty" when the "daylight" is "dear" (and is four-and-twenty the age of the persona or the price of daylight?). The sacrificial offering is also "dressed," sometimes in garlands as in Keats' "Ode on a Grecian Urn" and sometimes with seasonings. Removing one's clothing, getting undressed, is "undoing" one's clothing, so "their love is for their own undoing" continues the macabre pun. Men "scour about the world a-wooing [having 'undone' their clothing] / The bullet to their breast." As we shall see, bullets can be a metaphor for semen, so what is being wooed may be a male lover rather than a female mistress. Instead of the girl for whose "undoing" the man's clothing is most often "undone," the "undone" man "will lie" with his "leaden lover" to whom he cannot "lie." He cannot "undo" his union with this "lover," even if the "lover" is unresponsive ("leaden"), although he will "lie" alone in death, sharing his new bed, the grave, with no one. At the beginning of the poem, there are "two in haven," and who are they but the two lovers themselves in the "heaven/haven" of their shared bed, the bed he deserts for the bed of the grave where he will indeed "lie down again and sleep."

"Your hour is gone," the persona tells his girl, "but my day is the day of battle." It is the "hour for truth and her" following hard on "the lover's hour, / The hour for lies and him" in which he lay with her. If "truth" (or troth) to his friends who "are up and dressed and dying" is "treason" to her, so be it. Better to be true to them and a traitor to her than the reverse. We are back to "Lucasta," which also dealt with a "Deserter." The two personae would have understood each other perfectly. Nor is this merely a literary convention. Separation of the sexes was emphasized in the nineteenth century throughout a boy's schooldays. "Manliness came to be identified with exclusion of the female as soft and sentimental" (Adams, *Great Adventure*, 12). A boy early learned that "to be masculine was to be unemotional, in control of one's passions;" for the product of the Victorian educational system, "playing the man" meant not only the rejection and suppression of female traits in his own character. It also meant rejecting the company of women in favor of "an all-male world of brawn and physical power," a world in which lay the potential for "heroism and manliness." Such a code, emphasizing "dedicated self-sacrifice and manliness, pointed to a career in the military"(ibid., 24–25), and mandated that "women must be left behind in favor of the great pursuit of male competition. Being a man" meant "ultimately facing the challenge of death" (ibid., 87). There was more than one couple who could have stood as models for the personae in "The Deserter."

Housman's poetry as a whole is notorious for its coupling of love and death, and this too we have seen, for example in "Bredon Hill" (ASL 21) and "Along the field as we came by" (ASL 26). If there is any parody in these poems regarded as independent lyrics, it is so muted as to be all but invisible. The parodic element derives from the part that I have assigned them in the cycle as a whole.

A great deal has been said in the previous chapter about the inherent instability of heterosexual attachments, but in some poems such a passion can transcend even death. One aspect of "Is my team ploughing" (ASL

27) is the pathetic eagerness of the ghost to know if his girl has remained true to him, since he is clearly still concerned with her, although the ultimate (and thus most important) question concerns the well-being of his friend. However, just as the characters in the cycle are generally faithless, there are others who are faithful to the grave—and beyond, although Housman, to be sure, never treats this theme as seriously as does Browning in "Prospice." In the following poem, there is an element of burlesque, totally foreign to Browning, and an air of overwrought fidelity. Not all the ghosts in Housman's poetry are young men visiting their still-living friends. Some of them are lovers, like those in the Scottish border ballads, whose visits are, to say the least, unsettling.

The True Lover

The lad came to the door at night,
    When lovers crown their vows,
And whistled soft and out of sight
    In shadow of the boughs.

"I shall not vex you with my face
    Henceforth, my love, for aye;
So take me in your arms a space
    Before the east is grey.

"When I from hence away am passed
    I shall not find a bride,
And you shall be the first and last
    I ever lay beside."

She heard and went and knew not why;
    Her heart on his she laid;
Light was the air beneath the sky
    But dark under the shade.

"Oh do you breathe, lad, that your breast
    Seems not to rise and fall,
And here upon my bosom prest
    There beats no heart at all?"

"Oh loud, my girl, it once would knock,
    You should have felt it then;
But since for you I stopped the clock
    It never goes again."

> "Oh lad, what is it, lad, that drips
>   Wet from your neck on mine?
> What is it falling on my lips,
>   My lad, that tastes of brine?"
>
> "Oh like enough 'tis blood, my dear,
>   For when the knife has slit
> The throat across from ear to ear
>   'Twill bleed because of it."
>
> Under the moon the air was light
>   But dark below the boughs
> The still air of the speechless night,
>   When lovers crown their vows.

(ASL 53)

Some critics unabashedly dislike this poem. It has "a melodramatic quality, a leaning toward too much gesturing" (Robinson, *Angry Dust,* 35). It is filled with "lurid fancies" (Watson, *Divided Life,* 147). The last two stanzas "are the most tasteless in *A Shropshire Lad*" (Marlow, *A. E. Housman,* 75). None of his poems tops it "for sheer silliness" and it is "Housman's most dreadful work" (Coulthard, "Flawed Craft," 30). But let Hamilton speak at length about how unsatisfactory this poem is. Here, Housman "gives us what must be one of the worst and most ludicrous poems in the language," a "melodrama" in which he "descended to the emotional level of the fat boy in Pickwick—'I wants to make your flesh creep' " with "absurd metaphor and exaggerated irony, the wailing repetition of 'Oh' and 'lad,' " and commonplace language that is "at times ludicrous," (Hamilton, *Housman the Poet,* 39), so much so that "nothing can excuse . . . [its] sheer badness" (Hamilton, "A. E. Housman," 26).

Hamilton does not consider the poem as a ballad, but there are also critics who consider this poem specifically as such, and a bad one at that. They assume this is because Housman did not know how to handle the form. Poems cast "in the form of a ballad . . . are among the least successful of his poems" (Marlow, *A. E. Housman,* 71).[3] There are other critics who consider this a serious (and not entirely unsuccessful) attempt to write a ballad.[4] Indeed, Sylvia Bruce has perspicaciously noted that "when Housman has been accused of self-parody, usually he has been deliberately parodying the ballads." To be sure, she is not referring to this poem when she goes on to say "either it is quite a good parody of a lesser ballad or it is a shocking bad poem" (*Essays,* 41). Her comment is not particularly relevant to the poem about which she is writing ("In the Morning," LP 23), but it is entirely relevant to "The True Lover."

Many critics have been bemused by the implications of the title, which they think ambiguous. They find the meaning of "true lover" unclear.[5] Long have been the arguments over what precisely the word "true" means here, but it would be tedious to review the various interpretations, and needless for my purpose, which is to examine this poem as a ballad—but a ballad with a difference. Rather surprisingly, none of the critics has pointed out that in the ballad vocabulary, "true love" has a very specific meaning: "affianced" or "accepted" lover. We have seen this used earlier in the term "true lover's knot." In the ballad it is therefore possible to refer to a "false true love," which is indeed one of the stock phrases of the mode.

Again, I shall start by assuming that Housman knew just what he was doing and that he did what he intended to do. He did not customarily set out to write "bad" poetry, he was well acquainted with the style and conventions of the ballad, and he was his own most exacting critic. Before looking at this ballad to determine precisely what he was up to, it might be well to review the characteristics of the English folk ballad in order to see what it is—and what it is not. Then these characteristics can be matched against "The True Lover" to see where it conforms to ballad style and where it does not. Only then can we begin to draw some conclusions about it.

The folk ballad is characterized by simple stanza forms, use of stock phrases and epithets, incremental repetition, a question and answer dialogue, abrupt alternation between narrative and speech, and narrative that is both objective and impersonal. It begins *in medias res* and picks up the prior action only by implication. Its brevity is due to telling only the essential points of the story while leaving the rest to the auditor's own imagination. There is acceptance of the supernatural as normal and natural (especially the motif of the returning dead with overtones of tragic love), acceptance of gross improbabilities in the plot, blunt unsentimental acceptance of tragedy and death, and a plot that deals with love (innocent or illicit) with an unhappy ending. If there is one thing universally absent from the ballad, it is verbal humor. The folk ballad takes itself very seriously and, although it can accommodate knockabout farce occasionally, it does not easily incorporate more subtle forms of humor than that in "Get up and Bar the Door."

Simple stanza forms? Yes, this poem is written in the standard ballad meter. Stock phrases and epithets? Yes, but they are not the stock phrases and epithets used in the ballad. Incremental repetition? Yes, but whereas in "Edward" or "Lord Randal" it is designed to gradually reveal who has been murdered or that there has indeed been a murder, it is ludicrous as applied to a suicide whose murderer is himself. Question and answer dialogue? Unquestionably. The questions, however, unlike those in the folk ballad, are grotesque, and the answers even more so. Abrupt alternation between narrative and speech? Clearly, but what kind of narrative? Objective and impersonal? Not in the least. This poem drips with both blood and subjectivity, and the viewpoint is a strictly personal one. Brevity resulting from telling only the essential parts of the story? Rather verbosity in underlining those that are not essential, like the physical setting (which is rarely found in a folk ballad). Although the darkness is relevant since it prevents the girl from seeing her lover's injuries, it is implicitly or specifically referred to six separate times in the nine verses ("at night," "out of sight / In shadow," "Before the east is grey," all in the first two verses, "dark under the shade" in the fourth verse, and again "dark beneath the boughs" and "speechless night" in the last verse). This seems like overkill. The unsurprised acceptance of the supernatural and the returning dead? Most emphatically yes. Overtones of tragic love? Rather, I should say, overtones of farce or burlesque. Gross improbabilities? Yes, but not the sort, such as talking animals and birds, which are found in the folk ballad. Blunt, unsentimental acceptance of tragedy? No, and I doubt that many are convinced that this is a tragedy at all. Love with an unhappy ending? Assuredly so.

The basic plot (the lover returning from the grave to claim his sweetheart) is found in many versions in European as well as English balladry (and in Yiddish is known as "The Dybbuk," a variation on the same theme). It is the "Demon Lover" plot. The lover, or the husband, who has been missing for seven years (a stock number), knocks on the door before day. The girl admits him or goes out to him, and he tells her either that she is his affianced bride (who has in some versions been untrue to him, having during his absence married another man) or that only she is fated to be his bride. In either case, he has come to claim her. She demurs, but is at last won over (usually by his informing her that he is extremely rich, and it is all for her) and goes with him. It becomes gradually apparent that he is a ghost who must return before dawn to his grave (or to hell)—bearing her with him. In all versions of the Demon Lover, the affair between the ghost and the girl has been a mutual one. The ghost is her affianced lover (or "true lover") returning from the grave for his promised bride (or wife) whom he will take back with him.[6]

It is clear that the formal techniques of the ballad (meter, incremental repetition, and so on) are used by Housman. It is equally clear that the tone is very different. Even the plot, which closely follows the broad folk outline, incorporates two crucial changes, and in these changes in the stock story we may begin to see what is going on. This is a rejected lover, not a previously accepted one, and he has no intention of carrying his bride back with him; he intends only a single tryst, and he tells her so ("When I from hence away am passed / I shall not find a bride"). These alterations eliminate the sense of fore-doomed fate that in a ballad hangs

over the encounter and makes its end inevitable. The girl *must* redeem
her promise and keep her pledged word by going, whether she will or no,
with her affianced sweetheart, even if this means being false to her new
true love. Housman also eliminates the ghost's bribery of his love, informing us that she "went and knew not why." In the English version, she
knows perfectly well why. In the German version, she is drawn without
any discernible reason, as she is here.

Housman's ghost displays a "grim wit" (Bayley, *Housman's Poems*, 112),
and so does Housman, whose wit is at the expense of the too earnest
critics. Is the "it" that "never goes again" in the sixth verse the ghost's
"heart," or is it the "clock"? And if the clock, which has no business
in a ballad anyway, any more than does Jack's "vaccination mark" in an
Augustan poem, does this mean that time has stopped? In which case,
can the east ever become "grey"? Or does it mean that the ghost has
stopped only his internal clock, his own "ticker"? We are told that it is
"dark under the shade." It surely is, for the ghost is the shade that the
girl is lying under. How else could blood drip into her mouth from a slit
throat that she has never even noticed? This is not only a "gross improbability in the plot," it is an impossible improbability in any serious terms.
What are we to make of the ghost's detailed explication of the self-evident? But Housman had used this device before in his very early comic
verse, verse that is not within the scope of this study. This poem has all
the earmarks of one of his parodies. Hamilton's observations were quite
correct, but he failed to draw the obvious conclusion.

Housman seems to have utilized all the technical devices of the ballad
but replaced the ballad tone with one of grand guignol or Gothic horror.
This "ballad" resembles the ballad as a skeleton decked out with a wig
and suspenders resembles the grim reality, and for the same reason. This
is a skeleton designed for vaudeville, not for the grave, and it carries Terence's trademark. The "stock words and epithets" are part of his normal
vocabulary, like the notorious "lad." We already know that Terence has
had some ghostly experiences of his own, that at least one ghost has addressed him from the grave and at least once a ghost has tapped at his
window calling "Hist, Terence, Hist." The ghost theme seems linked to
Terence and the cycle.

I suggest first of all that this poem was written by "Terence" not by
Housman, as the "Tale of Sir Thopas" is told by "Chaucer" and not by
Chaucer. The repeated "lad," the extreme colloquialism of some of the
diction ("my girl," "like enough," and the "knocking" of the heart), and
the insensitivity of the speaker's attitude toward the girl all indicate as
much. This may be the sort of thing Terence's friends preferred to his
more somber poetry.

Secondly, I suggest that what Housman did here was to parody the

Scottish border ballads of which he was so fond, just as he parodied the Greek drama, the English opera, and both the metaphysical and Augustan styles. Critics are so accustomed to thinking of Housman as a serious poet that Coulthard could say of this poem: "Were it not for the solemn conclusion . . . , this howler would pass for choice satire," ("Flawed Craft," 30) which is precisely what it is, even if the critic could not even entertain the notion that that is what it was intended to be. "Choice satire" is indeed *le mot juste*, although Coulthard did not realize it. As a parody of the ballad, it is a masterpiece so beautifully done that it has enticed numerous critics into treating it seriously as an art-ballad (which it surely is, but the "art" is in the parody, not in the ballad). In the same way they have lauded (or denounced) "The night is freezing fast" as a metaphysical poem rather than a parody of a metaphysical poem. Had Housman not made it abundantly clear that the "Fragment of a Greek Tragedy" and the "Fragment of an English Opera" were parodies, such is his reputation for being a depressingly pessimistic poet of despair with one eye always on the grave and the other always on the "iniquities" of life (despite his mass of comic verse) that the critics would doubtless have accepted them as serious (and dreadfully bad) attempts to write a veritable Greek tragedy and a libretto for a seriously intended English opera. And what they would have done with the Latin grammar–cum–Jack and Jill poem had Housman not kindly explained to them what he intended, only the Muse of Critical Interpretation can know.

This poem is drawn directly from the ballads of the Scottish border, and it seems quite as deliberate a parody of those ballads as some of the previous selections have been of other modes. One of Housman's friends was the ghost-story writer, M. R. James, and it has been mentioned that Housman and William Scawen Blunt sat up late telling ghost stories. It would be only natural that he would try his own hand at this form, but in his own mode, not in theirs. The art of the ghost story is, "by the use of the common prosaic details of every day to convince us of the concrete reality of some horror outside common experience" (Cecil, *Early Victorian Novelists*, 38). This explains the very non-ballad-like frame, the opening verse with the boy hidden under the trees whistling for the girl to slip out of the house to meet him, and the end with the moonlight outside the grove and the still air and darkness "below the boughs." Both frame pictures are on the whole romantico-realistic, in contrast to the eerily ludicrous events that occur within the frame.

There are other poems on heterosexual love, not even peripherally part of the cycle. As might be expected of one who is basically a late-Victorian poet, and a constitutionally conservative one at that, Housman's treatment tends to be allusive, using implication rather than direct statement. As might be expected from the foremost Latin scholar of his day, and one of the half dozen greatest classicists of the modern age (dating modern times back to the Renaissance), he found from the first congenial themes in mythology. From mythology is drawn the following poem, and like so many of the lyrics, it is a tale of the blighted love between a man and a woman, a love doomed by the passage of time.

The first verse, which I am appending to the poem as printed, is its original opening, either a first draft of what is now the first verse or what was intended as the first verse with what is usually so printed intended as the second verse. It was cancelled by Housman, but I am here replacing it in order to consider its implications for the poem's import (Burnett, *Poems*, 123 bottom).

> Last on, delight; we seldom meet.
> > Day peeps not yet, though soon it will.
> A star or two has still to flee
> > Beyond the western hill.
>
> Tarry delight; so seldom met,
> > So sure to perish, tarry still.
> Forbear to cease or languish yet,
> > Though soon you must and will.
>
> By Sestos town, in Hero's tower,
> > On Hero's heart Leander lies;
> The signal torch has burned its hour
> > And sputters as it dies.
>
> Beneath him, in the nighted firth,
> > Between two continents complain
> The seas he swam from earth to earth
> > And he must swim again.
>
> > > > > > > (MP 15)

In the Greek myth, Hero was, appropriately, a priestess of Aphrodite, dwelling in Sestos, across the Hellespont from her lover Leander's home in Abydos. Every night, guided by a signal torch she lit at the top of her tower, he swam across for an assignation with her, returning by the same route. On one night of storm, the torch was blown out by the wind. Leander, in the middle of his swim left without a guide, lost all sense of direction and drowned. Hero found his body washed up on the shore the following morning, and she killed herself.

It is immediately apparent that Housman has altered the myth so that Leander drowns on the return swim rather than on his way to Hero. Housman gives him one last night "on Hero's heart," in her arms and in her bed. This is an addition to the story; there is also a subtraction. Housman does not provide any explanation for the tragedy except that "the signal torch has burned its hour." There is no hint of the winds spawned by the storm in the original legend; not even the weather is to blame. It is simply the end of his hour, "the hour for lies and him." Here the word lacks its more usual double meaning, having only its erotic value, the time for lying together. That time has simply elapsed.

The poem opens with "a generalization on the transitory nature of all delight, moving into a description of Leander in his moment of bliss . . . , but then, in the midst of this, directing the reader's attention out the window and down—directly and immediately down to the 'nighted firth' . . . the void" (Brashear, "Trouble with Housman," 86). The poem provides "poignant image of the brevity of joy. . . . ['Complains' suggests] that the natural elements will conspire to destroy happiness whenever they find it" (Graves, A. E. Housman, 227). I would add that the sexual nature of the "delight" and "happiness," which of its nature is transitory and brief, is quite explicit, not only in the situation but in the imagery as well.

The punctuation of the appended verse makes it clear that the first two verses (as I have printed them) are the words (or at least the thoughts) of one of the characters and not intended as a generalization at all. As in Housman the narrators are, as we have seen, invariably male, they are to be ascribed to Leander. The "we" can then refer to "I and Hero" or to "I and delight." The ambiguity is typical of Housman's construction. In what I have printed as the second verse, the ambiguity is removed and it is specifically the "delight" and not the girl that is "seldom met." This setting up of an ambiguity in one verse that is removed in a later verse is also typical of Housman (as "here" in "'Soldier from the wars returning," LP 8, which in the first verse is indeterminate but by the last verse is clearly the land of the dead). This verse also explicitly rather than implicitly eliminates the weather as a factor in the death of the torch.

That "signal torch" that "sputters as it dies" is no more than it seems if one confines oneself to the modern meaning of "dies," but if one adds to the linguistic equation the Elizabethan meaning, the torch is not the only thing that "dies" with a "sputter." Its death not only graphically describes the physical end of Leander's "delight," which will not linger or "tarry" for long no matter how much the man attempts to prolong it (vainly requesting it to "Last on" and "fail not yet" in rejected lines). It also foreshadows his physical death in the other sense as he returns to the "seas he swam." We have already seen that for Housman the sea is a symbol of death as well as of birth.

What Housman does not do is to follow Marlowe, who, in his "Hero and Leander," ascribes Leander's death to a case of mistaken identity. In

Marlowe's poem, Neptune thinks the boy is Ganymede, Jupiter's cup bearer. A boy serving drinks "to the god" is a homosexual symbol (Woods, *Articulate Flesh*, 23). Ask not what drink he serves, nor from what cup, nor how he serves it. Thus, the diction in the passage is overtly erotic. Neptune attempts to seize (or embrace) the boy, rape (or seduction) in mind, but when Leander begins to drown Neptune realizes his mistake too late (ibid., 24–25). Housman's poem is in all its aspects uncompromisingly heterosexual without any possibility of gender ambiguity. Leander lies "on Hero's heart." A veil is discreetly drawn over what took place before, although it is crystal clear. The words do not offend against Victorian reticence concerning sex, although the implicit eroticism of the words, the double meanings that I have been exploring, make it impossible to mistake the import.

Nor is it possible to mistake the import in another poem from the notebooks (Burnett, *Poems*, 171).

> And idle under sighing oak
>> Or near drowsing linden laid
> Maiden and youth in whispers spoke,
>> In whispers youth and maid.

This quatrain, so delicate and lovely, has an atmosphere of innocence, of evening and moonrise and nostalgia. Haber says it has an autumnal feel (A. E. Housman, *Manuscript Poems*, 33) presumably imparted by the "sighing oak." I do not agree; to me, it has a summer feel, the feel of the lazy, "drowsing" heat of August with the trees in full and concealing foliage, which Housman elsewhere evoked: "On the idle hill of summer, / Sleepy with the flow of streams" (ASL 35). Besides which, no sane English lovers would ever choose the outdoors for a lingering tryst in the autumn when England is not only muddy but also rainy and chill, not even (or perhaps especially not) in poetry.

It is instructive, in the light of Housman's own feelings about his sexual orientation, to be examined in chapter 9, to compare this poem with "In the morning" (LP 23), discussed above. In that poem, the emotions that follow the night together in the haystack are implicitly negative—shame, horror, disgust, etc. Here, the emotions are implicitly positive—joy, innocence, nostalgia. The haystack lovers look away from each other in disgust or shame, whereas these lovers converse in intimate whispers with each other. This seems to me to indicate once more that the lovers in the haystack are homosexual, unlike the lovers under the oak or near the linden, who are clearly heterosexual ("youth and maid") although both pairs have clearly been making love.

Housman did not make physical intimacy explicit; the closest he came to it was in "Tarry delight." Nor was he alone. In discussing Swinburne's poetry, he said that in English literature, Aphrodite "wages an unequal contest with another great divinity, who is called purity by her friends and hypocrisy by her enemies, and whom . . . one may perhaps call Mrs. Grundy." In 1910 Aphrodite is no longer persona non grata and English literature enjoys a "reasonable licence which it . . . seldom abuses" (A. E. Housman, "Swinburne," 278–79). Certainly he never abused it.

Housman was clearly privately amused by the excessive prudery of Victorian decorum. In 1929 he wrote his brother an account of the reaction of a reader who found A Shropshire Lad salacious and said, "I put it behind the fire. Filthiest book I ever read: all about—" The end of the sentence is not omitted in the original letter, but Laurence Housman, that champion of freedom of expression and enemy of censorship, considered it "unprintable" (L. Housman, A. E. H., 182, or A. E. Housman, Letters, 276). It is not hard, however, to guess what the words were. The reader was not wrong, although his reaction may seem rather odd to us who have become inured to the explicit description of the "facts of life" in modern literature. The humor and sprightliness of Housman's reaction to the accusation are delightfully reminiscent of his comic verse.

> Now all day long the horned herds
> Dance to the piping of the birds;
> Now the bumble-bee is rife,
> And other forms of insect life;
> The skylark in the sky so blue
> Now makes noise enough for two,
> And lovers on the grass so green
> —Muse, oh Muse, eschew th'obscene.

Nevertheless, he did "eschew th'obscene," at least on the surface. He did not, however, as we have seen, eschew the "facts of life," and if the birds do it and the bees do it, so do his lovers do it. The outraged reader indeed did not misinterpret A Shropshire Lad's lyrics. Housman treats the erotic "simply and very naturally." He is quite willing to write about "The lover and his lass / Beneath the hawthorne lying" (LP 7). Not easily shocked himself, and greatly enjoying both the bawdy and the vulgar (Hamilton, Housman the Poet, 17), he was yet in his poetry unwilling to shock others and so excluded both from direct, although not from indirect, expression.

Housman's serio-comic verse celebrating the aphrodisiac power, the "sensual music" of spring on all created things, not excluding "lovers on the grass," was dashed off in a private letter to his brother. It can be paralleled in Yeats, who said much the same thing in a poem written in an entirely serious mode for the ages, "Sailing to Byzantium"

. . . The young
In one another's arms, birds in the trees—
Those dying generations—at their song,
The salmon-falls, the mackerel-crowded seas,
Fish, flesh, or fowl, commend all summer long
Whatever is begotten, born, and dies
Caught in that sensual music . . .

(*Selected Poems*, 95)

Housman's greatest tribute to heterosexual love, however, was also his most agonizingly tormented expression of (his own) homosexual love. The subject was the same: Moses Jackson. When he finally learned that his friend had married, he began an epithalamium for him but composed only a small part before putting it aside. When he learned that his friend was dying, he completed it for inclusion in *Last Poems*.

Epithalamium

He is here, Urania's son,
Hymen come from Helicon;
God that glads the lover's heart,
He is here to join and part.
So the groomsman quits your side
And the bridegroom seeks the bride
Friend and comrade yield you o'er
To her that hardly loves you more.
　　Now the sun his skyward beam
Has tilted from the ocean stream.
Light the Indies, laggard sun:
Happy bridegroom, day is done,
And the star from Oeta's steep
Calls to bed but not to sleep.
　　Happy bridegroom, Hesper brings
All desired and timely things.
All whom morning sends to roam,
Hesper loves to lead them home.
Home return who him behold,
Child to mother, sheep to fold,
Bird to nest from wandering wide:
Happy bridegroom, seek your bride.
　　Pour it out, the golden cup
Given and guarded, brimming up,
Safe through jostling markets borne
And the thicket of the thorn;
Folly spurned and danger past,
Pour it to the god at last.

> Now, to smother noise and light,
> Is stolen abroad the wildering night,
> And the blotting shades confuse
> Path and meadow full of dews;
> And the high heavens, that all control,
> Turn in silence round the pole.
> Catch the starry beams they shed
> Prospering the marriage bed,
> And breed the land that reared your prime
> Sons to stay the rot of time.
> All is quiet, no alarms;
> Nothing fear of nightly harms.
> Safe you sleep on guarded ground,
> And in silent circle round
> The thoughts of friends keep watch and ward,
> Harnessed angels, hand on sword.
>
>   (LP 24)

Watson makes two telling points about this poem. He is the only one to note that it differs from all other epithalamia in its concentration on the groom rather than the bride, and he calls it "thematically disjointed and laboriously contrived" (*Divided Life*, 125). It does indeed differ from all other epithalamia—in English. There is, however, a precedent in Latin, in Catullus (*Odi et Amo*). Both of his epithalamia (61, "Collis o Heliconiei," and 62, "Vesper adest"), even while (briefly) lauding the bride, are clearly focused on the groom, who has "played with nuts long enough," enjoying "permissible pleasures" in the arms of "sweet slaves" and "idle bed-boy[s]," and who is "just as attractive" to the poet as to his bride, whose functions are limited to catering to his comfort and bearing him sons. The echoes of Catullus in Housman's poem are hardly accidental. "Hymen O Hymenaeus!" indeed.[7]

The source of the "disjointedness" and "laboriousness" upon which Watson commented has thus been hinted at although he shows no signs of recognizing it. Housman had so entirely assimilated Latin (and Greek and English) literature that echoes of other poets ring all through this poem, alternating stanzas with the more personal sections, although the two aspects are united and seamlessly woven together despite Watson's remark. It is as if when the personal emotion became overwhelming, Housman sought relief by retreating into the classical texts he knew and loved. This is a technique we shall meet again.

The opening lines in the second draft (Burnett, *Poems*, 91–93, bottoms of pages) differ in some vital aspects from that finally adopted. This draft has a bride in bower, afterward excised. Hymen is the god who intentionally joins the bridal couple *in order to* part the groom from the "groomsman" who must "abide," deserted by the groom. In the final version, there is no intimation of intention: joining and parting are naturally paired and inseparable. The joining of the bride and groom is, and must be, the parting of the friend and the groom. In the final version, also, it is the groomsman who "quits" the side of the groom, not the groom who leaves the groomsman to "abide." Both these changes serve to distance the poem from its inspiration. Parenthetically, the "groomsman" is the male equivalent of a "bridesmaid," not a best man or usher, and the role, now eliminated, was de rigeur up to the end of the nineteenth century (Ronald Pearsal, *Worm in the Bud,* 146). We remember that Housman, far from being a "groomsman," was not even informed of the wedding.

> Hie you hither, day is done,
> Hymen out of Helicon.
> Now to bower the bride is gone
> Happy [lover/bridegroom], light of heart,
> Hail the god that joins to part.
> Here the groomsman shall abide
> While the bridegroom seeks the bride.

Browne calls the line "so the groomsman quits your side" "a beseeching cry" (*Elegy in Arcady,* 31). How much more so it is in the rejected draft with its overtones of abandonment and faithful waiting. The "friend and comrade" who "yield[s] you o'er / To her that hardly loves you more" was, in the draft, "Friends and lovers." The use of the plural instead of the singular hardly cancels the naked revelation of the original noun. Hesper, be it noted, is another name for Venus, so the invocation to "the star from Oeta's steep" would carry a sexual charge even without the implications of "Calls to bed but not to sleep." The sun has "tilted from the ocean stream" and is called upon to "light the Indies." Housman's diary reveals how carefully he traced the ocean voyage that doubled as a honeymoon, tracking the ship that carried Moses Jackson away from England, and from him. The general reader would surely have missed the personal allusion, but it was not written for the general reader; it was written for one very special reader.

We have seen that the opening of the first verse is drawn from Catullus, and the second part of it and the second verse are very personal. In the third verse, Housman returns to classic literature, this time to the Greek of Sappho. No wonder that Marlow says that the description of sunset is "deliberately in the classical manner" (*A. E. Housman,* 119). It is not only "in the classical manner," it is a direct translation, and Davenport considered it "the best translation I know of Sappho's 'Espere ponta pheron' [Oh, evening star, . . .]." ("Terrier and the Rat,")[8] Let us look at another translation of the short lyric by Willis Barnstone (107), and judge for ourselves.

Evening Star

> Hesperos, you bring home all the bright dawn disperses,
> bring home the sheep, bring home the goat,
> bring the child home to its mother.

Housman replaces the goat with the bird, far more euphonious in English, and adds the thematic bridegroom. His version, a rendering rather than a translation, so beautifully flowing and mellifluous, is obviously not "best" as meaning the most exact translation, and as obviously is "best" as meaning the most beautiful. The same could have been said, by the way, of Housman's translation of Horace's Ode, "Diffugere Nives" (MP 5). This too is not literal but is nevertheless that used in anthologies of Latin literature in translation.[9]

The fourth verse is again personal and has faint echoes of "To an Athlete Dying Young" (ASL 19) and "Hell Gate" (LP 31). Is not the "golden cup" an echo of the athlete's "challenge cup" borne safely home? The "folly done and danger past," is this not the reverse of "Cureless folly done and said"? But that folly was done on the road to Ludlow fair, so is the "jostling market" through which the cup has been safely borne not Ludlow fair itself? The cup has been borne safely through "the thicket of the thorn," a line that could be very easily misidentified as coming from "Hell Gate" (LP 31). Is not this road also "the lovely way that led / To the slimepit and the mire"? (LP 31). Just what is the cup so safely borne through all the temptations of life until it is finally "poured out" to the god of marriage (LP 24)? Is it not the same cup from which Marlowe's Ganymede served Jupiter's needs, Ganymede who was also the bearer of a cup?

The imagery cannot be mistaken. The early drafts make it pellucidly clear. "Youth accomplished, manhood [ripe/come]" relates the cup to "manhood"; it is "[Full/high] and steady, not to tilt (alternatively it is ["Never shook nor turned a-tilt") / Safe, unsullied, nothing spilt."] It is "high" and "steady" and from it "nothing" has been "spilt," so it remains "unsullied" by the "folly" that was "spurned" and the "danger" that is now "past," the danger of illicit, and homosexual, carnal knowledge.

It is not only his friend whom Housman is "yielding" to "her that hardly loves you more." It is his own dream. This part of the poem is his acknowledgement that his friend has emerged "clean of stain" (AP 6) from their intimacy, despite his own efforts (actual or only dreamed of) to entice him into "folly" and the "mire." Perhaps without ever having analyzed the imagery, and certainly without having taken the personal references or intimations of homosexual attraction into account, at least one critic has seen this aspect of the poem clearly, calling it "a magnificent tribute to those who come chaste to marriage" (Sweeney, "Ethics," 124). And so it is, a "magnificent tribute" to one who did, one who was chased but not unchaste.

The sixth verse again retreats from the personal to the literary with its great echo of the end of Shakespeare's *Midsummer Night's Dream* in which Puck (strangely transformed here into Housman) pronounces a blessing on the marital bed, and its small echo of the beginning of his sequence of sonnets.[10] Sonnets 1 through 17 develop the theme of procreation, the getting of "sons to stay the rot of time." Shakespeare offers one primary reason for the getting of sons: to provide a copy of the beloved's lost beauty when "Time" has withered him. This sequence slides over into another in which a secondary reason is urged for the getting of a son: as a validation of the poet's description of the young man's beauty, which no one will believe if succeeding generations lack visual proof.

The only reason Housman offers, "to breed the land that served your prime / Sons," is completely original. However, let us return to Shakespeare's secondary reason. Woods points out that to produce a *son in response to the poet's urging* is "a proof of love—not for the mother . . . but for the poet himself" since it would serve as living "testimony to the erotic relationship between its father and the male lover, rather than the parental relationship of its father and his wife" (*Articulate Flesh*, 87). The mother is no more than a means to the continuation of the beloved's existence through his progeny and in herself is of little or no importance. We have seen this in Catullus and it fits in very nicely with Housman's lines that all but ignore the bride. The idea of the beloved's children as a link between two male friends is developed in Tennyson's "In Memoriam" where they will be the poet's nephews, sons of his sister and the friend who was to have been his brother-in-law, and perhaps they will be even more: ". . . boys of thine . . . I seem to meet their last desire, / To clap their cheeks, to call them mine" (Tennyson, "In Memoriam" 84, verses 3 and 5, 422).

As for the reason Housman urges, at least it could not be interpreted (or misinterpreted) by outsiders as Shakespeare's are. Let us not forget also that Jackson would understand the reference, which was all that was important to Housman. By the time this was written, he had indeed given Housman a son that he could call his: Gerry. The poem is just what Robb calls it, "a celebration of friendship" (*Four in Exile,* 40), but in a deeper sense than she ever meant. It ends with "harnessed angels, hand on sword," a fitting Miltonic echo to close Housman's personal *Paradise Lost.*

8

Dear Fellow

IN THE POSTHUMOUSLY PUBLISHED WORK, WE HAVE MUCH LESS MASK AND much more Housman. In reviewing *More Poems*, John Sparrow observed that the usual Terence conventions, the "my lads," the soldiers and deaths in battle, the graveyard settings, are largely absent, leaving us with "Housman speaking undisguisedly in the first person and not through the mouth of Terence." These poems show "the depth and nature of the emotion which needed that imaginary setting [Shropshire] and those half-real characters for its poetic expression. These poems reveal pretty clearly . . . the spring of Housman's personal emotions" (Review, 756). The poetry that grew on the banks of this particular spring will form the subject of the last part of this study. In this chapter, I wish to examine only the poems of loving friendship without the quotation marks.

Until the middle of the nineteenth century, "strong and emotional friendships between men were . . . easily accepted. Writers could celebrate one man's love for another without any thought of impropriety crossing their own or their readers' minds. . . . Homosexuals could therefore shelter behind the conventions of male friendship," and indeed "there was a fashion for intense male friendships that not only sublimated but in many instances probably disguised the practice [of homosexuality. Such friendships] were considered perfectly acceptable, and even admirable" (Chesney, *Victorian Underworld*, 390). After the Oscar Wilde trial, however, "there was a slump in sentimental friendships between men which hitherto wives had encouraged to keep their husbands from other women" (Croft-Cooke, *Feasting with Panthers*, 290). There was a "genteel tradition" in literature suffused with a non-erotic male bond that represented "real emotional relationships," which were spiritualized by the excision of phallicism, eroticism, and all indications of sexuality. In this tradition, "the most passionate emotional experience [between men] is . . . an idyllic afternoon on the grass, a deep look into a friend's eyes, or an understanding of brotherhood, rather vaguely defined" (Martin, *Homosexual Tradition*, 90). This tradition can be found in countless Victorian novels ranging from the Tom Brown books to the opening section of Forster's *Maurice*. Indeed, Forster combines the genteel tradition with the pastoral tradition over and over again to create an undercurrent of implicit homo-eroticism without, except in the body of *Maurice*, crossing the line. Hous-man straddles the line, using the genteel imagery to express real homoerotic passion.

Friendship posed a problem in the later nineteenth century. The pre-scribed male bond—friendships formed at school, the university, men's clubs, etc.—conflicted with the proscribed one. Therefore, "the intensity and sufficiency of male bonding needed to be strictly controlled by homo-phobic mechanisms" in order to reinforce the duty of men to marry and propagate. This created "a double bind in which 'the most intimate male bonding' was prescribed at the same time that 'the remarkably cognate' homosexuality was proscribed" (Dellamora, *Masculine Desire*, 195, in part quoting from Eva Kosofsky Sedgwick's "Beast in the Closet," 152). At a time when homosexuality was illegal—and a cause of persecution—the euphemism "romantic friendship" was used to designate homosexual rela-tionships. The difference between the normative male bond (friendship) and the illegal bond ("friendship") was the—often unconscious—erotic element. When the erotic element was sublimated, unexpressed and un-acknowledged, the emotion was designated as Platonic love. This is the relationship limned in the school section of Forster's *Maurice*, and it was a staple element in school stories in general. It is one of the bases of both *Tom Brown's School Days* and *Tom Brown at Oxford*; in neither book does the erotic element (apparent to the reader) rise into clear view. In actual-ity, however, single-gender schools, like other all-male environments (prisons, military units, ships at sea, etc.) were a breeding ground for "friendship" as well as friendship, and there was "a discernible wave of homosexual subculture" from the mid-nineteenth Century to the after-math of the Wilde trial (Reade, *Sexual Heretics*, 3).

In life the acceptability of strong and passionate friendships endured until the 1880s (Tannahill, *Sex in History*, 380–81) and beyond. In litera-ture, the decline of this fashion began somewhat earlier and can be traced from the explicit male bond in Shakespeare's *Two Gentlemen of Verona* to the Victorian novel along an ascending scale of reserve and self-con-sciousness until it culminates in the echoing silence of Trollope's *The Vicar of Bullhampton*.

This fashion for intense friendship was amply recorded in the poetry of the time as well as the prose. Tennyson's "In Memoriam" is the greatest expression of it. Whether Tennyson in fact ever addressed Arthur Hallam in life as he does in his poetry may be strongly doubted. The terms used in the poetry are what is important for my purpose.[1] The terms used for the poet's dead friend, "love," "dearest," and so on, seem to us terms of endearment appropriately addressed to or used by a man in regards to a woman (or by a woman to a man). They seem to us improper when used by a man to or about a man. For Tennyson this was clearly not the case. The terms in which he both addresses and refers to Arthur Hallam from the opening prologue through the closing epithalamium have for us an erotic charge.

The following excerpts bring together many, but not all, of the passages that most explicitly show this erotic transgender diction. Hallam is one "whom I found so fair," "My Arthur, whom I shall not see / Till all my widow'd race be run." Time is beseeched to "Come quick, thou bringest all I love." The poet, seeing his friend's dead body, "falling on his faithful heart, / Would breathing thro' his lips impart / The life that almost dies in me." Hallam is "the much-beloved," and the poet's "centred passion" will not "lessen from today" because "My spirit loved and loves him yet." He addresses the dead man: "So, dearest, now thy brows are cold," but had you not died, "More years had made me love thee more." He died, "But I remain'd, whose hopes were dim, / Whose life, whose thoughts were little worth, / To wander on a darken'd earth / Where all things round me breathed of him," "my prime passion in the grave," leaving me nothing to look forward to but "a meeting somewhere, love with love." The poet's heart is left "within a lonely place, / That yet remembers his embrace," and he cries in anguish, "Ah, dear, but come thou back to me! / Whatever change the years have wrought, / I find not yet one lonely thought / That cries against my wish for thee." His wish is granted in a vision where "The dead man touch'd me from the past, / And all at once it seemed at last / The living soul was flash'd on mine, / And mine in this was wound, and whirl'd / About empyreal heights." The figure in the vision , "tho' veil'd, was known to me, / The shape of him I loved, and love / For ever." He "fillest all the room / Of all my love," and that love has grown with the passage of the years. "Dear friend, far off, my lost desire, / So far, so near in woe and weal / O loved the most . . . / Mine, mine, for ever, ever mine; . . . / Loved deeplier, darklier understood; / Behold, I dream a dream of good, / And mingle all the world with thee" until "My love involves the love before; / My love is vaster passion now; / . . . I seem to love thee more and more / . . . I have thee still and I rejoice," and at last "love is more / Than in the summers that are flown."[2] There is of course much more than this in Tennyson's great elegy, but this is yet an integral part of the whole. Such poetry addressed to a male friend in terms of a sweetheart could still be written during the middle of Victoria's reign as it had been in Elizabeth's, but it could not be written much longer.

"In Memoriam" is unusual in its expression only in that it does not follow the elegiac tradition of the dead shepherd-singer mourned by his fellow shepherds, his tuneful friend, and all of nature, with its mythological paraphernalia, its muses, and its panoply of flocks of sheep, shepherdesses, and oaten pipes. Parenthetically, those pipes are perhaps the ultimate source of Terence's flute and some of the underlying pastoral apparatus in Housman's Shropshire cycle. "In Memoriam" brought the ancient elegiac tradition to a magnificent height, and Tennyson did this partly by using such personal, emotionally charged terms as we have been considering, sacrificing aesthetic distance in order to gain immediacy and direct impact.

By the time Housman was publishing his poetry, it was no longer possible for a man to speak of male friends in terms that carry, to our ears at least, an erotic charge. This posed a problem for him. He solved it by adopting a relaxed, easygoing, casual tone when speaking of male friendship, and a style of overtones and undertones drawing heavily on the buried pun and charged with erotic force in speaking of male "friendship." We have seen a sample of this technique of erotic intensity in the preceding chapter. Most of his poems celebrating friendship and comradeship he published only under the mask of Terence. Even if one confines oneself to the official poetry, however, it is clear that nonerotic male friendship and companionship, the mutual reliance and trust between men, implicit in "The Deserter" for example, were of great importance to him. The faithfulness and loyalty of male friends are among his recurring themes.[3] For Housman, friendship was one of the great values. It meant a total commitment to and a readiness for self-sacrifice for the sake of the friend. It involved instinctive sympathy and understanding that did not rely on clumsy words for communication. This ideal friendship is limned at the end of "Hell Gate" (LP 31), where the "pair of friends" journey together in silence, words being superfluous. This ideal relationship is rare indeed, but Housman was committed to the idea and used the term "friend" sparingly. There were few who could live up to his concept of friendship, but those few he cherished with loyalty and fierce devotion. He, at least, as a friend lived up to his own ideal conception.

His symbol for this ideal of loyalty, courage, and commitment is the soldier who is so common in his poetry. The soldier may also function as a sexually desirable (and available) male, of course, but the tone of carnality when this is his function is very different from that when the symbolism is non-sexual, and the carnal symbolism will be taken up in the next chapter. Here, we are concerned only with non-erotic friendship.

> When I would muse in boyhood
>   The wild green woods among,
> And nurse resolves and fancies
>   Because the world was young,
> It was not foes to conquer,
>   Nor sweethearts to be kind,
> But it was friends to die for
>   That I would seek and find.

I sought them far and found them,
    The sure, the straight, the brave,
The hearts I lost my own to,
    The souls I could not save.
They braced their belts about them,
    They crossed in ships the sea,
They sought and found six feet of ground
    And there they died for me.

(LP 32)

This poem, like so many of Housman's, can be read in two different ways. It was not "sweethearts to be kind, / But it was friends to die for / That I would seek" contains four ambiguities, "sweethearts," "kind," "friends," and "die." If these words are taken in the common sense, the lines mean, "I did not dream about girls of whom I could be fond and who would be indulgent to me but about friends for whom I could give my life." "Your sweetheart," however, is just what Housman calls himself in another poem referring to his bond with Moses Jackson (MP 24). Thus, despite its usual connotation, it can also refer to a male partner in a love-bond. "Kind" can specifically refer to a sexually compliant woman, as we shall see later, as well as being a gender-free term meaning "benign," "indulgent," or "accommodating." In homosexual usage, "friend" means "lover." And "die," as always, can carry the subterranean meaning of "sexual release." Taking all these words in their secondary meanings yields, "I did not dream about lovers of either sex who would give themselves to me but about male lovers with whom I could find sexual satisfaction." For the purposes of this chapter, we will assume the first, non-erotic, reading, remembering, however, that as Jebb has said, and without reference to the alternate meaning of "dying," "the notion of dying for one's fellow men . . . [is] the covert route by which A. E. Housman's homosexuality finds expression" (A. E. Housman, 85). The erotic reading is the basis of the two following chapters.

Neither heroism then, nor heterosexual love, but the self-sacrifice of friendship made up his adolescent dream. This dream was to be ironically fulfilled in two different ways. He outlived all his friends and most of his siblings, including Herbert, his soldier brother whose ghost haunts many of the poems. At the same time he did figuratively sacrifice himself for his friends, or rather for one friend alone, for whose sake "I went with half my life about my ways" (AP 7). This is the Monkey's Paw as it operated for Housman. He received what he most desired, but not as he had envisioned it.

Katherine Symons considered the following two poems as her brother's personal expressions of grief for Herbert, who fell in South Africa during the Boer War (Symons, Recollections).

Astronomy

The Wain upon the northern steep
    Descends and lifts away.
Oh I will sit me down and weep
    For bones in Africa.

For pay and medals, name and rank,
    Things that he has not found,
He hove the Cross to heaven and sank
    The pole-star underground.

And now he does not even see
    Signs of the nadir roll
At night over the ground where he
    Is buried with the pole.

                                            (LP 17)

    Sergeant George Herbert Housman, the poet's youngest and much loved brother, was killed in battle. His body remained in the rain on the field all night. When the casualty lists were at last published by the War Office, his regimental number was reported correctly but his name was entered as "Honsman" (Gasser, "A. E. Housman," 530). The "name," both one of the things for which he enlisted and his private identity, was swept aside, and only his "number" was correctly recorded. This is the parable of modern man in brief. His only official identity is as a number; his identity card number, his driver's license number, his passport number, his social security number, his army registration number, his PIN number, even his telephone number are more important than his name, his personal, unofficial self. This is why in the next poem he is "a name and a number" who is "cheap to the king / and dear to me." To official-dom he is "a number," and cheap, his value common. To the poet, "a name," and dear, and his value cannot be measured. To both, he is "price-less," though in opposite meanings of the word.

    Instead of gaining a "name," fame and reputation, he lost his "name," his personal identity. Nor were pay, medals, and rank to be his. He rose through the ranks to sergeant—and died. He was mentioned in dispatches for bravery, but was not decorated. And army pay at that level was not munificent. It is only by knowing the personal basis of the poem that its irony becomes overt. Herbert Housman apparently gave his life and gained nothing, not even the poetic immortality that, to-gether with the tears for "bones in Africa," his brother, by including this elegy in *Last Poems*, tried to bestow on him. Watson calls this poem "a tribute to every anonymous veteran" (175), effectively turning Sergeant George Herbert Housman into an "unknown soldier" (Forster, "Ancient and Modern," Gardner, *Critical Heritage*, p. 319). Thus the silence descends on him. The man, first reduced to a number, is finally reduced to a symbol, a "thing," or elevated rather than reduced for this is "the thing / He was born to be" (MP40 variation, Burnett, *Poems*, 139, bottom of page) a "flaming" symbol of Housman's ideal of "valour and truth," who "crossed in ships the sea" to find his "six feet of ground."

"Astronomy" is not "poetic." "He" does not, unlike Hardy's "Drummer Hodge," with which this poem is often compared, even have a name. Without the additional knowledge of who he is and what his history, the poem is bare and puzzling. As with "In Memoriam," knowledge of the poet's relationship with the subject of the poem is necessary for both clarity and a sense of the depth of the grief that makes the poet "weep." Hardy may marvel at Hodge's strange fate, but he neither weeps for him nor conveys the feeling that he is holding back his tears by force of will power. It is the sense of emotion that must somehow break forth into expression that gives strength and edge both to Tennyson's elegy for Arthur Hallam and Housman's poems for his brother, the preceding one and the following one alike.

> Farewell to a name and a number
>   Recalled again
> To darkness and silence and slumber
>   In blood and pain.
>
> So time coils round in a ring
>   And home comes he
> A soldier cheap to the King
>   And dear to me;
>
> So smothers in blood the burning
>   And flaming flight
> Of valour and truth returning
>   To dust and night.

(MP 40)

The poet's youthful vision was not, however, of friends who would die for him, although that was what he received. It was of "friends to die for," and this was denied him.

> I shall not die for you,
>   Another fellow may;
> Good lads are left and true
>   Though one departs away.
>   But he departs to-day
> And leaves his work to do,
>   For I was luckless aye
> And shall not die for you.

> (AP 20)

After the publication of *Last Poems*, Housman laid down his pen, thus bestowing on himself that symbolic death for his friend of which he had dreamed. The future held no personal or emotional prospects for him except the completion of his edition of Manilius and other professional work and the welcome one of his own demise. The only "completely new poem" he wrote after that was the hymn he composed to be sung at his own funeral (A. E. Housman, *Manuscript Poems*, 29). He could not physically die for his friend, but he could, and did, end his emotional and expressive life. It is impossible to know exactly when he wrote it, except that it was after January of 1925, after Moses Jackson's death. He was, after all, his own most "luckless" lad.

It has puzzled many why Housman chose to devote his professional life to an extremely obscure and unrewarding minor Latin poet like Manilius.[4] Garrod concluded that Housman hated poetry, that he found in scholarship an "anodyne" both for poetry and "all those parts of life that make up into poetry," and that he chose Manilius because it gave him "the savage satisfaction of detecting, and blazoning, . . . [the] incompetence of all the world save himself" ("Mr. A. E. Housman," 215). One might note that Garrod had himself published a commentary on Manilius 2 in 1911. Housman declined to review it but "wrote politely to him about it" (Gardner, *Critical Heritage*, 213) in October of that year, "I have no wish to prevent other scholars from editing Manilius, but rather the reverse; and I think the world is probably wide enough for both our books, as each contains a good deal which the other does not" (A. E. Housman, *Letters*, 121). In 1918, Garrod sent Housman a copy of his book of poetry *Worms and Epitaphs* (and many think Housman's poetry is morbid!), a book that Housman called, in acknowledging the gift, "interesting and spirited" (ibid., 167). Perhaps Garrod lacked Housman's active sense of fun and did not appreciate the pun, or perhaps he only felt the praise was insufficient. In time he took his revenge rather obliquely by proclaiming that Housman hated poetry. He did not specify what, or whose, poetry, the poet hated. The clear implication was that he hated it all, including his own, and especially hated writing poetry. These remarks were made in 1929. In 1930, in the preface to his edition of Manilius 5, Housman "severely criticized" Garrod's edition of Manilius 2.[5] Housman's forbearance had its limits.

Yet it is not so very difficult to understand why Housman devoted himself to a poet whose interest in astronomy matched his own, whose ingenuity in versifying arithmetic must have appealed to the man who could insert a subtraction problem into "Loveliest of trees" (ASL 2) and an addition problem into "When first my way to fair I took"(LP 35).[6] Manilius was also the poet who could write about a theme dear to Housman's own heart: "nature has never created from herself anything more precious or less common than the bond of true friendship. . . . There was but one Pylades, but one Orestes, eager to die for his friend. Once only throughout the ages have men disputed for the prize of death, in that one snatched at a doom the other refused to yield . . . the bond of loyalty is rare and granted to few" (*Astronomica* 2, 129–30). No, it is not at all difficult to comprehend: "It was friends to die for."

Friendship was indeed important to Housman although he knew that, like love, it was ephemeral. On the surface, he accepted, even while lamenting the fact, that time and loss would wither it. The tone, however, always pulls against this overt statement. The normative Victorian belief, so clear in "In Memoriam," that the passage of the years would increase and not lessen and ultimately destroy the love of the living for their dead friends, is apparently gone. Instead we find realism, and an aching void. In this and the following chapters it will be observed that lyrics from *More Poems* and *Additional Poems* outnumber those from the official poetry, although both *A Shropshire Lad* and *Last Poems* do not go completely unrepresented.

> The rain, it streams on stone and hillock,
>   The boot clings to the clay.
> Since all is done that's due and right
> Let's home; and now, my lad, good-night,
>   For I must turn away.
>
> Good-night, my lad, for nought's eternal;
>   No league of ours, for sure,
> To-morrow I shall miss you less,
> And ache of heart and heaviness
>   Are things that time should cure.
>
> Over the hill the highway marches
>   And what's beyond is wide:
> Oh soon enough will pine to nought
> Remembrance and the faithful thought
>   That sits the grave beside.

The skies, they are not always raining
　　Nor grey the twelvemonth through;
And I shall meet good days and mirth,
And range the lovely lands of earth
　　With friends no worse than you.

But oh, my man, the house is fallen
　　That none can build again;
My man, how full of joy and woe
Your mother bore you years ago
　　To-night to lie in the rain.

(LP 18)

It should first be made clear that this poem was completed only in the spring of 1922, although begun in 1895. Thus, it has only a fortuitous connection with the death, in October of 1901, of Herbert Housman, whose body was indeed left "to lie in the rain." The second thing to note is that like the "Epithalamium" it is a marriage of the poet's personal and professional concerns, a fusion between his own poetry and a translation of part of one of Horace's odes. However, let us follow the Red Queen's advice and start at the beginning, with the rain. In poetry, rain is usually a symbol of fertility, but this rain creates streams only in "God's Acre" where are planted the "seeds that never grow" (AP 11). This rain is a symbol of sterility, and of futility.

The first verse is built on a pun and an ambiguity. The pun is in "The boot clings to the clay." "Clay" is the human body ("dead clay that did me kindness" LP 30), and it is also the grave ("Clay's the house he [Fred] keeps" ASL 25), so there are three ways to read the second line. The mourner himself is metaphorically dead, and the "clay" is his own body, which continues to go through the motions of life, "To wash and dress and eat and drink / And look at things and talk and think / And work, and God knows why" (LP 11). The boot in this reading is a literal part of "To dress." Or the "clay" may be the body of the dead friend and the "boot" a metonymy for the foot, specifically the mourner's foot, which is reluctant to leave his friend in the grave. Or the "clay" may be the grave itself. The second and third readings then collapse into each other, and the "clay" is both the grave and its inhabitant. The two readings with which we are left, both being intended, set up a typical hovering ambiguity. At the moment, the second takes precedence, and in the next line, the persona, having rendered to the dead all that is his "due," tears (dew) having been shed as well as all the proper rites observed, says, "Let's home." Since the dead friend is already in his "long home," as it is called in the oldest English poetry ("Clay's the house he keeps"), to whom is this addressed? The persona is speaking only of himself, not of "you and

I" but of "me, myself, and I." We can hear his reluctance to depart in the apology he tenders to his dead. His "boot clings to the clay" and that boot no longer refers only to the foot it encases, but to the persona of whom that foot is a part. "I must turn away" implies "I must desert, I must abandon, I must forsake you," not simply "I must go to my own home."

The ambiguity is the never-stated word "bed" that underlies both the repeated "good-night" and the grave itself, the bed of earth. It is both literally the grave and metaphorically a cot or couch in which the dead man sleeps, having been bidden the last "Good-night." This dead metaphor is now in English almost inseparable into its component parts. Here, however, Housman is consciously exploiting it as he did in "Along the field," (ASL 26) which was discussed in chapter 6: "And time shall put them both to bed / But she shall lie with earth above, / And he beside another love."

There is an earlier draft of the second verse in the fourth notebook, begun only when Housman had determined to issue his *Last Poems*, which is relevant, and extremely illuminating (Burnett, *Poems*, 87–88, bottoms of pages).

> Good-night, my lad, for nought's eternal;
> > Not you nor I, for sure.
> Man and remembrance, both decay,
> The loving-kindness like the day,
> > Not even ills endure.

In the final version, it is the "league," (the friendship) that is not eternal. In the draft, it is "Not you nor I," our physical selves, our bodies. The body will inexorably decay, and the "remembrance" will keep pace with its decay. By the time the dead body has returned to the dust from which it was made, the memories will have disintegrated together with it. The love and the memories of friendship will fade away with the same inexorability as the light when evening creeps into the sky. Nothing, not the body, not remembrance, not daylight, not even grief at the loss of one's friend ("ills") "can endure." But do not these "ills" have the same referent as all Housman's other "ills"? The word usually connotes homosexuality. The rejection of this line may have been precisely because here this connotation is not intended. Indeed, this verse underlies the ultimate version, which contradicts its entire import. The persona asserts that each day "I shall miss you less," but he knows it is false. Time "should cure" an aching, heavy heart. "Shall" is superceded by "should," and what "should" be is by definition what will not be.

The next verse is an attempt to deny the implications of that "should," but the language is in direct opposition to the statement it makes. It starts out bravely enough, with the highway and the "wide" world beyond. Then appears another pun, the hinge. "Pine" is the "plain pine box" that has been consigned with the clay to the clay. Although the poem states that it is the "memories" and the "faithful thought" that will "pine to nought," it is in fact only the pine casket that will dwindle away until it disappears. The persona will continue to "pine," to long for what was and can never be again "the land of lost content, / . . . The happy highways where I went / And cannot come again" (ASL 40). That highway that "marches" "over the hill" may lead to "what's beyond" but it cannot lead to "what's beyond recall." "Remembrance and the faithful thought" will continue to sit beside the grave even when the "boot" has physically left the "clay" to sleep. It is, after all, a "faithful thought / That sits the grave beside." There it "sits" and there it will continue to sit forever. The "boot" may reluctantly abandon the grave, but the "thought" is immobilized there. This is evident in that "Good-night" of the first verse repeated as the opening word of the second verse. The emotion is overpowering. The same thing happens here as in the "Epithalamium" (LP 24). When the personal element becomes so strong as to be unbearable. Housman turns for words to the literature of the past, this time to Horace's Ode (book 2, no. 9, 192). "Clouds do not always veil the skies, / Nor showers immerse the radiant plain," Dr. Johnson rendered the passage. The context is the same but whereas Horace used the lines to persuade the auditor to stop his eternal mourning, Housman uses it to explain why his mourning is not to be eternal. Swinburne rendered the same thought in other imagery in "A Forsaken Garden" verse 7(*Swinborne*, 78).[7]

> Love deep as the sea as a rose must wither
> As the rose-red seaweed that mocks the rose
> Shall the dead take thought for the dead to love them?
> What love was ever as deep as a grave?
> They are loveless now as the grass above them
> Or the wave.

The sinuosity of this stanza from Swinburne, curling back on itself in intricate convolutions, is in stark contrast to the sinewosity, the simplicity of diction and form, which stiffens Housman's lyrics.

Having found refuge from his own emotion, as it were, in the two lines from Horace, thus creating a breathing space, Housman proceeds to return to his own persona. Again, the drafts in the notebooks throw light on what he is doing. There are two draft versions of this verse on the same manuscript page, so he may have written them at almost the same time. I shall print the draft of the complete verse first, followed by the second draft of lines 3 through 5 (Burnett, *Poems*, 87–88, bottoms of pages).

> The rain, it is not always raining,
>   or man the grave beside.
> Time and again shall I be glad,
> And [chance on/find me] friends like you, my lad,
>   The world it is so wide.
>
> I shall [be blithe/delight] in morning's blue,
> Be gay with friends as good as you,
>   Or why's the world so wide?

The second line of the Horace translation replaced the second line draft. Why? I would suggest that the original second line was too naked an expression of the implications of the preceding "ache of heart and heaviness," the "remembrance and the faithful thought / That sits the grave beside." The persona is still beside the grave. Not only the memory and the thought linger there; he himself does so. In the first verse, having done all that's "right," he intended to "turn away," but his "boot" still "lingers" at the graveside.

Despite all the intimations of movement, this is a poem of stasis. The persona will never replace the dead man emotionally, either by chance or intent, no matter how wide the world may be, although he will have some "good days and mirth" with other "friends no worse than you," "no worse than you" but not "like you." Removed is the direct comparison between these hypothetical new friends and the "vanish'd hand" and the "voice that is still," as Tennyson phrased it in "Break, break, break." The reason, I think, for rejecting the second draft version is interesting. The interrogative form of the last line—"I shall doubtless recover from the pain of your death, or else what is the reason for there being such amplitude in the world?"—can only serve to cast an overwhelming shadow of doubt on the thought expressed in the words. "Or" implies that "I shall never recover," denying the entire premise of the poem.

Parenthetically, it will not have passed unnoticed that in discussing the draft versions, I am not concerned with their poetic value (or lack of value). Housman doubtless rejected them for prosodic reasons as well as connotative ones. I am using them to excavate the underlying emotional and cognitive layers buried beneath the poems as we have them.

The last verse, with its cry of muted anguish, underlines the intimated denial of the premise that is never directly challenged. The poem closes as it began, with the rain streaming onto the grave, the tears of mourning that, never so stated, are yet the symbol of the persona's own repressed tears. Nothing has altered, nothing has moved, and the state of the weather, reflecting the persona's emotional state, is unchanged. One feels clearly that it never will change. Emotionally, the persona's grief is to be equated with that of a mother for a dead child, and not that of a mere friend, not that friends are ever "mere" in Housman. And the mother does not forget. The tone of this poem, with no resolution attained between the verbal movement and the emotional stasis of resignation, is quite different from that of "Parta Quies" (MP 48), based on the same metaphor of sleep for death (from the opening "Good-night" to the final "Sleep on, sleep sound"), but it imparts a sense of quiet finality. As Watts said, "love and friendship alike end in oblivion" ("Poetry of Housman," 123). But they will end only with the final coming of that same oblivion, when the persona is himself "clay," returning us to the first reading of the second line, with which we began.

One thing I have not considered is the identity of the dead man. The poem was not written for Moses Jackson, then still living. In any case, the poet would never see his friend's grave except in a photograph (which was sent to him and which he treasured with all the other mementos of his lost friend) and in his imagination, which it no doubt was. It would have been the ultimate in tactlessness, however, to have included it in the volume written in tribute to the still living (though barely) Moses Jackson. In addition, this poem does not carry that erotic charge that inevitably accompanies the verses directly addressed to or unquestionably about him. Moses Jackson, however, although the "friend" of Housman's dreams, was not his only friend.

There was another, equally dear to him though in a different way, one whose memorial verses would appropriately be included in the book intended for Moses Jackson, one beside whose grave Housman must certainly have stood with the emotions reflected in the above poem. That friend—who is definitely the subject of the next poem, probably of a second poem, and possibly of others, including the preceding one—was Moses Jackson's brother Add, Adalbert J. Jackson. The text was basically settled, although not finalized, late in the Boer War. The coincidence of the rain falling on the abandoned body of his own brother Herbert, in conjunction with the death of Moses Jackson's brother Add, may have resulted in a conflation in this poem of Herbert and Add as the poet's own young brother(s), the composite object of mourning, lying in the rain-soaked grave.

Before considering the A. J. J. poems, it may be useful to see what Laurence Housman had to say about his brother's relationship with the two Jackson brothers. In editing Laurence Housman's "De Amicitia" for publication, John Carter, after noting the fact that Adalbert's "photograph hung close to that of Moses Jackson . . . over Housman's fireplace at Trinity" until the time of the poet's death, appended extracts from two letters from Laurence Housman to Maude Hawkins on this subject. The parenthetical explanation is Carter's, the emphases are Laurence Housman's. "I still think there was more *mutual* attraction between those two [AEH and Moses Jackson]. . . . But Jackson *shied away* from the full implication, knowing he could not share it '*in kind.*' But . . . his attraction to the younger brother *was* reciprocated . . . I doubt whether Moses ever kissed AEH: but I have no doubt that AJJ *did*" (19 June 1958). And again, a month later, his "no doubt" was even less doubtful. He wrote to her, "I have no doubt whatever that A. E. H. was in closer and warmer physical relationship with A. J. J. than with his brother Moses" (21 July 1958) (L. Housman, "*De Amicitia,*" Appendix B, 41).

Carter cautiously accepts Laurence Housman's account. I do not. Let it not be overlooked that Laurence Housman seems never to have met either of the Jackson brothers more than once or twice, and then only by chance and fleetingly. Housman kept his life in compartments; friendship and family were not in the same compartment. Laurence Housman did not recognize Moses Jackson's picture on his brother's wall and asked him about it. He may have recognized that of Adalbert, or he may have felt it more discreet (although discretion was not prominent in his character) not to ask questions about the portrait of the handsome youth. For whatever reason, he asked only about the portrait of Moses Jackson, the unromantic, middle-aged man. Nor does Laurence Housman base his conclusions on any private conversations he had with his brother on the subject; there were none, or he would surely have made mention of them, at least obliquely.

Laurence Housman based his conclusions solely on the texts of the canonical poems themselves, for he makes no mention of any references in the notebooks or any other papers to either brother. The letters to Mrs. Hawkins were written in 1958, when he was already 93, a very old man with a failing memory, and his memory seems never to have been particularly accurate. In other words, his conclusions were based on guesswork, his private knowledge (no longer private) of his brother's homosexuality, and his own knowledge of his brother's character.

A. E. Housman and his brother Laurence were not particularly close either as children or young men. During the years they both lived in London they saw each other very seldom, either by accident or by appointment. It was only in the closing years of the poet's life that they spent any amount of time together. This is clear from both Laurence Housman's autobiography and his memoir of his brother. He did not, and *could* not, know the truth of his brother's relationships, physical or emotional, reciprocal or not, with either of the Jacksons. He could be sure of his opinions (as are most people), but they remain only his opinions and as such are worth only a little more than those of others.

Laurence Housman thought that the attraction between A. E. Housman and Moses Jackson was mutual. It probably was. Most people react to subliminal signals about the emotions of those whom they know well and with whom they are in daily contact. The two young men knew each other well. They roomed together at Oxford and shared premises in London, by mutual agreement. Later, Housman stood godfather to Moses Jackson's son. Additional data have been included in the first chapter. That the affection between them was mutual cannot be denied. Laurence Housman thought that Moses Jackson "*shied away* from the full implication, knowing he could not share it '*in kind.*'" Assuming the existence of an emotional state many years earlier in a person whom one never knew well, and then analyzing the reasons for it, seems to me to be going a bit far. It is at least possible, as I have already suggested, that Moses Jackson did share the emotion "in kind" but "shied away" from acknowledging to the world or to his friend, perhaps even to himself, that he did so. It seems to me unlikely that Housman would have been so deeply in love with Moses Jackson had there been no reciprocal attraction whatsoever "in kind." There are many reasons for marrying other than overwhelming love, and one of them may be to prove to the world (and to oneself) that one is "normal"; another, recommended to the titular character in E. M. Forster's *Maurice*, is to cure oneself of this "unnatural" passion. It is not unusual for constitutionally gay men to "marry to avoid the stigma of being homosexual or because they are unable to acknowledge that they are [gay]."[8] Indeed, John Addington Symonds married for precisely these reasons. I am not saying that such *was* the case with Jackson, but I am saying that it *could have been* the case.

Laurence Housman says that his brother was also attracted "to the younger brother." It may be so. It may also have been that A. E. Housman regarded Add Jackson primarily as Moses' brother, and his love for his friend was extended to include that friend's brothers (and sisters), that in some sense he thought (wishfully and wistfully) of Add Jackson rather as a sort of quasi brother-in-law. As Page acutely remarks, "to be the brother of Moses was in itself sufficient basis for Housman's interest and affection" (*A. E. Housman*, 54).[9] After Moses Jackson left for India, Add Jackson would also have been a conduit for the passing of casual messages between his brother and Housman. Housman's diary indicates that when Adalbert Jackson received letters from his brother in Karachi, Housman was informed of them (Housman, "*De Amicitia*," 38). Adalbert would have been the only one with whom Housman could speak easily and intimately about the absent man. That the friendship between them endured until Adalbert's death is all of which we can be sure. The exact nature of that friendship is something about which we (like Laurence Housman) can only speculate.

Page considers the idea of physical intimacy between them as possible, but unlikely (*A. E. Housman*, 54).[10] When Laurence Housman asserts that the relationship between A. E. Housman and Adalbert Jackson was reciprocal, there is no reason for doubting it. Just as subliminal signals indicate physical attraction, they also indicate friendly regard. Few people seek to become friends with those who clearly dislike them, and should they do so it is more than doubtful that they would succeed. The friendship between A. E. Housman and Adalbert Jackson is amply attested to.

Laurence Housman states categorically that he doubts that Moses Jackson ever kissed A. E. Housman, but does not in the least doubt that Adalbert did. He implies without ever quite saying so baldly that A. E. Housman and Adalbert Jackson were lovers. All this he insinuates without a single shred of evidence except that supplied by his own imagination, into the state of which I would not care to enquire. Perhaps Moses Jackson never kissed his friend, and perhaps he did—once—and was horrified at himself afterward. It is hard to forget that overwritten "we" in the poem about the lovers in the haycock.

That Adalbert Jackson and A. E. Housman had an affair, were physically lovers, or even exchanged passionate (as opposed to brotherly) kisses, I take leave to doubt. The psychology is all wrong; the few known facts are all against it. Adalbert Jackson was, first, last, and always, the young brother of Moses Jackson, the brother of the man whom Housman loved with a deep and abiding love. It does not seem to me probable that he should have consoled himself with this particular man as a substitute for what he was denied. Jacob did not go eagerly to Leah's bed when Rachel was beyond his reach. Any other man in the world would have been more likely. To have been intimate with Moses' brother when the one he wanted was Moses would have seemed to him both a betrayal and a cruel mockery. It is only fair to add that Professor Robert Friend, who as a gay man obviously had more understanding of the dynamics of such a relationship than is possible for me, completely disagreed with me on this point. However, I hold to my opinion.

Page considers, and I concur, that the friendship between Housman and Adalbert, though close, was casual. Once, on reading a letter from the poet, Adalbert was described by one of his sisters as "roaring with laughter over it." It could hardly have been a love letter. It was a month after Adalbert Jackson's death before Housman learned of it, and having learned of it, he was not himself ill for months afterward as he was after that of Moses Jackson. Instead, he wrote a condolence letter to the family in which Page reports him as having said that Adalbert's was "the most

amiable nature he had ever known." Despite Laurence Housman's innuendoes, I think Page is correct in calling this "a good relationship, happy
and relaxed, rather than a grand passion or even an infatuation." Page
also notes that the poetry, on which Laurence Housman based his certainty, does not support it. The A. J. J. poems "seem . . . to express real
affection but not passion: even at their most explicitly admiring . . . they
are on an entirely different emotional level from the ravaged, desolate
cries torn from him by his love for Moses" (*A. E. Housman*, 54).

In fact, they are on the same emotional level as the Herbert Housman
poems already examined, on the same emotional level as "The rain, it
streams." The tone is warm and affectionate and personal, heavy with
regret, but easy. These poems are not infused with erotic puns. One has
no sense of the boiling volcanic emotion erupting despite all attempts at
suppression that one cannot but feel in those "ravaged desolate cries" that
will be considered in the next chapter but one, that on the poetry about
himself and his "friend." Now, let us look at the A. J. J. poems.

A. J. J.

When he's returned I'll tell him—oh,
     Dear fellow, I forgot:
Time was you would have cared to know,
     But now it matters not.

I mourn you, and you heed not how;
     Unsaid the word must stay;
Last month was time enough, but now
     The news must keep for aye.

Oh, many a month before I learn
     Will find me starting still
And listening, as the days return,
     For him that never will.

Strange, strange to think his blood is cold
     And mine flows easy on,
And that straight look, that heart of gold,
     That grace, that manhood, gone.

The word unsaid will stay unsaid
     Though there was much to say;
Last month was time enough: he's dead,
     The news must keep for aye.

                                        (MP 42)

The "word," the "news" that "must keep for aye" since it was not told "last month," would have been of Housman's appointment as Professor of Latin at Adalbert's own old alma mater, University College, London. There would certainly have been "much to say" about this, on both sides, for Adalbert had read classics. The very fact that this great news had not been told "last month" indicates the easy nature of their friendship. Had Laurence Housman's certainties been facts, the first thing Housman would have done on receiving this position would have been to share the "news" with Adalbert.

Let us note that the A. J. J. poems were never intended for publication. They were written, like so many in the notebooks from which Laurence Housman took them, to relieve the pressure of Housman's emotions. This first of the A. J. J. poems was written early in 1893, only a few months after his friend's death in November of 1892 (Burnett, *Poems*, 453). If the verse seems filled with "impotent cliches" (Ashton, "Critical Study," 198) or to be weak and sentimental (Mortimer, "Housman Relics," 631), seems "rather pedestrian" and "mournfully pathetic" (Watson, *Divided Life*, 144), this is the reason. We have seen enough workshop material to realize that there is a vast gulf between even a second or third draft and a final version, one with which Housman was satisfied. He never worked this poem into such a final form, and it shows. The poem was written as an anodyne for the poet's own grieved bewilderment, his sense of futility. Having done this, there was no reason to do more.

The second poem that is generally accepted as referring to Adalbert Jackson, a reference suggested by his nephew, Moses Jackson's son, Housman's godson Gerald, in a letter to Laurence Housman (A. E. Housman, *Collected Poems and Selected Prose*, 495), records what was probably an actual experience. Most people have had the experience of seeing in a stranger an astonishing resemblance to someone one knows well. In this case, the stranger was a beggar, and his eyes and voice were those of Adalbert Jackson.

> He looked at me with eyes I thought
>   I was not like to find,
> The voice he begged for pence with brought
>   Another man to mind.
>
> Oh no, lad, never touch your cap;
>   It is not my half-crown:
> You have it from a better chap
>   That long ago lay down.
>
> Turn east and over Thames to Kent
>   And come to the sea's brim,
> And find his everlasting tent
>   And touch your cap to him.

(MP 41)

The man who begged for "pence" is given a "half-crown." When he tries to thank the munificently charitable gentleman, he is instructed to go east, cross the Thames, and journey to a certain cemetery in Kent "at the sea's brim" where he will find the grave of the one who was responsible for this unexpected largesse. Following these directions will take him to the graveyard at "Ramsgate, the home town of the Jackson family, where Adalbert was buried" (L. Housman, "*De Amicitia*," Carter addenda, appendix B, 41), and he may "touch" his "cap to him."

There is another draft of the last verse of this poem, which Burnett opts to use, although in this case I have preferred the version used by Ricks and all other editors. The alternate verse is provided in the notes.[11] As bad as it undoubtedly is, it has two virtues. The first is the depersonalization of the subject by removing the Ramsgate reference, thus rendering it less Jackson/Housman specific. Its other virtue is that in comparison with it "A. J. J." is touched with relative luster. The puns in this verse are something worse than bad; they are obvious. To "step out" is to "march." But since my friend cannot march the tramp must march—or tramp—to him at "the world's end." The poetic improvement (at the cost of universalization) in the version printed by Laurence Housman is evident, and it seems so simple: only the prosaic directions. But Housman had the knack of doing what Wordsworth had contended was the poet's task: investing the prosaic with poetic magic, a knack nowhere better seen than in the usual version of this last verse. "The world's end" is replaced by the "everlasting tent," the mundane spatial image by a combined temporal and spacial one, and such a temporal, spacial one!

"Tent" denotes a temporary and movable abode used by wanderers (gypsies or nomads); its connotations are as different as possible from those of the eternal and eternally fixed "house of clay." This is, however, not any common tent but an "everlasting" one, a quiet, understated, but brilliant oxymoron that suggests that even the grave cannot be considered the ultimate and final resting place. The nomadic tent dissolves into a revivalist's tent, with no pejorative overtones, with its emphasis on "the life and the resurrection." Those who dwell in such "everlasting" tents are assured of eventually moving on, to "fresh Woods, and Pastures new," as Milton put it in "Lycidas." Housman did not himself dwell in such a "tent," but he could understand and use the image.

It has not been previously suggested that the following brief lyric, like "The rain it streams" completed and polished for *Last Poems*, is also an A. J. J. poem, any more than it has been suggested that "The rain it streams" is one. However, I would suggest that these two poems are related to each other and to the preceding poem. If I am right they are all part of a fragmented elegy for his friend, Adalbert J. Jackson.

> The sigh that heaves the grasses
>   Whence thou wilt never rise
> Is of the air that passes
>   And knows not if it sighs.
>
> The diamond tears adorning
>   The low mound on the lea,
> Those are the tears of morning,
>   That weeps but not for thee.

(LP 27)

This poem began to take shape some time before 1902, when a fair copy was made, and Burnett thinks any date earlier than autumn of 1901 unlikely. Graves relates it to Herbert Housman's death and the Boer War cycle. He considers it "a poem about the cold indifference of the Universe" (*A. E. Housman*, 124). This seems to me an oversimplification. Adalbert's death is at least as likely as that of Herbert Housman to have inspired this poem. Its ambivalent hovering between the tonal staying and the verbalized going, between the endless mourning of the imagery and the stated intention of not mourning, are like those of "The rain it streams." The imagery is not about "cold indifference" but about ambivalence. Almost every key word is ambiguous, and those ambiguities reverse the tenor of the poem.

On the surface the lyric goes out of its way, too far out of its way, to deny the pathetic fallacy as the other went out of its way to emphasize over and over that the persona was leaving even while he remained. By using the "morning" spelling and underlining that it *is* "morning" and not "mourning," that the "sigh" is only and no more than the insensate wind, and that the "tears" shed are not in fact tears of mourning for the dead man in his 'low mound on the lea' but prosaic dew, the poem creates a sense that the persona is trying, and not very successfully, to convince himself that the sighs and tears and mourning are not his, and are not real. The poet doth protest too much, methinks. Those "heaving grasses" are a projection onto nature and thus a denial of the persona's real heaving of the breast. The sigh is not his but only the wind. The tears sparkling on the grave are only dew (or rain, or something else, anything but his tears). "I am not mourning, and I shall presently go away, but not yet, not yet." The last, and final, "good-night" has not been said. We have seen in Housman's earliest poetry his sense that the pathetic fallacy is emotionally valid even while it is objectively invalid. This poem is a condensed and transmuted development of that early work.

Empson, noting the tension between what the words say they say and what they mean but deny saying, thoroughly approved of it. He called it "a four-square healthy little poem (only the wind sighs over the dead friend's grave . . . and does not know if it sighs; only the dew weeps . . . and does not weep for the dead man; still, it weeps") ("Teaching Literature"). Incidentally, Browne thinks that the "diamond tears" are, or may be, not dew but rain brought by the Pleiads, traditionally associated with gentle summer rains (*Elegy in Arcady*, 103), apparently because Housman used this star cluster in connection with rain that symbolized his tears elsewhere, as we shall see. Stevenson sees no ambiguity (which is, after all, Empson's specialty) but ascribes the imagery to a combination of personification and irony which sets up a "tone of wry amusement and detached wisdom. The pose is a device for not giving way to the passion of the moment," and the poem is "charged with the emotions of the experience. . . . Housman's style is a pose, a mask for his awareness" ("Ceremony of Housman's Style," 53). What they are all aware of and try to explain in different terminology is that the pathetic fallacy is denied only on the surface. On a deeper level, it is accepted as, in some sense, valid. Empson is aware that the grave is that of a "dead friend." How? The poem does not say so, but the very words that deny the emotion clearly proclaim the friendship. Browne related the "diamond tears" to rain, which brings us into the ambience of "The rain it streams" (LP 18). Stevenson sees "the passion of the moment" and the emotions of the experience under the "mask," not a "mask" for his awareness at all, I would argue, but a mask for the very emotions felt at his friend's grave, denied as pertaining to himself, transferred to nature, and again denied. This is very like the denials of endless grief already discussed.

Even if it is agreed that this poem is akin to "The rain it streams," I have not yet clearly linked them with the death of Adalbert Jackson, although I suspect that there is indeed a linkage.

It may have been noted by the alert reader that Housman very rarely uses the pronouns "thee," "thy," or "thou." In all the canon, excepting this one poem, these obsolete pronominal forms occur in only six poems, all of which are in the unofficial volumes. One use is in the translation of "Diffugere Nives" (MP 5). Three of the appearances of these forms are in poems in which it is not the persona but a character in the poem who uses them. In the early "New Year's Eve" (AP 21) the "dead gods" use them. In the early "Atys" (AP 1), a poem drawn from mythology on the death of the son of king Croeses of Lydia, the king's companion uses them. And in "The Sage to the Young Man" (MP 4) the sage uses them. The hymn written "For My Funeral" (MP 47) where the context is religious makes use of such a form. An obsolete pronoun is also found in "Bells in tower at evening toll" (MP 17) where the context is at least quasi-religious since the bells are church bells and the poem deals with spiritual temptation. Such pronouns are *never* found in the official poetry.

The above poem is not a translation, nor a character's recorded speech, nor has it a direct religious context. Indeed, this is the only serious adult poem using such a pronominal form in a modern, non-religious setting where the speaker, although a persona, is not also a dramatic character.

Housman's diction in every other poem is colloquial and modern, not "poetic." Indeed, a simple and non-ostentatiously poetic vocabulary is one of the hallmarks of his poetic style. When archaic or "poetical" words are used they call attention to themselves, as do Latinate words, because of their very rarity. And such archaic words as occur frequently (a very short list, starting with the notorious "lads" that is still common in British speech and thus not really archaic at all) are usually characteristic of the Terence persona rather than of the poet behind the mask. Nor is the Terence vocabulary particularly archaic; most of his characteristic diction is still in common use in many of the more rural parts of England and among certain classes even in London, as regular listening to the British news media will easily confirm. These words retain their archaic *flavor* but have not in fact fallen out of usage even today, a hundred years later. Housman was a conscious artist who carefully chose his words for their effect and had cogent reasons for his choices.

Why, then, in this particular poem, do we find "thou" and "thee"? I would tentatively suggest that the use of "thou" was forced by the later use of "thee," and that "thee" was necessary for the rhyme that rang in the poet's ear, though not in the poem: "sea." The "low mound by the sea" becomes "the low mound on the lea," and "lea" is another poetico-archaic word unnatural to Housman. This is its single and unique use in all his poetry. Housman even when masquerading as Terence usually uses "fields" or "grass" or even "mead," but never—except here—"lea." And unlike so many others, this is not in any way a "Terence" poem. The diction is Housman's alone.

Those "diamond tears" may not be only dew or rain. There may be some ocean spray mixed with them. And we know who was buried at Ramsgate, in Kent, on "the sea's brim." The chain of reasoning is slender, but I think it will hold.

That the emotion so carefully denied actually permeates the poem was felt by Robb, who said of it that "the pain of lost love remembered sobs through this brief lament" (*Four in Exile*, 23). It is the pain of lost love never realized that is heard in the "ravaged desolate cries" of other poems, but in these poems of what, despite Laurence Housman, I believe to be loving friendship without quotation marks, it does not wail broken-heartedly. It only weeps quietly. It does not cry out, it only sighs, but those sighs will not cease while the winds blow.

There is a single notebook quatrain (Burnett, *Poems*, 173) with which I wish to end this examination of Housman's poetry on friendship, so much of which has already been discussed as part of the Shropshire cycle, and which links it to his poems on "friendship," to be taken up in the next chapters.

> I have desired to die,
>> That so this fire might cease.
> When you were lost, and I
>> Were perished and at peace.

"These lines," Haber suggests, "may commemorate Housman's grief at the death of his friend, A. J. Jackson. . . . His most significant tribute, 'A. J. J.' (MP 42), was written a few pages later" (A. E. Housman, *Manuscript Poems*, 42). In fact, only five pages separate the two. I quite agree with Haber but I think it may "commemorate" more than the death of Add Jackson.

If this poem relates to Adalbert, and only to him, its diction, for example "this fire," would tend to support Laurence Housman's insinuation about the relationship between the two men. Its tone also is quite different from that of the A. J. J. poems we have just seen. Like the diction, it seems far more akin to the Moses Jackson poems with their heartbroken cries and reiterated assurance that only death can end the poet's desire, that only in the grave will "this fire" at last "cease" and the speaker find "peace." If we recall, however, that for a long time Adalbert was Housman's primary link with Moses Jackson, this seeming contradiction is resolved. What was "lost" was not only "you," my friend Adalbert, but "you," one of my links with the man I love, severed by your death, and thus "you," Moses Jackson, were also in a way "lost." "I have desired to die / That so this fire might cease," but instead of finding "peace" in my own death, I "lost" you in many senses, and the fire still rages. "It was friends to die for," never friends who would themselves die. It was the inverse of the adolescent dream.

It is now appropriate to turn from friendship to "friendship," and in the next chapter we shall examine Housman's own attitude toward his sexual orientation before turning to the poetry of which Moses Jackson is undoubtedly the subject.

Melpomene

9

How Ill God Made Me

As we have seen, the tone of the poems in which Housman commemorates the non-erotic male bond is charged with grief and regret for lost comrades and the persona's own youth. The subjects are given fictitious names in the Shropshire cycle, but in writing about real people, Housman does not hesitate to use their initials ("A. J. J.") or their names. In his farewell to Venice, "Far known to sea and shore," in the last verse he also bids farewell to the gondolier whom he had employed for many years during his visits to that city.

> Far known to sea and shore,
>   Foursquare and founded well,
> A thousand years it bore,
>   And then the belfry fell.
>
> The steersman of Triest
>   Looked where his mark should be,
> But empty was the west
>   And Venice under sea.
>
> From dusty wreck dispersed
>   Its stature mounts amain;
> On surer foot than first
>   The belfry stands again.
>
> At to-fall of the day
>   Again its curfew tolls
> And burdens far away
>   The green and sanguine shoals.
>
> It looks to north and south,
>   It looks to east and west;
> It guides to Lido mouth
>   The steersman of Triest.

> Andrea, fare you well;
>> Venice, farewell to thee.
> The tower that stood and fell
> Is not rebuilt in me.

> (MP 44)

Graves says unhesitatingly that Housman and Andrea were lovers, and in this poem "he used the phallic image" of the tower that once stood and has now fallen, never to be rebuilt "in me," to express his having fallen out of love with both Venice and Andrea (*A. E. Housman*, especially 152). In fact, the tone of the poem is one of wistful regret, not dead passion. Its affinities are with the lyrics of the preceding chapter and not with those to be considered here. That the tower that Graves says *is* a phallic image can be so there is no doubt. The question is, *is it a phallic image for Housman?* A tower has many symbolic meanings, not one. It can represent the "ivory tower" of youthful idealism; it can represent the phallus of adult sexuality; it can represent the "sage's tower" of scholarship or the wisdom of age or, as often used, the "ivory tower" of retreat from the world, as suggested to me by Professor Robert Friend. No one has ever suggested that the tower in Milton's "Il Penseroso" is anything but the third.

Now, there is one tower to which Housman recurs quite often, Ludlow tower. No suggestion has ever been made that Ludlow tower has a phallic dimension or is in any way symbolic. It is accepted as part of the Shropshire "local color." If one were to give it a symbolic value, the most appropriate one might be the dual symbol of the apparently eternal but ultimately mortal spirit of traditional England and the aspirations, ideals, and enthusiasm of youth, both of which will endure only "Till Ludlow tower is down" (ASL 3). Like Ludlow tower, the Venetian tower is a church tower, a belfry complete with bells that toll the hours. In fact, it is St. Mark's ("The steersman of Triest / Looked where his mark should be"), and it similarly functions as a symbol both of traditional Venice and the dreams and enthusiasms of youth.

Housman paid his last long visit to Venice when he was almost fifty, and he returned very briefly only when he was sixty-seven years old, in response to a request from Andrea who thought he was dying. The first and second drafts of this poem were both written in April 1922, after that last long visit. The farewell to both the city and the man have the same poignancy of regret for what was and is no longer as we have seen in the last chapter. Housman was already old and tired. The fallen tower of Venice seems to have much the same significance as that of Ludlow, and it is not a phallic one.

Having disposed of the specifically phallic significance of the tower, what of Andrea? Despite the positive assertion of Graves and Browne (*Elegy in Arcady*, 156) that the Venice tower is a symbol of the ending of a love affair between Housman and his lame, one-eyed gondolier and/or of Housman's active sex life, Bayley, Page, and Jebb are more cautious. Bayley thinks the relations between Andrea and Housman "were probably wholly decorous" (*Housman's Poems*, 162), and Page concludes that "it needs a great deal of determination to detect a romantic motivation" in the reference to Andrea, since the death-bed visit was most likely an act of "noblesse oblige." He adds that the carnal reading distorts the poem, which "is not even superficially . . . about Andrea," who receives only four words near its end, but about Venice and "more profoundly, it is Housman's farewell to his own past" (*A. E. Housman*, 122–23). Jebb points out that real evidence of a love affair is wholly lacking (*A. E. Housman*, 42); Naiditch considers the evidence "insufficient" (*Problems*, 58, note 2). Page also points out that Housman quite casually mentioned Andrea in his letters to his stepmother and sister Katharine, which he was most unlikely to have done had the relations between himself and his gondolier been anything other than the ostensible ones (*A. E. Housman*, 122–23). I completely agree. Indeed, considering Housman's determination to keep his private life private, I would say that the use of Andrea's name in the poem is *prima facie* evidence that Andrea was never more than Housman's gondolier, an employee of long standing who had served his employer both faithfully and well as a gondolier—and nothing else. Goold compares the chauffeur who drove the aged Housman around France in the 1930s and cared for him when he was ill or injured to Andrea, and considers both of them young men to whom he had "taken a liking" that never "went beyond pleasurable friendship" ("Housman's Masnilius," 137).

The tone of the poem is charged with the same grief and regret we have seen in the preceding chapter and is quite different from that of the poetry we now have to consider. It lacks the supercharged sexual underlayer we have seen in "Tarry Delight" (MP 15). A similar tone of repressed intensity vibrates in Housman's poetry about the erotic male bond and is created in much the same way: diction that holds an unspoken pun or double entendre in its depths, obliquity, and misdirection.

Housman was not the only one who wrote homosexual poetry in this way. W. H. Auden, in 1945, refused publication permission for a study of the homoerotic patterns in his poetry partly on the grounds that a teacher is "particularly vulnerable" to scandal if rumors of homosexuality are whispered about him (Woods, *Articulate Flesh*, 169). In 1876, such rumors were partly responsible for preventing Walter Pater's appointment as a professor of poetry at Oxford (Small, Introduction to Pater's *Marius the Epicurean*, xii). If this was true of Pater in 1876 and of Auden in 1945, it was surely true of Housman in the years immediately following the Oscar Wilde trial. To prevent such rumors, Auden "systematically" concealed the maleness of his subject by using the genderless "you." The critics accepted the ambiguity and obscurity of his poetry, an ambiguity that acted "as a gag on any attempt to understand the experiences that were their source and often, indeed, their subjects" (Woods, *Articulate Flesh*, 168–70). At the other end of Europe, Cavafy in the original versions of his poetry also left the gender of his subject ambiguous.[1]

In heterosexual poetry names are customarily assigned to the love objects (Delia, Celia, Stella, etc.), but in homosexual poetry, the androgynous "you" is preferred. This is as true of Spender as of Auden. It is usually interpreted as a technique of universalization. It is not. It is a technique of self-censorship (Roditi, cited in Woods, *Articulate Flesh*, 170) and self-protection. Or a female name may be given to the male subject of the poem, as in Byron's "Thyrza" poems, inspired by a "beautiful [choir] boy" to whom he gave a female name, partly in order to make the poems publishable. The use of gender transfer as a smoke screen is both an act of self-defense and a response to the demands imposed by the mainstream culture (Paglia, *Sexual Personae*, 350). Housman did not use Byron's technique. It would have seemed to him, I think, both flamboyant and dishonest. Instead, like Auden and Spender, he simply used gender-free terminology in the poems now under discussion. In much of the poetry to be considered in the next chapter, however, Housman uses "he." These poems were never intended for publication. For Housman, there was only one "he."

Since physical love between men was most safely "left unexpressed . . . the strength of the literature of homosexuality lies in obliquity arising from the need to resort to metaphor to express sexual meaning" (Woods, *Articulate Flesh*, 2). It is Housman's metaphors that we will consider in this chapter.

Auden, despite being so reticent about his own sexual preferences (he was usually oral active), had no hesitation in identifying Housman as anal passive. He ascribed the self-disgust so often evident in his poetry to the Greek mode in which ephebes were anal passive and adult men anal active. An adult anal passive was an object of scorn, says Auden, and Housman accepted the judgement of ancient Greece ("A Worcestershire Lad"). In fact, most male homosexuals are both anal and oral, both passive and active, at different times with the same partner or with different partners although, like Auden himself, they have preferences one way or the other.[2] Since the most common homosexual metaphor in Housman's erotic poetry is "drinking," his preferred mode, as far as it is indicated at all, may have been the same as Auden's: the active role in fellatio.

Self-disgust is certainly one component of Housman's homosexual poetry. Auden ascribed it to the specific role that he assumes that Housman preferred. I would ascribe it simply to his preference for men, to the mere fact of his being a homosexual. Housman's is not a poetry in which homosexuality is celebrated. He did not glory in his sexual orientation. He only accepted it, sometimes stoically, sometimes defiantly, but one feels that he did so fatalistically and bitterly, having fought against it and lost the battle. It brought him neither joy nor satisfaction. His one public statement about homosexuality is puckish, and rather wry. When A. J. A. Symons requested permission to include some poems from A Shropshire Lad in his 1928 anthology, A Book of Nineties Verse, Housman refused. He wrote to his publisher, Grant Richards, "to include me in an anthology of the Nineties would be just as technically correct, and just as essentially inappropriate, as to include Lot in a book on Sodomites; in saying which I am not saying a word against sodomy, nor implying that intoxication and incest are in any way preferable" (A. E. Housman, Letters, 271). This reply is a "nice combination of accuracy and disingenuousness" with "ironic nuances" (Gardner, Critical Heritage 3). Needless to say, Richards was blind to these nuances.

Homosexuals are Housman's "luckless lads." Their love can result only in sterility, and "the smack of it is sour." (ASL 62) As Cavafy wrote in "Theatre of Sidon (A.D. 400)," ". . . those verses: all about a special kind of sexual pleasure, / the kind that leads toward a condemned, a barren love." (Collected Poems, 90). Housman would have agreed completely.

> When the bells justle in the tower
>   The hollow night amid,
> Then on my tongue the taste is sour
>   Of all I ever did.
>
>   (AP 9)

This terrible and bitter "cry from the heart" (Graves, A. E. Housman, 220) is built on two unspoken, and partly erotic, puns. Bells have "tongues:" their clappers. Mouths have tongues: organs of taste (Ricks, "Nature of Housman's Poetry,") and sour is one of the four basic taste sensations. Tongues are also the means by which words are articulated aloud, and they are the languages in which those words are framed. The first two meanings link the "bells" of the first line with the "taste" of the third. The second and third meanings link this quatrain with Terence/Housman's poetry, the "sour" brew which "out of a stem that scored the hand" he "wrung . . . in a weary land" (ASL 62). In retrospect, that "stem" about which there was so much debate has an additional meaning. The Bible says in Isaiah 9:1, "there shall come forth a rod out of the stem of Jesse." No fertile seed, no scion will "come forth" out of this "stem," the hollow stem both physically and metaphorically, in a homosexual union no matter how strongly or lovingly that "stem" is "wrung." The fourth meaning of tongue links Housman the Latin scholar and English stylist to rural Terence whose tongue not only speaks for him but also speaks in a slightly different tongue; the linguistic stigmata of his diction are not those of Housman.

That "sour" taste on the tongue flavors "all I ever did." All professional, poetical, and personal achievements alike are "hollow" like the "stem," because "Effacing clean and fast / Cities not built to last / And charms devised in vain, / Pours the confounding main" (MP 45). Are not those "charms devised in vain" both the poetry itself and the editions of Latin poets, incantations chanted in and by many "tongues"? All are reduced to the same level of futility. We have already seen this implicit in Housman's images of sterility. The bells "justle . . . /The hollow night amid." In the night "lovers crown their vows" (ASL 53), but this night is "hollow" because although it may create sound (as the hollow bell does when struck) it cannot create substance. It is sterile. The "seeds" planted in a man's body "never grow" into literal children. They can produce only the figurative nettle ("touch it and it stings" MP 32), which I earlier suggested as Terence's "stem that scored the hand," or, in the case of a poet, the flowers whose colors are "not the wear." But even though they may prove seeds that germinate in later poets and are reborn into new poems, these offspring can only be symbolic, literary but never literal.

This variety of complex pun, common in Housman's erotic poetry, is almost all beneath the surface; only the tip is clearly visible. Sometimes what shows is the pointed tip of the sword. In discussing "Hell Gate" (LP 31), it was indicated that a sword is, or can certainly be interpreted as, a phallic symbol. The sword that Sergeant Troy wields with such facility in his night meeting with Bathsheba Everdene and that so fascinates her in Hardy's *Far from the Madding Crowd* cries aloud to be read phallically. A gun can also be such a symbol. They are a man's weapons, and one need only recall that in Cleland's *Fanny Hill* such words, like "tool" and "weapon" itself, are invariably substituted for the words that uncompromisingly designate the male organ, to see how easily a phallic symbol can become a euphemism for the phallus.

Whether in any given context such words are literal, can be interpreted phallically, or are meant to be so interpreted, is matter for debate. However, when in the poetry of a given poet, in this case Housman, such a reading adds depth and clarity to poems otherwise pedestrian or only vaguely, if incontestably, symbolic, the scales become heavily weighted in favor of the erotic reading. This reading applied to Sin's sword and Ned's gun created firm linguistic support for the homosexual interpretation of the entire poem that, clearly felt by some, could still be overlooked by others in favor of the friendship-without-the-quotation-marks, the agape instead of the eros, reading.

When Housman intends the unsymbolic weapon, he makes this literal use very clear, sometimes by resorting to metonymy. The soldiers "braced their belts about them" ("When I would muse in boyhood," LP 32); the "Deserter" cries "Reach me my belt" (LP 13). Sometimes the context is clearly murder or suicide. We have seen the Woolwich cadet's pistol. There are the knives which "The True Lover" used to kill himself (ASL 53) and Maurice's brother used to kill him (ASL 8), and the knife for which the would-be suicide paid "eighteen pence" ("Good creatures, do you love your lives," MP 26). There are the hunting lances in "Atys" (AP 1). The only other weapons that are unambiguously weapons are the guns that "sing" to announce "The Day of Battle" (ASL 56). There is also, of course, the knife held at the neck of the "Queen of Air and Darkness" (LP 3), but since she, like Death in "Hell Gate" (LP 31), is the personi-fied female—and evil—the knife in this poem may also be considered a phallic one.

Sometimes the weapons are incontestably symbolic, but symbolic of what? There are swords in two of the following poems, but are they real swords or symbolic ones? If symbolic, what do they symbolize? Are they swords or, like Sin's sword in "Hell Gate," are they "swords"?

> As I gird on for fighting
>   My sword upon my thigh,
> I think on old ill fortunes
>   Of better men than I.
>
> Think I, the round world over,
>   What golden lads are low
> With hurts not mine to mourn for
>   And shames I shall not know.
>
> What evil luck soever
>   For me remains in store,
> 'Tis sure much finer fellows
>   Have fared much worse before.
>
> So here are things to think on
>   That ought to make me brave,
> As I strap on for fighting
>   My sword that will not save.
>
> (LP 2)

This clearly symbolic sword has been interpreted in five ways. It is cour-age, "the sort of courage . . . every man needs if he is to face up to life"

(Graves, A. E. Housman, 108–9). It is both courage and pride (Walton, "Not Mine, but Man's"). It is "the bitterness in their [common soldiers'] lot" (Tinker, "Housman's Poetry," 89). It is feelings of love, friendship, honour, and bravery for which Housman "is willing to face death" (Bronowski, "A. E. Housman," 221). And it is an active life: "a life of action even though it culminates in failure is nobler than a life of ease" (Whitridge, "Vigny and Housman," 161). That all of these readings are possible is clear, but their very multiplicity indicates that some element has not been factored into the equation. Some of these readings are mutually antithetical. What they have in common is the tacit assumption that this is a poem about physical or metaphorical war, and the sword a literal or figurative weapon in that war. This is precisely the assumption that I want to question. Those "old ill fortunes / Of better men than I," their "hurts" and "shames," the "evil luck," all have echoes in other poems, and they do not refer to war but to homosexuality.

We have seen sufficient of Housman's "luckless lads" to understand that for him "ill fortunes / Of better men than I" and "evil luck" can, at least potentially, mean the "ill fortune" or the "evil luck" of being a homosexual. This explains the otherwise rhetorical "hurts" that are "not mine to mourn for" and the "shames" that "I shall not know." The words tend to bring us back to "Sinner's Rue," the flower "of a heart whose trouble / Must have been worse than mine" (LP 30). And they bring us back as well to the Woolwich cadet, whose future life would have been one of "long disgrace and scorn," who was destined to "tread the mire you must," who, had he lived, would have inevitably become one of the "souls undone undoing others," but who is instead "Clean of guilt" (ASL 44). These thoughts "ought to make me brave," but when something "ought to" produce a particular effect, the implication is that it does not in fact do so. The identity of those "better men than I" is implied in "Others, I am not the first" (ASL 30) and will be taken up in connection with that poem, so let us leave it in abeyance for the moment and consider the "sword upon my thigh." The propinquity of the "sword" and the "thigh" on which it is "girded" for "fighting" make the implications clear. Sexual congress is often referred to metaphorically as a war, "the battle of the sexes." The man's "sword" on his "thigh" is the prime weapon in this "battle." Here, however, it is not a common sword, for it "will not save." It is an unproductive implement, a sword that will not fulfill its intended function. Like the thoughts "that ought to make me brave," the sword "ought" to save its wielder from "hurts" and "shames," but like those thoughts, it will not. Yet the persona straps it on regardless. This sword will not "save" him, and "save" has religious connotations. "Thou shalt not lie with mankind . . . it is abomination" (Lev. 18:22), and the Woolwich cadet wrote that he had not (yet) offended "as it is called in the Bible." Not having (mis)used his sword, and choosing "not to wrong" other men, his "brothers." by so doing, he killed himself and so was, presumably, "saved" in this sense, not by using his sword but by foregoing its use, forever. This persona, taking the opposite course of action, chooses to "strap on" his unproductive sword, wield it, and not be "saved." The military connotation of a sword is not lost, but the war in which it is a weapon is quite different from that usually assumed.

The sword is in its literal sense one of the weapons of the soldier. The concept of the soldier as a man whose commitment is to other men rather than to women has already been taken up, in discussing "The Deserter" (LP 13) for example. It is time to look at this concept a bit more closely. We have seen in earlier chapters some of Housman's poems celebrating the soldier as a symbol of constancy, courage, and loyalty. Let us turn now to those in which he is something quite different, a difference made clear by the alteration of tone and the technique of buried erotic metaphor.

> The street sounds to the soldier's tread,
>   And out we troop to see:
> A single redcoat turns his head,
>   He turns and looks at me.
>
> My man, from sky to sky's so far,
>   We never crossed before;
> Such leagues apart the world's ends are,
>   We're like to meet no more;
>
> What thoughts at heart have you and I
>   We cannot stop to tell;
> But dead or living, drunk or dry,
>   Soldier, I wish you well.
>
> (ASL 22)

The soldier holds a special place in Housman's poetry, both in the Shropshire cycle in which Terence is Housman's mask and in the unmasked poetry. We have already seen a good deal of this. The soldier's "gallant bearing and [the] ripe masculinity of men in uniform" merged with the evocation of "youthful idealism and impending adversity" (Watson, *Divided Life* 145) to invest Housman's soldier with a complex symbolism. Indeed, the prevalence of soldiers in Housman's poetry (one of the causes of its being characterized as "adolescent") is in fact one component of the code that provided entree into the homosexual subtext for those "in the know" (Robbins, "Very Curious Construction," 151). We have seen in the previous chapter that the symbolism of the soldier was partly compounded of brotherhood, self-sacrifice, and friendship, the soldier's "youthful idealism" and "impending adversity." He perfectly embodied those two recurring themes in Housman's poetry, exile and death, in addition to his implicit sexuality.[3] It is now time to turn to his "gallant bearing and ripe masculinity," in short, to his role as a sex-object, not only in Housman's poetry, but in Victorian life.

In Victorian homosexual and homoerotic literature, there was a long-standing tradition "that soldiers are especially attractive. What makes them so is their youth, their athleticism . . . their uniforms, and their heroic readiness for "sacrifice' " (Fussell, *Great War*, 278). Men in uniform were especially attractive to homosexual men, as is clear from Proust's *Remembrance of Things Past*. Indeed, the prostitutes in the notorious Cleveland Street affair were "men in uniform," telegraph boys and soldiers (Dellamora, *Masculine Desire*, 11).

Soldiers were "staple elements" in Victorian homosexual pornography (Ronald Pearsall, *Worm in the Bud*, 459), and not in pornography alone. "It need hardly be doubted," writes Chesney, "that a fair number of private soldiers took part in the casual [homosexual] prostitution that was a traditional evil among troops quartered in London" (*Victorian Underworld*, 391). And indeed, "the Guards . . . were well known in homosexual circles as a regiment where [male] prostitutes would be found" (Jebb, *A. E. Housman* 86). In fact, "soldiers were well-documented as having semi-professional careers as prostitutes alongside their more "manly" duties" (Robbins, "Very Curious Construction," 151). As Fussell notes, for active pre-World War I homosexuals, "soldiers [were] specifically the object of desire" and the guards "had *of course* been notoriously employable as sexual objects since early in the nineteenth century" (*Great War*, 279). The emphasis is mine). Nor were they necessarily only the objects of homosexual relations; they were also the initiators. J. A. Symonds recorded that in 1865 he was accosted by a Grenadier Guardsman who, after "a few commonplace remarks . . . broke abruptly into proposals, mentioned a house we could go to, and made it quite clear for what purpose" (Grosskurth, *Memoirs*, 186), nor was this his only such encounter. In the early 1890s, he was taken by a friend "to a male brothel near the barracks in Regent's Park and he arranged to take a trooper he met there to a private room and had relations with him" (Croft-Cooke, *Feasting with Panthers*, 122). We may recall that in Forster's *Maurice* there is an incident involving a soldier who was not so employable, to the complete confusion of the man who had approached him assuming that he was amenable. There is ample evidence that soldiers were not only theoretical sex objects but practical and available as sexual partners. It may be recalled that in considering Terence's hypothetical military service, I suggested that the "eye that measures me" was that of a quartermaster, "too unhappy to be kind," whose owner hated his "fellow man." If "kind" is given its secondary sexual meaning of "accommodating," to be discussed in the next chapter, then the implication is that the eye belongs either to a heterosexual, "unhappy" and "undone with misery," "lost" because he has given his "heart and soul" to a woman (ASL 14), or else to a homosexual who has denied and repressed his natural instincts. In either case, he is one who "hates" his "fellow man," at least in the role of a possible sexual partner. He does not look him in the eye.

Robinson calls "The street sounds to the soldier's tread" a poem on "a momentary flash of friendship between a bystander and a passing soldier" (*Angry Dust*, 36). Robertson says that in it "all the poet's longing for friendship, . . . all the generosity and warmth of his reserved and frustrated nature bursts forth" ("Housman and Hopkins," 99). For both commentators, then, this is a poem of friendship without the quotation marks. It is, however, as one might suspect, a good deal more complex than that. The word "troop" in the second line, with its military connotation, creates a verbal link between the persona and the redcoat, a verbal link reinforced by the direct eye contact. Nor is this "a feverish little item . . . which operates by inflation of one passing glance to extreme intimacy and significance" (Robert Pearsall, "Vendible Values," 87). Far from "inflation," it operates by deflation, excising everything but the bare fact and permitting the meaning to be expressed only covertly.

The momentary meeting of the eyes of a man and a woman in popular song "across a crowded room" is an acknowledgement of their mutual attraction. It is so here as well. When a homosexual man makes eye contact with another man, the response he receives indicates interest—or lack of interest—just as in a first eye contact between a man and woman. We may contrast Housman's poem with Cavafy's "The Window of the Tobacco Shop":

> They stood among many others
> close to a lighted tobacco shop window.
> Their looks met by chance
> and timidly, haltingly expressed
> the illicit desire of their bodies.
> Then a few uneasy steps along the street
> until they smiled, and nodded slightly.
> And after that the closed carriage,
> the sensitive approach of body to body,
> hands joined, lips meeting.
>
> (Collected Poems, 57)

What is important is the mutuality between the persona and the "soldier [who] seem not only to understand each other but to find their intimacy—total though but of a second's duration . . . in the knowledge that it is finished and complete" (Bayley, *Housman's Poems*, 32–33). Does that glance "but of a second's duration" mean only that their eyes met for a second and that then the contact was "finished and complete," or is it a metaphor for something more? That meeting of eyes, that momentary "glance," can be read as an image of physical, homosexual intercourse (Woods, *Articulate Flesh*, 164).[4] As a single "passing glance," it connotes not a long affair but a one-night stand, and this implies that the union is a commercial transaction and not a love affair.

Bayley has analyzed the shades of meaning in the designation of the soldier as the poem progresses. In the first stanza, he is a "simple redcoat." In the second, he is "My man," and in the third he is "plain soldier," a cycle from the impersonal meeting through possessive intimacy to an impersonal farewell. "My man" is "a complex mode of address, going all the way from the patronizing . . . to the comfortably possessive, as in German *mein Mann* my husband." Housman's mode of address excludes patronage "but not possessiveness: for at this moment he owns the soldier's being and thoughts, in the way that lovers own each other" (*Housman's Poems*, 33). But is patronage really excluded? "Patronage" has more than one meaning, and one of them is commercial. "Dead or living, drunk or dry" seems a rather simple pair of antitheses. However, if "dead" and "dry" connote the state of the male organ after coitus, and "living" and "drunk" that of the same organ during fellatio (the "stolen waters" of MP 22), the antithesis is single rather than double and the sexual subtext rises to the surface.

This same erotically charged undertext can be observed in another "soldier" poem, one that was never published, perhaps because it is a shade too obviously readable as a parable of male prostitution. It is, however, still in the notebooks (Burnett, *Poems*, 181).

> Says the grenadier to me,
> "Give me half-a-crown," says he.
> To the grenadier says I,
> "Very well, my lad, but why?"
>
> "Why," says he, "for standing cheer
> To a British grenadier."
> So I put the money down
> And he took my half-a-crown.

Whether this is the record of an actual commercial transaction or not, the imagery makes the sexual connotations rather obvious. The price is negotiated, and the service to be purchased is agreed. The payment is for "standing cheer" to a soldier, and that soldier is "my lad," the possessive and intimate connotations of which we have just considered. The word "standing" can imply the stance of the soldier or his condition. Are we talking about a "one-night stand," or perhaps a very quick standing one? The money is "put down," nor is it the only thing that is "put down" as a result of the agreement. The implied commercial transaction is narrated in terms of providing a drink. "Cheers!" And this will again be a serving of bitter from Ganymede's cup, one with a "sour" aftertaste on the tongue.

J. R. Ackerley in his semi-autobiographical work *My Father and Myself* provides the factual background of the poem. He writes, "His Majesty's Brigade of Guards had a long history in homosexual prostitution . . . they were easily to be found of an evening in their red tunics standing about in the various pubs they frequented, over the only half-pint they could afford . . . and alert to the possibility that some kind gentleman might appear and stand them a few pints, in return for which and the subsequent traditional tip—a pound was the recognised tariff for the Foot Guards then, the Horse Guards cost rather more—they were perfectly agreeable to . . . a 'bit of fun' " (126–27). It seems that the Grenadier in this poem, if my reading of it is plausible, cost a great deal less! It is very easy to understand why this poem was not published by either A. E. Housman himself or by his brother.

There is one other "soldier" poem that must be examined in this context of sexual imagery. It is possible to make sense of it even if the erotic subtext is ignored. It can be read as a poem about the reconciliation of enemies on the field of battle itself (Robert Pearsall, "Vendible Values"). This reading aligns Housman's poem with Hardy's "The Man He Killed." It emphasizes the last two lines in which fellowship is extended to the enemy "chap," his courage and panache acknowledged and admired. This non-erotic reading requires the reconciliation of the romantic tone and the grimly realistic field details, and they can indeed be reconciled. The "plumes" are in keeping with the lush atmosphere of the first two lines and epitomize the romantic image of preindustrialized war. They were still a feature of military uniforms in Housman's day (and indeed still are a feature of ceremonial military uniforms today), so they were not precisely archaic then, although their time of practical use was passing. They are confronted by smoke, flame, and bullets, elements not yet fully integrated into the popular image of "war" but on the verge of being so, and the plumes are overwhelmed. The poem, like the plumes themselves, wavers between archaic and contemporary, romantic and realistic. The idealistic or ceremonial "plumes" are fallen, trampled "under heel," and made irrelevant by modern weapons. The enemy's gesture at the end restores the romantic, nostalgic ambience destroyed by the modern reality, ultimate gallantry in the face of death. This reading—based on the facts that a "sabre" need not be a phallic image, "died" need not have its Elizabethan meaning, and the lead "flying" in the first verse and structurally parallel to the "sabre" in the second has no hidden meaning—is satisfying. It accepts the imagery of the first two lines as serving only to establish the romantic atmosphere that will be "blown" apart by the bullets and restored by the dying youth's gesture. Let us look at the poem with this reading in mind.

> I did not lose my heart in summer's even,
> > When roses to the moonrise burst apart:
> When plumes were under heel and lead was flying,
> > In blood and smoke and flame I lost my heart.
>
> I lost it to a soldier and a foeman,
> > A chap that did not kill me, but he tried;
> That took the sabre straight and took it striking
> > And laughed and kissed his hand to me and died.
>
> (MP 37)

It is quite possible to make sense of this poem without examining the sexual imagery, as it is possible to read the previous poems thus. The problem with reading them in this way is that their depths are lost beneath the surface that is the focus of concentration. I have assumed the existence of an erotic undertext for them, and on the same assumption let us examine the imagery of "I did not lose my heart in summer's even" a bit more closely. The poem can be taken as symbolic and allusive. So much is agreed and one level of its symbolism and allusiveness has been seen. There is a deeper level, however, which is far less obvious than in the earlier poems. The vocabulary of the sexual imagery is a somewhat specialized one, clear enough once one has the key but otherwise rather opaque. It is necessary to first discover this key and unlock the imagery.[5]

It was observed above that the gun, the lead emissions from which penetrate the body, as well as the sword or knife, or saber, which itself does the penetrating, can be a phallic metaphor. Another metaphor for the phallus, or for its head, can be the moon that emits rays or beams of light as the gun does bullets or the phallus the ejaculate. The Elizabethan "die" meaning "ejaculate" has also been referred to earlier, as has the rose as a feminine symbol. With all this in mind, let us look at the poem again to see in what way it is "a homosexual fantasy" (Graves, *A. E. Housman*, 221), beginning with the first two lines. Here is what Bayley called "the unexpected clue to the poem [which] is surely in the contrast between the traditional world of love—summer, moonlight, and roses, which are boisterously and almost violently presented—and the world of war, which is yearning, langourous, and gentle . . . the battle itself is all graceful movement and languid surrender, the softness of plumes and heels, a gentle mime of swordplay, erotic abandonment, culminating in the laughing surrender to consummation. The poem has knowingly rejected the moonlit garden, as a place of conventional and mechanical loving, and chosen instead the bizarre softness and abandoned grace of a battlefield" (*Housman's Poems*, 40).

I disagree with his comments about the softness, gentleness, and languor of the battlefield. I do agree that the contrast is between the traditional world of heterosexual love symbolized by the moonlit rose-filled summer garden and the "bizarre," and male-dominated, world of homosexual love symbolized by the flying bullets and piercing saber of the battlefield. However, there is still something missing. If the "roses" that "burst apart" to the "moonlight" are girls whose virginity has been "burst" by the "moon" of the glans, and if "soldier" and "foeman" are as aggressively male as "roses" are passively female, the entire poem is a clear rejection of heterosexuality and a declared preference for homosexuality. The loved one who is killed and the lover who kills him both hope to "die" in the Elizabethan meaning, but here the "foeman" only "tried" to kill me (I did not attain orgasm), but I did cause him to "die" with my "sabre," and I "lost my heart" to him when he "laughed and kissed his hand to me" even as my lovemaking brought him to climax. Since antiquity, military and sexual terminology have overlapped, and in the nineteenth century "dying" on one's "enemy" was a staple figure in love poetry (Fussell, *Great War*, 270). It was not only the Elizabethans who used "die" with two meanings; so did the Victorians.

It is not unusual for war poetry, and non-war poetry as well, to "make much of the quasi-erotic desire of the bullet (and . . . the bayonette) to 'kiss' or 'nuzzle' the body of its adolescent target" (ibid., 160). Allen Ginsberg used the phallus/sword metaphor in "Howl" (line 40), and "Please Master" (lines 37–40). So did Robert Friend in "Dangerous" ("that the gun / he points at me / from his shadowy undergrowth / may shoot at last," *Dancing with a Tiger*, 2:34, ll. 8–11) and in "In Mexico" ("His naked cries / mingle with my cries / as the knife thrusts," ibid., 2:23, ll. 1–3). D. H. Lawrence also utilized this image in "Eloi, Eloi, Lama Sabachthani?" (*Complete Poems*, 742):

> So when I run at length thither across
> To the trenches, I see again a face with blue eyes.
> A blanched face, fixed and agonized,
> Waiting. And I knew he wanted it.
> Like a bride he took my bayonet, wanting it,
> Like a virgin the blade of my bayonet, wanting it,

> And it sank to rest from me in him,
> And I, the lover, am consummate,
> And he is the bride, I have sown him with the seed
> And planted and fertilized him.

These lines could almost be a paraphrase of this level of Housman's poem. Ginsberg and Friend are, of course, much later than Housman, but D. H. Lawrence was almost contemporary with him, indeed predeceased him. Both Housman and Lawrence were writing poetry during the second decade of the twentieth century, but Housman was a traditionalist and D. H. Lawrence was an iconoclast whose poetry points forward rather than backward.

In all these later poets, beginning with Lawrence, the image is so obvious as hardly to warrant the name of "metaphor." I suggested in the introduction that the emergence of homosexual poetry from the underground and its acceptance into the mainstream were attended by a loss of subtlety and poetic force. These two poems illustrate what was gained and what was lost. What was gained was directness and force; subtlety was lost. The later poets like Robert Duncan are not obliquely allusive in the way that Housman is. Duncan, in "The Venice Poem," for example, is hardly subtle ("Nature barely provides for it. / Men fuck men by audacity," cited by Gunn, "Homosexuality in Robert Duncan's Poetry,"), nor is Friend, in "Letter of the Law" ("Because 'Thou shalt not lie with mankind' / spoke to his rigid understanding, / he rammed home / standing," *Dancing with a Tiger*, 23), nor is Ginsberg, in "Sweet Boy, Gimme Yr Ass."

Some observations about Greek art were made in discussing "To an Athlete Dying Young" (ASL 19), and reference was also made to Housman's comment on the proposed Lovat Fraser illustration for a poem about a Greek statue, an illustration that featured a "mutilated statue," to Housman's intense disgust. Here is the poem which that "mutilated statue" was intended to illustrate. The poet's disgust is readily comprehensible.[6]

> Loitering with a vacant eye
> About the Grecian gallery,
> And brooding on my heavy ill,
> I met a statue standing still.
> Still in marble stone stood he,
> And stedfastly he looked at me.
> "Well met," I thought the look would say,
> "We both were fashioned far away;
> We neither knew, when we were young,
> These Londoners we live among."
> Still he stood and eyed me hard,

An earnest and a grave regard:
"What, lad, drooping with your lot?
I too would be where I am not.
I too survey that endless line
Of men whose thoughts are not as mine.
Years, ere you stood up from rest.
On my neck the collar prest;
Years, when you lay down your ill,
I shall stand and bear it still.
Courage, lad, 'tis not for long:
Stand, quit you like stone, be strong."
So I thought his look would say;
And light on me my trouble lay,
And I stept out in flesh and bone
Manful like the man of stone.

(ASL 51)

On a first reading, this may give the impression of being only a "whimsical little poem" expressing a mood of "stoical endurance" (MacDonald, "Poetry," 120) in which the modern persona, faced with the contrast between his weakness and the statue's strength, both learns humility and takes inspiration from it. If that were all it is, it is curiously over-elaborated. Is that, however, all it is?

The persona's eye is "vacant" until it meets the statue's with its "earnest and a grave regard." Direct eye contact is at once established, not with a modern soldier but with a representation (and representative) of Greek male beauty whose look is "grave." The word has the force not only of "serious" but also of "pertaining to the grave," to the dead world in which the spirits of both are at home, and perhaps also to the sterility and futility that for Housman so often underlies such references. The persona was "brooding on my heavy ill," his "trouble," and that "ill" or "trouble" is the specifically homosexual lover's "ail," "Greek love," to which the Greek statue of the ephebe is relevant. Housman's self-written "Epitaph" (AP 12) speaks of "how ill God made me." His "trouble," which gazing at the statue helps to lighten, is the same "trouble," the "griefs," the "luggage I'd lief set down" (ASL 50), the "lot" with which he is "drooping." The statue inspires him to "stand" and be, not "manly," but "manful," like a man and also man-full, filled with, or filling, men. What was "drooping" and has been encouraged by regarding the (unmutilated) Greek statue to "stand," to be erect in fact, need hardly be spelled out. It is as obvious as the phallus itself when it "stands." The persona resolves to follow the statue's exemplary advice: "quit you like stone, be strong." One of the salient characteristics of stone, the one relevant here, is that it is hard; it does not "droop." The statue is "standing still," and "still" carries its own load of double meanings. The Greek statue is un-moving, it is standing quietly, but it is still standing, even among this "endless line" of Londoners who will have children and thus continue their "line," their lineage, endlessly. They are "men whose thoughts are not as mine"—or as the persona's. The statue seems to recognize a kin-ship with the gazer, or rather the gazer feels a kinship with the statue (as in an earlier poem he did with a "redcoat"). The nature of both was "fashioned far away" and long ago also, in classical Greece where homo-sexuality was an accepted mode of life. Can there be any real doubt that the persona is here the poet? This poem, far from being a celebration of stoic fortitude in the abstract (Robb, *Four in Exile*, 36), is indeed what Page called it: a "personal and tragic response" (Page, *A. E. Housman*, 193) to his personal "heavy ill," that same "ill" that he shares with his "luckless lads," with those "much finer fellows" who had before him strapped on the "sword that will not save" (LP 2), and also with the Greek statue.

That statue, and the museum itself, says Giordano, represent the an-cient Greek experience as a whole and is a symbol of both "classical art and of the spirit and values that created it" ("Art and Imagination," 47). As homosexuality was part of that classical Greek ethos, I would add, it *must* be included as part of the "spirit and values" that created Greek art. The statue is thus an alter ego of the persona, "a second though stronger self, bearing a burden much like" his, both "aliens, out of context in the unfriendly London" (ibid., 47). This critic considers the statue's lesson is "a stoical resignation to life's woes generally," which I would narrow to one specific woe in place of Giordano's "troubles which life brings to all of us" (ibid., 47). His interpretation clearly subsumes mine, but I feel it makes the point of the poem more diffuse and thus less immediate. My disagreement is not with Giordano's basic interpretation but with its ap-plication.

> Others, I am not the first,
> Have willed more mischief than they durst:
> If in the breathless night I too
> Shiver now, 'tis nothing new.
>
> More than I, if truth were told,
> Have stood and sweated, hot and cold,
> And through their reins in ice and fire,
> Fear contended with desire.
>
> Agued once like me were they,
> But I like them shall win my way
> Lastly to the bed of mould
> Where there's neither heat nor cold.

But from my grave across my brow
Plays no wind of healing now,
And fire and ice within me fight
Beneath the suffocating night.

(ASL 30)

The phrase "if truth were told" in the second verse seems to be mere
padding. If this is what it indeed is, it would be a curious lapse for a poet
who is more inclined to leave things out than to include words whose
only function is to fill out a line. The manuscript shows that the first form
of this line was "Men whose very graves are old," (Burnett *Poems*, p. 32
bottom) which serves to emphasize the contrast between the living persona and the unspecific long-dead "others" of the first stanza. "If truth
were told" was deliberately substituted for what seems a more meaningful
line. Perrine has clearly demonstrated, however, that the phrase is quite
the opposite of padding. It is the key to the poem ("Housman's 'Others,
I am not the first' "). Its meaning is, however, obscured.

Before we come to that meaning and the reason why Housman obscured it, let us look at some of the imagery. The shivering, the sweating,
the "heat and cold," the "ice and fire," are basic to the imagery. They are
in each stanza, repeated in different forms. What are they meant to connote? For Scott-Kilvert, they are the "emotions of youth, the period when
untried ideals and untutored desires . . . first encounter a hostile or indifferent world" (*A. E. Housman*, 37). White suggests that what is represented is illness, a "sickness physical as well as in . . . [the] soul"
establishing a trope that leads directly to the "winds of healing" ("*Shropshire Lad*," p. 261). For Leggett, the point of the poem is that they represent the guilt-accompanied desire that is the young persona's first
reaction to experience, the "strong feelings" of the persona from which
he seeks relief in philosophy, a response the poet demonstrates to be inadequate, (*Poetic Art*, 50–51) and thus "the burden of human guilt which
comes with knowledge" (*Land of Lost Content*, 25). It seems that these
shivers and agues represent the fruit of the Edenic tree of knowledge, usually understood as heterosexual "knowledge." We have already seen that
when there are widely differing interpretations of a Housman symbol, the
basis for that symbol is often something quite different from any of the
proffered explanations. The same is true here.

In the manuscript there are three possibilities recorded for this image.
"Agued" was one, the others "thwarted" and "frustrate." If this is not
sufficient to cast doubt on the above readings, let us look at the source of
the image. This particular image has classical roots. Sappho sang of her
reaction to being near the one she loved: "thin fire runs through my body.
. . . Sweat pours down over me. I shudder" (*Sippho*, 11). Plato used the

same metaphor of chills and fever in the *Phaedrus*. The love in both cases is homosexual. This is not to deny that these symptoms are used in classical literature in reference to heterosexual love, but only to point out that they are not confined to inter-gender relationships. In Housman's case, their classical use for both varieties of love provided a warrant for his use of them to imply heterosexuality while in fact denoting homosexuality. The chills and fever in Housman's poem are obviously to be taken as symbols for "the contending desires and fears that oppress him" (Perrine, "Housman's 'Others'," 135), "oppress him" and not the persona. Let us take it as established that they in fact represent not only illicit love, but homosexual love, the fruit not of the heterosexual "tree of knowledge" but of Housman's other arboreal symbol, the "tree of man."

In the letter to Grant Richards concerning the Fraser illustrations, Housman rather ingenuously explained that this poem contrasts "the passions of youth and the unwholesome excitement of adultery with the quiet and indifference of death" (Grant Richards, *Housman*, 183). Marlow has no hesitation in accepting this explanation (*A. E. Housman*, 37, and again 114). That the contrast is indeed between "the quiet and indifference of death" and an "unwholesome excitement" of a sexual nature no one would or could question. The imagery makes the nature of the "excitement" very clear. The only question is whether or not "adultery" is the only, or even the most likely, such "unwholesome" passion. Northrop Frye provides a comprehensive answer:

> As long as poetry follows religion towards the moral, religious and poetic archetypes will be very close together . . . the incestuous, the homosexual, and the adulterous . . . [will be linked]. The qualities that morality and religion usually call ribald, obscene, subversive, lewd, and blasphemous . . . can achieve expression only through ingenious techniques of displacement. . . . true love may be symbolized by the triumph of an adulterous liaison over marriage . . . , by a homosexual passion . . . or an incestuous one. (*Anatomy of Criticism*, 156–57)

Housman gave his sanction to "an adulterous liaison." An "incestuous" one can be ruled out. The third, "homosexual passion," whether as a symbol of "true love" or a source of "unwholesome excitement," is the true reading.

Who then are those "others" who preceded the persona in this predicament, for "I am not the first"? They are those who, "if truth were told," were "like me," only "better men than I" and "much finer fellows" (LP 2). Their identity *had* to be obscured to preserve Housman's public mask. Today we can give them names; Socrates, Plato, Aristotle, Julius Caesar, Catullus, Petronius, and other ancient authors highly regarded are the "others," but only "if truth be told," homosexuals about whom the "truth" was not told in the Victorian period when homosexuality was "not only socially unacceptable . . . , it was an unacceptable subject for polite conversation" and anything suggesting it was "hushed up" (Perrine, "Housman's 'Others'," 137). Obviously homosexual lines in classical literature were excised, and the text of at least one classic, the *Satyricon*, was even altered so that the recipient of Trimalchio's long embrace after his feast was transformed from a boy to a girl.

Housman had a translation of "Trimalchio's Banquet" in which he "had had to underline the word 'girl' and write in the Latin word for 'boy' against these lines: 'amongst those who had last arrived, there was a good-looking girl whom Trimalchio approached and held kissing for a while' " (Graves, *A. E. Housman*, 204). It is only proper to record that this passage is now translated more accurately: "Among the incoming slaves there was a remarkably pretty boy. Trimalchio literally launched himself upon him and . . . began to cover him with rather prolonged kisses" (Petronius, *Satyricon*, 80). One trusts that Housman's ghost is pleased with the Arrowsmith translation. "If truth were told" as it now is, he was indeed "not the first."

Mortimer calls the poem an expression of the conflict between Housman's wish to be part of the "rough and hazardous" life embodied in Terence and his duty to the life of scholarship. The conflict is real, but it is hardly the result of that postulated. As Perrine says, the speaker "suffers from the burden of forbidden desires. He is torn between desire and fear—fear of the consequences of fulfilling his desires, fear of punishment if he [even] seeks to fulfill them" (Perrine, "Housman's 'Others'," 135), which is quite a different matter. The consequences in this case will be considered shortly. For the moment, it is sufficient to note that, as in Auden's poetry, specifically homosexual, and therefore illicit, love seems to exist "behind a door which was locked on both sides" (Woods, *Articulates Flesh*, 171). It was on one side of this "locked door" that Housman's persona "stood and sweated, hot and cold" while "ice and fire" ran through his reins.

Those "reins" have proved problematical. In 1940, it was seriously suggested that although the printer's proofs had been scrutinized by Housman with an alert eye and very little tolerance for errors, this is a misprint for "veins."[7] The manuscript version of this verse (Burnet, *Poems*, 32 bottom) clarifies the matter. The third and fourth lines in the earliest draft are "And [in their marrow, ice to fire/through their reins in ice and fire] / Fear [did battle/contended] with desire." The word "reins" is perfectly clear and unmistakable in the manuscript. Its archaic meanings included "kidneys" as well as "seat of the feelings, passions, and affections." Housman's hesitation over using "marrow" instead links the word with the "kidneys" meaning. Housman preferred "reins" because in addition to the physiological meaning it had the "seat of the passions" meaning, and another meaning as well.

The usual denotation of "reins" is the "means of controlling a horse." The horse has more than once been used as a symbol for carnal appetite, and the reins for the restraints against indulgence of this appetite. "Reins" is thus a key word, for the subject is the necessity, and the difficulty, of controlling unbridled desire, the need for which will end only with death. It is indeed only death that can provide the "wind of healing" for which the Housman persona yearns, as we shall see shortly.

The manuscript shows that where "lastly" is printed in Housman's third stanza, the original word was "safely," which echoes the end of the Woolwich cadet poem: "Turn safe to rest" (ASL 44). Ague and fever, fear and shame, afflict "me." Perrine argued that for understanding the poem, the "homosexual interpretation is not only possible but necessary" ("Housman's 'Others'," 137). This being so, clearly the persona is a direct projection of the poet who has quite deliberately obscured much of the meaning of the lines for reasons that are obvious.

The obscurity that covers the undertext of the above poem is not to be found in the following one. The subtext is still obscured, but the technique is different. No gender-specific words are used for the beloved, and the reader can be depended upon to assume that the male persona ("lad") is appealing to a girl to ease his "ail." After all, "most writing has traditionally been heterosexual, not by declaration but by implication. Men . . . are assumed to be heterosexual until proved otherwise. And heterosexual assumptions are presumed to be universal" (Martin, *Homosexual Tradition*, xv–xvi). Haber certainly assumes just that: "the living lover . . . calls to the maiden to undo her door for him. He pleads that he is about to slay himself, asks for love's embrace. . . . What A. E. H. suggests here is this: the consummation of love is the prologue to suicide; the sex-act and death are cause and consequence, hardly distinguishable from each other" ("Downward Eye," 310). With all due respect, these are Haber's suggestions and not Housman's. The maiden he assumes; the threat of suicide he also assumes, perhaps on the basis of the action of Housman's "True Lover" (ASL 53). Neither is in this poem. This lyric could easily have been included in the chapter "On Hero's Heart Leander Lies" since, as Haber so well demonstrates, it echoes the heterosexual poetry. Both the dramatic situation and the chain of association, however, are such that the words addressed aloud here to the sweetheart on the other side of the locked door seem to reflect the unspoken thoughts of the persona in "Others, I am not the first." It is as if that were the internal and this the external record of the same moment.

On your midnight pallet lying,
    Listen, and undo the door:
Lads that waste the night in sighing
    In the dark should sigh no more;
Night should ease a lover's sorrow;
Therefore, since I go tomorrow,
    Pity me before.

In the land to which I travel,
    The far dwelling, let me say—
Once, if here the couch is gravel,
    In a kinder bed I lay,
And the breast the darnel smothers
Rested once upon another's
    When it was not clay.

(ASL 11)

Again, we begin with the lover's agues, here softened to "sighs," and proceed to the grave "where there's neither heat nor cold" (ASL 30). "The dramatic situation [is reduced] to a few essential features" (Page, A. E. *Housman*, 194) but the most essential feature is carefully left for the reader to provide: the gender of the one on the other side of the door. The reader will almost certainly provide a "maiden" for the sighing "lad." The persona begs to be able to say that he "rested once upon another's" breast, the breast of the object of the plea. In "Tarry delight" (MP 15), Leander "lies" on Hero's heart. Does this make the listener incontestably female? It might seem so, but in Trollope's novels, it is always the girl who lies on the man's bosom.[8] This is also true in Yeats's "He Bids His Beloved Be at Peace": "Beloved, let your eyes half-close, and your heart beat / Over my heart" (*Selected Poems*, 23). But we know that it is a "lad" who wants to lie in a "kinder" bed than the grave, one in which his "breast" will rest "upon another's." The ambiguity is easily resolved by the simple assumption that the sweetheart behind the door is as male as is the "lad" who wishes to lie on his breast.

In the manuscript, there are three versions, other than the one finally selected, of the last two lines but one. We have [breast/ heart], and the "darnel" was alternately [tombstone/cerecloth/knotgrass]. These do not concern us, but they make the following reconstruction of the line to follow it possible (Burrett, *Poems*, 5, variants at bottom), thus: "[And/ Once] the [heart/breast] the darnel [smothers/covers] / [Beat one night upon a lover's/Breathed against a happy lover's/ Rested once upon a lover's]." The gender of the sweetheart is as unspecified in the manuscript as in the final text, except that a "lover" is usually male. As with the other official poems, Housman carefully kept his mask in place.

When the eye of day is shut,
    And the stars deny their beams,
And about the forest hut
    Blows the roaring wood of dreams,

From deep clay, from desert rock,
    From the sunk sands of the main,
Come not at my door to knock,
    Hearts that loved me not again.

Sleep, be still, turn to your rest
    In the lands where you are laid;
In far lodgings east and west
    Lie down on the beds you made.

In gross marl, in blowing dust,
    In the drowned ooze of the sea,
Where you would not, lie you must,
    Lie you must, and not with me.

(LP 33)

Housman wrote to J. W. Mackail about this poem, "I must confess I do not know what lines 3 and 4 mean" (A. E. Housman, *Letters*, 200). It would seem that they welled up directly out of the "hairy weid," bypassing the intellect. This is probably why they have such imaginative force. Housman said: "I think that to transfuse emotion—not to transmit thought but to set up in the reader's sense a vibration corresponding to what was felt by the writer—is the peculiar function of poetry. . . . Poetry is not the thing said but a way of saying it. . . . Meaning is of the intellect, poetry is not" (*NNP* 352, 364, 365). The intellectual content of these two lines is inchoate rather than organized. Each individual word seems the center of an image cluster that includes some but not all of the surrounding words, rather like a Chinese puzzle. The forest raises the wood, and the hut is associated in fairy tales with this environment. But is the "wood" to be equated with the "forest" at all? It is a "roaring wood." It may be a wood in which the wind is "roaring." but "roaring wood" primarily suggests a "roaring fire" that consumes the wood. It is the "roaring wood" and not the wind that "blows," and it is a "wood of dreams." Does this mean a wood existing in the dream world, or that the dreams feed the fire and are by it consumed? Or is this not "wood" but "would," the "I would" of the persona's dreams that never achieve reality? The lines have no intellectual meaning though they are pregnant with emotional meanings, and they are certainly poetry. Nor are these the only puns in these opening lines. In this poem, the usually buried sexual connotation of "lie" rises to the surface in the last phrase, which is directly preceded by the "would" that takes us back to the "wood of dreams." Only one thing clearly emerges: this is either a dream poem, or a poem about dreams, and its force is emotional, not intellectual.

The poem seems to be a dream vision of a looming darkness "when the eye of day is shut," night has fallen, and death has at last claimed (or is at last claiming) the "hearts that loved me not again," or one of them. It is, after all, in *Last Poems*, and Housman usually has a reason for his poetry. The persona expects to lie in his bed and be buffeted by an emotional wind, "the roaring wood [would] of dreams," haunting dreams of those "in far lodgings," their graves "in the lands where you are laid" even though they are "where you would not." As Graves says, "those who in the past have rejected his love are asked not to haunt him any longer" (*A. E. Housman*, 221). They are specifically begged to "Come not at my door to knock," do not enter my dreams, do not give me the mocking shadow of what can now never be more than a dream. When you were alive, although yours was "the head" that I dreamed of, you in turn would "not dream of me" (MP 11), and now even though you are dead you still haunt my slumber. "Turn to your rest," and leave me to mine. Or so it seems the persona is saying, but is he?

Two poems ago, it was the persona who stood at the door, torn between the desire to knock and the fear of the consequences. In the preceding poem the persona did knock, but it is safe to assume that the door did not open. Now it is the persona who is behind that locked door. Although he begs that the "hearts that loved me not again" not "knock" for admittance where they were previously unwilling to enter, still, as Bayley points out, "it seems likely that the second negative . . . in emphasizing how little he wants to be visited also suggests both that he yearns to be [so visited] and that he knows [that he will not be, except in his own dreams;] the hearts did not love him . . . it is a vision of the lost" (*Housman's Poems*, 152), those lost in more than one sense. As in the previous poem, the probable male gender of the addressee is obscured by the use of gender-free words ("hearts" and "you"). The pluralization of the addressee similarly obscures the (probably) singular identity of the man to whom this plea is made, the man whose image filled the poet's dreams. His was "the head that I shall dream of, / And 'twill not dream of me" (MP 11), the one who "loved me not again," the dying man for whom this volume of poetry was written.

I said above that Housman was fatalistic about his sexual orientation but would have been better pleased had he been like other men. Let us now turn to the poems that indicate his attitude, his sometimes stoic and sometimes defiant but always unhappy acceptance of his own sexual orientation.

The stars have not dealt me the worst they could do:
My pleasures are plenty, my troubles are two.
But oh, my two troubles they reave me of rest,
The brains in my head and the heart in my breast.

Oh, grant me the ease that is granted so free,
The birthright of multitudes, give it to me,
That relish their victuals and rest on their bed
With flint in the bosom and guts in the head.

(AP 17)

The theme of the poem is "fatal destiny" (Graves, A. E. *Housman*, 124) and it touches the "nadir of bitterness" (Haber, "What Fools," 450). That there is a personal reference was sensed by Housman's sister Katharine, who called the poem "his own biography" (Symons, et al., *Recollections*, 33 U.S. ed., referred to but not same words 25 U.K. edition). Without knowing the full biographical details, she had no doubt that these lines were relevant to her brother's life. The relevance of "the brains in my head" needs no explication, saving perhaps Housman's own. "Men hate to feel insecure; and a sense of security depends much less on the correctness of our opinions than on the firmness with which we hold them; so that by excluding intelligence we can often exclude discomfort," as he said in his Cambridge inaugural lecture (*Collected Poems and Selected Prose*, 310). Thus "the brains in my head" are one factor.

Auden, who understood the relevance of the second factor, "the heart in my breast," was coy in his remarks. Life, he says about this poem, offers two alternatives: being happy, healthy, and socially "ept" or sensitive but neither "happy, or successful in love, or at home in any company" because "there are two worlds and you cannot belong to them both. If you belong to the second . . . you will be unhappy because you will always be in love with the first, while at the same time you will despise it. The first world . . . will not return your love because it is in its nature to love only itself" ("Jehovah Housman and Satan Housman," 32). What he calls the first world, that of the socially "ept," is clearly the heterosexual world, "the birthright of multitudes" who "rest on their bed / With flint in the bosom." There is implicit here a suggestion that these heterosexual multitudes do not feel as deeply (if at all) as homosexuals, or at least as the particular homosexual who penned the lines. And we have seen enough of the heterosexual game of "musical beds" in the cycle poems to make this implication a logical one in understanding Housman.

What Auden calls the second world is the "gay" world, Housman's world, which created "the heart in my breast" because of which that "fear contended with desire." The heart suffered from "this cursed trouble,"

Housman's "fatal destiny" that made him, like Auden, "a stranger, and afraid / In a world I never made" (LP 12).

> The world goes none the lamer,
>   For ought that I can see,
> Because this cursed trouble
>   Has struck my days and me.
>
> The stars of heaven are steady,
>   The founded hills remain,
> Though I to earth and darkness
>   Return in blood and pain.
>
> Farewell to all belongings
>   I won or bought or stole;
> Farewell my lusty carcass,
>   Farewell my aery soul.
>
> Oh worse remains for others
>   And worse to fear had I
> Than so at four-and-twenty
>   To lay me down and die.
>
>   (MP 21)

This poem was completed after January of 1925, although the first draft is considerably earlier, so Housman himself may have been preparing the poem for inclusion in a posthumous volume (A. E. Housman, *Manuscript Poems*, 98). Laurence Housman was under the distinct impression that his brother wished the truth concerning his sexuality to be made public once he was safely dead (L. Housman, *"De Amicitia,"* 34). The reference in this poem is certainly less veiled than in those we have already examined where it had to be excavated and the encrustations removed before its nature was made manifest. Here, the problem is quite different. The poet is obviously speaking through a persona (the Woolwich cadet, perhaps?). The "four-and-twenty" reminds us of Terence who, complaining about the weather that has ruined Ludlow fair this year, rejects all comforting assurances that next year it will improve, saying, "but then we shall be twenty-four" (LP 9), and the "Deserter" who was perhaps "four-and-twenty" when "daylight" is "dear." The use of a persona, however, becomes clear only in the final verse. The first verse has a tone of conviction, an intensity that then seems to dwindle into posturing. When something like this seems to happen, it is wise to look at it from another angle, Housman's angle, to determine what does happen.

The first verse rings true: "this cursed trouble / Has struck my days and me." The early drafts and a single line of another poem, one that other-wise seems to have little or no reference to Housman's homosexuality, are relevant. The notebook draft of "Be still, my soul, be still; the arms you bear are brittle" (ASL 48) gives two early versions of that first line: "Be still, my soul, be still; it will not mend with grieving" and "Be still, my soul, be still; it never can be mended" (Burnett, *Poems*, 51–52, variants bottoms of pages). What the "it" is that can never be mended, and cer-tainly not with grieving, is unspecified. Need one doubt that "it" is "this cursed trouble"? In the last verse of this poem is the line "Horror and scorn and hate and fear and indignation," which is always taken to be the poet's reaction to the "injustice" rife in the world. Housman was a social conservative, if not a reactionary, who was not notable for his sensitivity to "injustice" in the abstract. This poem is thus anomalous unless we change our understanding of it.[9] If this is not a reflection on social injus-tice in general but rather a rumination on his own situation and the spe-cific injustice to which men like himself were liable to be subjected, it ceases to be an anomaly and becomes an especially powerful statement of one of his recurring themes. "Horror and scorn and hate and fear and indignation" would then refer to the public reaction to homosexuality and also to his own internalization of that public attitude toward his "cursed trouble," the "it" that "never can be mended," the "ancient evil" of the next poem. The last line then ("Oh why did I wake? when shall I sleep again?") is also transformed into a personal plea for that "wind of healing" that blows only from the grave.

Let us now return to "The world goes none the lamer" and take a closer look at the third verse, which seems singularly inane. The first two lines were not the original conception. The second draft has "And so farewell my [kingdom/fortunes] / That I could not control." This is at once superceded by "Good-bye to all [possessions / that ever / the havings] / I had or earned or stole" (Burnett, *Poems*, 127–28, variants bot-toms of pages). "My fortunes" bring us back to those "old ill fortunes" and the "luckless lads." They are something that "I could not control," any more than a man can control "the colour of his hair" (AP 18). I suspect that Housman felt this was a little too unmasked for publication, even posthumously, so the next version took its place, with the reference to those possessions "I had or earned or stole" replaced at last by "I won or bought or stole."

The verbs are interesting. If one assumes that the reference is indeed to homosexual activities, the "belongings" or "possessions" or "havings" being the men the persona possessed or had, and who thus belonged to him, each verb gains specificity. "Had" in one of its slang meanings is clear. One may "earn" love, or one may "steal" another person's heart, or another person's lover. There are also the "stolen waters" of MP 22,

mentioned above but not yet discussed, which refer to homosexual satis-
factions. The final choice of diction is yet more specific. "Won" means
received as a result of either effort or luck and "bought" refers to the patronage of male prostitutes. This takes us directly back to the first two
soldier poems. Only "stole" is used in both versions, referring metaphorically to fellatio as drinking "stolen waters." These references lead directly
to the "lusty carcass" in the next line, with its erotic physical connotations. In this reading, the four lines are anything but inane. They are a
mask concealing a history of tragedy, "this cursed trouble."

The last verse can then be seen to echo the suicide note of the Woolwich cadet, who died for fear of the "worse" things that awaited him otherwise, "souls undone, undoing others" (ASL 44). This persona also
decides to "lay me down and die," returning in "blood and pain" to
"earth and darkness." But is there a pun intended in "lay me down and
die"? Is the decision in favor of "to die" the death or "to die" the ejaculation, to kill himself, or to accept his "cursed trouble," blood, pain, and
all? Or is there finally only ambivalence that gives both of these readings
equal weight? This next poem may help to clarify the matter.

An Epitaph

Stay, if you list, O passer by the way;
Yet night approaches: better not to stay.
    I never sigh, nor flush, nor knit the brow,
    Nor grieve to think how ill God made me, now.
Here, with one balm for many fevers found,
Whole of an ancient evil, I sleep sound.

                                        (AP 12)

Mandel, reading the poem in isolation from many of the other poems
and from the poet's biography, concludes that the word "ill" may mean
either "badly made" or "made sick." If the first, it refers to man's rational-
ity that can comprehend death; if the second to madness. Both are states
that would produce the sufferer's symptoms. In either case, the persona is
clearly insane. One need not use such convoluted logic to understand the
epitaph if one begins by assuming an identity between "I" and the poet,
as well as among the "ancient evil," the "cursed trouble," and the "old ill
fortunes of better men than I" (LP 2) from which "if truth be told" many
"others, I am not the first" (ASL 30) have suffered, the "fortunes / That
I could not control," (MP 21 variant) the ill-luck of being a homosexual.
This is the chills and fever that can only be healed in the grave. In the
"Epitaph" (as it is usually titled although Burnett gives no title) the persona looks forward to having at last been fanned by the "wind of healing"
and made "whole" or "cured" (in the manuscript the choice is left open).

The classical form of the "Epitaph" underlines that this is indeed an "ancient" evil. Even though in the classical world it was not regarded as an "evil" at all, in Housman's world—and in Housman's psyche—it was. It is as old as civilization itself and Housman took a professional as well as a personal interest in it. The poem implies "that the ills of the ancient world are much like those of today; even though Housman, in his Victorian infirmity, looked for release from troubles which might not in ancient times have seemed so heavy" (Bayley, *Housman's Poems*, 36). The word "flush," which takes us back to the "fire," "heat," and "fever" we have seen so often, barely conceals the sexual dimension of the poem, which as a whole embodies "a comfortless yearning, . . . the feeling hidden in the centre of Housman's lines" (ibid., 9–10).

Haber says that this poem "memorializes the idea of release from life's ills and places their burden not on man but on his maker" ("What Fools," p. 454). This is true but too general. It is not "life's ills" from which release is anticipated, but one very specific ill. It is an "evil" and a "cursed trouble." Even now, homosexual men "must necessarily internalize some at least of the hatred of homosexuality with which they have been brought up" (Miles, *Rites of Man*, 182). How much more must a boy brought up in an orthodox Anglican home with strong ecclesiastical connections in the last third of the nineteenth century have internalized the biblical thunder ("It is an abomination . . ."). This is reflected in Housman's poetry.

Both Wilde's *The Picture of Dorian Gray* and Gide's *The Immoralist* also "suggest it is impossible to achieve homosexual pleasure without the inevitable accompaniment of fear, guilt, and self-hatred" (Meyers, *Homosexuality and Literature*, 14). "The fear of persecution, the guilt engendered within a homosexual by societal attitudes . . . [and the hostility of the primary culture] shape their identity and distort their lives"; the attitude expressed by normative society "makes a homosexual wary. It makes him . . . defensive, emotionally insecure . . . it may become internalized and damage the self-image of the oppressed. If you tell a person often enough that he is . . . a sinner . . . in time the victim may come to believe the insults, and either become indrawn, tense, and anxious . . . or adopt those characteristics which he is expected to have" Llewellyn-Jones, *Every Man*, 227–28).[10] Housman internalized these attitudes and became "indrawn, tense, and anxious" behind his mask. This internalization of the world's judgement is in part the subject of Yeats's poem "A Dialogue of Self and Soul," Part 2, verse 2 (Selected Poems, 125):

> How in the name of Heaven can he escape
> That defiling and disfigured shape
> The mirror of malicious eyes
> Casts upon his eyes until at last
> He thinks that shape must be his shape?

Housman created his mask to prevent his soul from appearing in his face. His first reaction on realizing he was a homosexual, "when he called himself to judgement . . . was unbounded self-condemnation followed by a passionate indictment of the 'ways of God and man' that had betrayed him . . . to an existence he hated for its barrenness and isolation. The second poem (dating in the mid 1880s) he entered in his earliest poetry notebook (A 61) is an epitaph he wrote for himself; now cured of the evils of life, he sleeps soundly, no longer grieving to think of God's mistake in making him" (Haber, *A. E. Housman*, 13). We have just looked at this "Epitaph." John Peale Bishop understood this. He remarked that in the poems about felons executed by hanging and suicides, the dead men all have the same face, and that face is A. E. Housman's. His was, psychologically, the head in the noose. He was a felon who had broken the laws of both man and God, and the consequences were punishment in life and damnation after.

> The laws of God, the laws of man,
> He may keep that will and can;
> Not I: let God and man decree
> Laws for themselves and not for me;
> And if my ways are not as theirs
> Let them mind their own affairs.
> Their deeds I judge and much condemn,
> Yet when did I make laws for them?
> Please yourselves, say I, and they
> Need only look the other way.
> But no, they will not; they must still
> Wrest their neighbor to their will,
> And make me dance as they desire
> With jail and gallows and hell-fire.
> And how am I to face the odds
> Of man's bedevilment and God's?
> I, a stranger and afraid
> In a world I never made.
> They will be master, right or wrong;
> Though both are foolish, both are strong.
> And since, my soul, we cannot fly
> To Saturn nor to Mercury,
> Keep we must, if keep we can,
> These foreign laws of God and man.
>
> (LP 12)

This is Housman's most direct statement about the dilemma of the homosexual who must keep the "foreign laws" imposed by "men whose thoughts are not as mine." The poem, which opens with rejection and defiance of the right of church and state to dictate his private life, closes with weary, resentful resignation and grudging acquiescence in the attempt to appear to conform, although the closing couplet makes it abundantly clear that there is no guarantee that the attempt will be successful.[11]

Escape to a more hospitable world, that symbolized by Saturn and Mercury, which represent the ancient past when homosexuality was an accepted option, or, at the worst, tolerated, is impossible. The poet who was first and foremost a classical scholar, however, could in a way escape to this world in his professional work with its literature. It was a world in which "loves such as his would not have found all the laws of God and man against them," a world long dead (Bishop, "Poetry," 143) to which he could and did fly if only in his imagination. Saturn was the god who ruled during the mythological golden age, and, since Housman uses the Latin rather than the Greek name, may reasonably be assumed to represent both Rome and Greece. Mercury was the patron of tricksters, those who went under false pretenses, as Housman and many others were forced to do. He is also the patron and guide of the dead who leads them to their final destination, the world of the dead, an ambiguous figure in both mythology and Housman's poetry, where he is "The Merry Guide" of ASL 42. These associations bring us back to the "wind of healing," the same wind that blows steadily through "The Merry Guide." Although one cannot escape to "Mercury" (a subtle rejection of suicide as a practical and desirable solution to the dilemma), one's soul will at the last go with him. "And since, my soul, we cannot fly / To Saturn or to Mercury" together, we must wait. "Be still, my soul," until we are no longer a "we," until "my lusty carcass" (MP 21) is in the grave and you, my soul, are free to fly. Here are the loneliness, anguish, and despair of those men who, living as the modern term has it "in the closet," must struggle to conform against their very nature. Society will exert all its power to "wrest" the deviant into at least an outward conformity to its laws. It demands abject submission, and the price of resistance is at the least jail, as Oscar Wilde found, at the most execution, and afterward damnation.

Let us pause, and look more closely at these laws of God and man. The law of God is made abundantly clear in I Corinthians 6:9–10: "Know ye not that the unrighteous shall not inherit the kingdom of God? Be not deceived: neither fornicators nor idolaters, nor adulterers, nor effeminate, nor abusers of themselves with mankind . . . shall inherit the kingdom of God." This is uncompromisingly the law of God. Homosexuals are equated, among other sinners, with adulterers, which may explain why Housman chose adultery as the ostensible temptation of the persona when writing to his publisher about "Others, I am not the first" (ASL 30). Grant Richards would have been appalled at the true source of the temptation. He was, after all, one of those who, like Katharine Symons, sprang indignantly to the defense of Housman when, after the poet's death, the truth began to be whispered. He could not and would not credit it.

Ever since the triumph of the cross against paganism, "the Christian Churches have been one of the strongest influences in society's condemnation of homosexuality and its persecution of overt homosexuals" (Llewellyn-Jones, *Every Man*, 218). The threat of "hell-fire" was very real in the earnest mid-Victorian mind. Housman could not have helped but absorb it even while rejecting it. Let us not forget the "hell-fire" of Ned's uniform in "Hell Gate" (LP 31).

What of the law of man? In classical Greece and Rome, homosexuality was a part of the social structure, but it was not carried over into European culture. This aspect of classical culture, like many others, was replaced by the Judeo-Christian tradition (the verses from Corinthians elaborate on that in Leviticus). After the collapse of Rome, the state as the center of power was replaced by the Church, which filled the power-vacuum. The moral law preached in the parish churches was backed by threats of eternal damnation, a more effective deterrent than any merely temporal penalty that could have been devised by secular authority. Christian morality was enforced, backed by the social as well as the religious authorities. The law of God was merged with that of man. The official penalty for homosexuality became gradually more severe until it included the death sentence. Hellfire after death was preceded by jail and the gallows. In 1535 under Henry VIII, the formerly ecclesiastical offense of sodomy was made a felony the penalty for which was death. This law was repeated and re-enacted under Queen Elizabeth I.

Let us look at the text of the "law of man" as it was in Housman's lifetime. In 1885, under the Labouchere Amendment (cited by Tannahill, *Sex in History*, 379–80), the criminal law was as follows: "Any male person who, in public or private, commits or is party to the commission of, or procures or attempts to procure the commission by any male person of any act of gross indecency with another male person" may be tried and imprisoned, with or without hard labor, for a maximum of two years. This criminalized "even a private, consenting homosexual relationship, and even one that stopped well short of full intercourse." The penalty for actual sodomy was far heavier. Housman had good and sufficient reason to feel himself "a stranger" and to be "afraid." Only in 1967 were private homosexual relations between consenting adults, with some exceptions, legalized (Tannahill, *Sex in History*, but especially 137 and 379–80). The conviction of Oscar Wilde under this law in 1895 "established the pattern of persecution that forced homosexuals to go underground for more than seventy years" (Meyers, *Homosexuality and Literature* 9). It is this cry

against persecution without specifying the "crime" of which the persecuted are "guilty" that gives this poem its universality, its power as the *cri
de coeur* of the generic outsider, the person who for any reason does not
belong, "a stranger, and afraid."

Housman's poem "effectively dramatizes the mingling of religious and
civil sanctions, all in the name of a superficial conformity on a matter
that is none of 'their' affair. . . . Housman [by using a dance metaphor]
emphasizes the triviality of the difference and the sense of disproportion
between the "crime" and the punishment. At the same time, the metaphor of the "stranger" and the "foreign laws" suggests the depths of Housman's alienation and his recognition that he would always live in a world
that he could never be fully a part of" (Martin, "Two Strategies," 17).

"Let them mind their own affairs," cries the poet/persona, and if "their
affairs" are heterosexual and mine are not, if "my ways" lead to the "mire"
of which we have seen so much, why, let them "please themselves" with
their variety of "affairs" and "look the other way" so as not to see mine.
"The other way" is the heterosexual "way" that leads to heaven instead
of that mire. Let them indulge themselves in the "adultery" and "fornica-
tion" and "idolatry" that the laws of God condemn equally with my
"ways," even though the law of man all but ignores them altogether. Such
unemphasized erotic puns as these on "affairs" and "ways" are the stigmata of the poetry in which Housman refers however obliquely to sexuality in general and to his own sexuality in particular. So are echoes of
other poems on the same theme, such echoes as the ones here of "Loitering with a vacant eye" about the Greek statue (ASL 51) and the healing
winds of the grave raised by the reference to Mercury (ASL 30).

The penalty for breaking the "law of man," if not that for trespassing
the "law of God," was no idle threat, as Oscar Wilde found. He did not
acknowledge the necessity to "Keep we must, if keep we can, / These
foreign laws of God and man." Instead, he did everything possible to draw
attention to himself and demonstrate that he cared not a whit what people might think. When his lover's father, the Marquis of Queensberry,
called him a "somdomite" [sic], Wilde sued him, lost the case, and was in
turn tried and sentenced to the maximum penalty under the above-cited
law, two years at hard labor in Reading Gaol. Housman, in his poem
based on this case, alters Reading Gaol to Portland, the prison where
someone in the Shropshire cycle (I suggested it was Ned) served his sentence and died. I also stated that the felon's crime might have been homosexuality. This assumes that it is Ned, who is apparently heterosexual,
and that he is based on Oscar Wilde, a married man (as was also John
Addington Symonds) and the father of two children before leaving the

closet and entering the prison cell. Oscar Wilde is the subject of the following poem.

Oh who is that young sinner with the handcuffs on his wrists?
And what has he been after that they groan and shake their fists?
And wherefore is he wearing such a conscience-stricken air?
Oh they're taking him to prison for the colour of his hair.

'Tis a shame to human nature, such a head of hair as his;
In the good old time 'twas hanging for the colour that it is;
Though hanging isn't bad enough and flaying would be fair
For the nameless and abominable colour of his hair.

Oh a deal of pains he's taken and a pretty price he's paid
To hide his poll or dye it of a mentionable shade;
But they've pulled the beggar's hat off for the world to see and stare,
And they're haling him to justice for the colour of his hair.

Now 'tis oakum for his fingers and the treadmill for his feet
And the quarry-gang on Portland in the cold and in the heat,
And between his spells of labour in the time he has to spare
He can curse the God that made him for the colour of his hair.

(AP 18)

The persona (or personae, since the poem seems to give a voice to the
mob rather than to any individual) is savage about the "colour of his
hair." We recall that in "Purple William" the unfortunate boy's words
served either to create a truth or to enable a hitherto hidden truth to
manifest itself and his complexion was altered to a "hue" that "was not
the wear" (ASL 63), which is, metaphorically, exactly what Wilde did.
In challenging the Marquis of Queensberry in court, he challenged his
opponent to pull his "hat off" and expose the native hue of his hair, upon
which they indeed "pulled the beggar's hat off for the world to see and
stare." Is it possible that "beggar" is a half-pun, suggesting the almost
identical "bugger"? In any case, there is no doubt that the "colour of his
hair" is a metaphor for homosexuality. J. R. Ackerley certainly so understood it. He wrote, "This obsession with [homosexual] sex was already
taking me . . . to foreign countries, France, Italy, Denmark, where civi-
lized laws prevailed and one was not in danger of arrest and imprisonment
for the colour of one's hair" ("My Father and Myself," 126). Martin
points out that in "C 33" (the number of Oscar Wilde's cell in Reading
Jail), Hart Crane deals with both "the alienation of the artist and the
persecution of the homosexual." This is not so in Housman's Wilde

poem. Although Housman's "poetry is generally written in a mood of longing for the 'land of lost content,' the remembered world of friendship with his beloved Mo, [he] was roused to anger by Wilde's fate and . . . denounced the society which condemned Wilde for a quirk of fate—'the colour of his hair' " (i.e., his homosexuality). Housman "is not interested in the fact that Wilde is an artist, and views his homosexuality as a merely physical arrtibute" (Martin, *Homosexual Tradition*, 117).

The metaphor makes its point with some subtlety. As he said in "The Application of Thought to Textual Criticism," Housman customarily translated the abstract into concrete metaphor.

> Mistakes are . . . made which could not be made if the matter under discussion were any corporeal object, having qualities perceptible to the senses. The human senses have had a much longer history than the human intellect, and have been brought much nearer to perfection. . . . I find . . . that a good way of exposing the falsehood of a statement or the absurdity of an argument . . . is to transpose it into sensuous terms and see what it looks like then. (*Complete Poems and Selected Prose*, 329).

Here, he exposes the absurdity of the ordinary reaction to the "matter under discussion," homosexuality, by transposing it into the "corporeal object," the sensuously perceptible characteristic of an unusual hair color, and "what it looks like then" is an overreaction, to say the least. The metaphor assumes that the felon is being punished for something that he did not choose and over which he has no control. Christopher Ricks has argued that there is a tradition in English literature of using hair color as an indictable offense, "a cruel perversion of injustice" and "a type of the arbitrarily unjust." He suggests that the color in question was red, and he links it to the anti-Semitic tradition that Judas Iscariot [and the devil] had red hair ("A. E. Housman and 'the colour of his hair'," 240). The religious and theological implications of Ricks's argument are outside the parameters of this study, but that Housman chose an appropriate analogy is indicated by current research suggesting that homosexuality is a genetic rather than a behavioural condition.[12] It seems to be in their genes that Housman and his lads are "luckless."

Laurence Housman has two comments about this poem. The earlier ascribes it simply to a "strong . . . expression of his feeling against social injustice" (L. Housman, *A. E. H.*, 105). The more revealing remark was in the much later, and posthumous, "*De Amicitia*" (34):

> It refers quite evidently to those who inescapably, through no fault of their own, are homosexual—having no more power of choice in the matter than a man has about the colour of his hair, which . . . he . . . cannot get away from.

Here . . . was a poem expressing contemptuous anger against society's treatment of these unhappy victims of fate, and a sympathy which went as far as
to imply no blame

The poem is certainly this, but I think it is more than this.

Nowhere is Housman's ambivalence toward his own sexuality more evident. He is not only the exposed man, the man in the dock, but he is
also the howling mob, the voice of public outrage. As Mendilow remarked about Tennyson's dramatic monologues, the personae both hide
and reveal "aspects of the poet's own personality" ("Tennyson's Palace,"
p. 156) and Housman's was, as we have seen, a conservative one. He was
horrified by the mob howling for Wilde's blood, a mob that could so easily be howling for his own. Because Aubrey Beardsley had illustrated some
of Wilde's writing, an untrue rumor circulated that he too was homosexual, and a mob stormed and stoned the offices of the *Yellow Book*. As a
result, Beardsley was dismissed from his position as its editor, as Gillette
explained in his introduction to Beardsley's *The Story of Venus and Tannhauser* (49). At the time, Housman was a professor at University College,
London, and allegations of homosexuality are always most dangerous to
those who, like teachers, are in close contact with young men, as Auden
was well aware. Shortly after Housman's birth, the father of John Addington Symonds had forced Rev. Vaughan, the headmaster of Harrow, to
resign—and had prevented him from accepting the high clerical positions
offered him—by threatening to expose his "affair" with a student. The
relationship between Vaughan and his student, Alfred Pretor, had not
involved coition but was limited to letters and caresses, and it was his
downfall (Grosskurth, *Memoirs*, 110–15). Both William Johnson (later
known as Cory) and Oscar Browning, who taught at Eton, had been summarily dismissed for inappropriate relations with their students, for being,
in the current terminology, "Arcadian schoolmasters" (Croft-Cooke,
Feasting with Panthers, 103). Nor was this possibility limited to lower
schools. In the early 1860s the authorities at both Oxford and Cambridge
were "only too aware . . . of the air of 'corrupt Greek ethics' which was
discernible in the books and lives of several of their leading classics men,
[and] of the exaggerated brotherliness among undergraduates." Indeed,
"this was a period in which the pederasty of schoolmasters . . . caused a
number of scandals in the schools" (ibid., 100–101). Browning, a Fellow
of King's College in Cambridge, had been "eased out" without any overt
scandal, but with rumor aplenty (ibid., 117). The situation in this regard
had not materially altered by the time of the Wilde trial. The emotional
storm it roused was potentially a threat to Housman's own mask and
safety. He could well imagine that same mob storming and stoning the
university buildings athirst for *his* blood. As Carey noted, he "responded

to the legalised victimisation of his kind with mingled guilt, shame, indignation and fury" ("Books of the Century," 9), but also with a degree of identification with the homophobic mob.

Like Housman, "the majority of homosexuals live quiet, unobtrusive, 'normal' lives, hoping to be invisible in society. . . . Even when living these quiet lives, fear of discovery or fear of oppression lurks constantly" (Llewellyn-Jones, *Every Man*, 229–30). The Wilde trial increased those fears. Housman was outraged by the mob that echoed his own internalized self-hatred; he was perhaps equally so by Wilde's own behavioral irresponsibility that had focused the attention of the press and the public on his "crime." All this outrage is poured out here, finding its voice in the poem in which Housman is at once the mob, the cause of its fury, and potentially its next victim. No name is given to the "him" whose hair is of an unacceptable shade. No name is needed.

Housman in this poem defines in metaphorical terms those choices available to the homosexual, the subject of "The laws of God, the laws of man" (LP 12). He can attempt to stay in the closet, "keep" the "foreign laws" by dying his hair or keeping his hat always on, and paying "a pretty price" in the coin of fear, loneliness, and isolation, as Housman himself did. Just how high that price is his poetry makes clear. Or he can come, or be dragged, out of the closet, "flayed" when his skin/disguise/hat is "pulled off," and be sent to prison. Once it would have been hanging or even burning as in Hart Crane's "Modern Craft" ("My modern love were / Charred at a stake in younger times than ours," *Complete Poems*, 132), but now it is merely "oakum," the "treadmill," and the "quarry-gang," and all for being as God made him.[13]

As "he" is nameless, so is his crime "nameless and abominable." The second epithet is from Leviticus; Wilde's lover, Lord Alfred Douglas, bestowed the first on it, coupled with the concept of "shame," in his poem "Two Loves."[14]

> . . . "What is thy name?" He said, "My name is Love."
> Then straight the first did turn himself to me
> And cried, "He lieth, for his name is Shame,
> But I am Love,
>
> .   .   .   .
> I am true Love, I fill
> The heart of boy and girl with mutual flame."
> Then sighing said the other, "Have thy will,
> I am the love that dare not speak its name."

Housman's contemporary reaction to the Wilde case may be compared to Robert Friend's "At the Tomb of Oscar Wilde," (*Dancing with a Tiger*, 13):

> Hounded to death by a prurient age
> that coyly itched beneath white sheets
> you sleep, while the same ignorant rage
> beyond these gates foams through the streets,
> Those who spit are those who leer
> where can-cans have their frenzy on
> in burlesques of their one idea—
> Leda and the dirty swan.
>
> In your lost name the lost confess,
> .   .   .   .

For Friend, as for Housman, the "ignorant rage" of the mob "foams through the streets," and Wilde's is a "lost" name. The difference is that whereas Friend could write explicitly in his poetry about his homosexuality, Housman could not. It was not only Wilde who was sent to jail. He was a symbol of personal and imaginative freedom as well as a person, and he himself summed up the situation perfectly in *De Profundis*: "imagination was as much in prison as I was. Vanity had barred up the windows, and the name of the warder was Hate" (64). What was also in the prison of social and poetic conformity erected by "a prurient age" was Housman's poetic vocabulary. However, he was still able to defy the "warder of hate" imaginatively and declare, in metaphoric terms, his choice.

> Ho, everyone that thirsteth
>   And hath the price to give,
> Come to the stolen waters,
>   Drink and your soul shall live.
>
> Come to the stolen waters,
>   And leap the guarded pale,
> And pull the flower in season
>   Before desire shall fail.
>
> It shall not last for ever,
>   No more than earth and skies;
> But he that drinks in season
>   Shall live before he dies.
>
> June suns, you cannot store them
>   To warm the winter's cold,
> The lad that hopes for heaven
>   Shall fill his mouth with mould.

(MP 22)

It is easy to see why E. M. Forster said of this poem: "The manner is scholarly and churchified . . . the dean might be giving out a hymn. The matter is blood-hot or death-cold" ("Ancient and Modern," Gardner, *Critical Heritage*, 319). Let us start with the "churchified" manner, as did he. Housman opens with a phrase from the Bible: "Ho, everyone that thirsteth, come ye to the waters . . . hear, and your soul shall live" (Isaiah 55:1, 3), but Isaiah's waters are the waters of salvation and need not be "stolen." They are not Housman's. His come from a different passage: "stolen waters are sweet" (Proverbs 9:17). These are proverbially the waters of carnal indulgence, and the "blood-hot" matter to which Forster referred. In this scriptural opening, Housman proclaims that drinking the "stolen waters" entails a price if caught. We know what that price is: "jail and gallows and hell-fire" (LP 12). The paradox is that drinking them will give life to the soul ("Drink and your soul shall live").

When one is dying of thirst, one must choose between drinking the "stolen waters" despite the price, and a living death, a life deprived of that which gives it meaning and makes it worth living. It may be argued that the deprivation is essential to attain salvation. A hell in this life is the price for an afterlife in heaven, and a hell on earth will result in eternal life, whereas heaven in this life will be paid for by an eternal life in hell. For Housman, however life was already hell: "Who made the world I cannot tell / 'Tis made, and here am I in hell" (MP 19). Nor did he accept the concept of an afterlife of reward and punishment. As the last verse makes manifest, soul and body are coterminous. Both the drinker and the abstainer ("the lad that hopes for heaven") will fare alike. Nothing is eternal, not even "earth and skies," so eternal life is irrelevant. As "Breath's a ware that will not keep" ('Reveille,' ASL 4), breath, or life, must be used before, like other wares, it moulders. Breath, youth, warmth, energy are for *now*; they cannot be stored in life's June against the coming winter. This is the "death-cold" matter of Forster's comment. All that is in question is the quality of earthly life, and it is better to live richly than to merely exist. "The lad that hopes for heaven" and the drinker of the waters will fare alike after death. This is explicit in a verse from the manuscript of "The Sage to the Young Man" (MP 4): "The loser hath not less, / They have not more that win: / One wage for righteousness / And one like wage for sin" (Burnett, *Poems*, 117, notes at bottom of page).

Here is the voice of defiance that rang at the beginning of "The laws of God, the laws of man" (LP 12), but even here Housman is careful to obscure the true nature of his "stolen waters." The walled garden, the forbidden pale, from at least its use in the *Song of Songs* throughout the course of literature, with its most elaborate eastern expression in Firdausi's *Perfumed Garden* and European expression in the medieval French *Roman de la Rose*, has been a metaphor for the woman immured and forbidden. In the early 1840s, the female body was "the valley sequester'd, inviting, / That shelters the fountain, of purest delight."[15] Parallel to this, as Eden, the garden of the Hesperides, or the garden of Proserpine, the "guarded pale" is a metaphor for heaven. Housman's "stolen waters" are in a "guarded pale."

We have considered the "pale." What of the "waters"? In Freud, water is a symbol of the female, as the walled garden is in literature. This seems to lead to three conclusions: sex with a woman is the forbidden experience, the only real heaven is to be found in a woman's embrace, and it is not eternal. This reminds us of "Tarry, delight," (MP 15) The word "leap" connotes youth and vigor, which are reinforced by the "June suns." Youth, vigor, even "desire" ultimately "must fail." All of this is clear—and conventional—but we know that for Housman, heaven was not a woman's embrace but a particular man's, "the heaven that I / Perish and have not known" (MP 2 in Ricks or Sparrow editions).

Despite the association of walled gardens with the female, Housman's "stolen waters" are not feminine. They are the "drink" for which I suggested the grenadier received "half-a-crown." the "bitter brew" that leaves a "sour" taste on the tongue, the proscribed "waters of life" for drinking which Oscar Wilde spent two years in Reading Gaol. They are the waters of fellatio in Robert Friend's "By the Sea of Galilee" ("there was a spring and we drank from it . . . I swallowed the wafer of your flesh, / you drained the wine from my lips," *Dancing with a Tiger*, 33). These are very masculine waters. E. M. Forster, who understood the implications of the image for Housman, wonders: "Did he [Housman] ever drink the stolen waters which he recommends so ardently to others? I hope so" ("Ancient and Modern," Gardner, *Critical Heritage*, 321).

Housman did indeed drink those "stolen waters," at least during his summer visits to Paris,[16] but it may be doubted that they provided more than bodily satisfaction. It would seem that his greatest source of contentment was not "friendship" but friendship, and that the very special "friendship" which lay at the center of his emotional life was the source not of contentment but of torment, a torment apparent in the poetry addressed to its object. This poetry is the subject of the next chapter.

10

The Soul that Was Born to Die for You

IN THE PRECEDING CHAPTER, THE EMPHASIS IN ALMOST EVERY POEM WAS on "I" and "my" feelings about my "cursed trouble." In this chapter, the emphasis shifts. The lyrics tend to focus on "you" and our relationship to each other or on "him" and "my" feelings about him, expressing what Page called "the tragedy of unfulfilled desire" (*A. E. Housman*, 194). Tennyson understood this tragedy and put it into words in "Tears, Idle Tears" from *The Princess*. Tennyson's song sums up a good deal of the Housman poetry considered in this chapter:

> Dear as remembered kisses after death,
> And sweet as those by hopeless fancy feign'd
> On lips that are for others; deep as love
> Deep as first love, and wild with all regret.
>
> (*Tennyson*, 267)

Housman's "best poetry is love poetry, and the tone of it is almost uniformly unhappy. Much of it seems to be addressed to a man, a revered friend passionately sought or surrendered" (Haber, *A. E. Housman*, 11–12). In answering some of the questions put to him by Pollet, Housman said, "Oxford had not much effect on me, except that I there met my greatest friend" (*A. E. Housman, Letters*, 328). For Housman, only one man was "my greatest friend." There was only one "him," one "friend and comrade," "my love," the real, but nameless, subject of much of his poetry. Cavafy puts this into words in "December, 1903":

> And if I can't speak about my love—
> If I don't talk about your hair, your lips, your eyes,
> still your face that I keep within my heart
> the sound of your voice that I keep within my mind,
> the days of September rising in my dreams,
> give shape and color to my words, my sentences,
> whatever theme I touch, whatever thought I utter.
>
> (Collected Poems, 139)

We have examined "When I was one-and-twenty" as a prologue to the Shropshire cycle. It is Housman's best-known poem on the price one pays for giving one's heart, but it is not the only one, nor the most personal. He himself gave away his heart and soul and paid the price throughout his life, not "jail and gallows and hell-fire" (LP 12) but pain, loneliness, and an aching heart. In this chapter, we shall look at the poems that are in my judgement (and that of others) the record of this price. I shall assume that no persona stands between the poet and the poem in the unofficial verses, that "I" is Housman speaking in his own voice. Seven lyrics are from *A Shropshire Lad*. One is from *Last Poems*. In these, the techniques examined in the previous chapters are prominent. The rest, about two-thirds of the individual poems considered here, are from the unofficial verse, and in them there is little or no attempt at indirection, gender disguise, or ambiguity. They are as close as one can get to the poet's naked heart.

I am not alone in considering the following poem semi-biographical rather than theoretical. Sparrow was of the opinion that in it Housman is "speaking apparently in his own person" (Symons et al., *Recollections*, 57 U.K., 76 U.S. ed.). So was Browne: in this "rueful" poem the second stanza "indicates his despair at the sudden break" six years previously when he moved out of the lodgings he shared with Moses Jackson (*Elegy in Arcady*, 16).[1] It was thus Housman's own heart that was "laden" with "rue" (ASL 54). As we have already seen, much of Housman's poetry has a personal basis transmuted by art into universality, a transmutation incomplete or never even attempted in many of these poems.

> There pass the careless people
>   That call their souls their own:
> Here by the road I loiter,
>   How idle and alone.
>
> Ah, past the plunge of plummet,
>   In seas I cannot sound,
> My heart and soul and senses,
>   World without end, are drowned.
>
> His folly has no fellow
>   Beneath the blue of day
> That gives to man or woman
>   His heart and soul away.
>
> There flowers no balm to sain him
>   From east of earth to west
> That's lost for everlasting
>   The heart out of his breast.

Here by the labouring highway
With empty hands I stroll:
Sea-deep, till doomsday morning,
Lie lost my heart and soul.

(ASL 14)

In his French article, "A. E. Housman," Pollet splits the reference of the third verse into two separate emotional relationships, speaking of the poet's imprecations against both love and friendship, but the text offers no support for such a division. The poem clearly equates the giving of one's "heart and soul" to a man with giving them to a woman. Either the poem is about friendship, or it is about love, and we have seen that the tone of the poems about simple friendship is quite different from this. Friendship may be ended by death, causing grief, but it is never, in Housman, "folly." This is not, then, a poem about simple friendship. The phrase "that gives to man or woman / His heart and soul away" can mean only one thing. It cannot refer to girls who give their hearts away to men as well as men who give theirs away to women, because it is specifically "his folly," "his heart and soul," and "his breast," and there is "no balm to sain him." The reference can only be to the man whose love is unrequited.

The "people" of the first line are "careless" in several senses in addition to the obvious one. They have no "care" not only because they "care less" for those women they love than does the speaker for the man to whom he has given his heart but because they have no cause for "care." They have no soul-sickness and are spared the "cursed trouble" because of which "I loiter" by the road, "idle and alone." They "call their souls their own" because when they give their hearts and souls away they can marry the new owners and so reclaim them. As for the "souls" of those they love, they can also own them by marrying and so legally possessing both them and their former owners. Are those "seas I cannot sound" not also the "stolen waters" (MP 30) that "I cannot sound" both in the sense of measure and of speech, the seas to which the tongue is forbidden to give sound since that to which they refer is nameless?

Housman equates the love of a man for a man with that of a man for a woman. Nor is he wrong, for "homosexuals can feel as much passion and can love as deeply as heterosexuals" (Llewellyn-Jones, Every Man, 221). They can give their hearts away as irretrievably to a man (and incur as much misery as a result) as a man can to a woman or a woman to a man. Love is love and it exacts the same price whether heterosexual or homosexual.

The price exacted for homosexual love, however, may be higher, as it cannot eventuate in the accepted union of the couple. For a homosexual, the "heart and soul" thus given cannot be legally reclaimed by means of the rites of marriage. This is clear if we return to the "balm" that does not exist to "sain him," for in a poem closely related to "Shot?" (ASL 44), and also referring to the Woolwich cadet, we find that "here are salves to friend you, / And many a balsam grows on ground" for the curing of physical maiming, but they are useless "when your sickness is your soul" (ASL 45). That same soul-sickness associated with the giving away of one's "heart and soul," for which there is no cure, is specifically homosexuality and a man's giving of his "heart and soul" to another man. There is no cure "from east of earth to west." The image is temporal as well as geographical: "from east to west" can also mean "from birth to death." This reading takes us directly back to the poetry of the preceding chapter.

In the first verse "Here by the road I loiter," and in the last "Here by the labouring highway / . . . I stroll." The two images of purposeless movement act as a frame for this poem, but in the next poem the movement is no longer purposeless. The same structure is used, the circularity emphasized by the repeated line that makes the road a frame for the poem. This road, like the poems themselves, ends where it began. This is "the ceaseless way," "my way," not the way of the "careless people," the heterosexuals, of whom Housman said "my ways are not as theirs" (LP 12). This is the road where Terence lay in "lovely muck" (ASL 62), "the lovely way that led / To the slime pit and the mire" (LP 31). This is the way to Ludlow Fair where the persona walked with his "friends" drunk with the "sour" brew that "should do good to heart and head / When your soul is in my soul's stead" (ASL 62). When "you" accept the fact that you are like me homosexual, when you walk the same "way" as I do, then you will understand my poetry and accept me, and "I" will "friend" you and at last be your "friend." That "dark and cloudy day" (ASL 62) never dawned, the implicit invitation was not accepted, and Housman forever walked his "way" alone.

> White in the moon the long road lies,
>   The moon stands blank above;
> White in the moon the long road lies
>   That leads me from my love.
>
> Still hangs the hedge without a gust,
>   Still, still the shadows stay:
> My feet upon the moonlit dust
>   Pursue the ceaseless way.

The world is round, so travellers tell,
    And straight though reach the track,
Trudge on, trudge on, 'twill all be well,
    The way will guide one back.

But ere the circle homeward hies
    Far, far must it remove:
White in the moon the long road lies
    That leads me from my love.

(ASL 36)

In the poem "Others, I am not the first" (ASL 30) what seemed to be merely a "filler," the apparently inane "if truth were told," proved the key to the poem. Here, we have a similarly inane phrase, "so travellers tell." Firchow pounced on the phrase as "colossal naivete. . . . Even in 1896 and even in Shropshire, flat-earthers were not commonly to be met. Housman's contention that a peasant would rely on "travellers" for reports of the world's roundness and that such reports would come as a novelty to him, is simply preposterous" ("Land of Lost Content," 110). Let us first correct a misapprehension evident in this indictment. Assuming the speaker to be Terence, he is not a "peasant" but a "yeoman" as stated in "On Wenlock Edge" (ASL 31). He is also Housman's mask, and neither Terence nor his creator is particularly naive. Let us assume that, as in previous cases, Housman knew what he was doing and he did not intend to be "preposterous." We have examined his intentionally preposterous comic verse, and it is marked by a zest, a light-heartedness, which is conspicuous here by its absence. Let us assume rather that Housman's meaning is, as so often in his official poetry, veiled, and see what lies behind the veil. Who, exactly, are these travellers of the third verse who assert firstly that the "world is round" and secondly that if one continues to "trudge on" one will return to one's starting point?

Clearly, we are not talking about "flat-earthers" since it had been known since antiquity that one could not "trudge" around the world. For one thing, there is a great deal of water in the way. Columbus's voyages, and those of Balboa, Drake, Cook, and so on, had shown just how much. Let us then ask what else could be meant by a round world the circling of which would, "as travellers tell," bring one back to one's starting point. The answer is to be found in Manilius 1 (*Astronomica*, 21). Round "is the shape that continues for ever and most resembles that of the gods: nowhere in it is there beginning or end" like the "orb of the moon"; and "so too the Earth is rounded and reflects the shape of the heavens." The sun and moon are travellers that move in a circular orbit that always returns to its starting point. I would suggest that they are the specific travellers to which the poem refers. The sun, however, does not shine on this road. It is lit only by the moon.

That moon that "stands blank above" is a traveller that circles the world every twenty-four hours. It is the earth's shadow on the moon during eclipse that provides visual proof of the earth's rotundity. The moon is then the traveller that "tells" us that the world is round. It also demonstrates that following a circular "track" (the word is Housman's and also that used in astronomy) that appears "straight" to the human eye will lead inevitably back to the point from which we chose to begin tracking, although such a path properly speaking has neither beginning nor end but is spacially "ceaseless." In addition, roundness has neither temporal beginning nor end and "most resembles . . . the gods"; it is, one might say, the metaphysical shape of "ceaseless" eternity. Housman's "long road" is "White in the moon" because it reflects the moon's color. All of this is implied in the phrase that seems so "preposterous." It draws our attention directly to the moon, the source of the image.

The moon in antiquity was hermaphroditic, equally Luna and Lunus (what Robert Duncan calls "My Lord-and-Lady Moon" in "The Moon," line 23, *Bending the Bow*, 18), as Housman may well have known. There was the triple goddess who was, in the dark of the moon, Hecate, the "queen of air and darkness," a symbol of malign femaleness. There was the full moon, the "fecundating god: the male moon," full, round, and white, "a fecund repository of light," that emits rays, as the glans is the round and fecund repository of seed that it emits (Woods, *Articulate Flesh*, 35). We have seen this aspect of the moon in the "moonlight" to which the roses "burst apart" (MP 37). The persona in this poem, separated from his beloved, walks endlessly on the path of eternity in the light of the full moon. One need hardly specify that this "blank" moon does not represent any phase of the female moon goddess whether called Selene or Diana or Luna. This moon is Lunus, male, and the source of the "moonlight pale" that lit Terence"s road to and from Ludlow Fair (ASL 58).

The stasis of eternal circling is not limited to the moon, the road, and the speaker. The word "still" is repeated three times in the second verse. The first time it is associated with the "hangs" of the hedge that no "gust" agitates, and this imparts the connotation of "motionless." The second and third times, "still" picks up the following "shadows stay" and connotes the silence and changelessness of the shadows. Shadows are also shades, ghosts of the dead. "The shadows continue to remain silent" is one possible paraphrase. "The shadows remain very, very silent and/or motionless" is another. Further permutations are clearly possible. However one opts to adjust the relative weight of the meanings of "still" in each use (and Housman is clearly evoking all its meanings at once), one of its components is silence. This "way" is a silent way; he that treads it must not speak its name. Its silence is also the silence of death.

Its surface is "dust," and the grave is "the house of dust." But this dust is still, always and forever, lit by the "blank" moon under which it "lies." This road is thus also the "way" of the homosexual who "lies" under the male moon in two senses. Kreuzer points out that "lies" here connotes "complete inactivity, an absence of all motion" in a scene dominated by "the dead white of the moonlight." The motionlessness is emphasized by that moon which "stands" as the road "lies" and the hedge "hangs." This is the motionlessness of death reflected in the lifeless moon and emphasized by the repeated "still" and by "stays." It is a "scene of sterility," and sterility we have seen evoked before.[2] Its symbols are "God's acre" and the nettle. The poem, like the moonlit road itself, is lifeless, without even a "gust" of the wind that for Housman is the symbol of life and also of "healing." It is not merely, in fact, the road that leads to death; it is the road of death, but not death as a sleep in which "the wind of healing" (ASL 30) will replace "the gale of life" (ASL 31) and "I" will "sleep sound" (AP 12) healed of the "ancient evil," (AP 12) my "cursed trouble." (MP 21) Here there is no wind at all, neither the "wind of healing" nor "the gale of life." The poem suggests that homosexuality, symbolized by the hermaphroditic dead moon, still lights "my way" after death.

That this road is indeed the one trodden ceaselessly by the still shadows of the dead is also indicated by the repetition of the line that frames the poem. "The terminal repetition of an initial stanza [or in this case line] . . . by returning to the original point of departure, . . . suggests that there is no place else to go and consequently, that the journey has been completed" (Smith, *Poetic Closure*, 67). This is the road of death that one must tread after the journey of life is over. The imagery, approached from several points and from several angles, still leads to the same conclusion.

To give one's "heart and soul away" to "man or woman," and for Housman this means to another man, is to be "lost," to "lie drowned" till "doomsday morning." Housman gave his and was lost.

> Look not in my eyes, for fear
>   They mirror true the sight I see,
> And there you find your face too clear
>   And love it and be lost like me.
> One the long nights through must lie
>   Spent in star-defeated sighs,
> But why should you as well as I
>   Perish? gaze not in my eyes.

> A Grecian lad, as I hear tell,
>   One that many loved in vain,
> Looked into a forest well
>   And never looked away again.
> There, when the turf in springtime flowers,
>   With downward eye and gazes sad,
> Stands amid the glancing showers
>   A jonquil, not a Grecian lad.
>
> (ASL 15)

We recall the words of the hopeful seducer in "Oh see how thick the goldcup flowers," considered as part of the Shropshire cycle, where the youth tells the girl, "Oh, look in my eyes then, can you doubt?" (ASL 5) His insincerity in seeking only his own physical satisfaction is thrown into relief by the poet's contrary request to the man he loves whose welfare is dearer to him than his own.

Although Housman seldom drew directly on mythology, when he did, as in "Tarry delight" (MP 15), "Crossing alone the nighted ferry" (MP 23) to be discussed below, and here, "he used ancient idiom and allusion with unique effect" (Bush, *Mythology*, 475). I suspect that he achieves this effect by being at once within the poem and outside it in three separate ways, so the poem reflects the poet in three distinct modes. As a classicist using a classical myth he maintains a professional aesthetic distance; as the poet shaping the words, he maintains control; and as the "star-defeated" lover, he projects himself directly into the persona and gives the poem its sense of emotional intensity.

The specifically mythological second verse acts as a gloss on the personal first verse in which the beloved's gender is inexplicit. Hamilton calls this "a flawless poem . . . in which the lover fears his girl will see her own image therein [in his eyes], and love, not him, but herself" (Hamilton, *Housman the Poet*, 66). In its way, this is a great tribute to Housman's skill at indirection and gender ambiguity. We have seen the efficacy of this skill demonstrated in the last chapter by Haber's assumptions concerning the gender of the person "On your midnight pallet lying" on the other side of the locked door (ASL 11). The poem may be "flawless," but Hamilton's explication is not. It ignores the gloss that Housman so kindly provided, and should read, "the lover fears his *friend* will see *his* own image therein, and love, not him, but *himself*," as did Narcissus. Should this happen, both would be "lost" and "perish." As it is, only the speaker whose love is "disastrous," literally "star-defeated," is "lost" and will "perish." The nature of that loss and that death is indicated by the buried puns on "lie" and "spent." This is Housman's familiar technique for obscuring the actual import of his words. Indeed, in direct contrast to Hamilton's reading, Robbins finds here a "fear of involvement" that is "explicitly the fear of same-sex love. . . . the danger is to be found in the love of the same by the same, imaged as the love of one's own reflection" ("Very Curious Construction," 149). But, like Hamilton, Robbins ignores Housman's implicit gloss, to which we must now turn.

We have seen twice that a seemingly innocuous filler line, "if truth were told" and "so travellers tell," has pointed the way to the heart of the poem. There is such a half-line filler in this poem also, "as I hear tell," and like them it suggests that we turn our attention to the ancient world, and to the source of the fable. The story of Narcissus is told in Ovid's *Metamorphoses*, book 3, lines 3390–510, and contrary to the usual modern rendering, Echo has little to do with it. The female is not only marginal but also irrelevant. I shall recount the myth as Ovid told it at some length as much of Housman's imagery is drawn from it, not only in this poem but also elsewhere in his poetry.

The prophet Tiresias predicts that the boy Narcissus will live long provided that he never knows himself, that is, that he never becomes acquainted with his own essential nature. He is a beautiful youth whose love is sought by both maidens and other youths, but he is too proud to respond to any of them. The nymph Echo falls in love with him, but he spurns her as he has all others. A youth whom he has thus rejected prays that he should love someone as others have loved him, and as fruitlessly. Nemesis hears and grants his prayer. Resting by a spring of pellucid water, Narcissus desires to quench his thirst, bends over the pool, and "inside him, deep within him, / Another thirst was growing, for he saw / An image in the pool and fell in love." He is "Charmed by himself, spellbound, and no more moving / Than any marble statue," and "He wants himself." He attempts "to kiss the image in the water / Dips in his arms to embrace the boy he sees there" and "almost drowns / In his own watching eyes." Narcissus cannot understand his failure to embrace the boy who "is eager / For me to hold him." He appeals to the image, "You promise, / I think, some hope with a look of more than friendship. / You reach out your arms when I do, and your smile / Follows my smiling." At last realizing the truth, he yearns to die since death "takes my trouble from me. I am sorry only / The boy I love must die: we die together." Seeing the image fade, he cries out, "Where are you going? Stay: do not desert me, / I love you so. I cannot touch you; let me / Keep looking at you always, and in looking / Nourish my wretched passion!" After he dies, his soul in Hades continues to gaze at its own image in a Stygian pool, and his body is transformed into the flower that bears his name.

The story is a perfect source of metaphor for homosexual poetry. Narcissus must never know himself. His life depends on his remaining in ignorance of his essential nature. Self-knowledge, the forerunner of public exposure, equals disaster. In the United States in the 1920s "homosexual men were liable to be disowned by their families, dismissed by their bosses, condemned by their peers and priests, castrated or drugged or imprisoned by their doctors, or driven to suicide by the prurience of neighbors and press" (Woods, *Articulate Flesh,* 151). If the situation of the homosexual in England was not quite so life-threatening, it was not otherwise much better. We have seen what happened to the Woolwich cadet and to Oscar Wilde, and "The laws of God, the laws of man" (LP 12) demonstrate Housman's own assessment of it.

Narcissus not only rejects girls but also boys (to whom he is just as attractive) who also seek his love. One of these boys causes his downfall by being responsible for his coming to know himself. Metaphorically, the boy awakens to his own homosexuality through the agency of another male. Narcissus at last falls in love.

Narcissus almost drowns in the pool that holds the image he desires to embrace. This becomes the water where "My heart and soul and senses, / World without end, are drowned" (ASL 14). He and his image gaze into each other's eyes. Housman appeals to the object of his love, "Look not in my eyes . . . gaze not in my eyes" (ASL 15), for should you do so, we will both be in love with you, which would not much improve matters. We would both be "lost" instead of only I. In the last chapter, we saw the significance in homosexual poetry of such direct eye contact. Allen Ginsberg reverses Housman, and in "Please Master" he begs for eye contact.[3] Robert Friend describes the result that Housman predicts if the beloved does see his reflection in the lover's eyes: "you wander . . . / deep in a mirror world, in your own eyes drowned; . . . / Drinking in delight as from a spring, your lost / gaze is the only haunting look" (*Dancing with a Tiger,* "The Impossible Sea," 27). He also here provides a gloss on "Ho everyone that thirsteth" (MP 22). The delight drunk from this spring is the delight of the "stolen waters" (MP 22).

Narcissus longs to die. This will end his "trouble." We have already seen the "wind of healing" (ASL 30) that Housman evokes from the grave that will make him "whole of an ancient evil" (AP 12) and end "this cursed trouble" (MP 21). However, as is intimated in "White in the moon" (ASL 36), and as we shall see in other poems yet to be examined, it doesn't. Narcissus and his beloved will "die" together, linking death and sex as Housman is notorious for doing. Although he cannot touch his beloved, any more than Housman could touch his (however different the reasons) Narcissus begs that he will stay to be gazed at, and we shall soon see the use Housman makes of this. "My wretched passion," that same "cursed trouble," can only thus be "nourished." The notebooks record an earlier version of the beginning of the second verse: "[A/The]

Grecian lad, as [I hear/fables] tell, / One [that many loved/like you be-
loved] in vain" (Burnett, *Poems*, 18, variants at bottom of page). The rejected version of the second line was far more personal—and more
explicit—than its final form. It leaves no doubt of the identity of either
the speaker or his beloved.

Bayley puts the implications of the verse together with the author's
biography and extracts an appealing reading: the poem is a wry joke.

> Housman's tone is private, and tender, because the joke is shared only be-
> tween two non-lovers, for whom (or at least for one of them) a shared joke
> will be the nearest thing to love's intimacy. It is highly comical that you might
> chance to look in my eyes and fall in love with your own image; and then the
> pair of us would be in the same plight, both together and apart. If you were
> Narcissus the added absurdity is that you would never stop gazing . . . and to
> have brought that about would be an odd fate for me, even odder than the
> one I have. It is a love poem which imagines two people, one indifferent, shar-
> ing the joke two lovers might have at the moment of discovering each other.
> And the tone is both tender and tough—tender to the other but hard on
> himself, knowing the joke's on him. The effect of intimacy lies in its being
> almost unnoticeable. . . . Housman is adept at concealing the intimate behind
> the obvious. (*Housman's Poems*, 140)

This is, as I have said, an appealing reading. The only trouble is that it
assumes that both parties are in on the joke, but I doubt that this is so. It
seems to me less a shared joke than a wryly humorous private reflection.
As a shared joke, the humor would have been drowned in the overt expression of the emotion. The mask would have been off, and the masquerade over.

Narcissus is "an ideal subject for those . . . whose love of boys' bodies
had to masquerade as an interest in matters mythological and aesthetic.
. . . Narcissus . . . was a boy who fell in love with another boy . . . [and
his passion] can be used as a symbolic portrayal of the love" of a male for
a male, with two dimensions: homosexuality (a male for another male)
and self-love (a male for himself, his own reflection). In this particular
poem, "the boy to whom the poem is addressed would be . . . captivated
by himself, but erotically involved with the substance behind the illusion
of self: the other" (Woods, *Articulate Flesh*, 19–22). Both dimensions are
involved in this poem, homosexuality on the part of the speaker and at
least the potential for narcissism on that of the beloved.

The term "narcissism" has been appropriated for the concept of self-
love rather than the love of a man's reflected image, which is to say another man. Housman used this aspect of the myth in another poem that
does not directly concern us here. It is sufficient to give an excerpt from
"Oh fair enough are sky and plain" (ASL 20) to show the difference. He

is describing the reflection in the water as more beautiful than the "real" world. "These are the thoughts I often think / As I stand gazing down / In act upon the cressy brink / To strip and dive and drown; / But in the golden-sanded brooks and azure meres I spy / A silly lad that longs and looks / And wishes he were I." The one who falls in love with himself rather than another is "a silly lad," but falling in love with another is also "folly." The persona rejects the idea of deliberately drowning himself in those "azure meres" into which Narcissus looked. His "heart and soul and senses" (ASL 14) were indeed drowned, but not because of narcissism.

There is a third implication in the legend that seems to have been ignored. Narcissus fell in love with another male (homosexuality) who was himself (narcissism) and wanted to make love to him(self). This also makes him a symbol of masturbation. If we now look again at those buried puns in the first verse, "One the long nights through must lie / Spent in star-defeated sighs," we can hardly miss the implications. The speaker "lies" with himself at night, making love to himself while thinking of the unattainable beloved and imagining that, like Narcissus, he is not only himself but also the other. In this way he is at last "spent" and "perishes." We must indeed look at the fable as Ovid told it and not as it has been rewritten for an age willing to accept only the eponymous narcissistic meaning.

Housman was as adept at concealing the nature of his affection behind a veil of ambiguity and recondite allusion in his poetry as behind the veil of his mask in his life. The double meaning of "friend" acted as such a veil. It meant one thing to Moses Jackson and another, something far more emotionally charged, to Housman. For the one, it had only its common and usual meaning of casual, if deep, affection. For the other, there was nothing casual about this affection, another name for which was love. When Housman says "friend" in reference to himself, he means "lover."

> You smile upon your friend to-day,
>   To-day his ills are over;
> You hearken to the lover's say,
>   And happy is the lover.
>
> 'Tis late to hearken, late to smile,
>   But better late than never:
> I shall have lived a little while
>   Before I die for ever.
>
> (ASL 57)

Those "ills" are the lover's "ail," and they are cured by the friend's smile, a smile that eases the "lover's sorrow." If he cannot say that "the breast the darnel smothers / Rested once upon another's" (ASL 11), at least he can say "You smile upon your friend to-day." In addition to "better late than never," he implies "better a crumb of comfort, a symbolic sip of the water of life, than nothing." A single moment of shared intimacy, even if it is friendly rather than "friendly," means that "I shall have lived a little while."

Again, the notebooks reveal an earlier draft of the first verse, one more emotionally charged and far more personal—and revealing—than that which was ultimately printed (Burnett, *Poems*, 60, variants at bottom of page).

> You smile today, you hearken now,
>   So sighs and griefs are over;
> You give again the lover's vow,
>   And happy is the lover.

In the final version, "you" smile and listen to the lover's declaration, and this is enough to make the lover "happy." But "You hearken to the lover's say," implies only passive willingness to listen. It replaces the original third line in which there is an active—and positive—response. "You give again the lover's vow" indicates that the lover's feeling is indeed returned "in kind," to use Laurence Housman's delicate euphemism, thus putting an end to his "sighs and griefs" and providing far more cause for his happiness. The rather pathetic willingness to subsist on crumbs if cake cannot be had (which permeates the final version) is not in the original draft, which indicates that just perhaps that "symbolic sip of the water of life" may have been, if only once, less symbolic than has usually been assumed.

Love is a sharing of intimacy, not a giving on one side and a taking on the other but a mutual giving and taking. Housman's poetry is as strong an intimation of a desire to give as of a desire to take, perhaps stronger.

> Say, lad, have you things to do?
>   Quick then, while your day's at prime.
> Quick, and if 'tis work for two,
>   Here am I, man: now's your time.
>
> Send me now, and I shall go;
>   Call me, I shall hear you call;
> Use me ere they lay me low
>   Where a man's no use at all;
>
> Ere the wholesome flesh decay,
>   And the willing nerve be numb,
> And the lips lack breath to say,
>   "No, my lad, I cannot come."

(ASL 24)

Here, again, the buried puns carry the burden of the underlying mean-ing. The repeated "quick" in the first verse not only lends an air of ur-gency to the appeal but also carries in it the older sense of "alive." It stands in opposition to the death imagery of the second and third verses: "lay me low," "flesh decay," "nerve be numb," "lips lack breath," and, the buried pun, "I cannot come." The OED informs us that "come" in its specifically sexual meaning is mid-twentieth century slang. However, in the mid-nineteenth century it already had the denotation of "a flow or flood of water," and thus, by analogy, of those "forbidden waters" that Housman recommends to the thirsty. Here, I suggest, is the link between these two senses.

"Willing nerve" implies both that the "nerve" is "willing" (as Barkis was) and that it is the source of determination, the "will" which activates the flesh and wills "more mischief than it durst" (ASL 30). The appeal "use me," in the very center of the poem, is also an erotic pun: "I want you to use me, use my flesh and nerve and lips before I die and "they," others, take what you reject, make use of me themselves, and 'lay me low' in the death that is a euphemism for sexual repletion." One need not ask what "work" is being contemplated in "If 'tis work for two, / here am I." This reading, if accepted, means that Housman is in this poem skirting the cliff's edge by making the male gender of the addressee explicit, pre-cisely what he carefully avoided in the rest of his official poetry. He skirted the danger line, but did not cross it—quite.

I am not suggesting this reading in place of the obvious one in which the puns remain decorously buried; I am only noting that this erotic level does exist and contributes to the erotic tone of the poem that most critics feel without having quite analyzed why. Even Bayley has not disinterred all the implications of the diction. He says that this poem "hides its inner shrinking self behind its urgent note and form. "Here am I, man; now's your time" would be almost intimidating, like "Use me," but both con-ceal a real and plaintive longing, a feminine wish for a feminine role. The longing can be hidden by a tougher query—what use am I alive anyway—but the incongruity between feelings persists" (*Housman's Poems*, 140–41). It seems that Bayley has accepted Auden's diagnosis of Housman's role preference. "Use me" can indeed mean "Make use of me" as a passive recipient of your desire, the female role, although this is a bit more am-biguous than it seems on the surface. The notebooks may help to resolve this ambiguity. In them, we find an earlier draft in which the lines in the middle of the first two verses are quite different (Burnett, *Poems*, 26, vari-ants at bottom of page):

> Say, lad, have you things to do?
>   Do them quick while life's at prime
> [What's a friend for? Buckle to:/Quick, and if 'tis work for two,]
>   Here am I, man: now's your time.

> Send me now, and I shall go;
>   Call me [while I hear you/I shall come at] call;
> Wait not till they lay me low
>   Where a man's no use at all.

The question "What's a friend for?" can be read innocently or, by placing the friend in quotation marks, as a homosexual invitation to copulation. "Buckle to," or colloquially "Get to work," would tend to support the speaker's preference for a feminine role, but "I shall come at call" equally indicates the masculine role. It certainly leads directly into the last phrase, "I cannot come," whichever role is preferred.

The unerotic reading, "Once I am dead I shall not be able to respond to your summons," is glossed by another poem, which is itself not without its erotic undertones. Its imagery is drawn from the same source as "Look not in my eyes" (ASL 15), Greek mythology. The ferryman is Charon, and the "one coin" is the fare for passage into the land of the dead.

> Crossing alone the nighted ferry
>   With the one coin for fee,
> Whom, on the far quayside in waiting,
>   Count you to find? Not me.
>
> The fond lackey to fetch and carry,
>   The true, sick-hearted slave,
> Expect him not in the just city
>   And free land of the grave.

(MP 23)

"Send me now, and I shall go; / Call me, I shall hear you call; / Use me" (ASL 24), cried the speaker to his friend, "to fetch and carry," to be your "fond lackey," your "true, sick-hearted slave," "ere they lay me low" (ASL 24) in the "free land of the grave" where I will be neither able nor willing to answer your call. This conflation of the two poems clarifies both. Part of the ritual of crossing into the land of death is to drink from Lethe, causing forgetfulness of one's past life. One draft of the third line (that usually printed) is "Whom, on the wharf of Lethe waiting" (Burnett, *Poems*, 129, variants at bottom of page). Here, the implication is that nothing except the waters of Lethe, and perhaps not even they, can transform the "fond lackey" of "Say, lad" (ASL 24) to the indifferent speaker of "Crossing alone." We have seen in many of his poems that Housman looked forward to the death that would free him of the "luggage I'd lief set down" (ASL 50) his "disastrous love" (Burnett, *Poems*, 21, 177). Other poems clearly imply that his love is stronger than death. Like the poetry that embodied it, it "will last for long" (AP 4) if not quite so long as the world.

Randall Jarrell has subjected this poem to the closest possible reading, and any discussion of it must start with a summary of his remarks. The first verse consists of a rhetorical question, the obvious answer to which is, "Me." The given answer is instead the "denying and elliptical 'Not me.' " "The implied corollary" of the rhetorical question is "And I'll satisfy your expectations and be there?" The reply "Not me" is a denial of "flippant and brutal finality . . . [that] implies that the expectations are foolish." The diction of this verse implies, thinks Jarrell, three things: "You do expect to find me and ought not to," "You're actually such a fool as to count on my being there?" and "So I'll be there, eh? Not me." The tone of that "Not me" is one of "casualness, finality, and matter-of-fact bluntness," "the crudest of denials. There is in it a laconic brutality, an imperturbable and almost complacent vigor; it has certainly a sort of contempt. Contempt for what . . . himself for his faithlessness . . . his obsessing weakness?" Or is it contempt for "you" who expect to "keep things as they are, for being stupid enough to imagine that they will be so always? The tone is both threatening and disgusted," sardonic and venomous ("Texts from Housman," 51–54).

Jarrell offers several possible paraphrases of the third and fourth lines, all emphasizing either the speaker's own self-contempt or his contempt for the person he is addressing, or both. Jarrell, like so many, is misled by his own expectations and assumes the "you" is a girl. All of these paraphrases suggest that the speaker is triumphant, that he has in some sort won a victory, defeating "you" by not doing what "you" expected "me" to do. The tone of self-contempt that Jarrell finds, explicating it with such great eclat, is remarked upon by many critics. Ricks says of this poem that love slides "over into contempt and self-contempt, so that two poems occupy the same space."[4]

Jarrell proceeds to the second verse, pointing out the implications of the terms used. "Fond" is both "foolish" and "loving" as he says. The standard version of the fifth line is "The brisk fond lackey to fetch and carry." "Brisk," he points out, is both a positive term, meaning "lively, alert, and energetic," and a negative one, connoting officiousness and lack of dignity, "leaping at your every word." A lackey is a servant but the term is "contemptuous and degrading," a servile follower, a toady. Thus "fetch and carry" means "you thought so poorly of me that our love was nothing but the degrading relationship of obsequious servant and contemptuous master." "True" is constant, loyal, devoted, and faithful. "Sick-hearted" connotes, among other things, "cowardly," "weak," "ignoble," and "discouraged." Jarrell takes it to mean here "sick at heart at . . . his own helpless subjection" (ibid., 54–55). "Slave" is a dead metaphor for "a conventional lover," and in its literal sense both unpleasant and dishonorable, so as a term used between lovers it is both indecent and horrible. Jarrell then proceeds to carefully analyze the "just city / And free land of the grave," and this is the most convincing part of his explication. However, it is not germane to my purpose, so I reluctantly omit it and present only his summation. This poem "is an accusation that embodies every strong statement of the underlying antagonism, the real ambivalence of most such [love] relationships. . . . these plaints are always pleas" (ibid., 56). His final remark about a "plaint" being also a "plea" I heartily endorse.

Jarrell has justly noted that an aspect of a poem may be misleading in isolation, its full meaning and significance becoming apparent only when read as part of the larger unit, which may modify or "even in extreme cases completely" (ibid., 53) reverse the implications of the part in isolation. It is only unfortunate that while recognizing that the part in isolation from the whole may be misleading, he did not extend this critical principle to the poem in isolation from the whole oevre and the poet's biography. Had he done so, he would have avoided two errors. He would not have assumed that "you" was a "she," nor would he have assumed that the poem deals with two people in a mutual love relationship. Placing the poem in its own context cancels the probability, even the possibility of all his first verse paraphrases and much of the significance he gives to the diction of the second verse.

I do not find the "flippancy" and "brutality" that Jarrell does. Instead, I see a wry humor and tenderness. The poem seems to me to imply that the only reason why "I" will not be there to greet "you" is that "I" will already be dead myself, and the dead "cannot come" (ASL 24). Nor do I find the "self-contempt" that seems so obvious to so many. The diction in the fifth and sixth lines, the source of the supposed "self-contempt" (on which Jarrell exercised his ingenuity) is not A. E. Housman's. It is Laurence Housman's. He made an arbitrary choice of several words that had been left open, and chose "brisk," "fond," and "lackey." In *More Poems* he does not list these open alternates, but the manuscript fragment clearly indicates that both "fond" and "lackey" were afterthoughts. The alternate for "lackey" was "vassal" and that word carries a completely different set of connotations, a vassal being a loyal and faithful subordinate bound to his lord by solemn oath. The open adjective rejected by Laurence Housman was "prim" (see also Bayley, *Housman's Poems*, 135). "Prim" was an adjective often used by his friends to describe Housman, as he was well aware. It was the adjective that Wilfrid Scawen Blunt had used. It was the adjective used in the unsigned review of *More Poems* and Gow's Sketch in the *Times Literary Supplement:* "the sensitive affectionate spirit that lay concealed behind an exterior which was both prim and grim." In this context it constitutes a private joke, one which was never shared. This poem was not included in *Last Poems* because, I suspect, the situation envisioned in it was reversed. Moses Jackson was dying and the poem would have been not only incongruous and painful but, in the circumstances, macabre.

Accepting this poem as one of a number of similar lyrics related to the known facts of Housman's life (his classical expertise, and the enduring mutual affection between himself and the male "you" to whom it is addressed), I would tentatively suggest the following paraphrase: "Arriving at Lethe, the source of the waters of forgetfulness, but not yet having drunk of them, you will still remember me and the way I used to love you, but do not expect that I, who have already drunk that water, will remember you and be waiting for you, still your "prim," doting, oath-bound, and tormented lover. I have waited for you all my life, as you know, and you could indeed count on my waiting for you each time you came to London, but now, "Not Thames, not Teme is the river, / Not London nor Knighton the town." I have set my "luggage" down at last (ASL 50). The lad who was once so eager to be of use to you in any capacity you chose, who loved you with all his heart, is now "no use at all," (ASL 24) freed by death of his "cursed trouble" and the "folly" of his love for you. His "willing nerve" is at last "numb," (ASL 24) though I could wish it otherwise. You should not expect anything else. I, too, am now dead."

This may lack the eclat of Jarrell's lively reading, but it at least places the part in the whole, which modifies and perhaps indeed completely reverses the implications of the part in isolation, transmuting both "contempt" and "self-contempt" into wry humor, tenderness, and regret. The only victory is that of the grave, and ah! the pity of it.

Bayley, whose analysis is opposed to Jarrell's and not in essence very different from mine, does not offer a paraphrase, but his remarks are certainly pertinent. He sees the poem as just a bit flippant, but not brutal, sardonic, nor venomous. Instead he finds it "relaxed, cheerfully good-natured, as if the poet were sharing the joke in his question with his friend to whom he is speaking. 'Not me,' 'count me out,' are the sort of comments, jovially made. . . . The idea of waiting on the platform of Hades to meet such a friend is one that gives him a special amusement. I won't be hovering around you down there, as I have been here in Bayswater" where you and I and Add shared our lodgings. The keynote, Bayley suggests, is a kind of humour "coming not only from the incongruity of the imagined situation but from the interchangeability of sexual roles. A member of either sex might be there, clutching the coin like a busfare, and expecting the faithful partner, to whom he or she used to offer a cheek . . . to be waiting at the terminus. . . . [It is] not so much bitter as deeply touching" (*Housman's Poems*, 134–35).

Housman may have amused himself with the vision of "the far quay-
side" (or Lethe wharf), but he did not take it seriously. In the next poem
we also have a vision of the conditions that will obtain after death, not
this time a relaxed, amused, cheerful one but one both serious and
somber.

> When I watch the living meet,
>   And the moving pageant file
> Warm and breathing through the street
>   Where I lodge a little while,
>
> If the heats of hate and lust
>   In the house of flesh are strong,
> Let me mind the house of dust
>   Where my sojourn shall be long.
>
> In the nation that is not
>   Nothing stands that stood before;
> There revenges are forgot,
>   And the hater hates no more;
>
> Lovers lying two and two
>   Ask not whom they sleep beside,
> And the bridegroom all night through
>   Never turns him to the bride.
>
> (ASL 12)

Here, Housman sets up four specific antitheses between life and death:
being, flesh, emotions, and brevity against nonbeing, dust, forgetfulness,
and seeming endlessness. (Leggett, *Land of Lost Content*, 57). "Where I
lodge a little while" is ambiguous. It can mean either the street where I
am temporarily domiciled in a lodging house or the body in which my
soul is temporarily "lodged," the "house of flesh," both of which are contrasted to the grave, the "house of dust," where "my sojourn shall be
long." The word "sojourn," however, indicates that this lodging too is
only temporary, although not so much so as that of the first verse. Both
'a little while" and "sojourn" implicitly deny permanency. "Lodge" pivots
from its meaning in the opening lines, the "house of life" in either of its
possible connotations, to its meaning in the second verse, the "house of
dust."

The "heats of hate and lust" are "strong" in the "house of life." They
are the heats and fire of "Others, I am not the first" (ASL 30). In the
manuscript, there are two alternates to "the." "My" and "this," both
more personal than "the," indicate that there is a biographical underlayer
that was carefully removed by the change to the general, universal, "the."
Who, then, might be the recipients of Housman's "hate and lust"? Let us
hold the question in abeyance briefly.

The "heats" refer us back to the "heat" and "fire" of "Others, I am not the first" (ASL 30). It also glances at the other meaning of sexual receptivity as applied to animals that are "flesh" only and not human flesh/soul hybrids. They need not "mind" the "house of dust." The sexual connotations of "heat," especially when defined in terms of "lust," are picked up by a buried pun in the following verse: "Nothing stands that stood before." One need not spend much time speculating about what "stood before" and has ceased to stand. This pun is buried in a double sense! Again the manuscript offers an indication of what is going on. The original line was "None remembers [what/wrongs] they bore" (Burnett, *Poems*, 16, variants at bottom of page), and yet again the impersonal replaces the personal. There may be another reason as well. As a result of this change, death is equated specifically with the end of sexual desire. Because desire is no longer possible there is no cause for either hate or revenge; both are related to sexual exclusivity and jealousy. Although "lovers" may lie in the grave "two and two" like Noah's guests, they are no longer "lovers." Death ends the capacity for love as it ends the capacity for hate. Even the "bridegroom" is no longer interested in his bride.

Is it fanciful to link the "hate and lust" to the "bride" and the "bridegroom"? There is a peculiarity in both the manuscript of this poem and the printer's copy. Housman's handwriting was usually meticulous, yet he "inadvertently" wrote "bridge." He then "carefully inserted an e between d and g, altered the final e to a none-too-clear r, and went on to add the last three letters of his wanted word. Oddly enough, he made the identical error and correction in the copy he prepared for the printer" (Haber, "A Shropshire Lad," 85). This error is still clear in both the manuscript copy and the printer's copy. I have very little doubt that it indicates Housman's reluctance (and his determination) to accept Moses Jackson's marriage. I have already mentioned that having begun the "Epithalamium" Housman found it such a painful subject that he abandoned it for many years. Just as Moses Jackson was always "he," always "my friend" and "my love," he was also *the* bridegroom, and to refer to him as such must have been an exquisite torment for Housman. Haber considers Housman's difficulty in writing this word "odd" but he offers no explanation. I suggest that this is scribal stuttering over the word, logical and not odd at all. In this case, "the pen" was "mightier than the wrist," as Housman said in another connection in "De Nihilo" (*Classical Papers*, 3:1012). Housman also noted: "Instinct, more sensitive to danger than the conscious intellect, takes alarm betimes; and the pen automatically glides into a form of words that will help the truth to escape detection" ("Thyestes of Varius," *Classical Papers*, 3: 941–944). These two comments neatly explain what happened when Housman tried to write the word "bridegroom."

There is no other indication that Housman felt any "hate" toward

Rosa Chambers, who had married his friend and with him moved half way around the world. There was even some correspondence between them. But it would indeed be "odd" had Housman not felt at least some resentment toward her. Only in his poetry was it possible that "the bridegroom all night through / Never turns him to the bride." That "bridegroom" at last indifferent to his bride was the recipient of Housman's love, and of his poetry.

> If truth in hearts that perish
>   Could move the powers on high,
> I think the love I bear you
>   Should make you not to die.
>
> Sure, sure, if stedfast meaning,
>   If single thought could save,
> The world might end to-morrow,
>   You should not see the grave,
>
> This long and sure-set liking,
>   This boundless will to please,
> —Oh, you should live for ever
>   If there were help in these.
>
> But now, since all is idle,
>   To this lost heart be kind,
> Ere to a town you journey
>   Where friends are ill to find.
>
>   (ASL 33)

Even those who had no clue about the identity of "you" were aware that this poem had a biographical dimension. The ambiguity veiling all such references in *A Shropshire Lad* could not disguise the personal intensity of the feeling, although it could and did disguise the nature of its object. Katharine Symons understood it, like "I promise nothing" (MP 12) below, to refer to her brother's having once had a love affair about which she knew nothing (Symons et al., *Recollections*,). The reviewer of the *Times Literary Supplement* in 1936 recognized that here is "the expression of an emotion which . . . has not been dressed up for the occasion of print; the poet is speaking in the first person, and with his own voice, undisguised" (Review of *More Poems* and a Memoir, p. 845), and John Sparrow speaks of it as "inspired . . . by personal affection" (Sparrow, "A Shropshire Lad at Fifty," 130). Robb notes its "tortured sincerity" and "passionate tenderness" (*Four in Exile*, 12, 41). Later critics who have the advantage of knowing a good deal more about Housman than was at that time available are united in agreement that the poem relates directly to his feelings about Moses Jackson. Haber speaks of its "burden of hopelessness" ("What Fools," 452). Rosebury calls it "a direct statement of feeling," ("Three Disciplines," 221). Browne associates it with "Shake hands" (MP 30) and "Because I liked you better" (MP 31), both discussed below, and calls all three "glimmer-of-hope-if" poems referring directly to Housman's love for Moses Jackson (*Elegy in Arcady*, 18).

Whether there is even a small such glimmer of hope in any of these poems or only a wistful wish that such a glimmer did indeed exist is moot. I agree with Haber that what is expressed is not hope but hopelessness. The drafts make this patent and also link the poem with "Crossing alone" and its "sick-hearted slave" (MP 23). There are two drafts and a stray fragment (Burnett, *Poems*, 34, variants at bottom of page). Combining them, as I have done below, provides a composite version of the first three verses in which the "accumulation of alternative phrases, all in the single vein of grief and despair, . . . produces here an effect that is not paralleled elsewhere in Housman's notebooks" (Haber, "*A Shropshire Lad*", 171, note 1).

> If truth in hearts that perish
>   Could [move/touch] the [powers/heavens] on high,
> I think the love I [bear you/cherish]
>   Should make you not to die.
>
> Sure, sure if [stedfast meaning/single thought]/If [truth, If/care or]
>   [stedfast/single] meaning
>   [Or/If] [strong resolve/desire/life poured out] could save,—
> The [world/skies] might [end/fall] tomorrow,
>   You should not see the grave.
>
> [Long/Vain] [thoughts/care] [Hot hope] and [endless/useless]
>   [longing/labour]/[stedfast
>   meaning/grieving]/ [Long fear and
>   hope and striving/Fear and hot hope
>   and thinking/Cold fear and fires
>   burning/Tired days and nights of
>   waking/Care and sick fears and
>   thinking]
>   And [fruitless hope/sleepless care/endless toil/hopeless
>   pain(s)/endless thought/boundless will/
>   sick despair] to please,—
> Oh, you should live forever,
>   If there were help in these.

Any glimmer of hope at all to be found here is a will o' the wisp indeed. What is abundantly clear is both Housman's devotion and his conviction that it and his "hot hope" are "vain" and "fruitless" alike. That "hot hope" and the "cold fear and fires burning" carry us back to the heat of "Others, I am not the first" (ASL 30) and the "heats of hate and lust" (ASL 12), and the "sick despair" is that of the "true, sick-hearted slave" (MP 23). The "boundless will to please" echoes the theme of "Say, lad, have you things to do?" (ASL 24). The use of poetry to give life to the beloved is a staple of poetry, but here its power to do so is explicitly denied by that word "If," together with the power of love itself.

The last verse contains two ambiguities. One has been considered by Page, who asks, "is the supposed journey to another point of this world, or to the next? If the 'town' . . . echoes the "stiller town" of ASL 19 ["To an Athlete Dying Young"] the latter interpretation seems possible" (A. E. Housman, 194). I would go further and say that if the poem is read in near isolation from the biography, it seems most likely. However, given the incontrovertibly personal reference, it may not be. The poem is certainly, since it is in A Shropshire Lad, an early lyric, and the last verse may possibly refer not to Moses Jackson's journey to the next world but to his removal only as far away as Karachi.

The second ambiguity is another buried pun, this one on "kind," an ambiguity previously mentioned but undetailed. "To this lost heart be kind," pleads the speaker. That "lost heart" was drowned in "seas I cannot sound" (ASL 14). The word "kind" in this context is used in two senses, as Ford Madox Ford makes clear in The Good Soldier: "She did not want to be unkind to him; but she could see no reason for being kind to him" (33). The context is an attempted seduction, and the common meaning of the word is as clear in its first use as its erotic meaning is in its second. C. S. Lewis explains that "kind" is specifically used to refer to the woman who agrees to heal a lover's "ail." "It must not be hinted that the lady has any passions or senses, and so her favours must be attributed . . . to mercy. . . . The woman who yields to your suit is . . . kind" (Studies in Words, 33). In this poem, Housman uses the word simultaneously in both its meanings, the usual one and the recondite one, and in this second meaning he seems to be reserving the male role for himself even if this upsets Auden's theory. It was the male persona who pleaded with the girl to "Be kind, have pity" (ASL 5) in his attempted seduction of her.

The preceding poems have relied on those techniques I have considered in discussing Housman's erotic poetry in general. In those that follow, few such ambiguities or misdirections occur. They are open and explicit. They are all patently biographical. As Grigson noted, they "make the nature of his 'unlucky love' much more obvious" (Review, in Gardner, Critical Heritage, 325) than in A Shropshire Lad or Last Poems, although for Robertson the following poem (and presumably all the Moses Jackson poems) is about "misunderstanding [that] clouds friendship," ("Housman and Hopkins," 101) nothing more complex or ambiguous. Whether the problem is one of misunderstanding or one of understanding too well, the reader may decide. Although Robertson wrote well after the revelations in the *Encounter* article, he closed his eyes to the problem of sexual orientation, not for understanding Housman alone but also in regards to Hopkins.

> Shake hands, we shall never be friends; give over:
>   I only vex you the more I try.
> All's wrong that ever I've done and said,
> And nought to help it in this dull head:
>   Shake hands, goodnight, goodbye.
>
> But if you come to a road where danger
>   Or guilt or anguish or shame's to share,
> Be good to the lad that loves you true
> And the soul that was born to die for you,
>   And whistle and I'll be there.
>
>   (MP 30)

This poem, finished in April of 1922, had been begun in 1893, but was presumably too personal to be published during Housman's lifetime. It reflects his "futile yearning" and deep "sorrow over his separation from Moses Jackson." In no other poem is "the yearning so fervent," and "the wistful second verse is uniquely Housman's." It is not only "commitment; it is also an impassioned gesture . . . in the form of immortal verse. . . . What more could Housman offer?" (Browne, *Elegy in Arcady*, 18, 83–84).

The poignancy of the first verse is even greater in the superceded draft, where one potential first line is "No, no, all's over, I'll try no longer" and the second line is "Shake hands forever, no more's to say" or "The more I try and break my heart" (Burnett, *Poems*, 131–32, variants at bottoms of pages). The full meaning and force of the emotion are only implied in the final version, where they become evident as soon as one places "friends" in quotation marks. Otherwise, the outbreak of agonized devotion in the second verse seems disproportionate. Although the words that both reveal and mask the emotion are uttered, the emotion itself is suppressed only to break out even more passionately as a result of the attempt at suppression.

The "danger / Or guilt or anguish or shame" that is "to share" is the shared danger, guilt, anguish, and shame of two homosexual lovers. We have seen both the danger and all of the emotions that accompany homosexual expression in other poems. The "road" where these await is the "my way" of "The laws of God, the laws of man" (LP 12), the way of homosexuality. The second verse may then be taken to mean, "If the time should ever come when you find yourself able to respond to my love in kind, remember that I love you; "call me, I shall hear you call" (ASL 24) for "what's a friend for?" (ASL 24 variant) I am "the soul that was born to die for you" with either or both of the meanings of die.

In the Victorian Age, "certain characteristics recurred in the poetic treatment of polite love. There is the assumption that there was a Destined One . . . [and] that the Destined One was out of reach forever" (Ronald Pearsall, *Worm in the Bud*, 163). These conventions, I think, underlie the use of the concept in this poem. Bayley finds a reference to "the supreme Christian sacrifice" (*Housman's Poems*, 133) instead of one to Victorian love conventions. I do not find this explanation totally convincing. That the reference is instead to popular culture is indicated by the last line "And whistle and I'll be there," taken directly from Robert Burns's ballad "O whistle and I'll come to you, my lad," which was sufficiently embedded in the psyche of the time to be referred to in both Trollope's *Dr. Thorne*, where the entire verse is quoted, and in Eliot's *Felix Holt*, as well as providing the title for one of M. R. James's ghost stories. Alan Holden has suggested in *The Housman Society Journal* 18 that the "my lad" in Burns, which is not in Housman's lines, was yet so well known that the reader could be expected to provide it, "thus hinting at the sex of the friend." However, since Housman never intended this poem to be published, he would have had no expectations of any sort about what the reader would or would not provide. It seems more likely to me that the echo was in his own mind, and as he knew perfectly well the gender of the friend to whom the poem was addressed he had no reason to make the reference more explicit.

We have not heard that whistle before, sounding from beyond the grave, but only because it was excised in the final version of "In midnights of November" (LP 19). The seventh and eighth lines of that poem, as finalized by Housman, are "And the dead call the dying / And finger at the doors." In the first draft of those two lines, they read "The dead call to the dying / And whistle at the doors" (Burnett, *Poems*, 88, variants at bottom of page). There was only one friend whom he bade "whistle and I'll be there." I have suggested in a previous chapter that this friend is the one for whom the message of "When the eye of day is shut" was intended ("Come not at my door to knock / Hearts that loved me not again") (LP 33). The two requests are antithetical, but the desire that those "who loved me not again" not return to haunt me was, as we have seen, spoken without the intense conviction of "whistle [at the doors] and I'll be there."

The stanza that eventually became the fourth ("Oh, to the bed of ocean, / To Africk and to Ind, / I will arise and follow / Along the rainy wind") (LP 19) at first began thus: "I hear my comrades hollo, / Too long we friends are twinned" (Burnett, *Poems*, 89, variants at bottom of page). In discussing this poem earlier, I pointed out that the references to India and Africa might both be taken literally did we not know that Moses Jackson did not die in "Ind," although Herbert Housman indeed laid down his life in "Africk." The manuscript indicates that these two references are indeed biographical, the one to Moses Jackson metaphorically and the one to Herbert Housman literally. What died in "Ind" where Moses Jackson lived for much of his life after his marriage was not the friend but the dream of eventual "friendship." More than one sea lay "between the twain" (LP 26), and these are the "twain" that were "twinned" too long. It is possible that the word "twinned" was intended as a half-pun, referring both to the "twain" (the speaker and the friend from whom he was divided) and the "twin," (the speaker and the brother he had lost). In this case, one reason the verse was completely recast for inclusion in *Last Poems* would have been to remove this too-personal reference.

> He would not stay for me; and who can wonder?
> He would not stay for me to stand and gaze.
> I shook his hand and tore my heart in sunder
> And went with half my life about my ways.

> (AP 7)

That this is closely related to the preceding poem is clear from the reference to shaking hands and parting that is prominent in both. It also shares with the first verse of "Shake hands" the combination of a "striking emotional intensity with a curious flatness of style." Both verses seem to represent the same experience "in direct and literal terms . . . [with] the immediacy of a diary entry" (Page, *A. E. Housman*, 184). The act of shaking hands becomes synonymous with tearing the heart apart (Bayley, *Housman's Poems*, 18), and that tearing of the heart in the prior poem precipitated the emotional outburst of the second stanza. The phrase "my ways" reinforces and is reinforced by all the previously noted mentions of "my ways" that are "not as theirs"—or his (LP 12). Narcissus in Ovid's narration of the story begged his image to "stay and be gazed at." This underlies the present poem. "He" was unwilling to stay where "I" could "stand and gaze," where I could be erect and feed my love on his looks if on nothing else. This buried pun on "stand," might one say, rises to attention. We have here a lyric in which "all the writer wishes to do is to stand and gaze, like a lover; but the object of devotion . . . will not stay to answer what is in this case an unspoken question" (ibid., 18). The question may not be spoken verbally, but it is implicit in the imagery.

In this poem, the adored image does not "stay," but let us not forget that in Hades Narcissus spent eternity gazing at that image reflected in a

pool in the land of the dead, and there it did not dissolve. This is unspoken but implicit and perhaps the ultimate source of that "glimmer of
hope" in some of these poems. Browne is not explicit about whether he
thinks that the reference is to Moses Jackson's departure for Karachi (the
"town" where "friends are ill to find," ASL 33) or to his marriage (*Elegy
in Arcady*, 23). I would suggest that it is to both; the two events were
inextricably interwoven.

"I only vex you the more I try" (MP 30), and doing so "I break my
heart" (MP 30 variant), wrote Housman. Both the emotion and the
words in which it was expressed had to be suppressed, locked in his heart,
a sacrifice on the altar of his love. That parting was relived in still another
poem. The promise not to express his love was implicit in the preceding
poems. Here it is explicit, but again the impossibility of keeping that
promise in his heart, however well he may succeed in his struggle to keep
it in his words, is evident.

> Because I liked you better
>   Than suits a man to say,
> It irked you and I promised
>   I'd throw the thought away.
>
> To put the world between us
>   We parted stiff and dry:
> "Farewell," said you, "forget me."
>   "Fare well, I will," said I.
>
> If e'er, where clover whitens
>   The dead man's knoll, you pass,
> And no tall flower to meet you
>   Stands in the trefoiled grass,
>
> Halt by the headstone shading
>   The heart you have not stirred,
> And say the lad that loved you
>   Was one that kept his word.
>
>   (MP 31)

Note that in the third line from the end, the standard reading is "The
heart no longer stirred." Here I agree with Laurence Housman's reading
and disagree with Burnett's. The logic of the poem seems to me to require
that the heart beneath the headstone was indeed "stirred," since we are
told immediately thereafter that the dead lad was one "that loved you,"
and it was clearly "you" whose heart was "not stirred." Davis, too, considers Burnett's reading "clearly inferior" to Laurence Housman's, which is

the standard reading, "since it hardly makes sense" ("Blue Remembered Hills," p. 4).

This poem is very early, dating in draft to the beginning of 1893. That, of course, is actually only the latest possible date of composition, not the earliest date of its first conception. I myself would date the germ of this, "Shake hands" (MP 30) and "He would not stay for me" (AP 7) (no manuscripts found, but dated by Burnett between 1900 and spring 1902, Poems, 468) to a period between the beginning of 1888 and the spring or summer of 1891. On 10 December 1887 Moses Jackson had sailed for India, and Housman began keeping a diary in the first week of January. It has been noted above that the style of "He would not stay for me" (AP 7) resembles a diary entry, and the same could be said of the description of the parting in both "Shake hands" (MP 30) and "Because I liked you better." On a certain Sunday in 1898, when, after what was to prove one of his last visits to England, Moses Jackson again sailed for India, Housman made an entry in his diary, using the page marked "Friday, May 22, 1891": "10:45 p.m. said goodbye" (Housman, "De Amicitia," 38). That laconic "goodbye" was almost the last of many such partings. I feel quite sure that the poems in question, whenever they were actually written, reflect these periodic leave takings.

The first and last verses of "Because I liked you better" in a superceded notebook entry show some significant variations from those finally reached (Burnett, Poems, 132–33, variants at bottoms of pages, notes p. 468). The manuscript page is partially erased and overwritten, but, as Haber remarked anent his reconstruction, which follows, "it is much more explicit than the printed text of the four stanzas" (A. E. Housman, 144).

> Because I liked you better
>   Than friends in liking may,
> It irked you and I promised
>   I'd cast the thought away.
>
> And now the headstone naming
>   The heart no longer stirred
> Will say the lad that loved you
>   Was one that kept his word.

We notice that in the first verse the original implies a liking that goes beyond the limits of the permissible. This is changed in the final text from a question of what one is allowed to feel into a question of what one is allowed to say. Social convention replaces morality. And in the last verse, in the original draft the headstone itself will bear witness to the keeping of the promise. In the final version, it is the beloved who will come to this conclusion. These two changes, I think, reveal something of Housman's own deepening understanding—and acceptance—of his own feelings. The earlier version indicates a regard for accepted morality (this is a liking that should not be felt rather than one that should not be spoken of). There is also a belief that the persona can and will cease to love. The headstone may be taken as the spokesman for the heart buried beneath it, which knows the truth. "You," however, can only judge by appearances, which may—and do—belie the truth. The alteration in the thrust of the poem is embodied in the word that stands at its very center: "If."

Again, as in "Shake hands" (MP 30), the tone of the poem before "if" is dry and restrained, the voice that keeps its promise. Robinson ignores the "if" and assumes that the poem in its entirety records "ecstacy that has palled" (*Angry Dust*, 35). By ignoring the "if," the poem can be read to imply that the graveside visits of the bereaved are a matter of complete indifference to the dead. The dead man is understood to have been rejected by the living, and now repentant, lover, who was "vexed" by the dead man's devotion. Housman seems to be looking forward to a visit by the loved one to his grave as an opportunity to prove that he has indeed "kept his word."

The emotion, and the true meaning of the poem, both burst out following the "if," when what is heard is the voice that breaks the promise "to throw the thought away." It seems that thoughts are not so easily discarded. Brashear, who understands the implications, is appalled at a poem so "unwholesome" ("Trouble with Housman," 84). Browne remarks, "the almost casual plainness of speech is interrupted halfway as the emotion breaks through. . . . It is the hesitant, hopeful stanzas after the pivotal 'If' that reveal Housman's need to feel some glimmer of hope in his situation" (*Elegy in Arcady*, 17–18). Bayley sees the "if" and dismisses it, suggesting that the "thought" "like a stiff suit that doesn't fit, cramps a man and is better thrown away," and " 'the lad that loved you' has kept his word to forget that love, because he is dead" (*Housman's Poems*, 133). Bayley's likening of the "thought" to a "stiff suit" is interesting, because although he clearly uses "suit" sartorially, it has another meaning as well, one far more applicable: the suit of the wooer pleading that his beloved be "kind" to him. It is the organ of this suit that is not only "stiff" but also "dry." It is a rejected "suit," not a cramping one.

What follows the pivotal "if" is part of a poetic tradition that was used by both William Morris in "The Blue Closet" and by Tennyson in "Maud," among others. When the beloved visits the place where the dead lover is buried, a flower springs forth ("starts") to greet him. What Housman says is that "if" this does not happen, then—and only then—

you may say that I have "kept" my "word," that "my heart" is no longer "stirred" by your presence. Not otherwise. The poem clearly implies that what will in fact happen is that a "tall flower" will indeed "start" from the grass-grown grave "to meet you." The very terms of the denial make it instead an affirmation. It seems that "I" may well be waiting "on Lethe wharf" (MP 23 variant) after all.

This affirmation is verbalized in the next poem, which refers directly to that promise, and revokes it: "I promise nothing." Bayley finds here "obscure comedy" and offers a paraphrase explicating the humor. "I can't make any absolute promise, mind you, but yes, there is every chance of the arrangement being a permanent one. . . . The buried humour in the verses is part of a buried logic. Since there is no other party to the contract there is all the more chance that the arrangement should hold up. Yes, this unlucky love *should* last" ("Housman and Larkin," p. 153 emphasis Bayley's).

> I promise nothing: friends will part;
>   All things may end, for all began;
> And truth and singleness of heart
>   Are mortal even as is man.
>
> But this unlucky love should last
>   When answered passions thin to air;
> Eternal fate so deep has cast
>   Its sure foundation of despair.
>
>   (MP 12)

Again, "friends" is clearly to be understood as being in quotation marks. The promise exacted may be kept, "All things may end" including my love for you. Even "singleness of heart" is mortal, as I myself am, "but" . . . What follows the "But" depends on whether one reads "should" as meaning "ought to" or as meaning "is bound to," as Bayley reads it. If the first, it will not last, for things that "should be" in this sense are, ipso facto, things that will not be. This is the implication of the first verse. If the second meaning is intended, however, the second verse is an affirmation that this "unlucky love" is as "eternal" as fate itself.

Unlike other passions, which were at least for a time mutual, "answered," this passion will not "thin to air." Taking into account the implications of all of the poetry in this chapter, I would say that "should" here carries its second meaning. For his homosexuality in general, Housman uses such terms as "cursed trouble" and "ancient evil," as we have seen. For his love for Moses Jackson specifically, his terminology is different: "star-defeated," "disastrous," and "unlucky" do not imply "cursed" or "evil." All three terms have precisely the same meaning, "ill-fated," caused by contrary stars, matters of "eternal fate." Nothing, not even the end of the world, can remove this unhappy—but destined—love.

> Then, in the hour when iron is sand,
> And mountains crumble, this should stand,
> Nor falling firmament remove
> The landmark of disastrous love.
>
> (Burnett, *Poems*, 177 No. 21)

"All things may end, for all began," but it is not so. Even that last hour when the world ends, when iron disintegrates, "mountains crumble," and the heavens finally fall, cannot "remove" the monument of my love, causing it to fall; "this," this "landmark of disastrous love," will still "stand." Not even the final cataclysm can bring "this" to an end. The symbol of love that "stands" at the thought of the beloved need hardly be named. It is self-evident.

In the following poem, Haber says, Housman himself and Moses Jackson "are the principals. . . . [The poem] is a lament for his comrade" (*A. E. Housman*, 133). Parenthetically, I completely agree with Haber that "comrade," whether in "The West" (LP 1), the "Epithalamium" (LP 24), or elsewhere means Moses Jackson. This is "a romantic poem," also about Moses Jackson (Graves, *A. E. Housman*, 222), "fantasy-making" in which the first two verses are a "sexual fantasy" and the third "bluntly states the bleak contemporary fact" (Page, *A. E. Housman*, 185).

> Oh were he and I together,
>   Shipmates on the fleeted main,
> Sailing through the summer weather
>   To the spoil of France or Spain.
>
> Oh were he and I together,
>   Locking hands and taking leave,
> Low upon the trampled heather
>   In the battle lost at eve,
>
> Now are he and I asunder
>   And asunder to remain;
> Kingdoms are for others' plunder,
>   And content for other slain.
>
> (AP 2)

The dream incorporates and reinterprets that good-bye handshake which appears or is implied so often, turning the symbol of rejection into one of comradeship. "Locking hands and taking leave" is objectively no different from "Shake hands, here's luck, good-bye" (MP 30 variant, Burnett, *Poems,* 131 bottom) but subjectively it reverses the implications of that farewell. In the other poems, the heart-breaking reality is succeeded by the vision that attempts to negate it, here the vision precedes the miserable reality that "he and I" are separated and will remain so, and "content" is for another, not for me.

An especially gentle and tender expression of "star-defeated" love from ancient Greece seemed so perfectly to express Housman's own feelings that he translated it three times. The first version of Sappho's lines that I want to discuss was actually the last one written. It is a much looser translation than the others; indeed, it is a rendering rather than a translation, a variation on the theme of "I lie down alone." Perhaps because it was allusive rather than a close translation like his other treatments of Sappho's lyric, Housman could assume that most people would not notice its origin as a definitely homosexual poem and therefore felt no hesitation in publishing it himself. It is completely changed from the original brief, frank love poem, and Keyser ("Variations on Sappho,") suggests that the reason for the change was specifically to conceal the Sapphic original. The metrics are completely different from Sappho's. It is also different from Housman's two earlier renderings, in that here the Pleiades are gone, the rain is already streaming down rather than simply probable, and there is no sense of time passing. However, as in them, it is still midnight, the persona is still alone and sleepless, and the beloved remains unresponsive and unavailable. The word "wester," otherwise used only once in an unpublished fragment (discussed below), occurs in all three versions. The core of Sappho's lines is the lying alone at midnight, and it is this Sapphic element that is neither changed from nor added to the Greek original.

> The half-moon westers low, my love,
>   And the wind brings up the rain;
> And wide apart lie we, my love,
>   And seas between the twain.
>
> I know not if it rains, my love,
>   In the land where you do lie;
> And oh, so sound you sleep, my love,
>   You know no more than I.

(LP 26)

This lyric was certainly written in 1922 specifically for inclusion in *Last Poems.* It is unusual only in that the sole measure taken to disguise the identity of "my love" is the avoidance of any gender-specific word. There are no buried puns, no ambiguities. It is a naked declaration to the dying man that his friend's feelings are unchanged. The reference to "seas between the twain" would have been clear to him if to no one else. He was in western Canada, and Housman in England; it would have been difficult to "lie" more "wide apart." But he is still "my love," now and forever.

This is one of the loveliest of the Moses Jackson poems, in part because its "emotional intensity . . . is never loud nor thunderously passionate; but calm and controlled, gentle and restrained it has increased force and effectiveness" (Brenner, *Ten Modern Poets*, 187–88). The lines are so clearly personal that contemporary "literary critics . . . tried to identify the departed loved one—who they presumed was a woman" (Browne, *Elegy in Arcady*, 105). Needless to say, they did not succeed. Nor did they notice the origin of the poem.

Here are the other two alternate renderings of Sappho's lines, side by side.

The weeping Pleiads wester,
    And the moon is under seas;
From bourn to bourn of midnight
    Far sighs the rainy breeze:
	The rainy Pleiads wester,
	    Orion plunges prone,
	The stroke of midnight ceases,
	    And I lie down alone.

It sighs from a lost country
    To a land I have not known;
The weeping Pleiads wester,
    And I lie down alone.
             (MP 10)
	The rainy Pleiads wester
	    And seek beyond the sea
	The head that I shall dream of,
	    And 'twill not dream of me.
	             (MP 11)

In the manuscript of the second version, the word "rainy" in both verses is a replacement of the original "weeping." (Burnett, *Poems*, 121, variants at bottom of page). We saw Housman's reason when we took up the question of the pathetic fallacy. He rejected this mode for himself while continuing to use it as part of the Terence style of diction. It is clear that Sappho's lyric held a special attraction for him.

MP 10 is the more allusive of the two final versions with its line "From bourn to bourn of midnight" where "the bourn is one of time ['the stroke of midnight' here and far away] and distance, . . . One land [the nostalgic past, the 'land of lost content'] is irrecoverable; the other [India where Moses Jackson then was] unattained," and the other version, MP 11, "makes the grievance too explicit" (Bayley, *Housman's Poems*, 58).

In order to see just what Housman found and used and just what he added, we must turn to Sappho's lines. There is an excellent English translation to be compared to Housman's.[5]

The moon and Pleiades
are set. Night is half
gone and time speeds by.
I lie in bed, alone.

Unlike F. L. Lucas, who recognized MP 10 as an adaptation rather than a translation and considered it "even more poignant than its Greek original" ("Personality and Poetry," 207), Caclamanes, assuming that Housman's poem was intended as a translation of Sappho and nothing more, made some uncomplimentary remarks about it. Housman's version is "more wordy, its emotion is expressed with some prolixity and the first two lines in the second stanza have a touch of mysticism unknown to Sappho's poetry" ("Source of Another Poem," p. 244). Caclamanes has unerringly put his finger on the element that Housman quite knowingly added to the original, which he used only as a foundation for his own work: the "touch of mysticism," the "bourns" and the "lost country." In MP 11, Housman substitutes "Orion" for Sappho's moon; otherwise, the first verse is a fairly close rendering. The addition of Orion, however, serves to add an additional allusive touch: Orion's incessant pursuit of the Pleiades was in vain, and the reference insinuates into the poem a sense that the speaker's quest is equally eternal—and equally doomed to failure. Neither Orion nor the speaker will ever attain the beloved.[6]

The first three lines of verse 1 and the fourth of verse 2 in MP 10 also render Sappho's lines fairly closely. In both of his versions, Housman repeats the first, Sapphic, line in the second stanza. In each version, Housman's own addition to the source poem constitutes three lines at which we shall now look more closely.

MP 10	MP 11
Far sighs the rainy breeze:	And seek beyond the sea
It sighs from a lost country	The head that I shall dream of
To a land I have not known	And 'twill not dream of me.

The "touch of mysticism" also lies in the associations of the water imagery that is Housman's addition to Sappho. The "tears of morning/ mourning," the weeping or rainy nature of the Pleiades, is a projection of his own feelings into the natural world, a projection facilitated by the traditional association of this star group with rain. The seas that the moon is under or Orion plunges into are, like the "seas between the twain" of the preceding poem (LP 26), both the metaphoric seas in which "lie lost my heart and soul" (ASL 14) and the physical ones that separate England from India. That Housman in the guise of a translation from Sappho is actually expressing his own emotions about his separation (physical and metaphysical) from his friend is as obvious from the added water imagery as from the three un-Sapphic lines added to each of his versions. Those lines all refer directly and unambiguously to Moses Jackson, both to the Oxford-London years when they were together ("a lost country") and to India ("a land I have not known") in MP 10 (Calder, "Housman," 31). They also refer specifically to Jackson himself in MP 11 as "the head" sleeping "beyond the sea" that haunts my dreams, although " 'twill not dream of me." The tone of this group of poems is as valedictory as that of "Tell me not here" (LP 40).

We remember the poet's boyhood dream, "it was friends to die for" (LP 32) in the second reading of the line. It was indeed a specific "sweetheart to be kind," a sweetheart who was also a "friend to die for," of whom Housman dreamed, but the person in question would not be his "sweetheart" and was not "kind." Moses Jackson is not only "My love, that I was born to die for," he is also "My love, for whom I cannot die" and "My love that I shall not be true to" in lines in Notebook C (written between December 1895 and February 1900) that acknowledge that, however true the heart may be, the body has its own demands that must be met (Haber, *Manuscript Poems*, 69). These lines are not only a leave-taking from "my love," they are a leave-taking from that boyhood dream of uncomplicated friendship and from the young man's dream of physical intimacy. "I" am "the soul that was born to die for you" (MP 30), and you are the one "that I was born to die for." Fate meant us for each other, but that fate was laid under unlucky stars; "I was luckless aye / And shall not die for you" (AP 20). Indeed, I not only "shall not" but I "cannot" since you will not have it so. Therefore, though you remain my love, and always shall, "I shall not be true to" you. I shall and must find someone else to "die" for, so good-bye, my love, good-bye my dream, good-bye my hope, good-bye my ideal of myself as a "true" lover, good-bye. I have only "half my life" (AP 7) without you, and my heart is ripped in twain, but I will and must live to the hilt with that half-life and half-heart that are all that are left me.

This reading is glossed in another fragment from 1886 at the latest (Burnett, *Poems*, 171, notes 486) that Haber associates with the "controversial lyrics," especially "Because I liked you better" and the other Moses Jackson poems "in which estrangement between men is the theme" (A. E. Housman, *Manuscript Poems*, 32). It seems to be the conclusion of a dialogue between body and heart. Such debate poems are common in the medieval literary tradition and not unknown in Housman. If this one is so read, "my heart" in the first line is the "you" of the second with whom the body has been arguing and to whom this closing exhortation is addressed. Any other reading is grammatically impossible. Housman was meticulous about his grammar.

The first part of the debate is not given but is implicit in the closing lines. "Heart" has been defending its faith and love for its friend, its hope of winning him, "spelling" over, reliving the past, the dead memories that fed that hope, and "Body" has been urging realism and the demands of life in such terms as we have heard in "Ho, everyone that thirsteth" (MP 22). Death is approaching. "Day falls, night climbs," a nice reversal of the usual diction in which it is day that "up the eastern stair / Marches, azuring the air" (AP 11) and night that falls. What is left of life must be lived without constantly harking back to vain, dead hopes that only break one's heart, and the buried past. One must forget the ideal of eternal friendship and devotion to the man one was "born to die for." One must cease to rebel against one's fate in having given one's heart and soul away to one who rejects the gift. The dead hopes are buried beneath the "gravestone" by which "you" linger. Instead of clinging to them, you must accept both your rejection and your sexual proclivities. You must give them free rein. You must "leap the guarded pale" (MP 22) and steal the waters even if they are from a cup other than the one for which you thirst. You are what you are. Now go forward and drink life to the lees in your own "way."

> Nor break my heart with hoping any more,
>   Tomorrow you shall have the grave to wife:
>   Now, in the accepted time, make friends with life.
> To have missed no chances when you come to die
>   Haste, for the heaven is westered since you came:
>   Day falls, night climbs, the hour has lost its name;
>   Quick, quick! the lightning's pace were weary, slow,
>   And here you loiter spelling gravestones: go.

As in "The rain it streams" (LP 18) where despite all the talk of movement the persona still lingered at the graveside, here despite all the urgency of the language, the heart remains at the grave of dead love, dead hope, hoping still against all hope, breaking, until that final imperative "go." The body has the last word. Life is for living, not for "loitering by the road" while "heart and soul and senses, / World without end, are drowned" (ASL 14). Waters are for drinking, stealing them if necessary, and not for drowning oneself.

The ending of emotional intimacy and the spacial separation were succeeded by the irreversible separation of death, not Moses Jackson's death after his own life had ended, as Housman had visualized it in more than one poem, but the prior death of his friend. There was wry tenderness and humor in the poems in which he had played with the idea of this final resolution of his situation. The actuality was quite different. It seems to me to be captured in a poem written between 1895 and 1900, long before Jackson's death, a cry of unalloyed anguish, pain, betrayal, and jealousy.

> Now to her lap the incestuous earth
> The son she bore has ta'en,
> And other sons she brings to birth
> But not my friend again.

(AP 8)

The imagery takes us back to the concept of the earth as mother, a mother who "because my heart was sore, / Sorrowed for the son she bore." "Mother nature" is also "mother earth," female as the sky is male. C. S. Lewis notes that "the marriage relation between Father Sky . . . and Mother Earth forces itself on the imagination. He is on top; she lies under him. He does things to her (. . . rains upon her, into her): out of her, in response, come forth the crops—just as . . . babies out of wives. In a word, he begets, she bears" (*Discarded Image*, 32). Manilius called fall "the season when men commit the corn to the furrows, whilst the soil, relaxed by autumn's warmth, opens to clasp the seed" (*Astronomica*, 3:217), a verse that Lewis's words might have been designed to explicate. It makes the sexuality of the image overt. This ancient concept is part of what makes rain an image of fertility, an image that in Housman is reversed so that the rainy emission of the male god becomes instead an image of sterility. It does not enter "mother earth" to fertilize her but rather "God's acre," the grave, where it produces nettles, one of his many symbols of sterile homosexuality.

To return to the ancient paradigm that this poem reflects, the Great Mother, earth, bears sons who are both her lovers and the sacrifices offered on her altar. Adonis, Osiris, Attis, and Tammuz are all both the sons she bore and her lovers, slain, buried in her, and reborn from her to start the cycle again. Housman uses this concept in the opening two lines where the earth is "incestuous" because she has taken to her "lap" "the son she bore." In the manuscript fragment there is an open alternative to the motherly "lap," and that alternative is the incestuous "bed" (Burnett, *Poems*, 152, variants at bottom of page). "Bed" in Housman can mean either the bed of earth or the sleeping couch, as it does in "The rain it streams" (LP 18) where the dead friend is bid "Good-night" in his grave as one would a sleeping child tucked into its cot. Or it can mean the bed in which two people lie, but do not sleep, in each other's arms, as in "Is my team ploughing" (ASL 27) ("I lie as lads would choose" in the bed where "I cheer a dead man's sweetheart"). "Bed" can have any combination of these three meanings. Here, however, the "bed" is coupled with the "incestuous earth" and to it she, not mother but lover and slayer, not Mother Earth but the Great Mother whose sons are also her lovers and her victims, has taken "my friend" and is there coupling with him. This note of jealousy, muted in the alternative that Laurence Housman chose, sounds loudly and clearly in the rejected word.

Bayley lays more stress on the "mother" concept than I do:

The first line seems a pent-up whisper of resentment. . . . Earth couples with her dead son, and the thought is torment to his jealous lover . . . there is none the less something tender. The earth mother's embrace . . . is also the consolation and repose of the death in which she cradles him. "Incestuous" is a bitter word, but the speaker knows that the lap or bed of earth is a place of satisfaction for her son, his friend. . . . In the last line all jealousy of the incestuous mother is forgotten, as is resentment of her unmeaning fecundity. (*Housman's Poems*, 21–22).

I find no sense of consolation in the lines, nor do I think that, although jealousy is "forgotten," resentment also evaporates in the last line. The note I hear in that line is instead one of unalloyed suffering, a cry of ultimate pain. Adonis, Osiris, Attis, Tammuz, all are reborn from the earth, but "not my friend again," never again, never more. It is the cry of Lear over Cordelia's dead body, his, "Never, never, never, never, never!" that echoes in my ears in the silence that follows the end of the poem.

Although obviously not written about Jackson's death, the poem seems to me to express precisely what Housman felt when he learned of it. We have seen that the death of Moses Jackson was the death of Housman's poetic muse, and we have seen more than one expression of his farewell to his friend and poetry together. His abandonment of poetry after his friend's death was quite deliberate. This decision is expressed in an exquisitely sad valedictory. Here there is a brief backward look, but no lingering. Moses Jackson had looked on "the West" (LP 1), had left his mortal clothing on the shore, had "sped his soul on before," and had entered the "sunken bourn." Housman sent his love and his poetic gift to join his friend there.

> Once in the springing season,
>   When earth made gallant show,
> Out of the mine a jewel
>   Was given me, years ago.
>
> Long worn, its lustre's tarnished,
>   It's no more pride to me:
> I go tonight to fling it
>   In the cold and solvent sea.

This fragment (Burnett, *Poems*, 185, notes 500) cannot be dated at all, but the imagery suggests a date shortly after Housman learned of Moses Jackson's death. The metaphor here is one that Housman used nowhere else. The phrase "springing season" carries an appropriate cargo of connotations. It is the springtime of life, vigor, beauty, youth, and love, for "sweet lovers love the spring." The "jewel" that represents friendship, his gift of poetry, and his capacity for love was dedicated to the service of Moses Jackson, and with him gone it became meaningless and lost its value; "it's no more pride to me." It followed Jackson into the "cold and solvent sea" of death, bearing him company on his journey to "the West" (LP 1). The imagery here is the same as that of a notebook fragment that was written in August of 1895, the date's having been entered by Housman on the notebook page (Burnett, *Poems*, 50, variants at bottom of page).

> Lock your heart and sink the key
> With the millstone in the sea.

The reviewer of the *Times Literary Supplement* was unaware of the existence of this couplet. Nonetheless, he uses its imagery in discussing Housman. "Poetry did not free his spirit; it was a key for the locking, and not for the unlocking, of his heart" (Sparrow, "*A Shropshire Lad* at Fifty," 131). With that key he both opened his heart for those able to read between the lines and locked it; that key is a metaphor for his poetry. It is this which, together with the "millstone" of "the heart in my breast" (AP 17), was flung "in the cold and solvent sea," there to "sink" and be lost forever.

That "key" with which Housman locked his heart was once envisioned as having a different function. The lines that were printed as "Speak now, and I will answer; / How shall I help you, say' " (ASL 32), in a poem that has both the same urgency and meaning as "Say, lad, have you things to do?," was in the second draft "How would you have me help you / [Unlock/ Show me] your soul and say" (Burnett, *Poems*, 34, variants at bottom of page). Since Moses Jackson would not use the key to "unlock" his heart, Housman used it instead to lock his own and then sank it fathoms deep where his own "heart and soul and senses" (ASL 14) were drowned, just as did the Hebrew poetess Rachel Blaubstein (known as "Rachel Hameshureret" or "Rachel the Poetess"), who was deeply in love with a married man: "I will lock the door of my heart, / I will throw the key into the seas."[7] The parallel situation evoked a parallel response.

We looked above at a poem in which Housman visualized a visit to his grave "where clover whitens / The dead man's knoll" by the friend he had promised to "forget" (MP 31). It was implied by the closing imagery that the promise was broken and the dead lover had remained true to his devotion. In the following poem, the setting is the same, and the visitor is the same, but the promise has been kept, and the imagery of enduring love has vanished. Or has it?

Stone, steel, dominions pass,
  Faith too, no wonder;
So leave alone the grass
  That I am under.

All knots that lovers tie
  Are tied to sever.
Here shall your sweetheart lie
  Untrue for ever.

(MP 24)

"My love that I shall not be true to," the poet said in the lines from Notebook C, "Good bye, my love, good bye." And now that "I" have ceased to "hope" and have instead "made friends with life" (Burnett, *Poems*, 171), "I" would rather that you did not visit my grave after all. Now that "I" have betrayed you, "my love," and betrayed both my love for you and my own desire to "gaze" (AP 7) forever at your adored image, now indeed there is no point in your coming to my grave. Now indeed "no tall flower to meet you" (MP 31) will ever spring forth from it. I have at last been "true" to my promise and thereby "untrue" to both you and myself, and I have forfeited thus my right to respond to your presence. Even though "I" still feel myself to be "your sweetheart," the bond between us is severed at last, not by my death but by my betrayal of that bond. This is the obvious meaning of the lines, and as such they are touching and pathetic in their humility. In the notebook, there is an even more tender version of the penultimate line, "Here your old sweetheart lies" (Burnett, *Poems*, 29, variants at bottom of page). It seems very final. There is a "sense of betrayal" (Muir, "A. E. Housman," 63) and "a suggestion of guilt" (Graves, *A. E. Housman*, 223) in the last two lines. This seems clear, but is it as clear as it seems?

"Here your old sweetheart lies / Untrue for ever." What is the lie and what is the truth? Is the implication that the promise has at last been kept itself the "lie," a "lie" that "I" shall continue to avouch "for ever," so being "untrue for ever"? Does "here" refer to the grave or to the poem? "All knots that lovers tie / Are tied to sever" refers to the love-knot in Thomas Campbell's song "How Delicious is the Winning." Hardy used the line as the title of the wedding chapter in *Under the Greenwood Tree* to refer to the marriage knot: "the knot there's no untying." Housman's poem clearly refers to the bond of love, the love-knot between himself and the man whose "sweetheart" he yearned to be, but the two authors were friendly and Housman was thoroughly conversant with Hardy's work. Is there then, just possibly, a reference to the marriage bond as well as the love bond? "All" such knots are "tied to sever," not just the one that links us, and since the other bond may be some day severed, "Here shall your sweetheart lie," admittedly "untrue" in some sense, but yet waiting for you "for ever." This reading is clearly possible, and we have seen that in Housman's poetry of misdirection the probable reading is not necessarily the true one. Housman was adept at making his poetry ambiguous and keeping his secret hidden in his own breast.

> Ask me no more, for fear I should reply;
>   Others have held their tongues, and so can I;
> Hundreds have died, and told no tale before:
>   Ask me no more, for fear I should reply—
>
> How one was true and one was clean of stain
>   And one was braver than the heavens are high,
> And one was fond of me: and all are slain.
>   Ask me no more, for fear I should reply.

(AP 6)

The first four words are of course Tennyson's. Tennyson's poem "Ask Me No More" (*Tennyson*, 313) was deeply significant to Housman, and especially the line "Thy fate and mine are sealed" which certainly expressed "what he felt about himself and Moses Jackson; . . . it is not hard to think how much that would have affected the poet who took up the Tennysonian refrain which haunted him." It seems that Moses Jackson did everything possible to maintain "a close relationship" with Housman until his departure for India, and even thereafter he "never spurned the friendship, or broke it off. Housman's love none the less had to remain unspoken and poetry . . . had to remain its form of speech. Reticence was not only the price of love but the seal of it" (Bayley, *Housman's Poems*, 23–24).[8]

Housman's only poem that is publicly connected with Moses Jackson is the Latin "*Sodali Meo*," "My Comrade," "My Companion," which speaks in terms of the deepest affection and closest fellowship but not love, of friendship without any hint of "friendship." However, the devotion indicated, it is implied, is all but eternal. This is, I think, a little more explicit in the Latin (Burnett, *Poems*, 289–91) than in the English rendering by Edmund Wilson that is reprinted by Ricks in *A. E. Housman: Collected Poems and Selected Prose* (254–55), but it is also implicit there: "to-morrow runs before . . . To dull with all-benumbing thrust / Our wits that wake not from the dust, / Nor spare, with learning's lettered leaf, / The bonds of fellowship as brief" (255). The "bonds of fellowship" are brief, but "as brief" as what? They are as "brief" as "learning's lettered leaf," as "brief" as the longevity of classical Greek and Latin literature, as "brief" as the longevity of scholarly exegesis of this literature. It is "*non immortalia*" and "*non aeterni*." The specific reference is to Manilius, a poet whose book was almost two thousand years old, and the implied reference is to all ancient literature. The longevity of "learning's lettered leaf" is three, four, five thousand years or more. It is "*non aeterni*," but neither is it what one would call precisely "brief." "The world will last for longer, / But this will last for long" (AP 4).

It is hard not to attempt to decipher the names behind the adjectives in Housman's "Ask me no more," but to decipher them is not. "And one was braver than the heavens are high," and that one was George Herbert Housman who gave his life in the Boer War. "And one was fond of me," and that one was Adalbert Jackson, "fond of me" but not, despite Laurence Housman's certainty, "in love with me." "One was true," and that one must be taken as Housman himself, true throughout his life to a hopeless love. "And one was clean of stain," and that one was Moses Jackson, the bridegroom that carried the cup to his marriage bed without spilling a single drop. "And all are slain," all, for I myself am but a hollow voice speaking from the grave where my heart and soul lie buried with my friend.

Clio

11
The Pearl in the Oyster

In "the period of the french revolution," a review of *The Cambridge History of English Literature*, volume 11, Housman wrote that "the centre of interest in a poet is his poetry: not his themes, his doctrines, his opinions, his life or conduct, but the poetical quality of the works he has bequeathed to us" (A. E. Housman, *Collected Poems and Selected Prose*, 316). The exclusion of his own themes, doctrines, and opinions from critical consideration would at least halve the amount of commentary on Housman's poetry, and the exclusion of "his life or conduct" would dispose of most of the remainder. Relatively little has been written on "the poetical quality of the works" alone, nor could such a commentary easily be written, as Housman's works are intimately bound up with his themes, doctrines, opinions, and, most of all, with his life and conduct. The autobiographical element, however carefully disguised in the official poetry, was sensed from the beginning. There was speculation about Housman's "life or conduct" from the first publication of *A Shropshire Lad*, although the guesses were wide of the mark.

However relatively unimportant such things may or may not be to the understanding of Wordsworth, to whom Housman is referring, it is essential for an understanding of Housman's own poetry. Laurence Housman apparently cared little whether or not the poems were understood. He said in *"De Amicitia,"* in discussing the biographical significance of his brother's poems, that he wanted that understanding for his brother, not for his brother's poetry, and he believed that this was A. E. Housman's wish as well:

> Alfred's craving to be liked was also a craving to be understood; and in order that understanding might be possible, he left these records to be found. . . . And though the foolish and the obdurate . . . may reprobate what is here disclosed, many—the more intelligent, the more charitable, the more kindly of understanding—will . . . think differently; and having fuller knowledge will be able to have more liking also for the man who, in his own lifetime, could not let himself be better known (39).

In considering which of the lyrics in the notebooks were worthy of publication, Laurence Housman discovered in them

> certain matters of a very intimate character about himself, of which previously he had never spoken to me, although I had reason to think that he was aware both of my knowledge of what had so deeply affected his life, and of my sympathy for the unhappiness which it had caused him. . . . I found that most of these [unpublished poems] were more autobiographical than any which had appeared previously. Several of them were . . . as good as the majority of those which he had himself published; and their place in the M. S. notebooks showed that they were of no later date. The only reason I could find for his not having allowed them to appear was that they were too autobiographical, and that they referred to certain persons (or to one person) still alive. But from the fact that he had not destroyed them I judged that their publication had been left to my discretion, and that he had no objection to their autobiographical nature being recognized after his death. . . . [Some of the poems in *A Shropshire Lad*] may have been autobiographical; but there was no poem which for certain could be so regarded. In my judgment those which are most closely autobiographical in feeling are . . . XXX ["Others, I am not the first"], XXXI ["On Wenlock Edge"], XXXII ["From far, from eve and morning"], and XXXIII ["If truth in hearts that perish"]. . . . Of these four, I believe that no. XXX is the most direct expression of personal experience—and suffering (ibid. 34).

The only one of these lyrics not considered here is "From far, from eve and morning" (ASL 32), which is not included because it is parallel to "Say, lad, have you things to do?" (ASL 24) ("Take my hand quick and tell me / What have you in your heart. / Speak now and I will answer; / How shall I help you, say; / Ere to the wind's twelve quarters / I take my endless way"), and any remarks about it would be repetitious.

Laurence Housman continues: "In *Last Poems* there is far less material of an autobiographical character. In *More Poems* and *Additional Poems* . . . there is far more. That material my brother . . . held back . . . [but] he left me free to decide otherwise; and my interpretation of these two facts is that he was willing for those more personal poems to be published—but not in his own lifetime" (ibid. 34). Laurence Housman then proceeds to provide a list of "those [poems] which I reckon to be the most direct expression of personal feeling, or experience," (ibid. 34) a list that includes a few poems that I have not discussed: "The mill-stream, now that noises cease" (MP 19), "Like mine, the veins of those that slumber" (MP 20), "To stand up straight and tread the turning mill" (MP 27), and "O thou that from thy mansion" (MP 47).

The last was the poem that Housman composed to be sung at his own funeral. The autobiographical erotic element in one of the other four is less central to its imagery than other personal elements are (MP 27). The imagery of one (MP 20) is identical to that incorporated with much else in "Others, I am not the first" (ASL 30). The other, MP 19, has been referred to, although not considered in depth, and its technique (and some of its imagery as well) repeats that used in "Others, I am not the first" (ASL 30) (". . . here am I in hell / . . . And so, no doubt, in time gone by, / Some have suffered more than I, / Who only spend the night alone / And strike my fist upon the stone"). The other poems that Laurence Housman considered had a biographical basis are the following: "I to my perils" (MP 6), "They say my verse is sad: no wonder" (MP Prefatory Poem), "I promise nothing: friends will part" (MP 12), "Ho, everyone that thirsteth" (MP 22), "Shake hands" (MP 30), "Because I liked you better" (MP 31) "Farewell to a name and a number" (MP 40), "He looked at me with eyes I thought" (MP 41), "When he's returned I'll tell him—oh" (MP 42), "Far known to sea and shore" (MP 44), "It is no gift I tender" (AP 4), "Ask me no more" (AP 6), "He would not stay for me" (AP 7), "Now to her lap the incestuous earth" (AP 8), "The stars have not dealt me the worst they could do" (AP 17), "Oh who is that young sinner" (AP 18), and (actually from *Last Poems*) "The laws of God" (LP 12). All of these poems have been discussed at length in the appropriate place.

These are the poems that A. E. Housman's brother considered had a "personal note." All of them

> have some degree of connection with the trouble which overshadowed the whole of my brother's life. As I read them for the first time, they pointed quite clearly to the fact, which I already knew, that his deepest friendships were with men, that those friendships caused him trouble and grief, and that . . . he gave a far greater devotion than he ever received in return. In that greatest of all his friendships . . . there was no response in kind. . . . Nobody . . . can have any doubts about the emotional nature of my brother's love for Jackson; it was deep and lasting, and it caused him great unhappiness. Even in memory the emotion of it remained" (ibid., 35, 39).

It is that trouble and that love that I believe to be at the heart of Housman's poetry, poetry that originated in the tormented depths of his mind and rose to symbolic verbal expression as a dream does, the elements all present but disguised by the dreamer's self-censorship. It is this element, so essential for the understanding of the lyrics, that I have explored in this book.

Laurence Housman continues,

> When I found the poems which he had left to my discretion, when I found the diaries which had so obviously been preserved for one purpose only, when

I found other things among his papers . . . which told me clearly the direction
of his interest in beauty of human form, I became convinced that he had a
purpose, and that purpose was to let me know the secret of his life and to give
me liberty to make it known. . . . I am quite sure that . . . he had no false
shame in the matter: "the laws of God, the laws of man" were none of his
making—the responsibility for them was not his. . . . [T]hat was how he himself stated the case: and he was of too proud a nature to wish that he should
be misunderstood" (ibid. 39).

That Laurence Housman was, in this case at least, justified in his belief
is indicated by the misdirection with which A. E. Housman disguised the
intent of the official poetry, a misdirection that yet leaves it open to the
reader not to misunderstand him. It is the stage magician's technique of
deliberately drawing the spectator's eye to what is not in fact significant
while leaving open the possibility of his seeing what is truly important if
those misdirections are ignored. I have ignored them in this study; what
has emerged is not only Housman's agony but his pride and his willingness to reveal the truth to those who desire to see the meaning of his
poetry. As he himself said, poetry usually does have a meaning. In his
Leslie Stephen memorial lecture, *The Name and Nature of Poetry* (NNP),
Housman said:

Even when poetry has a meaning, as it usually has, it may be inadvisable to
draw it out, . . . I think that the production of poetry . . . is less an active than
a passive and involuntary process . . . a secretion; whether a natural secretion,
like turpentine in the fir, or a morbid secretion, like the pearl in the oyster. I
think that my own case, though I may not deal with the material so cleverly
as the oyster does, is the latter. (*Collected Poems*, 364, 370).

It was "inadvisable" to draw the meaning out of his poetry even in
1933 when these words were spoken. Today, I think he would be pleased
to have his poetry recognized as the pearl that he constructed around the
irritants of his homosexuality and his hopeless love to ease the discomfort
produced by them. The "morbid secretion" that welled out of his "hairy
weid" emerged as a string of pearls indeed.

Afterword

HOUSMAN RELISHED THE PARODIES OF HIS WORK, AND IT SEEMS LIKELY that the following versified biography would have both amused and pleased him. Being cringed at by critics and cherished by comrades constitute equally fitting tributes to a poet who took great pleasure in both.

A. E. HOUSMAN (1859–1936)
Mary Holtby

In Oxford town a lad's in trouble,
His friends and tutors groan aloud;
The one who should have notched a Double
Is now indubitably ploughed.

Ah, fate more fit for Shropshire yeoman,
Hard as the stool he sits upon
To him whose heart and tongue are Roman—
The clerk who'd rather be a don.

Ten years the civil servant labours
And cons the classics late at night;
Ovid and Virgil are his neighbors,
Propertius keeps his lamp alight.

Till Time, his midnight toil rewarding,
Redeems the unpropitious past,
A professorial post affording
At London first, and Cambridge last.

He now prefers his poets boring:
What treasures may Manilius yield!
There's half a lifetime spent in scoring
Off fellow-workers in the field.

Yet still he finds his thoughts returning
To fan an unrequited flame,
Bright in his burdened bosom burning
The love that dares not speak its name.

No balm shall sain him, save to show it
In Art's dissembling armour clad:
Dry don becomes impassioned poet
And Bromsgrove boy a Shropshire lad.

Still the stern Latinist discovers
Minute distortions in a text,
While redcoats march, and lonely lovers
Lie down deserted and perplexed.

So critics cringe, and comrades cherish
This man of wit and sentiment,
Who told the truth in hearts that perish
And limned the land of lost content.

Notes

Introduction

1. LeMire, "Irony and Ethics," remarks, a propos of "Is my team ploughing" (ASL 27) and ASL in general: "The reader first sees that this is not the way things should be and then, almost simultaneously, that this is the way things often are" (114).

2. Wilfred Scawen Blunt, *My Diaries*, part 2, 371–72, quoted by MacDonald, "Poetry of A. E. Housman," 114–115.

3. See, for example, Garrod, "Mr. A. E. Housman."

Chapter 1: The Bogle of the Hairy Weid

1. Tom Burns Haber, A. E. Housman, *Manuscript Poems*, 93. Archie Burnett, *The Poems of A. E. Housman*. Dr. Burnett provides the date as January 1925 or thereafter, 499. All poetry texts are taken from this edition unless otherwise noted.

2. John Keble, a review of Lockhart's *Life of Scott* (1838) in *Occasional Papers and Reviews* (Oxford and London, 1977), 6, quoted in Abrams, *Mirror and the Lamp*, 48 and again 145 in full.

3. A. E. Housman, letter to Maurice Pollet, 5 February 1933, Maurice Pollet, "A. E. Housman ['Etude Suivie d'une Lettre Inedite']," *Etudes Anglaises* (Sept. 1937), 385–404, or Housman, *Letters*, 329.

4. See Naiditch, *Housman at University College, London*: 100–2, 109, and 191–203; and Naiditch, "A. E. Housman and W. H. Mallock," 13–16, for a full discussion of the matter and one or two solutions not considered in this book.

5. Only *after* I had come to the conclusion that it was not a coincidence did I find that I had been anticipated. Tom Burns Haber, in *A. E. Housman* (50) had suggested that Moses Jackson "doubtless had exerted some influence in expediting his friend's appointment," (although how much influence he had and just what he could have done in this respect are moot). Keith Jebb in *A. E. Housman* (25) had concluded that "Obviously it was a happy coincidence, if it had not been partly engineered by the two friends."

6. Preface to *Last Poems*, A. E. Housman, *Collected Poems and Selected Prose*, 95. All prose quotations are taken from this edition unless otherwise noted.

7. That the phrase is both intimate and affectionate is beyond doubt. The "dear old . . ." construction is used with this emotional connotation by both Dickens and George Eliot, among others. J. B. Priestley remembered that in World War I soldiers tended "to use *old* to indcate half-affectionate familiarity," indicating acceptance, recognition, and something close to affection; this "curious adjective 'old' . . . preserved the affection" (Fussell, *Great War*, 179–80).

8. Although Haber states in *A. E. Housman*, 197, note 8, that Housman "preserved all of the forty-year correspondence from Jackson," he cites as his source only Laurence

Housman's account of finding this final letter. Laurence Housman in fact neither mentions any other letters from Jackson nor comments on their absence. Haber's assumption is thus unwarranted unless based on other evidence, evidence he does not see fit to mention.

9. A. C. Benson records in his diary in March 1925 that Housman "said that his first poems were caused by a deep personal attachment which had lasted for fifteen years and left a deep mark on him. He said that he had twice felt a loss of vitality in life—at 36 when even his devotion failed—and again lately when he found himself less interested in life," quoted in Naiditch, *Problems*, 142, note 4. The "fifteen years" can be taken to refer roughly to the period between Housman's meeting Moses Jackson at Oxford in 1877 and Jackson's marriage in 1889. Housman was thirty-six when *A Shropshire Lad* was published, and "lately" can perhaps refer to Jackson's death in 1922, a few years earlier than Benson's diary entry. The question is what, precisely, is implied by the phrase, "even his devotion failed." On the surface the remark indicates that his devotion ceased, but it can equally mean that his devotion failed for a time to sustain him, and this seems the more likely meaning in light of the repetition of the "loss of vitality" shortly before the date of the diary entry, a loss, that is to say, sustained twice, upon Jackson's marriage and upon Jackson's death. This, at least, is how I would understand the remark, remembering that Housman was most unlikely to have been specific about dates, time spans, or causes in discussing his personal affairs with anyone.

10. The biographical sketch and information about the fate of the notebooks are drawn from many sources, the primary ones being the following: Gow, *A. E. Housman*; A. E. Housman, *Manuscript Poems* and *Letters*; Haber, *The Making of 'A Shropshire Lad'*; A. E. Housman, Manuscript Fragments in the Library of Congress; Symons, et al, *Recollections*; Laurence Housman, *Unexpected Years*, "De Amicitia", and *A. E. H.*; Richards, *Housman*; Withers, *Buried Life*. The secondary sources are these: Graves, *A. E. Housman*; Haber, *A. E. Housman*; Marlow, *A. E. Housman*; Naiditch, *Housman at University College, London*, and *Problems*, especially the section "Notes on the Life of M. J. Jackson"; Page, *A. E. Housman*; Watson, *A. E. Housman*.

CHAPTER 2: BE KIND TO UNICORNS

1. Stead, W. T. *Review of Reviews*, 15 June 1895, quoted in Tannahill, *Sex in History*, 381, and in Ronald Pearsall, *Worm in the Bud*, 456.

2. Page, *A. E. Housman*, 113. He ascribes the story and the verse to a letter from Leonard Whibley to Gow, 19 November 1936; the comment is of course his own.

3. A. E. Housman, "Swinburne," in *Collected Poems and Selected Prose*, 277. For Housman's general assessment of Utilitarianism, see his introductory lecture at University College, London, 1892, ibid. 259–74.

4. Different versions of this poem are provided by Katharine Symons and Laurence Housman. I am following Burnett in citing "a fair copy written out by AEH for his godson, Gerald C. A. Jackson," Burnett, *Poems*, text 263, comment 546.

5. Laurence Housman provides a text of this poem in *A. E.H.*, 233. He considered it a "much funnier version of the Amphisbaena poem" (66), but it seems to me to be not so much a version of the same poem as an independent treatment of the same mythical serpent. For the other "version," see Burnett, *Poems*, 274–76.

Chapter 3: State the Alternative Preferred

1. Grant Richards, *Housman*, 380, quoting Edward Marsh, *A Number of People* (London: n.p., 1939), 222. Burnett accepts the ascription to Housman and provides text, *Poems*, 285 and comment 563.

2. Quoted in introduction, Manilius *Astronomica*, lxxvii.

3. Katharine Symons. "Memories of A. E. Housman," the *Edwardian* 17, no. 3 (September 1936). This was the magazine of King Edwards School, Bath, of which her husband was Headmaster. Quoted in Graves, *A. E. Housman*, 23, reprinted in Burnett, *Poems*, 189.

4. I have accepted the title Laurence Housman provided. The basic idea may have been suggested to Housman by an anonymous twelfth–century Latin poem "Ganymede and Helen" (which he might, or might not, have known), in which Ganymede says, verse 35, "But things are sundered by disparity; / More elegant are men joined each to each. / Perhaps you're ignorant of rules of speech: / The adjective and noun must both agree." Coote, *Homosexual Verse*, 121–29.

5. I wish to acknowledge my debt to Professor Jerome Mandel of Tel Aviv University whose comments suggested this reading to me.

Chapter 4: The Garland

1. John Whitehead, it may be noted, is aware of the conscious humor in the poem but not appreciative of it, considering it only "hearty flippancy unsuited to Housman's unfrivolous talent" and a "heavy-handed attempt at humour" that is "apparently intended defensively as a mock-debunking of his own poetry," "A. E. Housman," 148. Whitehead is apparently unaware of the pawky vein of humor that runs like a fine thread through a great deal of Housman's poetry and finds its full outlet in the comic verse and parodies. He is also apparently unaware that there is a difference between Housman the poet and Terence the persona.

2. Housman was, of course, aware of Ovid's use of the image. In his comments on the Latin poet's "Ex. Pont. III," he translates the Latin, "the flowers are plucked and the garden rifled; what marvel then if I have twined no garland worthy of the victor for whose brows it was meant?" and he explains, "Ovid has indicted a poem on Tiberias' triumph . . . but other poets . . . have forestalled him; they have stripped the garden of flowers and left him none from which to twine a worthy wreath." See "Ovidiana," *Classical Quarterly* 10 (1916), reprinted in *Classical Papers*, 3: 917–39.

3. Burnett, *Poems*, 353–54, provides the full text of the suicide note given in Housman's cutting from *The Standard*. This account is based on the report of the *Malvern News* quoted by Nosworthy, "Woolwich Cadet." Burnett also cites this account. See also White, "Suicide and the Poet."

4. Leviticus 18:22, "Thou shalt not lie with mankind as with womankind: it is abomination." Note, however, that according to Riskin, "Gays Sacrifice Their Future," 8, "abomination" is a mistranslation as the Talmudic sages suggest that the Hebrew "to'eva" is "To'eh ata ba," or "a tragic mistake" due to the consequent impossibility of generating offspring ("be fruitful and multiply"), a suggestion which Housman, with his constant images of sterility, would have heartily endorsed, although it seems highly unlikely that he was familiar with it (but see Efrati, "A. E. Housman's Knowledge of Hebrew").

5. For a full explication of this aspect, see Siegel, "Pastoral Elegy."

6. The movement between "not the wear" and "will wear them" was first brought to my attention by Professor Robert Friend, but I alone am responsible for the interpretation I have placed on it.

7. For a complete consideration of the relationship between Housman's lyric and the French model, see James Brannin, "Alfred Housman."

CHAPTER 5: WHAT TUNE THE ENCHANTRESS PLAYS

1. Ricks, "Nature of His Poetry" and "Nature of Housman's Poetry" (in almost identical terms); Brooks, "Alfred Edward Housman;" Page, *A. E. Housman*, 199. The quotation is from Page. See also the comment by Horwood in A. E. Housman, *Poetry and Prose*, 9 and 10: This is "a love story, a hopeless passion for a most beautiful and seductive enchantress" who is "a beautiful but imbecile mistress; she smiles, but is indifferent. But how heartbreakingly lovely she is!"

2. This is the image that informs Robert Duncan's line, ". . . a man that was Day came / shaking my heart like a storm in old trees," from "Night Scenes" (part 2, ll. 12–13, *Roots and Branches*, 7).

3. For a fuller astronomical analysis of this image, see Wysong "Housman's Use of Astronomy."

4. Strozier points out that the "silver-tufted" wands and the "daffodils" echo the gold and silver of the opening stanza and, noting the kinship with "Corinna's Going A-Maying," comments that "The real reason for the boy's and girl's being afield and awood is that lovers should be, want to be, will be loved again—as surely as the sun's silver gives way to its gold" ("Image, Illogic and Allusion," p. 259).

5. For a complete discussion of the *carpe diem* theme in Herrick's poem, see Cleanth Brooks, "What does Poetry Communicate?" in *Well Wrought Urn*, 67–79. One should note, however, that Whitehead identifies the "palms" as "willow wands tipped with silver buds." He associates them and the daffodils with the Christian festival of resurrection rather than with the decayed remnants of pagan fertility rites, saying that "the flowers and willows are being gathered to decorate the church in readiness for the service on Easter morning," "A. E. Housman," 147. This reading does not seem to me consonant either with Housman's habitual practice or with the general tenor of the poem itself.

6. Haber, *A. E. Housman*, 133, notes that this poem "illustrates [Housman's] frequent tendency to put himself into the action: he is speaking throughout to his comrade, who is *of course* Moses Jackson." The emphasis is mine.

7. See also A. E. Housman, *Manuscript Poems*, 94, and Haber, "Poem of Beeches," or his *A. E. Housman*, 112–13, for his suggested finished version.

8. The closest parallel in literature is in Trollope, *The Small House at Allington*, 573–74 and 599, respectively, for the two parts of the quotation. Johnny Eames, balked in his love for Lily Dale, goes to the wooden bridge on which he had in hope once "scored" her name. "He stood on the centre of the plank . . . and rubbing his hand upon the rail, cleansed it. . . . There, rudely carved in the wood, was still the word Lily. . . . [H]e took out his knife, and, with deep, rough gashes in the wood, cut out Lily's name from the rail."

9. Haber remarks, in *A. E. Housman*, 96, that "we can feel . . . the presence of Moses Jackson mediating between Horace and Housman in this scene; we can hear in his tremulous voice another declaration of the old undying passion and his cry of protest at the hopeless inadequacy of all that comradely affection could do when confronting the unfeeling rulers of human destiny."

10. See Whallon, "Love of Comrades." For the location of Housman's copy, I am indebted to P. G. Naiditch, letter of 1 January 1997.

Chapter 6: Rose Harland

1. One of the very first commentators saw this. In a review of *A Shropshire Lad* in *The Bookman*, June 1896, A. MacDonnell found in the volume several linked stories but "no continuous narrative" (83). The poems that made a "continuous narrative" out of the linked dramas were not included in this volume.

2. I believe that LeMire is mistaken in saying, "We have no reason to believe that he [Terence] ever dons a uniform and literally takes up soldiering" ("Irony and Ethics," p. 126 n. 9) I believe we do have warrant for such a belief, as will be made clear in the course of this chapter.

3. A. E. Housman, in a letter to J. W. Mackail, 25 July 1922, said that he had only put ASL 20 "in for variety." *Letters*, 200.

4. As LeMire notes, "all of Terence's experiences with women seem to be unfortunate. At best, his romances are tragic . . . at worst, they are sardonically twisted betrayals brought on the lovers by their own natures. Nowhere, however, do Terence's experiences add up to an affirmation of the sentimental love convention" ("Irony and Ethics," 122). The same is true of all the heterosexual relationships in the Shropshire cycle.

5. MacDonald, "Housman." See also John Erskine, "What Is Contemporary Poetry?" reprinted in *A. E. Housman: The Critical Heritage*, Philip Gardner, ed., hereafter cited as Gardner, *Critical Heritage*.

6. See Houghton, *Victorian Frame of Mind*, for a complete discussion of the Victorian ideals of masculinity and femininity.

7. Whitehead also identifies the "Ned" of "When I came last to Ludlow" with the "Ned Lear" of the notebook fragments, "A. E. Housman," 137.

8. The Greek original is in the *Palatine Anthology*, 9: 138. The translation is in Marlow, "Earliest Influences," 168.

9. The phrase "friendship triumphant" is used by both S. M. Ellis and Theresa Ashton. Horwood considers this "nothing but an allegory of friendship which can cheat Hell itself" (34).

10. Milton, *Paradise Lost* 2, ll. 649–73, pp. 247–48. In both Milton and Housman, the portress is female. Housman has reversed the identifications, not the functions.

Chapter 7: On Hero's Heart Leander Lies

1. See Millard's entire chapter, "A. E. Housman and the perils of cheat and charmer" for an interpretation of Housman's poetry that meets mine on this one point only. His entire reading is based on a totally different approach. For Housman's own attitude, see "Prosody and Method [I]," *Classical Quarterly* 21 (1927) reprinted in A. E. Housman, *Classical Papers*, 3:1119, where Housman speaks of "the frame of mind in which Tereus ravished Philomela: concupiscence concentrated on its object and indifferent to all beside."

2. Since Housman used a phrase from this poem ("a new Mistresse now I chase") as the source of the title of his own "The New Mistress," discussed in the preceding chapter, which also dealt with the "desertion" of the persona's sweetheart for the call of the mili-

tary, it is obvious that he knew Lovelace's poem well and had it in mind in writing both poems.

3. Also note LeMire's comment: "The scene is almost a caricature of the stark, ballad drama. . . . The imitation of ballad actions and ballad sentiments is too obvious" ("Irony and Ethics, 122). My contention is that Housman intended it to be "too obvious" because it was not "almost a caricature" but rather a full-blown—and intentional—caricature. If I am right, it is obvious that its intent was not sufficiently obvious.

4. See, for example, Brooks, Purser, and Warren, *Approach to Literature*, 4th ed., 298; Robb, *Four in Exile*, 17 and 38; Allison, "Poetry," 282–83; Brenner, *Ten Modern Poets*, 188–89; Brown, "Poetry," 8–9; Haber, "Influence of the Ballads," 118–29; and Marlow, *A. E. Housman*, 73–75.

5. Leggett, *Land of Lost Content*, 35–38. See also Abel, *Explicator*, 23; Hawkins, *Explicator*, 8; and Stevenson, "Martyr As Innocent," 82.

6. For the classic version in English, see Childe, *English and and Scottish Popular Ballads*, 243, 4: 360–69. Whitehead ("A. E. Housman," 134) suggests as a model "The Unquiet Grave" (Childe, no. 78, 2: 234–38), but here I believe he is mistaken as in this ballad it is the living lover who demands a kiss from the "clay-cold lips" of the dead, whose grave s/he haunts (in different versions it is the woman who haunts the man's grave and the man who haunts the woman's). For a German version that is a close parallel to Housman's, see "Wo die schonen Trompeten blasen" in Gustav Mahler's composition, *Das Knaben Wunderhorn*.

7. For a complete consideration of the classical element, see Calder, " 'Epithalamium,' " 25–30, who demonstrates that Housman has in fact cast the epithalamium in the form of a tragic ode or dirge.

8. That this is a translation of Sappho was noted in the anonymous Review of *Last Poems*, as well as by Davenport, "Terrier and the Rat." For a complete discussion of this and of the classical conventions of the epithalamium, see Reedy, "Housman's Use of Classical Convention."

9. See, for example, *Latin Literature*, 200–201.

10. Among the critics who have noted and/or analyzed these echoes are Haber, "What Fools These Mortals Be!"; Hamilton, *Housman the Poet*, 57; Burnett in *Poems of A. E. Housman*, and Naiditch in his index to Burnett, *Poems*.

CHAPTER 8: DEAR FELLOW

1. For a further consideration of the homoerotic element of the poem, see Ebbatson, *Tennyson*, chapter 8, and especially 97–100.

2. Tennyson, "In Memoriam," passages taken from prologue verse 10, lyrics 9, 17, 18, 42, 59, 60, 74, 81, 85, 90, 95, 103, 112, 116, 117, 129, 130, 131, and the epithalamium, verse 5, 331–484.

3. That "In Housman's poetry . . . the fickleness of women is often unfavourably contrasted with the constancy of men," as Whitehead remarks ("A. E. Housman," 135), is a basic tenet of Housman commentary. It is, however, desirable to stress that "often" is not "always."

4. For a consideration of the professional and technical reasons why Housman chose to work on Manilius, see Jebb, *A. E. Housman*, 116–19.

5. Philip Gardner, *Critical Heritage*, 213. For Housman's unwillingness to review Garrod's edition of Manilius 2, see Carter's reprint (*A. E. Housman, Selected Prose*) of a larger portion of Housman's preface to his edition of Manilius 5 than is provided by Ricks

(A. E. Housman, *Collected Poems and Selected Prose*). For Housman's remarks on Garrod's edition of Manilius 2, see ibid., 388–89.

6. For a complete discussion of this aspect of Housman's poetry, see Haber, "Astronomer-Poet."

7. The comparison was suggested by Ellis.

8. Isay, Letter to the editor. See also Isay, *Being Homosexual*, 65 and 105–8.

9. Page also remarks on Adalbert's importance to Housman "as a source of information about Moses and as someone to whom Housman could speak of him" (*A. E. Housman*, 54).

10. P. G. Naiditch considers the evidence insufficient, *Problems*, 58, note 2.

11. Burnett *Poems* places "brought" at the start of line 4. This is due to what he has called, in notes for a second impression that he has kindly provided to me, "the vagaries of computer setting." I have corrected this misplacement. Burnett also substitutes for the standard final verse the alternate (*Poems*, 139–40, variants at bottoms of pages):

> Once he stept out but now my friend
>   Is not in marching trim
> And you must tramp to the world's end
>   To touch your cap to him.
>
> *Poems*

Here, since the alteration depersonalizes the poem, I am quite sure that he is correct. However, the traditionally accepted last verse is so poetically superior that I have retained it.

CHAPTER 9: HOW ILL GOD MADE ME

1. Both Cavafy's "The Next Table," 91, and "The Afternoon Sun," 92, for example, were later rewritten to specify that the subject is male (notes, 175).

2. As Robert Friend put it in "Waste Not, Want Not," "if it is hard, you can suck it. / And if it is soft, you can fuck it," *Dancing with a Tiger*, 19. See also Isay, *Being Homosexual*, 90, and Joe Orton's diary entries for 19 May and 11 June, 1967, "I lay and allowed him to fuck me," and "At one moment with my cock in his arse," as cited by John Lahr, *Prick up Your Ears*, 17 and 18, respectively.

3. Whitehead also notes in this poem an indication of "a suppressed but pervasive element in Housman's poetry, namely his homosexuality," "A. E. Housman," 133. Also note that, as cited by Manegold in "Odd Place of Homosexuality in the Military," in 1941 "the psychiatrist William Menninger described the typical soldier's wartime relationship as one of 'disguised and sublimated homosexuality.'" The complexity of Housman's soldier symbolism is a reverse reflection of clinical psychology.

4. Woods is referring to Hart Crane's use of the image in his poetry, and consider also Robert Duncan's "I shy a glance that he too shies. / The authors of the look / write with our eyes / broken phrases of their book," from "Two Dicta of William Blake," part 2, ll. 4–6, *Roots and Branches*, 49.

5. For an explication of the homo-erotic vocabulary, see Woods, *Articulate Flesh*, from which I have extracted the relevant symbolism

6. The statue has been identified as the Farnese Mercury. See Robin Shaw, "From Housman's Places," 54, with photograph.

7. Peters, "Cynical Classicist." Perrine in his article on this poem ("Others I am not the first") admits that he too made this assumption at one time.

8. Trollope, *Last Chronicle of Barset*, 36, "Could she have lain on the man's bosom for

twenty years . . . ?"; *Can You Forgive Her?* 397, "Must she submit to his caresses,—lie on
his bosom"; *Eustace Diamonds*, 2:23, "She should lie on his breast and swear that she loved
him"; *Phineas Redux*, 448, "how her spirit would bear this accusation against the man
upon whose bosom she had slept."

9. The standard reading, in Whitehead's words, is "a general grudge against the
world's injustice coupled with Housman's usual longing for the grave" ("A. E. Housman,"
139). P. G. Naiditch informs me in a letter of 1 January 1997 that as he reads it, the "it"
is "existence" and that "the reactions . . . are enmeshed in religious imagery. 'Be still' is
a hymn; the references to blood and sweat, to Jesus." That "blood and sweat" can indeed
refer to Jesus, as in MP 1 ("Easter Hymn"), is clear, but I do not think that it is nearly so
clear that in this poem they do. It seems to me that the "it" may indeed be existence as
Naiditch thinks, but the pronoun lacks an antecedent and is itself so vague that it is open
to other interpretations.

10. See also Isay, *Being Homosexual*, especially 48 and 120.

11. Compare the following summation from Noël Coward's "Me and the Girls" with
the defiance of the opening of Housman's poem, to which Coward is apparently indebted:
"He loved me . . . and I loved him . . . , and if the happiness we gave each other was
wicked and wrong in the eyes of the Law and the Church and God Almighty, then the
Law and the Church and God Almighty can go dig a hole and fall down it" (*Noel Coward:
The Short Stories*, 475).

12. See, for example, Angier, "Biology of What It Means to be Gay"; Siegel-Itzkovich,
"Gay Genes"; "Born or Bred?"; CNN International, *Health Works*, Isay, *Being Homosexual*,
especially chapter 1, 135 note 2, and 137 note 1; and Small, "Gay Debate."

13. "Throughout the Middle Ages and later, Christian law-givers thought that nothing but a painful death in the flames could atone for the sinful act [of sodomy]. In England
. . . burning was the due punishment. . . . In France, persons were actually burned for this
crime in the middle and latter part of the eighteenth century." Edward Westermarck,
"Homosexual Love".

14. Lord Alfred Douglas, "Two Loves," ll. 66–69 and 71–74, in Coote, *Homosexual
Verse*, 264.

15. Cited by Ronald Pearsall, *Worm in the Bud*, 59, from *The Exquisite*, a pornographic
magazine, 3 vols., 1842–44.

16. Graves, *A. E. Housman*, 155 and 282–83, note 18. But see also Page, *A. E. Housman*, 121–22 and 222, second note to 121.

CHAPTER 10: THE SOUL THAT WAS BORN TO DIE FOR YOU

1. Adalbert had moved out previously. His absence would have exacerbated Housman's emotional difficulty as there would no longer have been a third person present to
act as a restraining influence on his words and actions.

2. See Kreuzer, *Elements of Poetry*, 132–34, for a full discussion of both the metrical
variations and the diction.

3. See Woods, Articulate Flesh, 208–10, for an analysis of this particular imagery.

4. See Haber, "Downward Eye"; Bronowski, "A. E. Housman"; and Ricks, "Nature of
Housman's Poetry," and "Nature of His Poetry." The Ricks quotation is from the former
but the idea is expressed in almost identical terms in both.

5. Sappho, *Sappho*, 9. Caclamanes offered his own translation in "Source of Another
Poem," but while his understanding of Greek is presumably excellent, his facility in trans-
lating it into English leaves something to be desired, so I am not citing his translation.
See also Keyser, "Variations on Sappho" for additional translations as well as for metrical

analysis and consideration of the resemblances and differences among Housman's three variants.

6. I am indebted to J. N. Wysong for this insight, which Keyser ("Variations on Sappho") also notes and upon which he elaborates.

7. Rachel, "B'mo Yadi" ["By my own hand"] in *Rachel's Poems*, 145. The translation is mine.

8. See Bayley, *Housman's Poems*, 23–24, where there is a brilliant analysis of the relevance of this and other of Tennyson's poems to Housman.

Abbreviations

CE—College English
HSJ—Housman Society Journal
JEGP—Journal of English and Germanic Philology
MLQ—Modern Language Quarterly
MTQ—Mark Twain Quarterly
N&Q—Notes and Queries
PMLA—Publications of the Modern Language Association
RES—Review of English Studies
SAQ—The South Atlantic Quarterly
SRL—The Saturday Review of Literature
TLS—The Times Literary Supplement
VN—Victorian Newsletter
VP—Victorian Poetry

OTHER ABBREVIATIONS

ASL—*A Shropshire Lad*
LP—*Last Poems*
MP—*More Poems*
AP—*Additional Poems*
NNP—The Name and Nature of Poetry

Bibliography

Abel, Darrel. *The Explicator* 8 (December, 1949), 23.

Abrams, M. H. *The Mirror and the Lamp*. London, Oxford University Press, 1933.

Ackerley, J. R. "My Father and Myself." In *The Penguin Book of Gay Short Stories*, edited by David Leavitt and Mark Mitchell, 109–30. (London: Viking, 1994).

Adams, Michael C. *The Great Adventure: Male Desire and the Coming of World War I*. Indianapolis: Indiana University Press, 1990.

Aldington, Richard. *A. E. Housman and W. B. Yeats: Two Lectures*. The Peacock Press, 1955.

Allison, A. F. "The Poetry of A. E. Housman." *RES* 19, no. 75 (July, 1943), 276–84.

Angier, Natalie. "The Biology of What It Means to be Gay." *The New York Times Weekly Review* (1 September 1991): 1.

Archer, William. "A. E. Housman." *Poets of the Younger Generation*, 183–95. London: John Lane, 1902.

Ashton, Theresa. "A. E. Housman: A Critical Study," *Poetry Review* 29 (1938), 191–200.

Auden, W. H. "Jehovah Housman and Satan Housman." *A. E. Housman: A Collection of Critical Essays*, edited by Christopher Ricks, 32–34. Englewood Cliffs, N. J.: Prentice-Hall, Inc., 1968.

———. "A Worcestershire Lad," *New Yorker* (19 February 1922): 332; reprinted in W. H. Auden, *Forewords and Afterwords*, edited by E. Mendelson, 325–32. New York: Random House, 1973.

———. "The Virgin and the Dynamo.' In *The Dyer's Hand and Other Essays*, 61–71 London: Faber and Faber, 1962.

———, editor. *Nineteenth Century British Minor Poets*. Notes by George R. Creeger. New York: Dell Publishing Co., 1965.

Baker, Kenneth. *Unauthorized Versions*. London: Faber and Faber, 1990.

Bateson, F. W. "The Poetry of Emphasis." *A. E. Housman: A Collection of Critical Essays*, edited by Christopher Ricks, 130–45. Englewood Cliffs, N. J.: Prentice Hall, 1968

Bayley, John. "A. E. Housman's "The Night Is Freezing Fast.' " *The English Review* no. 3 (1991): 17–18.

———. "Housman and Larkin: Romantic into Parnassian?" *Essays in Criticism* 41 no. 2 (April 1991), 147–59.

———. *Housman's Poems*. Oxford: Clarendon Press, 1992.

Beardsley, Aubrey. *The Story of Venus and Tannhauser*. Introduction by Paul J. Gillette. New York: Award Books, 1967.

Bennett, Arnold. *Clayhanger*. Harmondsworth, Middlesex: Penguin Books, 1954.

Bishop, John Peale. "The Poetry of A. E. Housman." *The Collected Essays of John Peale Bishop*, edited by Edmund Wilson, 138–45. New York: Scribners, 1948.

"Born or Bred?" Newsweek International Edtion (24 February 1992): 38–44.

Bourne, Jeremy. *The Westerly Wanderer: A brief portrait of A. E. Housman*. Bromsgrove: The Housman Society, 1996.

Brannin, James. "Alfred Housman." *Sewanee Review* 33 (April 1925): 191–98.

Brashear, William R. "The Trouble with Housman." *VP* 7 (Spring 1969): 81–90.

Brenner, Rica. *Ten Modern Poets*. New York: Harcourt, Brace and Co., 1930.

Briggs, Katherine. *An Encyclopedia of Fairies*. New York: Pantheon Books, 1976.

Bronowski, J. "A. E. Housman." In *The Poet's Defense*, 209–28. London: Cambridge University Press, 1939.

Bronte, Anne. *Agnes Gray*. London: Penguin Books, 1988.

Bronte, Charlotte. *Shirley*. London: Penguin Books, 1974.

Brooks, Cleanth. "Alfred Edward Housman." In *A. E. Housman: A Collection of Critical Essays*, edited by Christopher Ricks, 62–84. Englewood Cliffs, N. J.: Prentice-Hall, 1968.

———. *The Well Wrought Urn*. New York: Harcourt, Brace and Co., Harvester Books, 1947.

———. "The Whole of Housman." *The Kenyon Review* 3 (Winter 1941). Reprinted in *The Kenyon Critics: Studies in Modern Literature from the Kenyon Review*, edited by John Crowe Ransom, 267–72, Cleveland: The World Publishing Co., 1951.

———, John Thibaut Purser, and Robert Penn Warren. *An Approach to Literature*. 4th ed. New York: Appleton Century-Crofts, 1964.

———, and Robert Penn Warren. *Understanding Poetry*. New York: Henry Holt and Co., 1938.

Brown, Stuart Gerry. "The Poetry of A. E. Housman." *Sewanee Review* 48 (July, 1940): 397–408.

Browne, Piers. *Elegy in Arcady: An Artist's View of Housman's Poetry*. 2nd ed. Southampton: Ashford, 1990.

Browning, Robert. *Robert Browning: The Poems*, 2 vols., edited by John Pettigrew, supplemented and completed by Thomas J. Collins. Harmondsworth, Middlesex: Penguin Books, 1981.

———. *The Ring and the Book*. Edited by Richard D. Altick. Harmondsworth, Middlesex: Pemguin Books, 1981.

Bruce, Sylvia. *Essays on Isak Dinesen and A. E. Housman*. Nottingham: Paupers' Press, 1994.

Buchan, Irving, ed. *The Perverse Imagination: Sexuality and Literary Culture*. New York: New York University Press, 1970.

Burnett, Archie, ed. *The Poems of A. E. Housman*. Oxford: Clarendon Press, 1997.

———. "Poetical Emendations and Improvisations by A. E. Housman." *VP* 36, no. 3 (Fall, 1998): 289–97.

Bush, Douglas. *Mythology and the Romantic Tradition in English Poetry*. New York: Norton, 1937.

Butler, Samuel. *The Way of All Flesh*. New York: New American Library, 1960.

Caclamenes, Demetrius. "The Source of a Poem by A. E. Housman." *N&Q* 178 (24 February 1940): 133.

———. "The Source of Another Poem by A. E. Housman." *N&Q* 178 (6 April 1940): 244.

Calder, William M. III. "A. E. Housman: 'Epithalamium' (=L-P 24)." *Classical and Modern Literature* 2 no. 1 (Fall 1981): 25–31.

Carey, John. "John Carey's Books of the Century." *The Sunday Times Books* (25 July 1999), 9.

Carroll, Lewis. *The Complete Works of Lewis Carroll.* London: Penguin Books, 1988.

Carter, John, editor. *The Collected Poems of A. E. Housman.* London: Jonathan Cape, 1939.

———. "Corrigenda & Addenda." Preprinted from *Encounter* 30 (1968): 2–5. Not used.

———, editor. *A. E. Housman: Selected Prose.* Cambridge: Cambridge University Press, 1961.

Catullus. *Odi et Amo: The Complete Poetry.* Translated by Roy Arthur Sivanson. New York: Bobbs-Merrill, The Library of Liberal Arts, 1959.

Cavafy, C. P. *Collected Poems.* Rev. ed., translated and edited by Edmund Keeley and Philip Sherrard. London: Chatto and Windus, 1998.

Cecil, David. *Early Victorian Novelists.* Harmondsworth, Middlesex: Penguin, 1934.

Chaucer, Geoffrey. *The Canterbury Tales. Chaucer's Poetry.* Edited by E. T. Donaldson. New York: Ronald Press Co., 1958.

Chesney, Kellow. *The Victorian Underworld.* Harmondsworth, Middlesex: Penguin Books, 1970.

Childe, Francis James, ed. *The English and Scottish Popular Ballads.* 5 vols. New York: Dover Publications, 1965.

Clemens, Cyril. "A. E. Housman and His Publishers: A Series of Unpublished Letters." *MTQ* (Summer–Fall, 1941): 11–15, 23.

———. "Editorial in Memory of A. E. Housman." *MTQ* (Winter 1936): 1–2.

———. "Housman as a Conversationalist." *MTQ* (Winter 1936): 8–10, 13, 18, 22.

Clucas, Humphrey. "A Note on A. E. Housman." *Agenda* 24 (Spring, 1986): 91–93.

———. *Through Time and Place to Roam: Essays on A. E. Housman.* Salzburg: Salzburg University Press, 1995.

CNN International. *Health Works: News for Living.* "Special Report on Homosexuality." 27 March 1993.

Cohen, Ed. "The double lives of man: narration and identification in late nineteenth-century representations of ec-centric masculinities." *Cultural Politics at the fin de siecle,* edited by Sally Ledger and Scott McCracken, 85–114. Cambridge: Cambridge University Press, 1995.

Coote, Stephen, editor and translator. *Penguin Book of Homosexual Verse.* 2nd ed. London: Penguin Books, 1986.

Coulthard, A. R. "The Flawed Craft of A. E. Housman." *VN* Fall 1993: 29–31.

Coward, Noel. *The Collected Short Stories of Noel Coward.* London: Minerva, Mandarin Paperbacks, 1985.

Crane, Hart. *The Complete Poems and Selected Letters and Prose of Hart Crane.* Garden City, N.Y.: Doubleday and Co., Inc., Anchor Books, 1966.

Croft-Cooke, Rupert. *Feasting with Panthers: A New Consideration of Some Late Victorian Writers.* London: W. H. Allen, 1967.

Culpepper, Thomas Allen. *Homoerotic Poetics in Housman, Owen, Auden, and Gunn.* Unpublished dissertation, 1998.

d'Arch Smith, Timothy. *Love in Earnest: Some Notes on the Lives and Writings of English "Uranian" Poets from 1889 to 1930.* London: Routledge and Kegan Paul, 1970.

Davenport, Basil. "The Terrier and the Rat." Review of *The Name and Nature of Poetry.* *SRL* 1 July 1933.

Davis, Dick. "Blue Remembered Hills." Review of Burnett's edition. *The Poems of A. E. Housman. TLS* (5 June 1998): 3–4.

Dellamora, Richard. *Masculine Desire: The Sexual Politics of Victorian Aestheticism.* Chapel Hill: University of North Carolina Press, 1990.

Deutsch, Babette. *Poetry in Our Time: A Critical Survey of Poetry in the English-speaking World 1900–1960.* New York: Columbia University Press, 1952; Garden City, N.Y. Doubleday Anchor, 1963.

Dobree, Bonamy. "The Complete Housman." *Spectator* 164 (5 January 1940): 23–24.

Dudley, Fred A. *The Explicator* 14 (October 1955): 2 B.

Duncan, Robert. *Bending the Bow.* New York: New Directions, 1968.

———. *Roots and Branches.* New York: New Directions, 1964.

Ebbatson, Roger. *Tennyson.* Harmondsworth, Middlesex: Penguin, 1988.

Efrati, Carol. "A. E. Housman's Knowledge of Hebrew." *HSJ* 25 (1999): 83–86.

———. "The Horses and the Reins." *VP* 34, No. 1 (Spring 1996): 53–71.

———. "Housman's Escape from the Turning Mill." *HSJ* 24 (1998): 22–29.

———. "Housman, Hardy, and the Boer War Elegy." *HSJ* 25 (1999): 73–78.

Ehrsam, T. G. *A Bibliography of Alfred Edward Housman.* Boston: F. W. Faxon, 1941.

Eliot, T. S. Review of *The Name and Nature of Poetry. The Criterion* 13 (October 1933): 151–54.

Ellis, S. M. "Housman." *The Fortnightly Review* 13, new series (1 January 1923): 164–68.

Empson, William. "Rhythm and Imagery in English Poetry." *Argufying: Essays on Literature and Culture*, edited by John Heffenden, 147–66. London: Chatto and Windus, 1987.

———. "Teaching Literature." *Argufying: Essays on Literature and Culture*, edited by John Haffenden, 93–97. London: Chatto and Windus, 1987.

Erskine, John. "What Is Contemporary Poetry?" *North American Review* 242 (Autumn 1936): 171–80. Reprinted in *A. E. Housman: The Critical Heritage*, edited by Philip Gardner, 292–99. London: Routledge, 1992.

Ferguson, J. Delancey. "The Belligerent Don." *SRL* 2, no. 35 (27 March 1926): 657–59, 663.

Fiedler, Leslie. "Archetype and Signature: A Study of the Relationships between Biography and Poetry." In *Perspectives on Poetry*, edited by James S. Calderwood and Harold E. Tolliver, 394–409. New York: Oxford University Press, 1968.

Fielding, Henry. *Joseph Andrews and Shamela*, edited by Martin C. Batteston. Boston: Houghton Mifflin Co., Riverside Edition, 1961.

Firchow, Peter E. "The Land of Lost Content: Housman's Shropshire." *Mosaic* 13, no. 2 (Winter 1980): 103–121.

Firkins, O. W. "Living Verse." *Yale Review* 12 (July 1923), 850–52. Reprinted in *A. E. Housman: The Critical Heritage*, edited by Philip Gardner, 172–74. London: Routledge, 1992.

Ford, Ford Madox. *The Good Soldier.* New York: Penguin Books, Signet Classic, 1991.

Ford, George H. "W. S. Gilbert." *Norton Anthology of English Literature.* 2 vols. 4th ed., edited by M. H. Abrams. New York: W. W. Norton, 1979.

Forster, E. M. "Ancient and Modern." Review of *More Poems* and Gow's sketch. *Listener* 11 November 1926: 921–22. Reprinted in *A. E. Housman: The Critical Heritage*, edited by Philip Gardner, 317–21. London: Routledge, 1992.

Franklin, Ralph. "Housman's Shropshire." *MLQ* 24 (1963): 164–71.

Friedman, Ellen. "The Divided Self in the Poems of A. E. Housman." *English Literature in Transition* 20, no. 1 (1979): 27–34.

Friend, Robert. *Dancing with a Tiger: Love and Sex Poems*. Jerusalem: The Beth-Shalom Press, 1990.

Frye, Northrop. *Anatomy of Criticism*. Harmondsworth, Middlesex: Penguin, 1957.

Fussell, Paul. *The Great War and Modern Memory*. London: Oxford University Press, 1975.

Gardner, Philip, editor. *A. E. Housman: The Critical Heritage*. London: Routledge and Kegan Paul, 1992.

———. " 'One Fraction of a Summer Field': Forster and A. E. Housman." *Twentieth Century Literature: A Scholarly and Critical Journal* 31 nos. 2 and 3 (Summer/Fall 1985): 161–69.

Garrod, H. W. "Mr. A. E. Housman." In *The Profession of Poetry*, 211–24. Oxford: Oxford University Press, 1929.

Gasser, Brian. "A. E. Housman: *More Poems* 40." *N&Q* 27, No. 6. New series (December 1980): 530.

Gillet, Louis. "A. E. Housman." *Revue des Deux Mondes* 39 (1937): 208–21.

Giordano, Frank R., Jr. "Art and Imagination in Lyric 51 of *A Shropshire Lad*." *HSJ* 3 (1977): 45–53.

Goold, G. P. "Housman's Manilius." In *A. E. Housman: A Reassessment*, edited by. Alan W. Holden and J. Roy Birch, 134–53. Basingstoke: Macmillan, 2000.

Goose, Edmund. "The Shropshire Lad Again." In *More Books on the Table*, 21–26. London: Heinemann, 1923.

Gow, A. S. F. *A. E. Housman: A Sketch*. Cambridge: Cambridge University Press, 1936; New York: Haskell House, 1972.

Graves, Richard Perceval. *A. E. Housman: The Scholar-Poet*. New York: Charles Scribner's Sons, 1979.

Griffith, Ben W. *The Explicator* 13 (December 1954): no. 16.

Grigson, Geoffrey. Review of *More Poems*. *New Verse* 23 (Christmas 1936): 22–24. Reprinted in *A. E. Housman: The Critical Heritage*, edited by Philip Gardner, 324–25. London: Routledge, 1992.

Grosskurth, Phyllis, editor. *The Memoirs of John Addington Symonds: The Secret Homosexual Life of a Leading Nineteenth-Century Man of Letters*. New York: Random House, 1984.

Gunn, Thom. "Homosexuality in Robert Duncan's Poetry." In *The Occasions of Poetry: Essays in Criticism and Autobiography*, 118–34. London: Faber and Faber, 1982.

Haber, Tom Burns. *A. E. Housman*. Boston: Twayne Publishers, 1967.

———. "A. E. Housman: Astronomer-Poet." *English Studies* 35 (1954): 154–58.

———. "A. E. Housman's Downward Eye." *JEGP* 53 (1954): 306–18.

———. "A. E. Housman's Secret Grief." Preprinted from *Encounter* 30 (1968): 1–2. Not used.

———. "The Influence of the Ballads in Housman's Poetry." *Studies in Philology* 39 (January 1942): 118–29.

———. *The Making of "A Shropshire Lad"*. Seattle. University of Washington Press, 1966.

———. "A Poem of Beeches from the Notebooks of A. E. Housman." *Dalhousie Review* 31, no. 3 (Autumn, 1952): 196–97.

———. "The Spirit of the Perverse in A. E. Housman." *SAQ* 40 (1941): 368–78.

———. "What Fools These Mortals Be! Housman's Poetry and the Lyrics of Shake-speare." *MLQ* 6 (1945): 449–58.

Hamilton, Robert. "A. E. Housman: His Outlook and Art." *London Quarterly and Holborn Review* (1950): 261–66.

———. *Housman the Poet.* Exeter, N.Y.: Sydney Lee, 1949.

Hardy, Thomas. *Selected Stories of Thomas Hardy.* Edited by John Wain. London: Macmillan, 1966.

———. *Tess of the D'Urbervilles.* Harmondsworth, Middlesex: Penguin Books, 1978.

———. *Thomas Hardy: Selected Poetry.* Edited by David Wright. London: Penguin Books, 1978.

Hawkins, Maude M. *A. E. Housman: Man Behind a Mask.* Chicago: Henry Regnery Company, 1958.

———. *The Explicator* 8 (June 1950): 61.

Heap, G. V. M. "Last Poems III: An Interpretation." *HSJ* 4 (1978): 4–11.

Hoagwood, Terence Allan. *A. E. Housman Revisited.* New York: Twayne Publishers, 1995.

———. "Poetic Design in More Poems: Laurence and A. E. Housman, Part 2." *HSJ* 13 (1987): 7–13.

Holden, Alan. No title. *HSJ* 18 (1992): 49.

———, and J. Roy Birch, editors. *A. E. Housman: A Reassessment.* Basingstoke: Macmillan, 2000.

Holtby, Mary. "A. E. Housman (1859–1936)." *How to Become Absurdly Well-informed about the Famous and Infamous,* Edited by E. O. Parrott, 135–36. London: Penguin, 1988.

Holy Bible. King James authorized version.

Horace. *The Complete Works of Horace,* Edited by Caspar J. Kraemer, Jr. New York: Random House, The Modern Library, 1936.

Horwood, F. C., editor. *A. E. Housman Poetry and Prose: A Selection.* London: Hutchinson Educational, 1972.

Houghton, Walter. *The Victorian Frame of Mind: 1830–1870.* New Haven: Yale University Press, 1957.

Housman, A[lfred] E[dward]. *A Shropshire Lad.* The printer's copy in the Library of Trinity College, Cambridge, England.

———. *A Shropshire Lad 1896.* Introduction by R. K. R. Thornton. Oxford and New York: Woodstock Books, 1994.

———. *The Classical Papers of A. E. Housman.* 3 vols. Edited by J. Diggle & F. R. D. Goodyear, Cambridge: Cambridge University Press, 1972.

———. *The Letters of A. E. Housman.* Edited by Henry Maas. London: Rupert Hart-Davis, 1971.

———. *The Manuscript Poems of A. E. Housman.* Edited by Tom Burns Haber. Minneapolis: The University of Minnesota Press, 1955.

———. The Manuscript Fragments in the Library of Congress, Washington, D.C., USA.

———. *More Poems.* Edited by Laurence Housman. London: Jonathan Cape; New York: Alfred A. Knopf, 1936.

———. *Unkind to Unicorns: The Comic Verse of A. E. Housman.* Edited by J. Roy Birch. Cambridge: Silent Books and the Housman Society, 1995, re-edited by Archie Burnett and reissued 1999.

Housman, Laurence: *A. E. H.: Some Poems, Some Letters and a Personal Memoir by his Brother*. London: Jonathan Cape, 1937.

———. "A. E. Housman's *De Amicitia*." Annotated by John Carter, and including excerpts from Housman's diary. *Encounter* 29 (October. 1967): 33–41.

———. "A Poet in the Making." *The Atlantic Monthly* (July 1946): 116–23.

———. *The Unexpected Years*. New York: Bobbs-Merrill, 1936.

Hunt, Jo. "The Immortal Memory of A. E. Housman". A toast proposed at the Housman Society Dinner, 1980. *HSJ* 7 (1981): 55–59.

Isay, Richard I., M. D. *Being Homosexual*. London: Penguin Books, 1989.

———. Letter to the editor, *The New York Times Weekly Review* (25 April 1993): 6.

Jarrell, Randall. "Texts from Housman." In *A. E. Housman: A Collection of Critical Essays*, edited by Christopher Ricks, 50–61. Englewood Cliffs, N.J.: Prentice-Hall, 1968.

Jebb, Keith. *A. E. Housman*. Bridgend, England: Seren Books, 1992.

Kane, Robert J. *The Explicator* 10 (May 1952): Q7.

Keyser, Paul. "A. E. Housman's Variations on Sappho, Frag. 52 BERGK[4.]" *Classical and Modern Literature: A Quarterly* 5, no. 4 (Summer 1985): 315–22.

Kowalczyk, R. L. "Horatian Tradition and Pastoral Mode in Housman's *A Shropshire Lad*." *VP* 4 (1966): 223–35.

Kreuzer, James R. *Elements of Poetry*. Toronto: Macmillan, 1955.

Lahr, John. *Prick up Your Ears: The Biography of Joe Orton*. Harmondsworth, Middlesex: Penguin Books, 1980.

Lamb, W. R. M. "A. E. Housman: 1859–1936." *The Listener* (28 October 1936): 822–23.

Landor, Walter Savage. *The Poetical Works of Walter Landor*. 3 vols. Edited by Stephen Wheeler. Oxford: Clarendon Press, 1937.

Latin Literature, an Anthology: Translations from Latin Prose and Poetry chosen by Michael Grant. Harmondsworth, Middlesex: Penguin Books, 1978.

Lawrence, D. H. *The Complete Poems*. New York: Penguin Books, 1964.

Lea, Gordon B. "Ironies and Dualities in *A Shropshire Lad*." *Colby Library Quarterly* 10 (1973): 71–79.

Lear, Edward. *The Nonsense Verse of Edward Lear*. Edited by John Vernon Lord. London: Mandarin Paperbacks, 1992.

Leggett, B. J. *Housman's Land of Lost Content: A Critical Study of "A Shropshire Lad."* Knoxville: University of Tennessee Press, 1970.

———. *The Poetic Art of A. E. Housman: Theory and Practice*. Lincoln: University of Nebraska Press, 1978.

———. "An Unpublished Housman Letter on the Preface to *Last Poems*." *VN* 33 (Spring 1968): 48–49.

LeMire, Eugene D. "The Irony and Ethics of 'A Shropshire Lad.' " *University of Windsor Review* 1 (Spring 1965): 109–27.

Lewis, C. S. *The Discarded Image*. Cambridge: Cambridge University Press, 1967.

———. "The Personal Heresy in Criticism." *Essays and Studies* 19 (1934): 7–28.

———. *Studies in Words*. 2nd ed. Cambridge: Cambridge University Press, 1967.

Llewellyn-Jones, Derek. *Every Man*. Oxford: Oxford University Press, 1991.

Lovelace, Richard. *The Poems of Richard Lovelace*. Edited by C. H. Wilkinson. Oxford: Clarendon Press, 1930.

Lucas, F. L. "The Personality and Poetry of Housman." In *The Greatest Problem and Other Essays*, 179–233. New York: Macmillan, 1961.

Maas, Henry. "Additions and Corrections to *The Letters of A. E. Housman*." *HSJ* 2 (1975): 33–35.

———. "On Editing Housman's Letters," *HSJ* 7 (1981): 19–21.

MacDonald, J. F. "The Poetry of A. E. Housman." *Queens Quarterly* 31 (October–December 1923): 114–37.

MacDonnell, A. "Review of *A Shropshire Lad*." *The Bookman* (June 1896): 83.

Mandel, Jerome. "Housman's Insane Narrators." *VP* 26 (1988): 403–12.

Manegold, Catherine S. "The Odd Place of Homosexuality in the Military." *The New York Times Weekly Review* (18 April 1993): 1–2.

Manilius. *Astronomica*. Translated and edited by G. P. Goold, Cambridge: Harvard University Press, 1977.

Marcus, Steven. *The Other Victorians: A Study of Sexuality and Pornography in Mid-Nineteenth-Century England*. London: Corgi Books, 1966.

Marlow, Norman. *A. E. Housman: Scholar and Poet*. London: Routledge and Kegan Paul, 1958.

———. "The Earliest Influences on *A Shropshire Lad*." *RES* n.s. 6, no. 22 (1955): 166–73.

Martin, Robert K. "A. E. Housman's Two Strategies: *A Shropshire Lad* and *Last Poems*." *VN* 66 (Fall 1984): 14–17.

———. *The Homosexual Tradition in American Poetry*. Austin: University of Texas Press, 1979.

Mellow, James R. *Charmed Circle*. Boston: Houghton Mifflin, 1974.

Mendilow, A. A. "Tennyson's Palace of the Sinful Muse." *Scripta Hierosolymitana* 17 (1966): 155–89.

Meyer, Randy Lynn. Unpublished dissertation. (Fall, 1984).

Meyers, Jeffrey. *Homosexuality and Literature, 1890–1930*. London: The Athlone Press, 1987.

Miles, Rosalind. *The Rites of Man*. London: Paladin Books, 1992.

Millard, Kenneth. "A. E. Housman and the 'perils of cheat and charmer.'" In *Edwardian Poetry*, 80–106. Oxford: Clarendon Press, 1991.

Miller, J. Hilles. "The Sources of Dickens' Comic Art." In *Victorian Subjects*. Hemel Hempstead: Harvester Wheatsheaf, 1990.

Milton, John. *John Milton: Complete Poems and Major Prose*. Edited by Merritt Y. T. Hughes. New York: The Odyssey Press, 1957.

Molson, Hugh. "The Philosophies of Hardy and Housman." *Quarterly Review* 268 (1937): 205–13.

Morris, Desmond. *The Naked Ape*. New York: McGraw-Hill Book Co., 1967.

Mortimer, Raymond. "Housman Relics." Review of *More Poems*. *The New Statesman and Nation* 12 (24 October 1936): 631, 634.

Muir, Edward. "A. E. Housman." Review of *More Poems* and Gow's Sketch. *The London Mercury* 35 (November 1936): 62–3.

Naiditch, P. G. *A. E. Housman at University College, London: The Election of 1892*. Leiden: E. J. Brill, 1988.

———. "A. E. Housman and W. H. Mallock." *HSJ* 20 (1994): 13–16.

———. "Notes on the Life of M. J. Jackson." *HSJ* 12 (1986): 93–114.

———. *Problems in the Life and Writings of A. E. Housman.* Beverly Hills, Calif.: Krown & Spellman, 1995.

———. Review of Burnett's edition of *The Poems of A. E. Housman. The Classical Bulletin* (27 January 2000): 109–14.

Nash, Walter. " 'Diffugere nives.' on Englishing Horace." *Language and Literature* 2, no. 1 (1993): 19–36.

Nielsen, Rosemary M., and Robert H. Solomon. "Horace and Housman: Twisting Conventions." *Canadian Review of Contemporary Literature* 13, no. 3 (September 1986): 325–49.

Nosworthy, J. M. "A. E. Housman and the Woolwich Cadet." *N&Q* n.s. 17, no. 9 (September 1970): 351–53.

Orwell, George. "Inside the Whale." In *Selected Essays*, 215–56. Harmondsworth, Middlesex: Penguin Books, 1937.

Ovid. *Metamorphoses.* Translated by Rolfe Humphreys. Bloomington: Indiana University Press, 1957.

Page, Norman. *A. E. Housman: A Critical Biography.* London: Macmillan, 1983.

Paglia, Camille. *Sexual Personae.* New York: Vintage Books, 1991.

Pater, Walter. *Marius the Epicurean.* Edited by Ian Small. Oxford: Oxford University Press, 1986.

Pearsall, Robert Brainard. "Housman Versus Vaughan Williams." *VP* 4 (Winter 1966): 42–44.

———. "The Vendible Values of Housman's Soldiery." *PMLA* 82 (1967): 85–90.

Pearsall, Ronald. *The Worm in the Bud.* Toronto: Macmillan, 1969.

Perkins, David. *A History of Modern Poetry.* Cambridge: Harvard University Press, 1976.

Perrine, Laurence. "Housman's Lovers." *CE* 36, no. 6 (February 1975): 708.

———. "Housman's 'Others, I am not the first,' " *VP* 28, no. 3–4 (Autumn–Winter 1990): 135–38.

Peters, E. Curt. "A Cynical Classicist." *Poetry Review* 31 (1940): 155–56.

Petronius. *Satyricon.* Translated by William Arrowsmith. New York: Penguin, New American Library, 1959.

Pollet, Maurice. "A. E. Housman: Etude Suivie d'une Lettre Inedite." *Etudes Anglaises* (September 1937): 385–404. Or see A. E. Housman, *Letters*, 319, for the letter itself.

Prescott, Frederick C. "The Imagination: Condensation and Displacement." In *Perspectives on Poetry*, edited by James S. Calderwood and Harold E. Tolliver, 379–93. New York: Oxford University Press, 1968.

Priestley, J. B. "The Poetry of A. E. Housman." *The London Mercury* 7 (December 1922): 171–84.

Pugh, John. *Bromsgrove and the Housmans.* Bromsgrove: The Housman Society, 1974.

Reade, Brian, editor. *Sexual Heretics: Male Homosexuality in English Literature from 1850 to 1900.* London: n.p., 1970.

Rachel Hameshureret (Rachel the Poetess) [Rachel Blaubstein] Rachel's Poems (Hebrew). Tel Aviv: Davar Press, 1974.

Reedy, Gerard, S. J. "Housman's Use of Classical Convention." *VP* 6 (1968): 51–61.

Review. "A. E. Housman: *More Poems* and a Memoir." *TLS* (24 October 1936): 845–46.

Review of *Last Poems. Outlook* 1, no. 1297 (9 December 1922): 500. Reprinted in *A. E.*

Housman: The Critical Heritage, edited by Philip Gardner, 132–34. London: Routledge, 1992.

Reynolds, Judith. "Housman's Humor." *The Western Humanities Review 22* (Spring 1968): 161–64.

Richards, Grant. *Housman 1897–1936*. Introduction by Katharine E. Symons. London: Oxford University Press, 1942.

Richards, I. A. *Practical Criticism: A Study of Literary Judgement*. New York: Harcourt, Brace, and World Inc., 1929.

Ricks, Christopher, editor. *A. E. Housman: A Collection of Critical Essays*. Harmondsworth: Penguin Books, 1968.

———, editor. *A. E. Housman: Collected Poems and Selected prose*. London: The Penguin Press, 1988.

———. "A. E. Housman and 'the colour of his hair.' " *Essays in Criticism* 47, no. 3 (July 1997): 240–55.

———. "A. E. Housman: The Nature of His Poetry." In *The Force of Poetry* 163–78 (Oxford: Oxford University Press, 1987).

———. "The Nature of Housman's Poetry." In *A. E. Housman: A Collection of Critical Essays*, edited by Ricks, 106–22.

Riskin, Rabbi Shlomo. "Gays Sacrifice Their Future." *The Jerusalem Post* (30 April 1993): 8.

Robb, Nesca A. *Four in Exile*. Port Washington, N.Y.: Kennikat Press, 1948.

Robbins, Ruth. " 'A very curious construction': masculinity and the poetry of A. E. Housman and Oscard Wilde." *Cultural Politics at the fin de siecle*, edited by Sally Ledger and Scott McCracken, 137–59. Cambridge: Cambridge University Press, 1995.

Robertson, Alec. "Housman and Hopkins." In *Contrasts: The Arts and Religion*, 93–117. Worcester: Stanbrook Abbey Press.

Robinson, Oliver. *Angry Dust: The Poetry of A. E. Housman*. Boston: Bruce Humphreys Inc., 1950.

Roditi, Edouard. *Gay Sunshine 36/37* (Spring/Summer 1978).

Rosebury, Brian. "The three Disciplines of A. E. Housman's Poetry." *VP 21* (1983): 217–228.

Rosenthal, M. L., and A. J. M. Smith. *Exploring Poetry*. New York: Macmillan, 1955.

Rossetti, Christina. *The Poetical Works of Christina Georgina Rossetti*. London: Macmillan and Co., Ltd., 1928.

Rothenstein, William. *Men and Memories*. 2 vols. London: Faber and Faber, 1932.

Ryley, Robert M. "Hermeneutics in the Classroom: E. D. Hirsch Jr., and a Poem by Housman." *CE* 36, no. 1 (September 1974): 46–50.

———. "Response to Laurence Perrine." *CE* 36 no. 6 (February 1975): 708.

Sappho. *Sappho: Lyrics in the Original Greek with Translations by Willis Barnstone*. Garden City, N.Y.: Doubleday and Co. Inc. Anchor Books, 1965.

Schmidt, Michael. *Lives of the Poets*. London: Weidenfeld and Nicholson, 1998.

Schneider, Elisabeth. *Aesthetic Motive*. New York: Macmillan Co., 1939.

Scott-Kilvert, Ian. *A. E. Housman*, Writers and Their Work Series, gen. ed. Bonamy Dobree, London: Longmans, Green, and Co., 1955, re-issued 1977.

Sedgwick, Eve Kosofsky. *Between Men*. New York: Columbia University Press, 1985.

Shakespeare, William. *The Complete Plays and Poems of William Shakespeare*. Edited by

William Allan Neilson and Charles Jarvis Hill. Cambridge, Mass.: Houghton Mifflin, 1942.

Shaw, Robin. "From Housman's Places." *HSJ* 20 (1994): 54.

———. *Housman's Places*. Bromsgrove: The Housman Society, 1995.

Siegel, Jules Paul. "A. E. Housman's Modification of the Flower Motif of the Pastoral Elegy." *VP* 2 (1964): 47–50.

Siegel-Itzkovich, Judy. "Gay Genes." *The Jerusalem Post* (30 December 1991).

Sinclair, F. D. *A. E. Housman: An Evaluation*. Pretoria: Communications of the University of South Africa, 1957.

Skutsch, Otto. *A. E. Housman: 1859–1936*. London: The Athlone Press, 1960.

Small, Meredith F. "The Gay Debate: Is Homosexuality a Matter of Choice or Chance?" *American Health* (March 1993): 70–76.

Smith, Barbara. *Poetic Closure: A Study of How Poems End*. Chicago: University of Chicago Press, 1968.

Southey, Robert. *Poems of Robert Southey*. Edited by Maurice H. Fitzgerald. London: Oxford University Press, 1909.

Sparrow, John. editor. *A. E. Housman: Collected Poems*. Harmondsworth: Penguin Books, 1956.

———. "A. E. Housman." Review of *More Poems* and Gow's Sketch. *Spectator* 47 (20 October 1936): 756.

———. "*A Shropshire Lad* at Fifty." *TLS* (30 March 1946): 145–46. Reprinted in *Independent Essays*, London: Faber and Faber, 1963, 124–32.

Stallman, Robert Wooster. *The Explicator* 3 (February 1945): 26.

Stauffer, Donald A. *The Nature of Poetry*. New York: W. W. Norton and Co., 1946.

Stevenson, John W. "The Ceremony of Housman's Style." *VP* 10 (1972): 45–55.

———. "The Durability of Housman's Poetry." *The Sewanee Review* 94, no. 4 (Fall 1986): 613–19.

———. "The Martyr As Innocent: Housman's Lonely Lad." *SAQ* 57 (Winter 1958): 69–85.

Stoppard, Tom. *The Invention of Love*. London: Faber and Faber, 1997.

Strozier, Robert. "A. E. Housman: Image, Illogic and Allusion." *Colby Library Quarterly* 7, no. 6 (June 1966): 257–63.

Sweeney, Francis. "The Ethics of A. E. Housman." *Thought* 20 (1945): 117–125.

Swinburne, Charles Algernon. *Swinburne*. Edited by Bonamy Dobree. Harmondsworth, Middlesex: Penguin Books, 1961.

Symons, Katharine E., A. W. Pollard, Laurence Housman, et al., *Alfred Edward Housman: Recollections*. Bromsgrove: The Bromsgrove School, 1936; New York: Henry Holt and Co. 1937.

Tannahill, Reay. *Sex in History*. New York: Stein and Day, 1980.

Taylor, George A. "A. E. Housman." *Queen's Quarterly* 43 (1936): 383–90.

Tennyson, Alfred, Lord. *The Poems of Tennyson*. Edited by Christopher Ricks. London: Longmans, 1969.

Tillyard, E. M. W. "The Personal Heresy in Criticism: A Rejoinder." *Essays and Studies* 20 (1935): 7–20.

Tinker, C. B. "Housman's Poetry." *Yale Review* 25 (Autumn 1935): 84–95.

Trollope, Anthony. *Can You Forgive Her?* Harmondsworth, Middlesex: Penguin Books, 1972.

———. *The Eustace Diamonds.* Oxford: Oxford University Press, 1983.

———. *The Last Chronicle of Barset.* Oxford, Oxford University Press, 1980.

———. *Phineas Redux.* Frogmore, Herts.: Granada Publishing Ltd., Panther Books, 1974.

———. *The Small House at Allington.* Oxford: Oxford University Press, 1980.

Walton, Eda Lou. "Not Mine, but Man's." Review of *More Poems. The Nation* 143 (7 November 1936): 552.

Watson, George L. *A. E. Housman: A Divided Life.* London: Rupert Hart-Davis, 1957.

Watts, Neville. "The Poetry of A. E. Housman." *The Dublin Review* 200 (January–June 1937): 117–33.

Wells, Robert. "Hidden and Unmasked." Review of Bayley's *Housman's Poems, TLS* (30 October 1992): 11.

Werner, William. *The Explicator* 14 (October 1955): 2A.

Westermarck, Edward. "Homosexual Love." In *The Origin and Development of the Moral Idea.* Macmillan and Company, Ltd., 1912. Reprinted in *Men: The Variety and Meaning of Their Sexual Experience,* edited by A. M. Krich, 216–32. New York: Dell Publishing Co., Inc., 1954.

Whallon, William. "A. E. Housman's 'The Love of Comrades'," *HSJ* 14 (1988): 51–54.

White, William, editor. *A Centennial Memento with Excerpts from "A Shropshire Lad" and "Fragment of a Greek Tragedy," A. E. Housman, including Twenty-five Letters to Joseph Ishill.* Berkeley Heights, N.J.: Oriole Press, 1959.

———. "*A Shropshire Lad* in Process: The Textual Evolution of Some A. E. Housman Poems." *The Library,* 5th series 9 (1954): 255–64.

———. "Suicide and the Poet: A. E. Housman." *Today's Japan* (June 1960): 41–46.

Whitehead, John. "A. E. Housman." In *Hardy to Larkin: seven English poets,* 129–63. Munslow, Shropshire: Hearthstone Publications, 1995.

Whitridge, Arnold. "Vigny and Housman: A Study in Pessimism." *The American Scholar* 10 (Spring 1941): 156–69.

Wilde, Oscar. *De Profundis.* Edited by Jacques Barzun. New York: Vintage Books, 1964.

Williams, Charles. *Poetry at Present.* Oxford: Clarendon Press, 1930.

Withers, Percy. *A Buried Life: Personal Recollections of A. E. Housman.* London: Jonathan Cape, 1940.

Woods, Gregory. *Articulate Flesh: Male homo-eroticism and modern poetry.* New Haven: Yale University Press, 1987.

Wright, George T. *The Poet in the Poem.* New York: Gordion Press, 1960.

Wright, Kit. "Never Mind What It Means." *The Times Saturday Review* (2 February 1991): 15.

Wysong, John N. "A. E. Housman's Surrogate Son, Terence." *The Arlington Quarterly* 2, no. 1 (1969): 139–53.

———. "A. E. Housman's Use of Astronomy." *Anglia* 80 (1962): 295–301.

Yeats, William Butler. *Selected Poems and Two Plays of William Butler Yeats.* Edited by M. L. Rosenthal. New York: Collier Books, 1962.

Zipes, Jack. *Fairy Tales and the Art of Subversion.* New York: Methuen, 1988.

Index

(Page numbers in bold type indicate primary discussion)

301, 346 n. 6 (chap. 4), 349 n. 2 (chap. 9)

Gay studies, 26–28
Gide, André, 27, 280
Gilbert, W. S., 74
Ginsburg, Alan, 39, 265, 266, 301
Gosse, Edmund, 25, 37
Gunn, Thom, 39, 49

Hallam, Arthur, 103, 225, 226, 230
Hardy, Thomas, 18, 19, 47, 64, 95, 115–16, 123, 141, 142, 143, 203, 230, 256, 263, 331
Heine, Heinrich, 114, 115, 116
Henley, William Ernest, 17, 18
Herbert, George, 99
Herrick, Robert, 143, 346 nn. 4 and 5 (chap. 5)
Holtby, Mary, 341–42
homosexual writing (late nineteenth century): 22–26, 39, 225
Hopkins, Gerard Manley, 26, 27, 161, 315
Horace, 56, 103, 113, 157, 222, 233, 235, 236
Housman, A. E.: biographies of, 15–16; biographical summary, 53–62; commentaries on, 16–17; critical reaction to, 11–12, 14, 17–18, 19–20; editions: poetry, 13; editions: prose 16; impressions of contemporaries: 34–35; memoirs concerning, 14–15; notebooks, 16, 62–64, 70; Opinion on Utilitarianism, 72–73; poetry—see A Shropshire Lad, Additional Poems, Last Poems, light verse, juvenilia, and Latin verse, More Poems, and notebook fragments; Prose— "Application of Thought to Textual Criticism," 286; "Cambridge Inaugural Lecture," 276; Classical Papers, 16, 311, 345 n. 2 (chap. 4); 347 n. 1 (chap. 7); diary, 55, 58, 59, 221, 239, 319, 136, 319; Introductions to Manilius, 90, 195, 232; Letters and Inscriptions, 12, 15, 61, 64, 72, 88, 105, 124, 129, 134, 167, 186, 218, 121, 231, 255, 266, 270, 274, 292, 347 n. 3 (chap. 6); Name and Nature of Poetry: method of composition, 69–70; on Augustan poetry, 93–94; on Metaphysical poetry, 185–86; on personification of nature, 131; on the function of

poetry, 274; on the meaning and production of poetry, 340; Preface to Last Poems, 61, 64; review of the Cambridge History of English Literature, Vol. 11, 337; "Swinburne," 218
Housman, (George) Herbert, 50, 60, 129, 154, 228, 229, 230, 233, 237, 241, 244, 317, 333
Housman, Katharine, 14, 15, 16, 37, 47, 54–55, 61, 68, 69, 116, 123, 129, 164, 228, 253, 276, 283, 312, 345 n. 3 (chap. 3)
Housman, Laurence, 14, 15, 16, 20, 22, 23, 24, 36, 37, 46, 54–55, 58, 61–63, 68, 87, 90–91, 97, 99, 119, 123, 128, 130, 135, 164, 218, 237–39, 246, 247, 277, 286–87, 304, 308, 318, 328, 337–40, 343–44 n. 8 (chap. 1), 344 n. 5 (chap. 2)
Housman Society, the, 15–16
Hughes, Thomas, 224, 225

In Memoriam. See Tennyson, Alfred, Lord

Jackson, Adalbert, 50, 56, 58, 59, 62, 64, 237–41, 242, 243, 244, 245, 246, 247, 309, 333, 349 note 9 Chapter 8; 350 note 1 Chapter 10
Jackson, Moses, 38, 50, 54, 55–62, 64, 108, 112, 113, 124, 125, 138, 148, 151, 152, 154, 164, 199, 219, 221, 222, 223, 228, 231, 237–41, 242, 247, 275, 286, 293, 303, 309, 311, 312, 313, 314, 315, 316, 317, 318, 319, 321, 322, 323, 324, 325, 326, 327, 329, 330, 332, 333, 339, 343–44 nn. 5, 8, and 9 (chap. 1), 346 nn. 6 and 9 (chap. 5)
James, M. R., 99, 214, 316
Johnson, Lionel, 17, 18
Johnson, Samuel, 77, 157, 235
Joyce, James, 51–52
Julius Caesar, 270

Keats, John, 19, 103, 104, 207
King, Edward, 103
Kipling, Rudyard, 11, 17, 18, 19

Labouchere Amendment, 21, 22, 24, 26, 58, 283
Landor, Walter Savage, 68
Last Poems: As I gird on for fighting (No. 2), 257–59, 268, 270, 278, 279; "Astronomy" (No. 17), **229–30**; Could